The Road to the White House 2012

The Politics of Presidential Elections

NINTH EDITION

Stephen J. Wayne
Georgetown University

Australia • Brazil • Canada • Mexico • Singapore • Spain • United Kingdom • United States

The Road to the White House 2012
Stephen J. Wayne

Senior Publisher: Suzanne Jeans

Executive Editor: Carolyn Merrill

Associate Development Editor: Katherine Hayes

Editorial Assistant: Scott Greenan

Marketing Manager: Lydia Lestar

Product Manager: Caitlin Green

Art Director: Linda Helcher

Print Buyer: Fola Orekoya

Rights Acquisition Specialist: Jennifer Meyer Dare

Production Service: PreMediaGlobal

Cover Designer: Rokusek Design

Cover Image: Frontpage/ © Shutterstock

Library of Congress Control Number: 2011923937

Student Edition:

ISBN-13: 978-1-111-34150-3

ISBN-10: 1-111-34150-8

Wadsworth
20 Channel Center Street
Boston, MA 02210
USA

Printed in the United States of America
1 2 3 4 5 6 7 15 14 13 12 11

Preface

We are in another presidential election cycle. It follows the longest and most costly election in U.S. history in 2008. The new electoral cycle occurs within an international setting in which terrorism remains a principal concern with thousands of American soldiers fighting in Afghanistan and stationed in or near "hot spots" around the world. It also occurs within an economic environment in which the United States is slowly and unevenly emerging from the worst recession since the 1930s and a political climate in which strident, ideological politics continues to divide partisans and turn off many independent voters. The 2012 campaign will be influenced by these conditions as well as by evaluations of the successes and failures of the Obama administration.

The campaign will last about two years. By the end of it, the electorate will be weary to the point of numbness; the presidential candidates will be exhausted and, with the exception of one, disappointed; and the costs of the campaigns will be in the billions of dollars. Is it really necessary to have such an extended election period, to spend so much money, and go through such a vigorous, oftentimes nasty, public debate? Perhaps not, but free and frequent elections are critical for a democracy. They are a means by which the electorate can judge the candidates, keep the winners accountable, and hold them responsible for the policy decisions they make.

Elections tie citizens to their government. But for the voters to make an intelligent judgment, they need information about the qualities of the candidates, the policies they propose, and the partisan labels they wear. Does the current presidential electoral system encourage the most qualified candidates to run? Does it force them to discuss the most important issues, present feasible policy alternatives, and talk candidly with the American people? Does the electorate get the kind of information it needs to make an enlightened voting decision?

Will the results of the election fairly and accurately reflect the opinions, interests, and needs of the population as a whole? Is the system consistent with principles and practices of a democratic electoral process?

A primary goal of this book is to answer these questions. It does so by describing and evaluating the presidential election system from the perspectives of the candidates, the parties, and the American people. As with its previous editions, *The Road to the White House 2012* discusses the following:

- Why particular strategies are being adopted;
- Why certain tactics are utilized (and others are not);
- Whether these strategies and tactics are likely to achieve the desired results and at what cost;
- How the campaigns are using new communications technology;
- Why particular appeals are made, to whom, and with what impact;
- How candidates try to influence the news media and how the news media cover the campaign;
- Why the election turns out the way it does;
- And what it augurs for the direction of public policy and the next administration's ability to govern.
- It will also address the changes that the last presidential election has brought about in the way people run for presidency: how they raise money, energize their supporters, communicate their messages, turn out voters, and transition to government.

OUTLINE

The book is organized into four parts. Part I discusses the arena in which presidential elections occur. Its three chapters examine the electoral system, campaign finance, and the political environment. Chapter 1 provides a historical overview of nominations as well as elections with an extended discussion of the Florida vote controversy in 2000 and its consequences. Chapter 2 examines recent developments in campaign finance, the Supreme Court's decision on corporate spending, the explosion of revenues and expenditures, and the apparent demise of public funding. The chapter will also describe the ways in which campaign finance rules have been circumvented by the candidates and parties and the impact of that circumvention on a democratic electoral system. In the third chapter, continuities and changes in the political environment serve as the principal focus and provide a perspective on how the environment in which the elections occur affects the turnout of voters, the attitudes of the electorate, and the composition of partisan electoral coalitions.

Part II describes and analyzes the presidential nomination process from its early beginning through the national nominating conventions. Chapter 4 discusses the reforms that the parties have made in the way they select their standard-bearers, the legal issues that have arisen from these reforms, and the impact the reforms have had on the electorate, the parties, and the candidates. Chapter 5 continues this discussion through the competitive stage of the caucuses and primaries until the nominee is effectively determined. This chapter pays particular attention to the strategies the candidates adopt and the hurdles they must overcome, illustrating these strategies with case studies from the 2008 nomination campaigns. Chapter 6 describes the period after the nominees have been effectively determined through the conventions that officially anoint them and launch their general election campaigns. It describes how the candidates attempt to heal divisions within the party; improve their leadership image, which may have been damaged during the nomination process; and begin to challenge their partisan opposition in the general election. It also discusses the impact of the conventions on the voters' knowledge and partisan preferences.

Part III examines the presidential campaign itself. Chapter 7 details the organization, strategy, and tactics of the candidates and assesses the new communication technologies that have been used to identify voters, target appeals to them, and measure the effect of these appeals as the election progresses. It illustrates this discussion by comparing the Bush-Kerry and Obama-McCain campaigns. Chapter 8 turns to the news media: how the press covers the campaign and how the candidates try to affect the coverage they receive as well as counter that coverage with paid advertising, scripted public performances, and participation in the presidential debates. The chapter evaluates the impact that media-driven forces can have on the voting behavior of the electorate.

Part IV of the book looks at the election and beyond. Chapter 9 discusses and evaluates the vote: What does it mean? Is there a mandate? How do the results affect the president's ability to govern? Illustrations of the 2008–2009 transition from election to government are used to highlight the difficulties of moving from campaign promise to presidential performance. Chapter 10 considers problems in the electoral system and possible reforms to alleviate these problems. It examines some of the major difficulties that have affected the political system from party rules to finance issues to media coverage. The chapter also looks at proposals being discussed for improving the electoral system, making it more equitable to the citizenry, more responsive to popular choice, less prone to human error and fraud, and more likely to guide those in government and facilitate their policy-making responsibilities.

PURPOSE

Elections link the people with their public officials, a vital component of a functioning democracy. However, that link is far from perfect. Voting is individualized, yet governing is a collective undertaking. Everyone does not participate in elections, but government makes rules for all the people. Presidential candidates regularly overpromise and underdeliver. They create unrealistic expectations that are impossible to achieve by the president alone in a system of shared powers and divided government and also to accomplish as quickly as the public demands. As a consequence, the hopefulness that a campaign generates frequently fades into disillusionment, apathy, and cynicism as an administration progesses.

How can we improve elections? How can we encourage more of the citizenry to participate? How can we persuade the most qualified people to run?

How can we level the electoral playing field? How can we ensure that the mood of the voters will be reflected in the results of the election and that government officials will pursue the public's interest as reflected in the vote? In other words, how can we make sure that elections achieve their principal goals: to select the most qualified people, to provide them with a blueprint for governing, and to hold them individually and collectively accountable for their decisions and actions in government?

Without information on how the system works, that is, whether it is functioning properly and meeting its objectives, we cannot answer these questions and assess the merits of our electoral democracy. We cannot cajole the citizenry to meet its civic responsibilities and vote; we cannot recruit the best and the brightest to give up their privacy, shift their family responsibilities to others and, in many cases, sacrifice financially to run for office; we cannot improve the people–government–public policy connection for which elections are the critical link. In the case of presidential politics, ignorance is definitely not bliss, nor is the norm always or usually the ideal.

The road to the White House is long and arduous. In fact, it has become more difficult to travel than in the past. Yet, surprisingly, given all the criticism, there continue to be many would-be travelers. Evaluating their journey is essential to rendering an intelligent judgment on Election Day. However, more is at stake than simply choosing the occupant of the Oval Office. The system itself is on trial in every presidential election. That is why it is so important to understand and appreciate the intricacies of the process and to participate in it. Only an informed and active citizenry can determine whether the nation is being well served by the way we go about choosing our president and have some say in determining who that president will be and what the victor will do in office.

ACKNOWLEDGMENTS

Few books are written alone, and this one was no exception. For the 2012 edition, I was fortunate to have an excellent editorial and publishing team at Cengage/Wadsworth: Carolyn Merrill, Executive Editor; Angela Hodge, Editorial Assistant; and Joshua Allen, Senior Project Manager.

I would also like to express my thanks to the political scientists who have reviewed one or more of the nine editions of this book: John Bruce, University of Mississippi; Richard L. Cole, University of Texas at Arlington; Anthony Corrado Jr., Colby College; Stephen C. Craig, University of Florida at Gainesville; James W. Davis, Washington University; Gordon Friedman, Southwest Missouri State University; Jay S. Goodman, Wheaton College; Anne Griffin, the Cooper Union; Marjorie Randon Hershey, Indiana University; Hugh L. LeBlanc, George Washington University; Kuo-Wei Lee, Pan-American University; Robert T. Nakamura, State University of New York at Albany; Richard G. Niemi, University of Rochester; Diana Owen, Georgetown University; Charles Prysby, the University of North Carolina at Greensboro; Michael Robinson, Georgetown University; Lester Seligman, University of Illinois; Earl Shaw,

Northern Arizona University; John W. Sloan, University of Houston; Priscilla Southwell, University of Oregon at Eugene; William H. Steward, University of Alabama; Edward J. Weissman, Washington College; and Clyde Wilcox, Georgetown University.

Finally, everyone makes personal sacrifices in writing a book. I want to thank my wife, Cheryl, for her patience and understanding and for allowing me to enjoy Vermont summers and Marlboro Music while I worked on the book. I also want to thank my sons, Jared and Jeremy, who have kept their careers and needs from imposing on mine.

Stephen J. Wayne
Georgetown University

DEDICATION

To the memory of my parents and grandparents, who encouraged my interests in politics and my pursuit of higher education, and to my wife, Cheryl, who keeps me balanced and pointed in the right political direction.

About the Author

Stephen J. Wayne has been a Professor of Government at Georgetown University since 1989. A Washington-based expert on the American presidency, he has authored or edited 12 books and more than 100 articles, chapters, and book reviews. In addition to *The Road to the White House,* he has coauthored *Presidential Leadership* (with George Edwards), *Conflict and Consensus in American Politics* and *The Politics of American Democracy* (both with G. Calvin Mackenzie and Richard L. Cole), all published by Cengage/Wadsworth, and two books on democratic elections and governance. His latest book is entitled *Personality and Politics: Obama For and Against Himself.*

A much-quoted source for journalists covering the White House, he frequently appears on television and radio news programs and consults for television documentaries. He has testified before Congress on presidential elections, appeared before both Democratic and Republican advisory committees on the presidential nomination process, directed a presidential transition project for the National Academy of Public Administration, and participated in the 2000 and 2008 White House transition projects conducted by the Presidency Research Group. Professor Wayne lectures widely throughout the United States and abroad on the contemporary presidency and presidential elections.

Contents

CHAPTER 8
Media Politics 247

PART IV
THE ELECTION 291

CHAPTER 9
Understanding Presidential Elections 292

List of Figures and Tables

FIGURES

TABLES

The Electoral Arena

Part I

I CHAPTER PRESIDENTIAL SELECTION: A HISTORICAL OVERVIEW

INTRODUCTION

The road to the White House is long, circuitous, and bumpy. It contains numerous hazards and potential dead ends. Those who choose to traverse it—and there are many who do so—need considerable skill, perseverance, and luck to be successful. They also need substantial amounts of time, money, and effort. For most candidates, there is no such thing as a free or easy ride to the presidency.

The framers of the Constitution worked for several months on the presidential selection system, and their plan has since undergone a number of constitutional, statutory, and precedent-setting changes. Modified by the development of parties, the expansion of suffrage, the growth of the news media, and the revolution in contemporary communications technology, the electoral system has become more open and more participatory but also more contentious, more complex, and much more expensive. It has "turned off" many people who, for a variety of reasons, have chosen not to participate. This chapter is about that system: why it was created; what it was supposed to do; the compromises that were incorporated in the original plan; its initial operation and the changes that have subsequently affected it; the groups that have benefited from these changes; and the overall effect on the parties, the electorate, and American democracy.

In addressing these questions, I have organized the chapter into four sections. The first discusses the creation of the presidential election process. It explores the motives and intentions of the delegates at Philadelphia and describes the procedures for selecting the president within the context of the constitutional and political issues of that day.

The second section examines the development of nominating systems. It explores the three principal methods that have been used to nominate presidential candidates: partisan congressional caucuses, brokered national conventions, and state primaries and caucuses. It also describes the political forces that helped to shape these modes of nomination and, in the case of the first two, destroyed them.

The third section discusses presidential elections. It focuses on the most controversial ones, those determined by the House of Representatives (1800 and 1824), influenced by Congress (1876), and decided by the Supreme Court (2000). The chapter also examines elections in the twentieth and twenty-first centuries in which the shift of a relatively small number of votes could have changed the outcome (1960, 1968, 1976, and 2004). In doing so, this section highlights the strengths and weaknesses of the Electoral College and assesses its consistency with the principles of a democratic electoral process.

The final section of the chapter examines the current operation of the electoral system. It describes its geographic and demographic biases and how they affect the national character of the presidential elections. The section also discusses the Electoral College's major-party orientation and its adverse impact on third-party candidacies.

THE CREATION OF THE ELECTORAL COLLEGE

Of the many issues facing the delegates at the Constitutional Convention of 1787 in Philadelphia, the selection of the president was one of the toughest. Seven times during the course of the convention the method for choosing the executive was altered. The framers' difficulty in designing electoral provisions for the president stemmed from their need to guarantee the institution's independence and, at the same time, to create a technically sound, politically effective mechanism that would be consistent with a republican form of government. They wanted a representative government based on consent, but not a direct democracy in which everyone had an opportunity to participate in the formulation of public policy. Their goal was an electoral system that would choose the most qualified person, but not necessarily the most popular. There seemed to be no precise model to follow; heredity was out of the question, and a direct popular vote was viewed as impractical and undesirable.

Three methods of election had been proposed. The Virginia Plan, a series of resolutions designed by James Madison and introduced by Governor Edmund Randolph of Virginia, provided for legislative selection. Eight states chose their governors in this fashion at that time. Having Congress choose the president would be practical and politically expedient. Moreover, members of Congress could be expected to exercise a considered judgment. Making a reasoned, unemotional choice was important to the delegates at Philadelphia, since many of them did not consider the average citizen capable of doing so.

The difficulty with legislative selection was the threat it posed to the institution of the presidency. How could the executive's independence be preserved if the election of the president hinged on popularity with Congress and reelection depended on the legislature's appraisal of the president's performance in office? Only if the president were to serve a long term and not be eligible for reelection, it was thought, could the institution's independence be guaranteed so long as Congress was the electoral body. But ineligibility also posed problems, as it provided little incentive for the president to perform well and denied the country the possibility of reelecting a person whose experience and success in office demonstrated qualifications that were superior to others.

Reflecting on these concerns, Gouverneur Morris urged the removal of the ineligibility clause on the grounds that it tended to destroy the great motive to good behavior, the hope of being rewarded by a reappointment.[1] Delegates for a majority of the states agreed. Once the ineligibility clause was deleted, however, the term of office had to be shortened to prevent what the framers feared might become unlimited tenure or, in the words of Thomas Jefferson, "an elective monarchy." With a shorter term of office and permanent reeligibility, legislative selection was not nearly as desirable because it could make the president beholden to the legislature. Moreover, there was still the issue of whether the Congress would vote as one body or as two separate legislative houses. The large states favored a joint vote; the small states wanted separate votes by the House and Senate (since they had equal representation in the upper chamber).

Popular election did not generate a great deal of enthusiasm. It was twice rejected in the convention by overwhelming votes. Most of the delegates felt that a direct vote by the people was neither feasible nor wise.[2] Lacking confidence in the public's ability to choose the best-qualified candidate, many delegates also believed that the size of the country and the relatively primitive state of its communications and transportation in the eighteenth century precluded a national campaign and election. The geographic expanse was simply too large to allow for proper supervision and control of the election. Sectional distrust and rivalry also contributed to the difficulty of holding a national election.

A third option, indirect election, in which popular sentiment could be expressed but would not dictate the outcome, was proposed by James Wilson after he failed to generate much support for a direct popular vote. Luther Martin, Gouverneur Morris, and Alexander Hamilton also suggested an indirect popular election through intermediaries. It was not until the debate over legislative selection divided and eventually deadlocked the delegates, however, that election by electors was seriously considered. Proposed initially as a compromise that incorporated previous convention agreements by a Committee on Unfinished Business, the Electoral College design was viewed as acceptable by weary delegates eager to return home and get the Constitution ratified.

The debate over the Electoral College was short and to the point. Viewed as a safe, workable solution to the election dilemma, it was deemed consistent with the constitutional and political features of the new government and resistant to the kind of cabal and corruption that a popular vote might permit. How the electors were to be selected was left to the states to determine. To ensure their independence, the electors could not simultaneously hold a federal government position.

The number of electors was to equal the number of senators and representatives from each state. At a designated time, they would meet, vote, and send the results to Congress, where they would be announced to a joint session by the president of the Senate, the vice president. Each elector had two votes since a president and vice president were to be selected separately. The only limitations on voting were that the electors could not cast both their ballots for inhabitants of their own states[3] nor designate which of the candidates they preferred to be president and which one vice president.[4]

Under the initial plan, the person who received a majority of votes cast by the Electoral College was elected president, and the one with the second-highest total, vice president. In the event that no one received a majority, the House of Representatives would choose from among the five candidates with the most electoral votes, with each state delegation casting one vote. If two or more individuals were tied for second, then the Senate would select one as vice president. Both of these provisions were subsequently modified by the Twelfth Amendment to the Constitution.

The electoral system was a dual compromise that incorporated provisions of the Connecticut and North–South compromises. Both dealt with representation. The first provided for one legislative body to be based on population (the House of Representatives) and one in which the states were equally represented (the Senate); the other compromise allowed three-fifths of the slave population to be counted in the determination of a state's popular representation. Both compromises protected slave owners in the South by making it difficult for the representatives of the more populous North to determine public policy on their own.

Designating the number of electors to be equal to a state's congressional delegation gave the larger states an advantage in the initial voting for president; casting ballots by state delegations in the House, if the Electoral College was not decisive, benefited the smaller states. It was anticipated that this two-step process would occur most of the time since there would probably not be a consensus national leader other than George Washington. In effect, the large states would nominate, much like the state primaries and caucuses do today, and the small states would exercise equal influence in the final election.[5]

The other compromise between the proponents of a federal system and those who favored a more centralized, national government allowed state legislatures to establish the procedures for choosing electors but had a national legislative body, the House of Representatives, decide among the candidates if there was no Electoral College majority. Finally, limiting the vote to the electors was intended to reduce intrigue, fraud, and cabal, fears that were expressed about the undesirability of state-based popular voting.

THE DEVELOPMENT OF NOMINATING SYSTEMS

Although the Constitution prescribed a system for electing a president, it made no reference to the nomination of candidates. Political parties had not emerged prior to the Constitutional Convention. Factions existed, and the framers of the

Constitution were concerned about them, but the development of a party system was not anticipated. Rather, it was assumed that electors, whose interests were not tied to the national government, would make an independent judgment and it was hoped they would choose the person they felt was best suited for the job.

In the first two elections, the system worked as intended. George Washington was the unanimous choice of the electors. There was, however, no consensus on the vice president. The eventual winner, John Adams, benefited from some informal lobbying by prominent individuals prior to the vote.[6] A more organized effort to agree on candidates for the presidency and vice presidency was undertaken in 1792. Partisan alliances were beginning to develop in Congress. Members of the two principal groups, the Federalists and the Anti-Federalists, met separately to recommend individuals for whom to vote in addition to Washington. The Federalists chose Vice President John Adams; the Anti-Federalists picked Governor George Clinton of New York.

With political parties evolving during the 1790s, the selection of electors quickly became a partisan contest. In 1792 and 1796, a majority of the state legislatures chose them directly. Thus, the political group that controlled the legislature also controlled the selection of electors. Appointed for their political views, electors were expected to exercise a partisan judgment. When in 1796 a Pennsylvania elector did not do so, he was accused of faithless behavior. Wrote one critic in a Philadelphia newspaper: "What, do I chuse Samuel Miles to determine for me whether John Adams or Thomas Jefferson shall be President? No! I chuse him to act, not to think."[7]

Washington's decision not to serve a third term forced Federalist and Anti-Federalist members of Congress to recommend the candidates in 1796. Meeting separately, party leaders agreed among themselves on the tickets. The Federalists urged their electors to support John Adams and Thomas Pinckney, while the Anti-Federalists (or Democratic-Republicans, as they began to be called) suggested Thomas Jefferson and Aaron Burr. Since it was not possible to specify presidential and vice presidential choices on the ballot, Federalist electors, primarily from New England, decided to withhold votes from Pinckney (of South Carolina) to make certain that he did not receive the same number as Adams (of Massachusetts). This strategy enabled Jefferson with sixty-eight votes to finish ahead of Pinckney with fifty-nine, but behind Adams, who had seventy-one. Four years of partisan differences followed between a president who, though he disclaimed a political affiliation, clearly favored the Federalists in appointments, ideology, and policy, and a vice president who was the acknowledged leader of the opposition party.

PARTISAN CONGRESSIONAL CAUCUSES

Beginning in 1800, partisan caucuses, composed of members of Congress, met for the purpose of recommending their party's nominees. The Democratic-Republicans continued to choose candidates in this manner until 1824; the Federalists did so only until 1808. In the final two presidential elections in which the Federalists ran candidates, 1812 and 1816, top party leaders, meeting in secret, decided on the nominees.[8] "King Caucus," as the partisan congressional caucuses were called, violated the spirit of the Constitution. Caucuses effectively allowed members of Congress to pick the nominees. After the decline of the Federalists, the nominees of the Democratic-Republicans, or simply Republicans as they became known, were, in fact, assured of victory—a product of the dominance of that party.

There were competing candidates within the Republican caucus, however. In 1808, Madison prevailed over James Monroe and George Clinton. In 1816, Monroe overcame a strong challenge from William Crawford. In both cases, the electors united behind the successful nominee. In 1820, however, they did not. Disparate elements within the party selected their own candidates.

Although the caucus was the principal mode of candidate selection during the first part of the nineteenth century, it was never formally institutionalized. How the meetings were called, who called them, and when they were held all varied from election to election, as did attendance. A sizable number of representatives chose not to participate at all. Some stayed away on principle; others did so because of the particular choices they would have to make. In 1816, less than half of the Republican members of Congress were at their party's caucus. In 1820, only 20 percent attended, and the caucus had to adjourn without formally supporting President Monroe and Vice President Daniel D. Tompkins for reelection. In 1824, almost three-fourths of the members boycotted the session.

The 1824 caucus did nominate candidates. But with representatives from only four states constituting two-thirds of those attending, the nominee, William Crawford, failed to receive unified party support. Other candidates were nominated by state legislatures and conventions, and the electoral vote was divided. Since no candidate obtained a majority, the House of Representatives had to make the final decision. John Quincy Adams was selected on the first ballot. He received the votes of thirteen of the twenty-four state delegations.

The caucus system was never resumed. In the end, it was a victim of the Federalist Party's decline as a viable political force, the decentralization of political power, and Andrew Jackson's stern opposition to this method of nomination. As the Republican Party grew from being the majority to the only party, factions developed within it, the two principal ones being the National Republicans and the Democratic-Republicans. In the absence of a strong opposition, there was little to hold these factions together. By 1830, they had split into two separate groups, one supporting and one opposing President Jackson.

Political leadership was changing as well. A relatively small number of individuals had dominated national politics for the first three decades following the ratification of the Constitution. Their common experience in the Revolutionary War, the Constitutional Convention, and the early government produced personal contacts, political influence, and public respect that contributed to their ability to agree on candidates and to generate public support for them.[9] Those who followed them in office had neither the tradition nor the national orientation with which to affect the presidential selection process nor the national recognition to build support across the country for their candidates. Most of this new generation of political leaders owed their prominence and political influence to states and regions, and their loyalties reflected these bases of support.

The growth of party organizations at the state and local level affected the nomination system. In 1820 and 1824, it evolved into a decentralized mode of selection, with state legislatures, caucuses, and conventions nominating their own candidates. Support was also mobilized on regional levels. Whereas the congressional caucus had become unrepresentative, state-based nominations suffered from precisely the opposite problem. They were too sensitive to sectional interests and produced too many candidates. Unifying these diverse elements behind a single national ticket proved extremely difficult, although Jackson was successful in doing so in 1828. Nonetheless, a system that was more broadly based than the old caucus and could provide a more decisive and mobilizing mechanism was needed. National nominating conventions filled the void.

National Nominating Conventions

The first such convention was held in 1831 by the Anti-Masons. A small but relatively active third party, it had virtually no congressional representation. Unable to utilize a congressional caucus, the party turned instead to a general meeting, which was held in a saloon in Baltimore, with 116 delegates from thirteen states attending. These delegates decided on the nominees as well as on an address to the people that contained the party's position on the dominant issues of the day. Three months later, a second convention was held in the same saloon by opponents of President Jackson. The National Republicans (or Whigs, as they later became known) also nominated candidates and agreed on a platform critical of the Jackson administration.

The following year, the Democratic-Republicans (or Democrats, as they were later called) also met in Baltimore. The impetus for their convention was Jackson's desire to demonstrate popular support for his presidency as well as to ensure the selection of Martin Van Buren as his running mate. In 1836, Jackson resorted to another convention—this time to handpick Van Buren as his successor. The Whigs did not hold a convention in 1836. Believing that they would have more success in the House of Representatives than in the nation as a whole, they ran three regional candidates, nominated by the states, who competed against Van Buren in their areas of strength. The plan, however, failed to deny Van Buren an electoral majority. He ended up with 170 votes compared with a total of 124 for the other principal contenders.

Thereafter, the Democrats and their opponents, first the Whigs and then their Republican successors, held nominating conventions to select their candidates. The early conventions were informal and rowdy by contemporary standards, but they also set the precedents for later meetings. The delegates decided on the procedures for conducting the convention, developed policy statements (addresses to the people), and chose nominees. Rules for apportioning the number of delegates were established before the meetings were held. Generally speaking, states were accorded as many votes as their congressional representation merited, regardless of the number of actual participants.

The way in which the delegates were chosen, however, was left up to the states. Local and state conventions, caucuses, or even committees chose the delegates. Public participation was minimal. Party leaders designated the delegates and made the deals. In time, it became clear that successful candidates owed their selection to the heads of the powerful state organizations, not to their own political prominence and organizational support. But the price they had to pay, when calculated in terms of patronage and other political payoffs, was often quite high.

Nineteenth-century conventions served a number of purposes. They provided a forum for party leaders, particularly at the state level. They constituted a mechanism by which agreements could be negotiated and support mobilized. By brokering interests, conventions helped unify the disparate elements within a party, thereby converting an organization of state parties into a national coalition for the purpose of conducting a presidential campaign. Much of the bartering was conducted behind closed doors. Actions on the convention floor often had little to do with the wheeling and dealing that occurred in the smaller "smoke-filled" rooms. Since there was little public preconvention activity, many ballots were often necessary to reach the number that was required to win the party's nomination, usually two-thirds of the delegates.

The nominating system buttressed the position of individual state party leaders, but it did so at the expense of rank-and-file participation. The influence of the state leaders depended on their ability to deliver votes, which in turn required that the delegates not exercise independent judgment. To guarantee their loyalty, the bosses controlled their selection.

Popular Primaries and Caucuses

Demands for reform began to be heard at the beginning of the twentieth century. The Progressive movement, led by Robert La Follette of Wisconsin and Hiram Johnson of California, aimed to break the power of state bosses and their machines through the direct election of convention delegates or, alternatively, through the expression of a popular choice by the electorate. Florida became the first state to provide its political parties with such an option. In 1904, the Democrats took advantage of it and held a statewide vote for convention delegates. One year later, Wisconsin enacted a law for the direct election of delegates to nominating conventions. Others followed suit. By 1912, fifteen states provided for some type of primary election. Oregon was the first to permit a preference vote for the candidates themselves.

The year 1912 was also the first in which a candidate sought to use primaries as a way to obtain the nomination. With almost 42 percent of the Republican delegates selected in primaries, former President Theodore Roosevelt challenged incumbent William Howard Taft. Roosevelt won nine primaries to Taft's one, yet lost the nomination. (See Table 1.1.) Taft's support among regular party leaders who delivered their delegations and controlled the convention was sufficient to win renomination. He received one-third of his support from southern delegations, although the Republican Party had won only a small percentage of the southern vote in the previous election.

Partially in reaction to the unrepresentative, "boss-dominated" convention of 1912, additional states adopted primaries. By 1916, more than half of them held a Republican or Democratic contest. Although a majority of the delegates in that year were chosen by some type of primary, most of them were not bound to support specific candidates. As a consequence, the primary vote did not control the outcome of the conventions.

TABLE 1.1 | THE NUMBER OF PRESIDENTIAL PRIMARIES AND PERCENTAGE OF CONVENTION DELEGATES FROM PRIMARY STATES, BY PARTY, 1912–2008

	Democratic		Republican	
Year	Number of State Primaries	Percentage of Delegates from Primary States	Number of State Primaries	Percentage of Delegates from Primary States
1912	12	32.9%	13	41.7%
1916	20	53.5	20	58.9
1920	16	44.6	20	57.8
1924	14	35.5	17	45.3
1928	16	42.2	15	44.9
1932	16	40.0	14	37.7
1936	14	36.5	12	37.5
1940	13	35.8	13	38.8
1944	14	36.7	13	38.7
1948	14	36.3	12	36.0
1952	16	38.7	13	39.0
1956	19	42.7	19	44.8
1960	16	38.3	15	38.6
1964	16	45.7	16	45.6
1968	15	40.2	15	38.1
1972	21	65.3	20	56.8
1976	27	76.0	26	71.0
1980	34	71.8	34	76.0
1984	29	52.4	25	71.0
1988	36	66.6	36	76.9
1992	39	66.9	38	83.9
1996	35	65.3	42	84.6
2000	40	64.6	43	83.8
2004	40	67.5	26[a]	55.5
2008	39	67.4	42	82.2

[a]Five Republican primaries with a total of 309 delegates were cancelled because only George W. Bush qualified as a candidate.

Source: Harold W. Stanley and Richard G. Niemi, *Vital Statistics on American Politics, 2009–2010.* Washington DC: Congressional Quarterly, 2010, Table 1–23, p. 55. Reprinted by permission of Congressional Quarterly Press, A Division of SAGE Publications, Inc.

The movement toward popular participation was short-lived, however. Following World War I, the number of primaries declined. State party leaders, who saw primaries as a threat to their own influence, argued against them on three grounds: they were expensive; they did not attract many voters; and major candidates tended to avoid them. Moreover, primaries frequently encouraged factionalism, thereby weakening a party's organization. In response to this criticism, the reformers who supported primaries could not claim that their principal goal, rank-and-file control over the selection of party nominees, had been achieved. Public involvement was disappointing. Primaries rarely attracted more than 50 percent of those who voted in the general election, and usually much less. The minority party, in particular, suffered from low turnout for an obvious reason—its candidates stood little chance of winning the general election. In some states, rank-and-file influence was further diluted by the participation of Independents.

As a consequence of these factors, some states that had enacted new primary laws reverted to their former method of selection. Others made their primaries advisory rather than mandatory. Fewer convention delegates were elected in them. By 1936, only fourteen states held Democratic primaries, and twelve held Republican ones. Less than 40 percent of the delegates to each convention that year were chosen in this manner. For the next twenty years, the number of primaries and the percentage of delegates hovered around this level.

Theodore Roosevelt's failure in 1912 and the decline in primaries thereafter made them at best an auxiliary route to the nomination. Although some presidential aspirants became embroiled in primaries, none who depended on them won. In 1920, a spirited contest among three Republicans (General Leonard Wood, Governor Frank Lowden of Illinois, and Senator Hiram Johnson) failed to produce a convention majority for any of these candidates and resulted in party leaders choosing Warren Harding as the standard-bearer. Similarly, in 1952, Senator Estes Kefauver, who chaired the highly publicized and televised Senate hearings on organized crime, entered thirteen of seventeen presidential primaries, won twelve of them, and became the most popular Democratic contender but failed to win his party's nomination.

The reason Kefauver could not parlay his primary victories into a convention victory was that a majority of the delegates were not selected in primaries in 1952. Of those who were, many were chosen separately from the presidential preference vote. Kefauver did not contest these separate delegate elections. As a consequence, he obtained only 50 percent of the delegates in states in which he actually won the presidential preference vote. Moreover, the fact that most of his wins occurred against little or no opposition undercut Kefauver's claim to being the most popular and electable Democrat. He had avoided primaries in four states in which he feared that he might either lose or do poorly.

Not only were primaries not considered to be an essential road to the nomination but running in too many of them was interpreted as a sign of weakness, not strength. It indicated a lack of national recognition, a failure to obtain the support of party leaders, or both. For these reasons, leading candidates tended to choose their primaries carefully, and the primaries, in turn, tended to reinforce the position of the leading candidates. Those who entered primaries did so mainly to test their popularity rather than to win convention votes. Dwight D. Eisenhower in 1952, John F. Kennedy in 1960, and Richard M. Nixon in 1968 had to demonstrate that being a general, a Catholic, or a once-defeated presidential candidate would not be fatal to their chances. In other words, they needed to prove they could win the general election if nominated by their party.

With the possible exception of John Kennedy's victories in West Virginia and Wisconsin, primaries were neither crucial nor decisive for winning the nomination until the 1970s. When there was a provisional consensus within the party, primaries helped confirm it; when there was not, primaries could not produce it.[10] In short, they had little to do with whether the party was unified or divided at the time of the convention.

Primary results tended to be self-fulfilling in the sense that they confirmed the front-runner's status. Between 1936 and 1968, the preconvention leader, the candidate who was ahead in the Gallup Poll before the first primary, won the nomination seventeen out of nineteen times. The only exceptions were Thomas E. Dewey, who was defeated by Wendell Willkie in 1940, and Kefauver, who lost his race for the nomination to Adlai Stevenson in 1952. Willkie, however, had become the leader in public opinion by the time the Republican convention met. Even when leading candidates lost a primary, they had time to recoup. Dewey and Stevenson, defeated in early primaries in 1948 and 1956, respectively, went on to reestablish their credibility as front-runners by winning later primaries.

This situation in which the primaries were not the essential route to the nomination changed dramatically after 1968. Largely as a consequence of the tumultuous Democratic convention of that year, in which the party's nominees and platform were allegedly dictated by party "bosses," demands for a larger voice for rank-and-file partisans increased. In reaction to these demands, the Democratic Party began to look into the matter of delegate selection. The party enacted a series of reforms designed to ensure broader representation at its convention. To avoid challenges to their delegations, a number of states that had used caucus and convention systems changed to primaries. As Table 1.1 indicates, the number of primaries began to increase as did the percentage of convention delegates chosen from them.

New finance laws, which provided for government subsidies for preconvention campaigning, and increased media coverage, particularly by television, also added to the incentive to enter primaries. By 1972, primaries had become decisive. In that year, Senator Edmund Muskie, the leading Democratic contender at the beginning of the process, was forced to withdraw after doing poorly in the early contests. In 1976, President Gerald Ford came close to being the first incumbent president since Chester A. Arthur in 1884 to be denied his party's nomination because of a primary challenge by Ronald Reagan. In 1980, President Jimmy Carter was also challenged for renomination by Senator Edward Kennedy, as was George H. W. Bush by Pat Buchanan in 1992. Bill Clinton and George W. Bush were not challenged for renomination, but nonetheless, both raised millions to ensure that a credible candidate would not oppose them.

Since the 1970s, primaries have revolutionized the presidential nomination process. They have been used to build popularity rather than simply reflect it. Challengers can no longer hope to succeed without entering them; incumbents can no longer ignore them. The impact of primaries has been significant, affecting the strategies and tactics of the candidates, the composition and behavior of the convention delegates, and the decision-making process at the national conventions. The contests for the nomination have shifted power within the parties. They have enlarged the selection zone of potential nominees. They have also made governing more difficult. Each of these developments will be discussed in subsequent chapters.

THE EVOLUTION OF THE GENERAL ELECTION

The general election has changed as well. The Electoral College no longer operates in the manner in which it was designed. It now has a partisan coloration. There is greater opportunity for the general public to participate, but the campaign is not geared to obtaining the most popular votes. Although the system bears a resemblance to its past form, it has become more subject to democratic influences while continuing to contain many electoral biases.

The electoral system for president and vice president was one of the few innovative features of the Constitution. It had no immediate precedent, although it bore some relationship to the way Maryland selected its state senators. In essence, it was designed by the framers, not synthesized from British and American experience, and it is one aspect of the constitutional system that has rarely worked as intended.

Initially, the method by which the states chose their electors varied. Some provided for direct election in a statewide vote. Others had the legislatures do the choosing. Two states used a combination of popular and legislative selection. As political parties emerged at the beginning of the nineteenth century, state legislatures maneuvered the selection process to benefit the party in power. This maneuvering resulted in the selection of more cohesive groups of electors who shared similar partisan views. Gradually, the trend evolved into a winner-take-all system, with most electors chosen on a statewide basis by popular vote. South Carolina was the last state to move to popular selection after the Civil War.

Partisan Electors

The development of the party system changed the character of the Electoral College. Only in the first two elections, when Washington was the unanimous choice, did the electors exercise a nonpartisan and presumably independent judgment in their vote for president. Within ten years from the time the federal government began to operate, electors quickly became the captives of their party and were expected to vote for its candidates. The outcome of the election of 1800 vividly illustrates this new pattern of partisan voting.

The Federalist Party supported President John Adams of Massachusetts and Charles C. Pinckney of South Carolina. Democratic-Republicans, who had emerged to oppose the Federalists' policies, backed Thomas Jefferson of

Virginia and Aaron Burr of New York. The Democratic-Republican candidates won, but, unexpectedly, Jefferson and Burr received the same number of votes. All electors who had cast ballots for Jefferson also cast them for Burr. Since it was not possible in those days to differentiate the candidates for the presidency and vice presidency on the ballot, the results had to be considered a tie, though Jefferson was clearly his party's choice for president. Under the terms of the Constitution, the House of Representatives, voting by state, had to choose the winner.

CONGRESSIONAL DECISIONS

On February 11, 1801, after the results of the Electoral College vote were announced by the vice president, who happened to be Jefferson, a Federalist-controlled House convened to resolve the dilemma. Since the winners of the 1800 election did not take office until March 4, 1801, representatives from a "lame-duck" Congress would have to choose the next president.[11] A majority of Federalists supported Burr, whom they regarded as the more pragmatic politician, a person with whom they could deal. Jefferson, on the other hand, was perceived as a dangerous, uncompromising radical by many Federalists. Alexander Hamilton, however, was outspoken in his opposition to Burr, a political rival from New York, whom Hamilton regarded as "the most unfit man in the United States for the office of President."[12]

On the first ballot taken on February 11, Burr received a majority of the total votes, but Jefferson won the support of more state delegations.[13] Eight states voted for Jefferson, six backed Burr, and two were evenly divided. This vote left Jefferson one short of the needed majority. The House took nineteen ballots on its first day of deliberations and a total of thirty-six before it finally elected Jefferson. Had Burr promised to be a Federalist president, it is conceivable that he could have won.

The first amendment to reform voting procedures in the Electoral College was enacted by the new Congress, controlled by Jefferson's party, in 1803. It was accepted by three-fourths of the states in 1804. This amendment to the Constitution, the twelfth, provided for separate voting for president and vice president. It also refined the selection procedures in the event that the president or vice president did not receive a majority of the electoral vote. The House of Representatives, still voting by state delegation, was to choose from among the three presidential candidates with the most electoral votes, and the Senate, voting by individual senator, was to choose from the top two vice presidential candidates. If the House could not make a decision by March 4, the amendment provided for the new vice president to assume the presidency until such time as the House could render a judgment.

The next nondecisive presidential vote did not occur until 1824. That year, four people received electoral votes for president: Andrew Jackson (ninety-nine votes), John Quincy Adams (eighty-four), William Crawford (forty-one), and Henry Clay (thirty-seven). According to the Twelfth Amendment, the House of Representatives had to decide from among the top three, since no one had a majority. Eliminated from the contest was Henry Clay, who happened to be Speaker of the House. Clay threw his support to Adams, who won. It was alleged that Clay did so in exchange for appointment as secretary of state, a charge that Clay vigorously denied. After Adams became president, however, he nominated Clay for secretary of state, a position Clay readily accepted.[14]

Jackson was the winner of the popular vote in 1824. In eighteen of the twenty-four states that chose electors by popular vote that year, he received 192,933 votes compared with 115,696 for Adams, 47,136 for Clay, and 46,979 for Crawford. Adams, however, had the backing of more state delegations. A Massachusetts resident, he enjoyed the support of the six New England states, and with Clay's help, the representatives of six others backed his candidacy. The votes of thirteen states, however, were needed for a majority. New York seemed to be the pivotal state and Stephen Van Rensselaer, a Revolutionary War general, the swing representative. On the morning of the vote, Speaker Clay and Representative Daniel Webster tried to persuade Van Rensselaer to vote for Adams. It was said that they were unsuccessful.[15] As the voting began, Van Rensselaer bowed his head as if in prayer. On the floor he saw a piece of paper with "Adams" written on it. Interpreting this as a sign from on high, he dropped the paper in the box. New York went for Adams by only one vote, providing him with the barest majority.[16]

Jackson, outraged at the turn of events, urged the abolition of the Electoral College. His claim of a popular mandate, however, was open to question. The most populous state at the time, New York, did not permit its electorate to participate in the selection of electors. Moreover, in three of the states in which Jackson won the electoral vote but lost in the House of Representatives, he had fewer popular votes than Adams.[17]

Opposition to the system mounted, however, and a gradual democratization of the electoral process occurred. More states began to choose their electors directly by popular vote. In 1800, ten of the fifteen states used legislative selection. By 1832, only South Carolina retained this practice. The trend was also toward statewide election of an entire slate of electors. States that had chosen their electors within legislative districts converted to a winner-take-all system to maximize their voting power in the Electoral College. This change, in turn, created the possibility that there could be a disparity between the popular and electoral vote. A candidate could be elected by winning the popular vote in the big states but losing most of the small states or vice versa.

The next disputed election did not occur until 1876. In that election, Democrat Samuel J. Tilden received the most votes. He had 250,000 more popular votes and 19 more electoral votes than his Republican rival, Rutherford B. Hayes. Nonetheless, Tilden fell one vote short of a majority in the Electoral College. Twenty electoral votes were in dispute. Dual election returns were received from Florida (4 votes), Louisiana (8 votes), and South Carolina (7 votes). Charges of fraud and voting irregularities were made by both parties. The Republicans, who controlled the three state legislatures, contended that Democrats had forcibly prevented newly freed slaves from voting. The Democrats, on the other hand, alleged that many nonresidents participated as did people who were not registered to vote. The other disputed electoral vote occurred in the state of Oregon. One Republican elector was challenged on the grounds that he held another federal position (assistant postmaster) at the time he was chosen and thus was ineligible to be an elector.

Three days before the Electoral College vote was to be officially counted, Congress established a commission to examine and try to resolve the dispute. The electoral commission was to consist of fifteen members: ten from Congress (five Republicans and five Democrats) and five from the Supreme Court. Four of the Supreme Court justices were designated by the act (two Republicans and two Democrats), and they were to choose the fifth. Their choice, Justice David Davis, a political independent, was expected to become a member of the commission, but on the day it was created, Davis was appointed by the Illinois legislature to the U.S. Senate. The Supreme Court justices then picked Joseph Bradley, an independent Republican from New Jersey. Bradley sided with his party on every issue. By a strictly partisan vote, the commission validated the credentials of all the Republican electors, thereby giving Hayes a one-vote margin of victory in the Electoral College.[18]

Prior to the election of 2000, the only other one in which the winner of the popular vote was beaten in an undisputed Electoral College vote occurred in 1888. Democrat Grover Cleveland had a plurality of 95,096 popular votes, but only 168 electoral votes compared with 233 for Republican Benjamin Harrison. Cleveland's losses in Indiana by about 3,000 votes and New York by about 15,000 led to his defeat.

JUDICIAL DETERMINATION

The 2000 election was different. Not only was the popular vote very close but the electoral vote was close as well. Al Gore was ahead in twenty states plus the District of Columbia with a total of 267 electoral votes. George W. Bush led in twenty-nine states with a total of 238 electoral votes. One state, Florida, was in dispute. Out of more than 5.9 million votes cast in that state, 537 votes separated the two candidates. Both sides alleged procedural irregularities, voter eligibility issues, and ballot counting errors.

Four legal issues had marred the Florida election: voter confusion over the design of the ballot in one county; disagreement over eligible voters and absentee ballots in several others; tabulation problems in counties that used punch-card ballots; and the date when the official results had to be certified by the secretary of state.

Voter confusion stemmed from a "butterfly ballot" used in Palm Beach County, where many retirees live. Designed by a Democratic campaign official, the ballot was intended to help senior citizens read the names of the candidates more clearly by using larger type. To fit all the names on a single punch card, however, two columns had to be used, with the punch holes for voting, or "chads" as they are called, between them. Although Democrats Al Gore and Joe Lieberman were listed second on the left-hand column, their chad was positioned third, after the chad of the candidates on the right-hand column, Pat Buchanan and Ezola Foster of the Reform Party. (See Figure 1.1.) Some voters, who claimed that they intended to vote for the Democratic candidates, punched out the second rather than the third chad, which registered as a vote for Buchanan. Others,

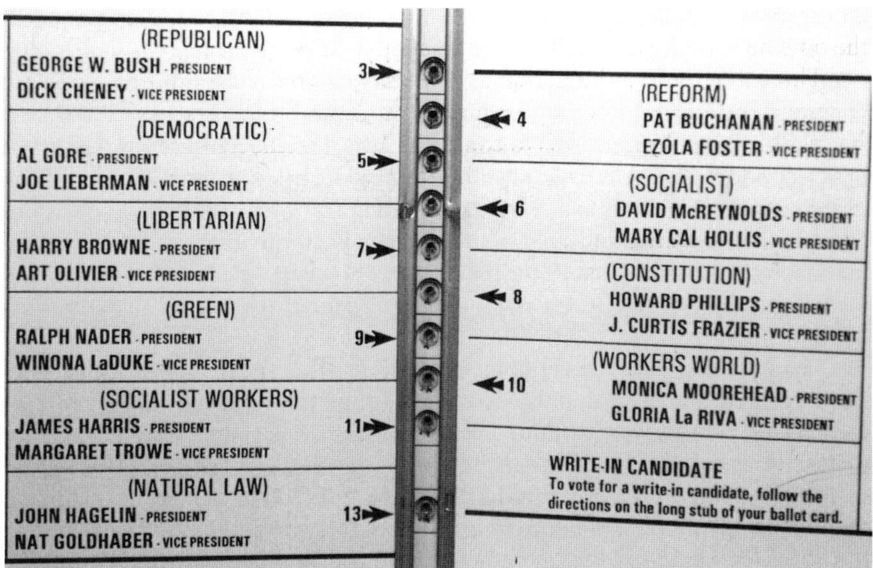

Figure 1.1 | The Palm Beach Ballot

Source: AP Photo/Gary I. Rothstein

in confusion, pushed out both the second and third chads, automatically voiding their ballots.[19] Aggrieved Democrats in the county immediately filed a lawsuit to contest the election and demand a new vote. A Florida state court, however, rejected their request, effectively terminating the revote option.

A second issue concerned ballots that were not properly included in the machine count. Many counties in Florida used a punch-card system of voting in which chads, a small perforated box on the card, must be removed with a specially designed instrument for the vote to be properly cast. The holes in the card were then tabulated by machine. However, if a chad was not completely removed, the vote may not have been recorded by the voting machine. The Gore campaign alleged that thousands of presidential votes in three Democratic counties—Miami-Dade, Broward, and Palm Beach—were not counted because part or all of a chad was still attached to the ballot. In other words, voters had not completely punched through the card. Democrats appealed to county officials for a hand count of these ballots.

One county, Palm Beach, began such a count; another, Miami-Dade, initiated a sample count to see whether a hand count was merited; the third, Broward, initially chose not to recount at all. Gore's representatives put pressure on the reluctant counties to proceed with a hand count of these uncounted ballots while Bush's attorneys went to federal court to stop it, arguing that a selective hand count in some counties was unfair to people in the other counties. Before the courts had rendered a judgment, however, Florida's secretary of state, a Republican appointee, certified the original county vote as the official one to which only absentee ballots, postmarked no later than election day and received by the counties within one week of the election, could be added. The secretary of state's certification prompted Gore's legal team to go to state court to force the secretary to accept hand-counted votes and an amended vote total submitted after the certification.

A Florida circuit court ruled that the secretary had discretion to accept or reject additional vote counts submitted by counties as long as she did not exercise that discretion arbitrarily. The secretary then asked the counties to justify why they wished to amend their original submission with an additional hand count of some votes. After they did so, however, she rejected their arguments, thereby forcing Gore's attorneys to take the entire matter to the Florida Supreme Court.

In an extraordinary session, televised across the country, lawyers for both sides debated the hand-count and vote deadline issues within the context of state and federal law and the U.S. Constitution. The Gore side claimed that the only way to ensure a "full, fair, and accurate" vote that represented the will of the Florida electorate would be to tabulate the disputed ballots by hand. But Bush's legal counsel contended that a hand count was blatantly unfair to those who had voted in accordance with the established rules and procedures of the state. Besides, they contended, extending the deadline for certified results violated an 1887 federal law that requires states to choose their electors by laws that are enacted *prior* to Election Day. The Florida Supreme Court, consisting of eight judges, all but one of whom were appointed by Democratic governors, sided with Gore and proceeded to give the counties an additional six days to submit a revised vote that included hand-counted ballots. Bush's lawyers appealed the Florida Supreme Court's decision to the U.S. Supreme Court.

What followed was a frantic hand count in two counties while a third, Miami-Dade, decided not to go ahead with one, in part because officials believed that they could not do so within the time frame established by the court.[20] Meanwhile, in another part of the state, Democrats filed suit to exclude all absentee ballots from certain counties because Republicans had been given an opportunity to add required voter registration numbers to the forms, omitted erroneously by a glitch in the software program that printed the request forms. Democrats had not been given a chance to add the numbers. However, a circuit judge ruled against the Democrats' claim.

On Monday, December 4, nearly a month after the presidential election, the U.S. Supreme Court vacated the Florida Supreme Court's verdict that had extended the deadline for hand-counted ballots in the three Florida counties on the grounds that its legal basis for this decision was unclear. The Court remanded the case back to the Florida Supreme Court for clarification and judgment. Later in the day, a Florida state court judge dismissed Gore's claims for an additional hand count of thousands of ballots from Palm Beach and Miami-Dade counties that had registered no presidential preference as well as the hand-counted ballots that had been submitted after the court-imposed deadline.[21] The judge also refused to overturn the certification of Florida's electoral vote for Bush. In a last-ditch effort to salvage a Florida victory, Gore appealed this state court judgment to the Florida Supreme Court.

Thus, the state supreme court was faced with two issues: One concerned its decision, and the legal basis on which it was predicated, for extending the state certification deadline for those counties that chose to submit an amended vote based on disputed hand-counted ballots; the other was Gore's appeal to overturn the lower court's decision that additional hand counts and time to certify results were not merited. The Supreme Court of Florida again sided with Gore, ordering an immediate recount of ballots that had not been included in the machine tabulation in all Florida counties. Bush's lawyers immediately appealed that decision to the U.S. Supreme Court.

The final legal maneuvering ended in the U.S. Supreme Court. After agreeing to hear the appeal, the Court stopped the recount of the disputed ballots, pending its judgment on the matter. On December 11, 2000, one day before Florida law required the designation of its electors, the Court heard oral arguments in *Bush v. Gore*. Its decision, announced the next evening, reversed the Florida Supreme Court's judgment that ordered the hand count to be resumed. The Supreme Court stated that the absence of a single standard to be used throughout the state by election officials violated the Fourteenth Amendment, which requires states to provide all their residents with equal protection under the laws. A majority of the U.S. Supreme Court went on to conclude that there was not sufficient time, given the state legislature's intent to designate Florida's electors by December 12, to establish such a standard. Hence, the certified vote that had Bush leading by 537 was final.

Four justices dissented from the finding that time had run out on the Florida Supreme Court. Two of these justices believed that the deadline for the designation of electors specified by U.S. law, the first Monday following the second Wednesday in December (the 18th in 2000) took precedence over the state legislature's date of December 12 and thus provided sufficient time for the state supreme court to establish a single statewide standard for recounting the votes. The two other dissenters felt that the Florida Supreme Court had acted properly, that the vote count was legal, and that it should not have been halted by the U.S. Supreme Court.

Following the disputed election, changes in the election laws occurred on both state and national levels. Florida enacted electoral reforms to prevent a repetition of the problems that occurred in 2000. Its new law provided more training for election workers, more accurate registration records, and provisional voting for those who claimed to be registered but whose names did not appear on county and precinct voting lists. The state also allocated money for counties to replace their antiquated punch-card machines with more updated scanning equipment and voting machines. National electoral reforms, along the lines of the Florida law, were also passed by Congress in 2002. The Help America Vote Act provided almost $4 billion in federal funds to the states to consolidate and computerize their voter registration lists by January 2006.[22]

Although registration problems, late absentee ballots, and long lines to vote were still apparent in the 2004 and 2008 elections, no controversy of the magnitude of the 2000 Florida election marred the outcome of either election. When the results of the vote are clear, minor disputes lose their saliency.

OTHER CLOSE ELECTIONS

There have been other close elections in which the vote choice of a relatively small number of people would have altered the results. In 1860, a shift of 25,000 in New York from Abraham Lincoln to Stephen Douglas would have denied Lincoln a majority in the Electoral College. A change of less than 30,000 in three states in 1892 would have given Benjamin Harrison another victory over Cleveland. In 1916, Charles Evans Hughes needed only 3,807 more votes in California to have beaten Woodrow Wilson. Similarly, Thomas E. Dewey could have denied Harry S Truman a majority in the Electoral College with 12,487 more California votes in 1948. A change in the votes of fewer than 9,000 people in Illinois and Missouri in 1960 would have meant that John F. Kennedy would have lacked an Electoral College majority. In 1968, a shift of only 55,000 votes from Richard M. Nixon to Hubert H. Humphrey in three states would have thrown the election into the House of Representatives, which at that time was controlled by the Democrats. In 1976, a shift of only 3,687 in Hawaii and 5,559 in Ohio would have cost Jimmy Carter the election.[23]

Not only could the results of these elections have been affected by very small shifts in voter preferences but in 1948, 1960, 1968, and 1992, there was the added possibility that the Electoral College vote would not be decisive. In each of these elections, third-party or independent candidates threatened to secure enough votes to prevent either majority-party candidate from gaining a majority. In 1948, Henry Wallace (Progressive Party) and Strom Thurmond (States' Rights Party) received almost 5 percent of the total popular vote, and Thurmond won 39 electoral votes. In 1960, fourteen unpledged electors were chosen in Alabama and Mississippi. In 1968, George Wallace of Alabama, running under the American Independent Party label, received almost 10 million popular votes and 46 electoral votes, and in 1992 H. Ross Perot received 19.7 million popular votes (almost 19 percent of the total) but none in the Electoral College. Four years later, he got 8.1 million popular votes but again, no electoral votes. Ralph Nader received less than 3 percent of the popular vote in 2000, but his 97,488 votes in Florida undoubtedly cost Gore that state and an overall election victory.

It is clear that close competition between the two major parties combined with a strong third-party or independent candidate provides the Electoral College with its most difficult test.

THE POLITICS OF ELECTORAL COLLEGE VOTING

The presidential campaign and election is shaped by the Electoral College. The strategies the candidates pursue, the resources they utilize, and the states in which they place their major efforts are all calculated on the basis of Electoral College politics, not the popular vote.

The Electoral College is not neutral. No system of election can be. The way votes are aggregated does make a difference. It benefits some of the electorate at the expense of others. The Electoral College usually works to the advantage of the candidate who wins the most popular votes. More often than not, it tends to exaggerate that candidate's margin of victory. Bill Clinton received only 43 percent of the popular vote in 1992 but 69 percent of the electoral vote; in 1996, he received 49 percent of the popular vote, 54.6 percent of the two-party vote, and 70.4 percent of the electoral vote. Similarly in 1968, Richard Nixon won only 43.4 percent of the popular vote but 56 percent of the electoral vote. In 1980, Ronald Reagan received 51 percent of the popular vote but a whopping 91 percent of the electoral vote; in 2008, Barack Obama won 53 percent of the popular vote but 68 percent of the vote in the Electoral College. Even in the very close elections of 2000 and 2004, Bush received a higher percentage of the electoral vote, 50.4 (2000) and 53.2 (2004), than the popular vote, 48 (2000) and 50.7 (2004).

Why does the Electoral College usually enhance the margin of the popular vote winner? The reason has to do with the winner-take-all system of voting that has developed in most states. In almost every instance, the presidential and vice presidential candidates who receive a plurality of the popular vote within the state get all its electoral votes.[24] This translates into a larger percentage of the Electoral College vote than it would with a direct popular vote.[25] According to one study of presidential elections from 1924 to 1992, the plurality winner who received more than 53.5 percent of the two-party vote received over 75 percent of the electoral vote.[26]

Advocates of the system see this enlarged Electoral College vote as an advantage for the new or reelected president. They claim that it increases the president's mandate for governing as well as the coalition of supporters on whom the president can rely. Most states also perceive a benefit from casting their votes as a unit. They believe that it enhances their political clout. In 2004, voters in Colorado soundly defeated a constitutional amendment that would have allocated their state's electoral vote in proportion to the popular vote that the candidates received. Such an amendment would have decreased that state's importance to the presidential candidates and the state's impact on the Electoral College vote.

The large states, theoretically, gain more influence in the Electoral College by winner-take-all voting. The very smallest states do so as well because they receive a minimum of three electoral votes regardless of the size of their population. As a consequence, their citizens have greater voting power than they would have in a direct election system. To illustrate, if Wyoming's population of approximately 520,000 in 2010 were divided by its three electoral votes, there would be one elector for every 173,333 people. Dividing California's estimated 2010 population of 38,067,000 by its fifty-five electoral votes yields one elector for every 692,127 persons.[27] Medium-sized states are comparatively disadvantaged.[28]

But the advantage that the largest and smallest states reap from the current Electoral College system pales by comparison to the benefit that the most competitive states receive regardless of their size. Since the advent of frequent public opinion polling during the election period, candidates have tended to concentrate their time, efforts, and resources in those states that seemed to be up for grabs—at least, according to the polls. Noncompetitive states, large or small, see little of the presidential campaign. The candidates rarely visit them;

they spend little, if any, money in them; run few, if any, political advertisements in their major media markets; and mount little, if any, grassroots effort. They are essentially ignored because their Electoral College vote is predictable.

And at the presidential level the number of competitive states had been declining until the election of 2008. In 1960, about half the states were deemed competitive; either of the major-party candidates had a realistic chance to win them. In the twenty-first century, only about one-third of the states have been seen as competitive at the beginning of the general election campaign (eighteen in 2008) and less than one-fifth at the end. In 2008, 98 percent of candidate visits and presidential advertising occurred in only fifteen states.[29] In short, the one national election in the United States has been reduced to a contest fought in a decreasing number of states.

Not only does the Electoral College in practice give disproportionate influence to the most competitive states but it also advantages the groups that live in them. Many of the larger battleground states are located in the Midwest and the smaller ones are in the Southwest. Minorities, such as African Americans, Hispanics, Asian Americans, and Native Americans, are less well represented in the large, more competitive Midwestern states and the Southwest. Thus the Electoral College also contains a *de facto* racial and ethnic bias, which may be reflected in the public policy initiatives of the winning candidate and party.

The Electoral College also benefits the two major parties at the expense of third parties and independent candidates.[30] The reason it does so is that the winner-take-all system of voting by states when combined with the need for a majority of the total electoral vote makes it difficult for third parties to accumulate enough votes to win an election. To have any effect, minor-party candidates must have support that is geographically concentrated, as Strom Thurmond's was in 1948 and George Wallace's in 1968, rather than more broadly distributed across the country, as Henry Wallace's was in 1948, H. Ross Perot's in 1992 and 1996, and Ralph Nader's in 2000.

Given the limitations on third parties, their most realistic electoral objectives would seem to be to defeat one of the major contenders rather than to elect their own candidate. In 1912, Theodore Roosevelt's Bull Moose campaign split the Republican Party, thereby aiding the Democratic Party candidate, Woodrow Wilson. In 2000, Ralph Nader's vote, though small, hurt Gore more than Bush and cost the Democrats a victory in Florida. In other elections, third parties may have dipped into the major two-party vote but do not appear to have changed the outcome of elections.

Which of the major parties is advantaged by the Electoral College has been much debated. The conventional wisdom held that the Republicans were advantaged more than the Democrats. Since 1968, their candidates have won seven of the last eleven presidential elections. The Republicans can rely on the support of more noncompetitive states, particularly those in the Rocky Mountain region and the South, although in 2008, Colorado and the three southern states of Virginia, North Carolina, and Florida voted for Obama. The Democrats' principal support comes from the states in the Northeast and on the Pacific Coast. However, the closeness of recent elections and the relative parity between the major parties today suggest that either one could win a majority in the Electoral College if they nominate a candidate with broad national appeal.

SUMMARY

The quest for the presidency has been and continues to be influenced by the system designed in Philadelphia in 1787. The objectives of that system were to protect the independence of the institution, ensure the selection of a well-qualified, national candidate, and do so in a way that was politically expedient and technologically feasible, given the state of communications and transportation in 1787. The Electoral College was also thought to be consistent with the tenets of a republican form of government.

Although many of the objectives remain the same, the system has changed significantly over the years. Of all the factors that have influenced these changes, none has been more important than the advent of political parties. Their development created an additional first step in the process, the nomination, which has influenced the selection and behavior of electors ever since.

The nomination process is necessary to the parties, whose principal interest is to get their candidates elected. At first, members of Congress, meeting in partisan caucuses, decided on the nominees. On the basis of common friendships and shared perspectives, they reached a consensus and then used their influence to mobilize support for the agreed-upon candidates. In effect, the ad hoc system that developed provided for legislative selection of the president in violation of the letter and spirit of the Constitution.

The caucus method broke down with the demise of the Federalists and the factionalization of the Republicans. It was never restored. In its place, a more decentralized mode of selection, reflective of the increasing sectional composition of the parties, emerged.

The new nomination process, controlled by state leaders, operated within the framework of a brokered national convention. There was little rank-and-file participation. Demands for greater public participation eventually opened up the nomination process, thereby reducing the influence of state leaders and decreasing the dependence of presidential candidates on them. Power eventually shifted from the political leaders to the candidates and their supporters, with party partisans making the final judgment.

Similar trends, rooted in the development of parties and the expansion of suffrage, affected the way in which the electors were selected and how they voted. Instead of being chosen on the basis of their personal qualifications, electors were selected on the basis of their partisan loyalties; instead of being elected as individuals, they were chosen as part of a partisan slate; instead of exercising independent judgment, the electors became agents of their party. The inevitable soon happened: bloc voting by electors in states.

The desire of the populace for greater participation in the presidential election process also had an effect. It accelerated the change to the popular election of the electors with the result that the electoral vote tended to reflect, even exaggerate, the popular vote. There have been only four times in U.S. history in which the plurality winner was not elected: 1824, 1876, 1888, and 2000.

In the presidential election of 2000, the electoral system was put to a severe test. Although allegations of voter intimidation, inaccurate registration lists, machine malfunctions, and tabulation disputes have characterized elections in the past and occasionally become contemporary issues, as in 1960, they rarely affected the overall result. In 2000, they did so, by focusing attention on the popular vote of one state, Florida, which ultimately determined the winner of the Electoral College vote.

The 2000 election and the ones following it have raised a multitude of issues that critically address the fairness and adequacy of the Electoral College as a national voting system. Critics allege that it is undemocratic, unequal, and unwise. It advantages the most competitive states. The presidential candidates spend the vast majority of their time and resources in these states and virtually ignore the rest of the country, thereby questioning whether the presidential election is truly a national election.

In summary, the electoral system works, but it does so imperfectly. It permits a partisan choice but has not generally facilitated partisan accountability or responsible party governance. It provides greater opportunities for public participation in the nomination and election processes but has not usually resulted in a broad cross section of partisans contributing money, working, or even voting in their party's primaries, nor has it encouraged all segments of the electorate to get involved and to vote in the general election. In some recent elections (1992, 1996, and 2000), the winning candidate received only a plurality of the vote. Considering that a substantial portion of the voting-age population does not vote, and the popular vote may be closely divided, the winner may not be able to claim the support of more than one out of three or four adults, hardly the mandate we might expect or desire in a democracy, nor one that is usually sufficient for governing effectively.

WHERE ON THE WEB?

General Sites

- **270towin.com**
  www.270towin.com
  Contains an interactive electoral map for current and past presidential elections.
- **C-SPAN: Road to the White House 2012**
  www.cspan.org
  Provides up-to-date information about the campaign.
- **Center for Voting and Democracy**
  www.fairvote.org
  An organization that promotes voter education and outreach, the center supports a national popular vote for president.
- **Democracy in Action**
  www.P2012.org
  A site sponsored by the Graduate School in Campaign Management of the George Washington University. It has a wealth of up-to-date information on the 2012 presidential campaign with links to other sources.
- **Google**
  www.google.com
  Comprehensive search engine.

- **National Popular Vote**
  www.NationalPopularVote.com
  An organization that has proposed an interstate compact in which states would agree to cast their electoral votes for the national popular vote winner.
- **Politics 1**
  www.politics1.com
  An online guide to current politics with links to other relevant sites for the 2012 campaign.
- **Yahoo**
  www.yahoo.com
  A comprehensive link for campaign news and information.

Government Sources

- **Election Assistance Commission**
  www.eac.gov
  The commission set up by Congress in the 2002 Help America Vote Act to facilitate voter registration and voting procedures in U.S. elections.
- **Federal Election Commission**
  www.fec.gov
  This commission collects and disseminates data on election turnout, voting, and most importantly, candidate, party, and nonparty group revenues and expenditures. It publishes the official results.
- **National Archives and Records Administration; Office of the Federal Register**
  www.archives.gov/federal-register/electoral-college
  Provides access to federal laws and presidential documents as well as statistics on past presidential elections and information on the Electoral College.
- **The White House**
  www.whitehouse.gov
  Provides information on the activities of the president and vice president: what they say, who they meet, and their positions on current issues.

Exercises

1. Prior to the completion of the next nomination process, obtain the most recent schedule of primaries and caucuses for the selection of delegates to the Democratic and Republican national nominating conventions for the year of the presidential election. You can do this on most major news networks' Web sites or at the Election Assistance Commission, the Federal Election Commission, or thegreenpapers.com. Try to figure out which of the declared and undeclared candidates for each party's nomination is most and least advantaged by this schedule. Then predict which of the candidates will be the popular-vote winner in the individual primaries and caucuses.
2. Get up-to-speed on the Electoral College by accessing and reviewing the material on the Electoral College at the National Archives and Records Administration site, (www.archives.gov/federal-register/electoral-college). Use the links available at this site to find out how the electors in your state are selected and the dates and procedures by which they will vote in 2012.
3. Access the Web site www.270towin.com. Explain how the Electoral College maps for the 2004 and 2008 elections differ. Then construct a winning Electoral College strategy for the Democratic or Republican candidate you prefer in 2012. Focus on the likely swing states in your analysis. Why do you think these states may go Democratic or Republican in 2012?

Selected Readings

Abbot, David W., and James P. Levine. *Wrong Winner: The Coming Debacle in the Electoral College*. New York: Praeger, 1991.

Amar, Vikram David. "The 2004 Presidential Election and the Electoral College: How the Results Debunk Some Defenses of the Current System" (Nov. 12, 2004). www.writ.news.findlaw.com/amar/20041112.html.

Bennett, Robert W. *Taming the Electoral College*. Stanford, CA.: Stanford University Press, 2006.

Best, Judith. "Presidential Selection: Complex Problems and Simple Solutions." *The Political Science Quarterly,* 119 (Spring 2004): 39–59.

Brunell, Thomas, and Bernard Grofman. "The 1992 and 1996 Presidential Elections: Whatever Happened to the Republican Electoral College Lock?" *Presidential Studies Quarterly,* 112 (Winter 1997): 134–138.

Destler, I. M. "The Myth of the Electoral College Lock." *PS: Political Science and Politics*, 29 (September 1996): 189–193.

Edwards, George C., III. *Why the Electoral College is Bad for America*. 2nd ed. New Haven: Yale University Press, 2011.

FairVote's Presidental Elections Reform Program. *Presidential Election Inequality: The Electoral College in the Twenty-First Century*. Takoma Park, MD: Center for Voting and Democracy, 2006.

Fortier, John C., ed. *After the People Vote: A Guide to the Electoral College.* Washington, DC: The AEI Press, 2004.

Gains, Brian. "Popular Myths and Popular Vote–Electoral College Splits." *PS: Political Science and Politics,* 34 (March 2001): 71–75.

Issacharoff, Samuel. "Law, Rules, and Presidential Selection." *Political Science Quarterly*, 120 (Spring 2005): 113–129.

Levinson, Sanford, Daniel Lowenstein, and John McGinnis. "Should We Dispense with the Electoral College?" *University of Pennsylvania Law Review*, 156 (2007): 10–37.

Longley, Lawrence D., and James D. Dana, Jr. "The Biases of the Electoral College in the 1990s," *Polity,* 25 (Fall 1992): 123–145.

Panagopoulos, Costas. "Electoral Reform." *Public Opinion Quarterly*, 68 (Winter 2004): 623–640.

Rakove, Jack. "Presidential Selection: Electoral Fallacies." *The Political Science Quarterly,* 119 (Spring 2004): 21–38.

Schumaker, Paul D., and Burdett A. Loomis, eds. *Choosing a President*. New York: Chatham House, 2002.

Troy, Gil. *See How They Ran: The Changing Role of the Presidential Candidate*. New York: Free Press, 1991.

U.S. Senate Committee on the Judiciary. *The Electoral College and Direct Election of the President*. Hearings, 102nd Cong., 2nd sess., July 22, 1992. Washington, DC: Government Printing Office, 1992.

Notes

1. Gouverneur Morris, *Records of the Federal Convention,* ed. Max Farrand (New Haven: Yale University Press, 1921), pp. 2, 33.
2. The first proposal for direct election was introduced in a very timid fashion by James Wilson, delegate from Pennsylvania. James Madison's *Journal* describes Wilson's presentation as follows: "Mr. Wilson said he was almost unwilling to

declare the mode which he wished to take place, being apprehensive that it might appear chimerical. He would say however at least that in theory he was for an election by the people; Experience, particularly in N. York & Massts, shewed that an election of the first magistrate by the people at large, was both convenient & successful mode." Farrand, *Records of the Federal Convention,* vol. I, p. 68.

3. This provision was intended to decrease parochialism and facilitate the selection of a national candidate. It forced Dick Cheney, George W. Bush's choice to be his vice presidential running mate in 2000, to move his official residence from Texas to Wyoming so that Texas' electors could vote for the entire Republican ticket if Bush and Cheney won the popular vote in that state, which they did.
4. So great was the sectional rivalry, so competitive the states, so limited the number of people with national reputations, that it was feared electors would tend to vote primarily for people from their own states. To prevent the same states, particularly the largest ones, from exercising undue influence in the selection of both the president and vice president, this provision was included.
5. George Mason declared, "Nineteen times out of twenty, the President would be chosen by the Senate." Farrand, *Records of the Federal Convention,* vol. II, 500. The original proposal of the Committee on Unfinished Business was that the Senate should select the president. The delegates substituted the House of Representatives, fearing that the Senate was too powerful with its appointment and treaty-making powers. The principle of equal state representation was retained. Choosing the president is the only occasion on which the House of Representatives votes by state.
6. Thomas R. Marshall, *Presidential Nominations in a Reform Age* (New York: Praeger, 1981), p. 19.
7. Neal R. Peirce and Lawrence D. Longley, *The People's President* (New Haven: Yale University Press, 1981), p. 36.
8. Marshall *Presidential Nominations,* p. 20.
9. Ibid., p. 21.
10. Louis Maisel and Gerald J. Lieberman, "The Impact of Electoral Rules on Primary Elections: The Democratic Presidential Primaries in 1976," in *The Impact of the Electoral Process,* eds. Louis Maisel and Joseph Cooper (Beverly Hills, CA: Sage, 1977), p. 68.
11. Until the passage of the Twentieth Amendment, which made January 3 the date when members of Congress took their oaths of office and convened, it was the second session of the preelection Congress that met after the election.
12. Lucius Wilmerding, *The Electoral College* (New Brunswick, NJ: Rutgers University Press, 1953), p. 32.
13. There were 106 members of the House (58 Federalists and 48 Republicans). On the first ballot, the vote of those present was for Burr. 53–51.
14. In those days, being secretary of state was considered a stepping-stone to the presidency. With the exception of Washington and John Adams, all the people who became president prior to Andrew Jackson had first held appointment as secretary of state.
15. Peirce and Longley, *People's President,* p. 51.
16. Marquis James, *The Life of Andrew Jackson* (Indianapolis: Bobbs-Merrill, 1938), p. 439.
17. He captured the majority of electoral votes in two of these states because the electors were chosen on a district rather than on a statewide basis. William R. Keech, "Background Paper," in *Winner Take All: Report of the Twentieth Century Fund Task Force on Reform of the Presidential Election Process* (New York: Holmes & Meier, 1978), p. 50.

18. The act that created the commission specified that its decision would be final unless overturned by both houses of Congress. The House of Representatives, controlled by the Democrats, opposed every one of the commission's findings. The Republican Senate, however, concurred. A Democratic filibuster in the Senate was averted by Hayes's promise of concessions to the South, including the withdrawal of federal troops. Tilden could have challenged the findings of the commission in court but chose not to do so.
19. The vote tabulated in this county provided some evidence of the confusion. Buchanan's vote was larger in Palm Beach than in any other Florida county. Palm Beach had a large, elderly Jewish population unlikely to have supported Buchanan. Moreover, Palm Beach had a larger percentage of ballots in which no presidential vote was recorded than all but two of the other sixty-seven counties in the state.
20. At the time of the court-imposed deadline, only one county, Broward, had submitted a recount that moved Gore to within about 500 votes of Bush. Palm Beach County was unable to get its votes in by the 5:00 PM deadline. That county submitted its revised tabulation several hours later, too late to be included in the revised state vote count. Still trailing his Republican opponent, Gore went back to state court to seek a court order forcing an immediate hand count in Miami-Dade, but a Florida appeals court refused to do so as did the state supreme court. These refusals prompted Gore to return to state court to ask for a court order to count the disputed ballots in Miami-Dade and include the revised vote totals from Palm Beach that had been completed after the deadline.
21. The judge held that Gore's attorneys had not provided statistical evidence to demonstrate the *probability*, not a mere *possibility*, that the results of the Florida election would be different if a hand count were to occur and be included in the vote totals.
22. The money was also used to buy more modern, touch-screen voting machines and make voting places more accessible to the disabled and ballots more understandable to non-English speakers. The law required states to allow provisional voting for people who believe that they were properly registered but who were not listed as registered at the precinct at which they voted.
23. Richard M. Scammon and Alice V. McGillivray, *America Votes 12* (Washington DC: Congressional Quarterly, 1977), p. 15.
24. Two states, Maine and Nebraska, do not always vote as a bloc because they do not select all their electors on an at-large basis. Two are chosen at large and the remaining ones are elected in each of the states' congressional districts. In 2008, Nebraska's electoral vote was divided, with McCain winning four and Obama one. McCain won the popular statewide vote as well as the vote in two of the state's three congressional districts. Obama won the other congressional district. The Maine vote went to Obama four to zero.
25. Thomas Brunell and Bernard Grofman, "The 1992 and 1996 Presidential Elections: Whatever Happened to the Republican Electoral College Lock?" *Presidential Studies Quarterly*, 112 (Winter 1997): pp. 134–138.
26. I. M. Destler, "The Myth of the Electoral Lock," *PS: Political Science and Politics*, 29 (Sept. 1996): p. 491.
27. The 2010 population estimates are from the Census Bureau. www.census.gov/compendia/statab/2010.
28. Lawrence D. Longley and James D. Dana, "The Biases of the Electoral College in the 1990s," *Polity*, 25 (Fall 1992): p. 134. There are two other, less obvious, biases in the Electoral College. The distribution of electoral votes is calculated on the

basis of the census, which occurs every ten years. Thus, the Electoral College does not mirror population shifts within this period. Nor does it take into account the number of people who actually cast ballots. It is a state's population, not its turnout, that determines the number of electoral votes it receives, over and above the automatic three.

29. "2008 Campaign Tracker" and "Following the Money—Campaign Donations and Spending in the 2008 Presidential Election," Center for Voting and Democracy. www.fairvote.org/tracker.
30. James C. Garand and T. Wayne Parent, "Representation, Swing, and Bias in U.S. Presidential Elections, 1872–1988," *American Journal of Political Science* 35 (Nov. 1991): pp. 1024, 1029.

2 CHAPTER | CAMPAIGN FINANCE

INTRODUCTION

Running for president is very expensive. In the 2007–2008 election cycle, $1.32 billion was spent by candidates for the presidency, almost twice as much as for 2004 and four times as much as 2000.[1] When party, group, and independent spending are added, total spending exceeded $2.4 billion. And that's just for the race for the presidency. According to the Center for Responsive Politics, a public interest research organization, $5.3 billion was spent on all federal elections in 2008.[2]

The magnitude of these expenditures poses serious problems for presidential candidates, who must raise considerable sums, closely watch their expenses, make important allocation decisions, and conform to the intricacies of finance laws during both the nomination and general election campaigns. In addition, the candidates must coordinate their financial activities with party leaders who must also solicit, distribute, and spend millions on behalf of their candidates for national office. Such large expenditures raise important issues for a democratic selection process. This chapter explores some of these problems and those issues.

The chapter is organized into five sections. The first details the costs of presidential campaigns, paying particular attention to the increase in expenditures since 1960. The following section looks at the sources of support and the questions that arise from the connection between candidates and donors. Should people's right to use their own money take precedence over the democratic principle of equity, limiting the size of contributions to level the playing field? Congressional attempts to set donation limits to federal elections, require disclosure, control spending, and subsidize elections are discussed in the third section. The fourth section examines the impact of campaign finance laws on revenues and expenditures in presidential campaigns and on the party system. In the final section, the relationship between campaign spending and electoral success is explored. Can money buy elections? Have the big spenders been the big winners?

THE COSTS OF CAMPAIGNING

Candidates have always spent money in their quest for the presidency, but it was not until they started personal campaigning across the country that these costs began to increase sharply.

A Brief Overview of Expenditures in American Elections

When electioneering was conducted within a highly partisan press environment before the Civil War, there were few expenses other than for the occasional biography and campaign pamphlet printed by the party and sold to the public at less than cost. With the advent of more active public campaigning toward the middle of the nineteenth century, candidate organizations turned to buttons, billboards, banners, and pictures to symbolize and illustrate their campaigns. By the beginning of the twentieth century, the cost of this type of advertising in each election exceeded $150,000, a lot of money then but a minuscule amount by contemporary standards.[3]

In 1924, radio was employed for the first time in presidential campaigns. The Republicans spent approximately $120,000 that year, whereas the Democrats spent only $40,000.[4] Four years later, however, the two parties together spent more than $1 million. Radio expenses continued to equal or exceed a million dollars per election for the next 20 years.[5]

Television emerged as a vehicle for presidential campaigning in 1952. Both national party conventions were broadcast on television as well as on radio. Although there were only 19 million television sets in the United States at that time, almost one-third of Americans were regular television viewers. The number of households with television sets rose dramatically over the next four years. By 1956, an estimated 71 percent had television, and by 1968, the figure was close to 95 percent; today it exceeds 98 percent, with most homes having two or more sets.[6]

The first commercials for presidential candidates appeared in 1952. They became regular fare thereafter, contributing substantially to campaign costs.

Film biographies, interview shows, political rallies, town meetings, and other campaign-related events have all been seen with increasing frequency.

In 1948, no money was spent on television by either party's candidate. Twenty years later, $13 million was expended for television advertising, approximately one-fourth of the total cost of the 1968 campaign. Forty years later in 2008, about $600 million was spent, 38 percent of the total candidate expenses.[7]

CONTEMPORARY CAMPAIGN COSTS

The advent of the electronic campaign following World War II was the principal reason campaign costs skyrocketed. In 1960, John Kennedy and Richard Nixon each spent a hundred times the amount Lincoln had spent 100 years earlier. In the 12 years following the 1960 general election, expenditures increased from about $20 million to over $90 million, an increase that far outstripped the inflation rate during that period. Table 2.1 lists the costs of the major party candidates in presidential elections from 1860 to 1972, the last general election in which campaign spending by major-party candidates was unrestricted until the Obama campaign of 2008.

Prenomination costs have risen even more rapidly than those in the general election, as indicated in Table 2.2. Until the 1960s, large expenditures were the exception, not the rule, for gaining the party's nomination. General Leonard Wood spent an estimated $2 million in an unsuccessful quest to head the Republican ticket in 1920. The contest between General Dwight D. Eisenhower and Senator Robert A. Taft in 1952 cost about $5 million, a total that was not exceeded until 1964, when Nelson Rockefeller and Barry Goldwater together spent approximately twice that amount. Since 1968, preconvention expenditures have generally exceeded those in the general election. The increasing numbers of primaries, caucuses, and candidates, combined with the willingness of several recent hopefuls to forgo federal matching grants entirely and the expenditure limits that go with them, have been largely responsible for the rise.

In the 1950s, the preconvention contests were optional; since the 1970s, they have been mandatory. Even incumbent presidents have to enter them, and they spend money even when they are not challenged. In 1984, the Reagan campaign committee spent almost $28 million during the nomination period, much of it on voter registration drives for the general election; in 1992, George H. W. Bush spent over $27 million in defeating Pat Buchanan, a conservative newspaper columnist who had not previously sought public office. In 1996, Bill Clinton spent almost $35 million running unopposed for the Democratic nomination; eight years later, George W. Bush spent over $250 million without a nomination opponent.

Why is it so expensive to run for a presidential nomination, much less in the general election? The answer is that it costs money to raise money, to hire a staff, and to travel around the country. Designing and airing advertisements, conducting public opinion polls, setting up an interactive Web site, and reaching out to potential supporters are also costly operations. Add to these office and equipment rentals, event organizers and advance teams, media consultants, grassroots organizers, online communication experts, researchers and

Table 2.1 | Costs of Presidential General Elections, Major Party Candidates, 1860–1972

Year	Democratic		Republican	
1860	Stephen Douglas	$ 50,000	Abraham Lincoln*	$ 100,000
1864	George McClellan	50,000	Abraham Lincoln*	125,000
1868	Horatio Segmous	75,000	Ulysses Grant*	150,000
1872	Horace Greeley	50,000	Ulysses Grant*	250,000
1876	Samuel Tilden	900,000	Rutherford Hayes*	950,000
1880	Winfield Hancock	335,000	James Garfield*	1,100,000
1884	Grover Cleveland*	1,400,000	James Blaine	1,300,000
1888	Grover Cleveland	855,000	Benjamin Harrison*	1,350,000
1892	Grover Cleveland*	2,350,000	Benjamin Harrison	1,700,000
1896	William Jennings Bryan	675,000	William McKinley*	3,350,000
1900	William Jennings Bryan	425,000	William McKinley*	3,000,000
1904	Alton Parker	700,000	Theodore Roosevelt*	2,096,000
1908	William Jennings Bryan	629,341	William Taft*	1,655,518
1912	Woodrow Wilson*	1,134,848	William Taft	1,071,549
1916	Woodrow Wilson*	2,284,950	Charles Evans Hughes	2,441,565
1920	James Cox	1,470,371	Warren Harding*	5,417,501
1924	John Davis	1,108,836	Calvin Coolidge*	4,020,478
1928	Alfred Smith	5,342,350	Herbert Hoover*	6,256,111
1932	Franklin Roosevelt*	2,245,975	Herbert Hoover	2,900,052
1936	Franklin Roosevelt*	5,194,751	Alfred Landon	8,892,972
1940	Franklin Roosevelt*	2,783,654	Wendell Willkie	3,451,310
1944	Franklin Roosevelt*	2,169,077	Thomas Dewey	2,828,652
1948	Harry Truman*	2,736,334	Thomas Dewey	2,127,296
1952	Adlai Stevenson	5,032,926	Dwight Eisenhower*	6,608,623
1956	Adlai Stevenson	5,106,651	Dwight Eisenhower*	7,778,702
1960	John Kennedy*	9,797,000	Richard Nixon	10,128,000
1964	Lyndon Johnson*	8,757,000	Barry Goldwater	16,026,000
1968†	Hubert Humphrey	11,594,000	Richard Nixon*	25,042,000
1972	George McGovern	30,000,000	Richard Nixon*	61,400,000

*Indicates winner.

†George Wallace spent an estimated $7 million as the candidate of the American Independent Party in 1968.

Source: Data based on *Financing Politics: Money, Elections, and Political Reform,* 3rd ed. By Herbert E. Alexander. Copyright 1984 by Congressional Quarterly.

TABLE 2.2 | COSTS OF PRESIDENTIAL NOMINATIONS, 1964–2008 (IN MILLIONS OF DOLLARS)

	Expenditures	
Year	**Democrats**	**Republicans**
1964	(uncontested)	$10.0
1968	$25.0	20.0
1972	33.1	*
1976	40.7	26.1
1980	41.7	86.1
1984	107.7	28.0
1988	94.0	114.6
1992	66.0†	51.0
1996	41.8	182.0
2000	95.8	247.2
2008	1,043.9	450.2

*During a primary in which Richard M. Nixon's renomination was virtually assured, Representative John M. Ashbrook spent $740,000 and Representative Paul N. McCloskey spent $550,000 in challenging Nixon.

†Estimates based on Alexander and Corrado, *Financing the 1992 Elections*, Tables 2.1 and 2.4.

Sources: 1964–1972, Herbert E. Alexander, *Financing Politics* (Washington, DC: Congressional Quarterly, 1976), pp. 45–47, Copyright © 1984 by Congressional Quarterly Press, a Division of SAGE Publications, Inc. Reprinted by permission.; 1976–1984, Federal Election Commission, "Reports on Financial Activity, 1987–88," *Presidential Pre-Nomination Campaigns* (August 1989), Table A.7, p. 10; Herbert E. Alexander, "Financing the Presidential Elections" (paper presented at the Institute for Political Studies in Tokyo, Japan, September 8–10, 1989), pp. 4, 10; 1988–1992, Herbert E. Alexander and Anthony Corrado, *Financing the 1992 Elections* (Armonk, NY: Sharpe, 1995), Copyright © 1995 by M. E. Sharpe, Inc. Reprinted with permission of the publisher.; 1996–2008, updated by author from data published by the Federal Election Commission, "Presidential Campaign Disbursements" (inception through July 31 of the 1996 and 2000 election years, and December 31, 2004 and 2008). (www.fec.gov)

speechwriters, a press operation, and the professional lawyers, accountants, policy advisers, and the money never seems to be sufficient.

Moreover, candidates are now forced to campaign simultaneously in several states for several months before those states' primaries and caucuses are held. To do so, they need to use the electronic media, radio, and television, which is also costly. By 2000, television expenses for the presidential race alone exceeded $205 million; in 2004, they were about $578 million when the congressional elections were included; in 2004 and 2008, they were about $600 million just for the presidential contest.[8]

THE PROBLEMS WITH LARGE EXPENDITURES

Three major issues arise from the high costs of contemporary elections. One pertains to the donors. Who gives, how much, and what do they get for their money? A second relates to the costs. Are they too high, and can they be controlled without impinging on First Amendment freedoms? The third concerns the impact of spending on the election. To what extent does access to large amounts of money improve a candidate's chances of winning? The next section turns to the first of these issues, that of private sources of financial support and the attempts by government to regulate them.

THE SOURCES OF SUPPORT

Throughout most of U.S. electoral history, parties and candidates have depended on large contributions. In the midst of the industrial boom at the end of the nineteenth century, the Republicans were able to count on the support of the Astors, Harrimans, and Vanderbilts, while the Democrats looked to financier August Belmont (American representative of the Rothschild banking interests) and inventor and industrialist Cyrus McCormick. Corporations, banks, and life insurance companies soon became prime targets of party fund-raisers. The most notorious and probably most adroit fund-raiser of this period was Mark Hanna. A leading official of the Republican Party, Hanna owed most of his influence to his ability to obtain substantial political contributions. He set quotas, personally assessing the amount that businesses and corporations should give. In 1896 and again in 1900, he was able to obtain contributions of \$250,000 from Standard Oil. Theodore Roosevelt personally ordered the return of some of the Standard Oil money in 1904 but accepted large gifts from magnates E. H. Harriman and Henry C. Frick. Roosevelt's trust-busting activities during his presidency led Frick to remark, "We bought the son of a bitch and then he did not stay bought."[9]

Sizable private gifts remained the principal source of party and candidate support until the mid-1970s. In 1972, the last year when the size of contributions was not restricted, Richard Nixon and George McGovern raised an estimated \$27 million from fewer than 200 individual contributors.[10] In general, the Republicans benefited more than the Democrats from wealthy contributors, known in the campaign vernacular as "fat cats." Only in 1964 was a Democrat, incumbent president, Lyndon B. Johnson, who enjoyed a large lead in the preelection polls, able to raise more money from large donors than his Republican opponent, Barry Goldwater. The reluctance of regular Republican contributors to support the Goldwater candidacy forced his organization to appeal to thousands of potential supporters through direct mail. The success of this effort, raising \$5.8 million from approximately 651,000 people, showed the potential of a popular appeal for funds and shattered what had been an unwritten "rule" of politics that money could not be raised by a mass appeal.

Despite the use of mass mailings and party telethons to broaden the base of political contributors in the 1960s, dependence on large donors continued. In 1964, more than \$2 million was raised in contributions of \$10,000 or more. Eight years later, approximately \$51 million was collected in gifts of this size or larger. Some gifts were in the million-dollar range. The magnitude of these contributions, combined with the heavy-handed tactics of the Nixon fund-raisers in 1971–1972, brought into sharp focus the difficulty of maintaining a democratic selection process that was dependent on private funding.[11]

Reliance on large contributors who did not want to be identified, the inequality of funding between parties and candidates, and the high cost of campaigning, especially in the mass media, all raised serious questions. Were there assumptions implicit in giving and receiving? Could elected officials be responsive to individual benefactors and to the general public at the same time? Was the need to obtain large contributors and keep them "happy" consistent with the tenets of a democratic society that all people have equal influence on the selection of and access to public officials? Did the high cost of campaigning, in and of itself, eliminate otherwise qualified candidates from running? Were certain political parties, interest groups, or individuals consistently advantaged or disadvantaged by the distribution of funding? Had the presidency become an office that only the wealthy could afford or that only those with wealthy supporters could seek?

THE HISTORY OF CAMPAIGN FINANCE LEGISLATION

Reacting to these issues, Congress in the 1970s enacted far-reaching legislation designed to reduce dependence on major donors who contribute large amounts of money, bring donors out in the open, discourage illegal contributions, broaden the base of public support, and control escalating costs at the presidential level. Additionally, the Democratic Congress that passed these laws wanted to equalize the funds available to the Republican and Democratic nominees. Finally, the legislation was designed to buttress the two-party system, making it more difficult for minor candidates to challenge successfully the major parties' nominees for elective office.

REGULATION, DISCLOSURE, AND PUBLIC FINANCING

The Federal Election Campaign Act (FECA), enacted in 1971, set ceilings on the amount of money presidential and vice presidential candidates and their families could contribute to their own campaigns.[12] It allowed unions and corporations, which had been prohibited from contributing, to form political action committees (PACs), consisting of their members, employees, and stockholders, to solicit voluntary contributions to be given to candidates or parties or to fund the group's election activities. The FECA also established procedures for public disclosure of contributions over a certain amount. A second statute, the Revenue Act of 1971, created tax credits and deductions to encourage private contributions. It also provided for public funding by creating a presidential election campaign fund. Financed by an income tax checkoff provision, the fund initially allowed taxpayers to designate one dollar of their federal income taxes to a special presidential election account.

These laws began a period of federal government regulation of national elections that has continued into the twenty-first century. The history of that regulation is a history of good intentions built on political compromise but marred by unintended consequences of the legislation and its implementation as candidates, parties, and nonparty groups have circumvented the letter and spirit of the law to gain electoral advantage.

Partisan compromises in the enactment of campaign finance legislation were evident from the outset. Although the original funding provision was enacted in 1971, it did not go into effect until the 1976 presidential election. Most Republicans, including President Nixon, opposed the policy of government financial support and regulation. In addition to conflicting with their general ideological belief that the national government's role in the conduct of elections be limited, the legislation offset their party's traditional fund-raising advantage. President Nixon was persuaded to sign the public funding bill, however, after Democrats agreed to delay the effective start of the bill until after his likely reelection.[13]

The 1972 election was marked by heavy-handed fund-raising tactics. The Nixon campaign in that election cycle raised more money than in any other previous presidential campaign. In addition to aggressive solicitation, the expenditures of the Nixon reelection effort also became an issue, albeit after the election. Investigative reporting by the *Washington Post* and hearings conducted by a Senate committee revealed that the Committee to Reelect the President, referred to by Nixon's opponents as CREEP, had spent some of its funds on "dirty tricks" and other unethical and illegal activities, such as the break-in at the Democratic National Committee's headquarters at the Watergate office building. These revelations aroused public ire and created the incentive for a Democratic Congress to enact new and even more stringent legislation.

In 1974, the FECA was amended to include public disclosure provisions, contribution ceilings for individuals and groups, spending limits for the campaigns, federal subsidies for major-party candidates in the nomination process, and complete funding for them in the general election. The law also restricted the amount candidates could contribute to their own campaign and the amount that others could spend independently on their behalf. Finally, it established a six-person commission, the Federal Election Commission (FEC), to implement and enforce the law.

The 1974 amendments were highly controversial. Critics immediately charged a federal giveaway, a raid on the Treasury. Opponents of the legislation also argued that the limits on contributions and spending violated the constitutionally guaranteed right to freedom of speech, that the funding provisions unfairly discriminated against third-party and independent candidates, and that Congress' appointment of some of the commissioners violated the separation of powers.

In the landmark decision of *Buckley v. Valeo*, 424 U.S. 1 (1976), the Supreme Court upheld the right of Congress to regulate campaign contributions and expenditures but negated the overall limits on spending by individuals and nonparty groups and the appointment by Congress of four of the six election commissioners. The majority opinion in that case contended that by placing restrictions on the amount of money a person or organization could spend during a campaign, the law directly and substantially restrained freedom of speech, a freedom protected by the First Amendment to the Constitution. The Supreme Court did allow limits on contributions to candidates' campaigns, however, and limits on expenditures of those candidates who accepted public funds but not those who refused these funds. By holding that contributions to and expenditures of presidential candidates could be limited, the justices acknowledged that large, often secret, contributions and rapidly increasingly expenditures did pose problems for a democracy, problems that Congress could address.

The Court's decision required that the election law be amended once again. It took Congress several months to do so. In the spring of 1976, during the presidential primaries of that year, amendments were enacted that continued public funding of the presidential nomination and election campaigns, based on a figure of $10 million in 1974 to be adjusted for inflation, but did so on a voluntary basis. Candidates did not have to accept government funds, but if they did, they were limited in how much they and others could contribute to their own campaigns and how much those campaigns could spend. The FEC was reconstituted with all six members to be nominated by the president and appointed subject to the advice and consent of the Senate. The law required that three commissioners be Democrats and three be Republicans to ensure that the commission would be fair to both major parties.

ADJUSTING THE FEDERAL ELECTION CAMPAIGN ACT

With limited amounts of money available, the candidates opted to spend most of it on television advertising. Gone were the buttons, bumper stickers, and other election paraphernalia that had characterized previous campaigns. Fewer resources were directed toward grassroots organizing. Turnout fell. The national parties lost influence. Congress was concerned.

In 1979, additional amendments to the FECA were enacted to rectify these problems. To encourage voluntary activities and higher voter turnout, the amendments allowed party committees at the national, state, and local levels to raise and spend unlimited amounts of money for party-building activities such as registration and getting out the vote. Known as the *soft money provision*, this amendment, as interpreted by the FEC, created a gigantic loophole in the law.[14] It permitted, even encouraged, the major parties to solicit large contributions and distribute the money to their state and local affiliates as they saw fit. Pandora's box had been opened, although it took another decade and a half to exploit it fully.[15] Later amendments to the FECA increased the base grant for nominating conventions of the major parties to $3 million in 1979 and $4 million in 1984.

It was not until 1993 that the law was amended again to increase the amount of money in the fund used to subsidize candidates for their party's presidential nomination and provide general election grants. Congress' failure to tie the amount of money taxpayers could designate for the fund to inflation, the decline in the percentage of taxpayers making such a designation, and the increasing number of candidates vying for party nominations all contributed to a shortfall that was only expected to get worse in the years ahead. To rectify the problem, Congress increased the income tax checkoff from $1 to $3, a little less than the cost-of-living adjustment since the provision had originally gone into effect. However, the portion of taxpayers designating a payment to the fund had fallen significantly from its high of 28.7 percent in 1980. For the tax year of 2010, only 7.3 percent of taxpayers contributed to the fund.[16]

A new problem of a very different magnitude emerged in 1996—the exploitation of the soft money loophole to circumvent the law's intended contribution and expenditure limits. This exploitation resulted from a very creative interpretation of the 1979 amendments by President Clinton's political advisers, the major parties, subsequently the FEC, and finally, the courts. Here's what happened.

In 1995, Clinton and his advisers began planning for the president's reelection campaign. Their strategy was to position Clinton as a centrist by airing a series of advertisements that touted his record and favorably contrasted it with that of the congressional Republicans. The ad campaign was costly. After $2 million was spent by the president's reelection committee in the summer of 1995, the president's advisers feared that there would not be sufficient funds left to handle a challenge for the Democratic nomination if one developed and also respond to a strong Republican opponent prior to the nominating conventions. They resolved this dilemma by turning to the "soft money" loophole created by the 1979 amendment. Since the commercials that the Clinton administration aired were policy-oriented and did not specifically and directly urge the president's reelection, the president's advisers argued that the Democratic Party could pay for the ads with soft money, which the president would help raise. Lawyers for the party agreed.

What followed was a frantic, no-holds-barred fund-raising effort in which the president and the vice president actively participated. Inducements to contribute included dinners with the president and vice president at expensive Washington hotels, sleepovers in the Lincoln bedroom in the White House, state dinners with world leaders, rounds of golf with Clinton, trips on Air Force One, VIP treatment at Democratic Party functions such as its 1996 nominating convention, even invitations to join the commerce secretary on official U.S. trade missions abroad. Naturally, Republicans were outraged by these activities, particularly the use of public office for partisan purposes. Their party officials and elected leadership protested and congressional investigations followed, but to no avail. In the end, the Republicans resorted to the same tactics as the Democrats, using their control of Congress as leverage to raise soft money. They eventually netted more of it than did the Democrats.

The soft money issue reemerged during the 2000 nomination campaign. Republican candidate John McCain and Democrat Bill Bradley promised, if elected, to support a ban on soft money. Although neither candidate's bid for their party's nomination was successful, the campaign finance issue remained salient; it put candidates Bush and Gore on the defensive and led to cries for reform. In April 2001, the Senate enacted the Bipartisan Campaign Reform Act (BCRA), also known by the name of its sponsors as the McCain–Feingold bill, to close the soft money loophole. The legislation also restricted the use of the principal instrument by which nonparty advocacy groups had tried to affect the election's outcome—issue advocacy advertising. Nine months later, the House of Representatives followed suit, and in March 2002, the legislation became law. Table 2.3 lists the major contribution limits of the new law as adjusted for inflation for the years 2011–2012.

TABLE 2.3 | CONTRIBUTION LIMITS FOR 2011–2012

	To Each Candidate or Candidate Committee Per Election	To National Party Committee Per Calendar Year	To State, District, & Local Party Committee Per Calendar Year	To Any Other Political Committee Per Calendar Year	Special Limits
Individual may give	$2,500*	$30,800*	$10,000 (combined limit)	$5,000	$117,000* overall biennial limit: • $46,200* to all candidates • $70,800* to all PACs & parties
National Party Committee may give	$5,000	No Limit	No Limit	$5,000	$43,100* to Senate Candidates per campaign
State, District, & Local Party Committee may give	$5,000 (combined limit)	No Limit	No Limit	$5,000 (combined limit)	No Limit
PAC	$5,000	$15,000	$5,000 (combined limit)	$5,000	No Limit
PAC (not multicandidate) may give	$2,500*	$30,800*	$10,000 (combined limit)	$5,000	No Limit
Authorized Campaign Committee may give	$2,000	No Limit	No Limit	$5,000	No Limit

The Bipartisan Campaign Reform Act of 2002 (BCRA) included provisions that indexed some contribution limits for inflation. The limit for individuals' contributions to candidates, for example, was set at $2,000 per election in BCRA and is adjusted at the start of each new election cycle. Adjustments are announced after the Department of Labor determines the inflation rate for the previous election year (in this case 2010). The new limit on contributions from individuals to candidates is effective retroactively to the day after the last general election (i.e., Nov. 3, 2010). The other new limits are effective retroactively to Jan. 1, 2011.

*These contribution limits are increased for inflation in odd-numbered years.

Source: "FEC Announces 2011–2012 Campaign Cycle Contribution Limits," Federal Election Commission, February 3, 2011. fec.gov/press/20110203newlimits.shtml

THE BIPARTISAN CAMPAIGN REFORM ACT AND ITS IMPACT

The BCRA banned the national party committees from raising soft money, but to compensate, the new law also raised individual and overall federal contribution limits to candidates and parties and restricted the use of issue advocacy ads, in which candidates were cited by name, to periods that exceeded thirty days before a primary and sixty days before the general election. Exemptions, however, remained for tax-exempt organizations.

Opponents of the law immediately questioned its constitutionality. Such disparate groups as the National Rifle Association, the American Civil Liberties Union, and the Christian Coalition argued that the ban on issue advocacy advertising in the final days of the campaign violated the First Amendment's protection of freedom of speech and freedom of the press. The Republican National Committee claimed that the prohibition on soft money violated the state parties' right to raise money to organize and mobilize voters in all elections in which state representatives were selected, while groups representing poorer Americans contended that the increase in amount of money that could be contributed by individual donors under the new law violated the rights of less wealthy people under the Fifth Amendment's equal protection clause. In contrast, the bill's sponsors, the FEC, Common Cause and other public interest groups, and twenty-one state attorneys general supported the law.

Anticipating a constitutional challenge, the drafters of the legislation included a provision for a quick judicial review. One year later, on December 10, 2003, as the Democratic nomination process was underway, the Court issued its ruling in the case of *McConnell v. FEC*, 540 U.S.93 (2003). By a 5-to-4 vote, the justices upheld most of the provisions of the BCRA, including the ban on soft money solicitation by the national parties and the limits placed on issue advocacy ads that identified specific candidates in the closing month of primaries and sixty days or less in the general election.[17] It was left to the FEC to regulate enforcement.[18]

The FEC issued a series of regulations, some of which were very contentious.[19] New legal challenges to these regulations immediately ensued. In the end, the courts invalidated a number of the FEC's regulations. One of the most controversial involved "nonpolitical" organizations, which the FEC had indicated were not subject to the soft money restrictions. But how was nonpolitical to be defined? Did it mean that the group could not engage in political activities, or that most of its expenditures could not be devoted to electioneering, or that its primary purpose could not be to elect a specific candidate?

The question was more than a theoretical one. It had very practical and immediate consequences. The reason is that Democrats, fearing that the prohibition on soft money would place their party at a competitive disadvantage, had turned to nonprofit, nonpartisan groups to raise unlimited amounts of money and spend it on election-related activities.[20] Sponsors of the BCRA and their supporters urged the FEC to regulate these groups in accordance with the intent of the law to prohibit soft money in national elections. Republicans who had previously opposed the law also urged the FEC to issue new regulations that prohibited nonparty groups from engaging in these activities. However, the commission voted 4 to 2 not to do so.

After the election, and with prodding from a federal judge, the commission said that it would regulate these groups on an ad hoc basis rather than prescribe general rules for all of them. It fined four of the groups, two Democratic and two Republican, a total of $1.38 million for not registering with the FEC as political organizations and for accepting contributions that exceeded the legal amount.[21] Since the groups raised millions, the fines were considered minimal—the cost of doing business. Fines of this magnitude did not deter similar groups from large-scale fund-raising during the 2007–2008 election cycle and probably will not in the 2012 election.[22]

Although the Supreme Court upheld Congress' right to prohibit advocacy ads in which candidates are identified by name in the final days before the election, the issue came up again in 2006 after a pro-life group in Wisconsin sued the FEC for ruling that the group's advocacy ads violated the sixty-day rule. During the fall of 2006, the pro-life group had urged people to write to their senators opposing the confirmation delay of several of President Bush's judicial nominations. Mentioned in the ad were the names of the state's two senators, Russell Feingold and Herbert Kohl, but not their voting records on nomination or abortion-related issues. Feingold was running for reelection in that year. A three-judge federal court reversed the FEC's ruling on the grounds that the group's freedom of speech was violated. In 2007, the Supreme Court agreed to review the lower court ruling in the case of *Citizens United v. Federal Election Commission.*[23]

During the 2008 nomination campaign, a conservative, nonprofit corporation, Citizens United, produced a documentary film attacking Hillary Rodham Clinton. The film was made available to movie theaters and sold as a DVD. The organization, Citizens United, also wanted to distribute it on cable television as a paid-for video; it intended to run advertisements informing the public of the film's availability. The FEC, however, ruled that a movie produced by a corporation at its expense violated the ban on corporate spending in federal elections. The commission also indicated that advertising for the film would be subject to the disclosure provision of the BCRA. A lower court that considered the controversy also ruled against Citizens United, prompting the corporation to appeal the case to the Supreme Court.

The Court heard oral arguments in March 2009 and then asked the parties to reargue the case in September of that year. Solicitor General Elena Kagan, later nominated by President Obama to the Supreme Court, defended the government's position validating the election law. In January 2010, a 5-to-4 majority issued a broad ruling that corporations have free speech rights that are protected by the First Amendment. In the words of the justice who wrote the majority opinion, Anthony Kennedy, "If the First Amendment has any force, it prohibits Congress from fining or jailing citizens, or associations of citizens, for simply engaging in political speech."[24] Justice John Paul Stevens, author of the dissent, replied, "At bottom, the Court's opinion is . . . a rejection of the common sense of the American people who have recognized a need to prevent corporations from undermining self government since the founding, and who have fought against the distinctive corrupting potential of corporation electioneering since the days of Theodore Roosevelt."[25] The Court did not invalidate the BCRA's disclosure requirements or the limits that the law placed on the size of contributions to candidates in federal elections.

The decision was criticized by Democrats. They feared that groups with access to large amounts of money would be able to exercise undue influence on American elections. In his 2010 State of the Union Address, President Obama said, "The Supreme Court reversed a century of law to open the flood gates for special interests—including foreign corporations—to spend without limit in our elections."[26] Republicans responded that freedom of speech, a basic right of Americans, individually and collectively, had been protected against those who would limit it. In response to the Court's decision, Democrats introduced legislation to prevent corporations that received $50,000 or more in government contracts and foreign corporations from spending in U.S. elections. The legislation was not enacted, however.

Despite the free speech controversy, the latest campaign finance legislation, the BCRA, has achieved some of its intended goals. It has encouraged the major parties to improve their fund-raising operations and to do so by soliciting contributions within the limits prescribed by federal law. In fact, the Republicans and Democrats actually raised more money in the last two election cycles without soft money than they had with it. (See Table 2.8.) The number of small donors, people who contributed $200 or less, has also increased dramatically—another goal of the legislation and one to which Internet technologies have contributed. Although some soft money has found its way back into the election process, it is likely to be a relatively minor factor compared with independent spending by corporations and labor unions.

REVENUE: WHERE DOES THE MONEY COME FROM?

The election laws had a significant impact on the base of contributors, the modes of solicitation, and the objects of spending in the 2008 presidential election. This section of the chapter explains how the legislation has affected donors, donations, and the overall revenues that candidates, parties, and nonparty groups receive.

INDIVIDUAL CONTRIBUTORS

One of the most important objectives of the BCRA as well as its predecessor, the FECA, was to reduce the influence that a small number of major contributors had on the presidential nomination and election. To a limited extent, both laws have achieved this goal. No longer can candidates depend on a few wealthy friends to finance their quest for their party's nomination. Since 2002, the limits on individual donors (see Table 2.3), the ceiling on matching grants, and the eligibility requirements for federal funds have made the solicitation of a large number of small contributors absolutely essential.

The costs of contemporary campaigns and the decline in the purchasing power of the dollar—it is less than one-fourth of what it was in 1976—have forced candidates to appeal to more donors than they did before the FECA went into effect, although they have also become increasingly dependent on contributors who give the maximum amount. In 2000, George W. Bush received about two-thirds of his funds from donors who "maxed out" at $1,000; in 2004, he received almost half (47 percent) from those who gave $2,000 or

BOX 2.1 | THE OBAMA MONEY MACHINE

The Internet was a critical component of the Obama campaign. It was used to communicate with supporters, raise money, attract volunteers, and expand the candidate's political base. The fund-raising component was essential.

Obama was not the first presidential candidate to use the Internet as a fund-raising tool. In 2000, Republican John McCain supplemented his campaign treasury by raising about $7 million online, much of it after his surprising victory over George W. Bush in the New Hampshire primary.[i] Similarly, Howard Dean used the Web during 2003 to gain money and attention in his quest for the 2004 Democratic nomination. In the words of Dean's campaign director, Joe Trippi, "On the Net, we were the first mover, and every day that no one tried to do anything to get in it meant it was another day we were getting closer to having that $200 million that we thought we could get to."[ii] A Web site with a blog for communication among Dean's supporters and officials of the campaign generated about $30 million from almost 1 million contributors made the campaign look like a spontaneous grassroots operation. The news media took notice.

Obama expanded the Dean model. His campaign assembled an experienced group of Internet entrepreneurs to maximize the use of this new communications technology. Included were Chris Hughes, one of the cofounders of Facebook, and Joe Rospers, who had worked on Dean's campaign and then set up his own Internet fund-raising company.

The Web site of the Obama campaign, My.BarackObama.com, was a multipurpose site. It directed prospective donors from major social networks, such as Facebook, MySpace, AsianAve, BlackPlan, and Twitter, to the Obama site on which they could press a button, make a contribution, and charge it to their credit card. Supporters were encouraged to make monthly donations that also could be automatically charged to their card. They were also encouraged to seek contributions from their friends and associates for Obama. His campaign staff told them how to do so.

The emphasis of the Obama Internet operation was to make people feel as if they were part of the campaign. Personalized communications helped in this effort. Having the e-mail addresses of thousands of small donors meant the campaign

---

more. John Kerry received 36 percent from this top donor group. In 2008, most of the candidates continued to rely on large donors, especially during the first phase of their nomination campaigns when they needed to establish their credibility as viable candidates. However, the most surprising financial development in the 2007–2008 election cycle was the increasing number of small donors, those who made contributions of $200 or less. Approximately one-fourth of the $746 million Obama received came from people who gave a cumulative total of $200 or less. About half came from those who gave $1,000 or more.[27] Republican Ron Paul was also successful in raising substantial sums (almost 40 percent of his total) from small donors.

The success that recent candidates have had in raising large amounts from small contributors has been primarily due to the Internet. Box 2.1 tells the story

could go back to them again and again for money. According to campaign manager David Plouffe, the Obama campaign raised over $200 million online during the nomination phase of the electoral process.[iii] Approximately 30 percent of Obama's total funds during this period came from donations of $200 or less; in the general election, it was more of the same, with 34 percent of his money coming from small donors.[iv]

Obama was not the only candidate to benefit from online contributions. Republican Ron Paul also received most of his money from the Internet, with 39 percent of his total coming from small contributors.[v] Raising these funds was a critical component of Paul's campaign strategy. According to his manager, Lew Moore,

> We calculated very early that we'd have no chance at all to be perceived as a first-tier candidate by anybody unless we raised quite a bit of money right away . . . We hired a videographer. He was one of the first people we hired in our campaign. We were making YouTubes every two or three days. Suddenly, we started noticing that 300,000 or 400,000 people were watching them . . . it was critical to our getting off the ground as a campaign.[vi]

The success of the Obama effort as well as those of other candidates demonstrates the potential of the Internet as a vehicle for broadening the financial base of presidential campaigns. It is fast, cheap, relatively easy, and can be used continuously throughout the campaign until the individual limits are reached. But to be successful, Internet fund-raising also requires candidates with special appeal to groups of voters, an appeal that Obama had for a cross section of Americans, particularly those under 30, and that Ron Paul had for a smaller group who shared his libertarian views.

---

[i]Neil Munro, "The New Wired Politics," *National Journal* (April 22, 2000), p. 1260.
[ii]Joe Trippi, *Campaign for President: The Managers Look at 2004* (Landam, MD: Rowman and Littlefield, 2006), p. 67.
[iii]David Plouffe, *The Audacity to Win* (New York: Viking, 2009), p. 237.
[iv]"All CFI Funding Statistics Revised and Updated for the 2008 Presidential Primary and General Election Candidates," Campaign Finance Institute, January 8, 2010. www.campaignfinanceinstiute.org
[v]Ibid.
[vi]Lew Moore, *Campaign for President: The Managers Look at 2008* (Landam, MD: Rowman and Littlefield, 2010), p. 51.

of how the Obama campaign did it—how it identified and energized donors. The Obama model has become the prototype that most other candidates will have to follow to enlarge their donor base.

In addition to gifts from individuals, the largest single source of revenues, candidates have found other ways to supplement their campaign funds. They can provide some of their own money. There is no restriction on the amount of personal funds that can be spent in the years prior to the election cycle. At the point of candidacy, a $50,000 personal contribution limit is imposed if a candidate accepts federal funds. There are no personal limits for candidates who do not accept federal funds. Thus, in 1992, H. Ross Perot was able to spend over $63 million of his own money on his campaign in lieu of taking government funds. He chose to accept federal funds in 1996, thus limiting his private contribution to $50,000. However, Perot ended up spending more than $8 million of his money to secure the Reform Party's 1996 nomination, fund its nominating conventions, and get the party on the ballot in all fifty states. Of the major-party candidates, the single largest personal contributors to their own campaigns have been Republicans Steve Forbes ($38 million in 1996 and $48 million in 2000) and Mitt Romney ($42.4 million in 2008) in their unsuccessful attempts to win their party's nomination.

Borrowing money is also allowed. Hillary Rodham Clinton lent her campaign $20 million in 2008 and John Kerry $6.4 million in 2004. Kerry's success in winning the Democratic nomination that year enabled his campaign to pay back to Kerry the money he lent his campaign; Hillary Clinton was unable to do so despite Obama's promise to help her retire some of her campaign debt.

Funds raised but not spent by candidates in their campaigns for other federal offices can be used in their quest for the presidential nomination. John McCain transferred $2 million from his Senate account to fund the initial stages of his 2000 campaign for the Republican nomination and $22 million in 2008. Hillary Clinton transferred $10 million in unspent funds from her 2006 Senate race for her presidential bid two years later; Democratic hopefuls Chris Dodd, Joe Biden, and Barack Obama transferred lesser amounts. The ability to tap funds raised in other federal campaigns encourages potential candidates in the House and Senate to raise as much money as they can prior to an anticipated bid for their party's presidential nomination.

Although cash contributions are restricted, voluntary goods and services are not. Artists and musicians, in particular, can generate considerable revenue for candidates by offering their time and talent. Concerts, and to a lesser extent, art sales, have become excellent sources of revenue. In fact, $2,000-plus dinners have become a particularly popular way to bring in large amounts of money early in the nomination process. Incumbents who run for reelection have used their fund-raising prowess to benefit themselves, other partisans, and their party in this manner.

NONPARTY GROUPS

Until the Supreme Court's *Citizens United* decision, corporations and labor unions were prohibited from making direct contributions to political candidates, but the FECA allowed their employees, stockholders, or executives to do so by forming Political Action Committees (PACs) and funding them with their voluntary contributions.[28] Since 1976, these groups have affected federal elections in general and the presidential election process in particular by endorsing candidates, by contributing up to $5,000 to their campaigns, by spending an unlimited amount of money independently for or against candidates, and by internal communications with their members and sympathizers.

With a $5,000 limit on contributions, corporations, labor unions, and PACs help presidential hopefuls more by the dollars their organization spends on campaigning than by the money they give to the candidates. Republicans have generally received more money from PACs than have Democrats, but still

PAC contributions represent only a small fraction of the funds they raise for a presidential campaign. In 2008, Republican candidates for their party's nomination received $2.4 million from PACs and Democratic candidates $2.6 million, a very small amount of the almost $1.5 billion in candidate revenues for the 2007–2008 election cycle. Barack Obama refused PAC contributions.[29]

In the prenomination period before candidates officially declare their candidacy and well before the primaries and caucuses are scheduled, candidates establish Leadership PACs to fund their preprimary activities. They use these PACs to pay for staff and travel, and give contributions to other campaigns during the midterm election cycle. Leadership PACs have also become mechanisms for identifying and tapping potential donors, not once but continually until the limit for individual contributions is reached. Candidates also set up advocacy PACs to promote their issues and policy positions. All major candidates for the 2008 party nominations established one or both types of PACs.

Some of the Republican candidates for their party's 2012 nomination have gone a step further. They created PACs in states that did not restrict the size of individual contributions. The money raised by these state-based organizations was used to supplement their national PAC funds in order to pay for political consultants, campaign staff, travel, as well as contributions made to various state and local candidates. Mitt Romney raised the most money in this manner, $1 million in the two years leading to the 2011–2012 election cycle. Others who used state PACs as well as advocacy PACs to supplement their national leadership included Haley Barbour, Mike Huckabee, Sarah Palin, and Tim Pawlenty.[30]

GOVERNMENT FUNDS

In addition to individuals and nonparty groups, a third source of money is the government matching grants for the nomination and grants for the national party conventions and the general election. Table 2.4 shows the government funds distributed by the treasury since 1976.

Matching Funds

Here's how matching grants work. Eligible federal candidates who receive individual contributions up to $250 in the election year or the year before can match those contributions by an equal amount from the federal election fund, not to exceed $250 per contribution. These funds, however, are only distributed in the calendar year of the election. To be eligible, candidates must raise $5,000 in twenty states in contributions of $250 or less, a total of $100,000. Remaining eligible for matching funds is harder than simply qualifying for them. To remain eligible, candidates must receive at least 10 percent of the vote in two consecutive primaries in which they are entered. If they are entered in more than one primary on a given day, they need to win 10 percent in only one of them. Failing to receive this percentage negates their eligibility for federal funds until such time as they receive at least 20 percent of the vote in a subsequent primary.[31]

The 10 percent rule helps front-runners and hurts lesser-known candidates. Twice during the 1984 campaign Democrat Jesse Jackson lost his eligibility

TABLE 2.4 | GOVERNMENT FUNDING OF THE NOMINATION PROCESS, 1976–2008

Year	Matching Funds	Convention Grants	General Election	Total
1976	$24.8	$4.1	$43.6	$73.6
1980	31.3	8.8	63.1	103.3
1984	36.5	16.1	80.8	133.5
1988	67.5	18.4	92.2	178.2
1992	42.9	22.1	110.5	175.4
1996	58.5*	24.7	152.7	236.0
2000	62.3	29.5	147.7	239.5
2004	28.4	29.8	149.2	207.5
2008	21.7	29.9	84.1	139.4

*In 1996, H. Ross Perot received partial general election funding as a third-party candidate, as did Pat Buchanan in 2000. In 2008, Barack Obama declined public funding in the general election.

Source: Federal Election Commission, "Public Funds in Presidential Campaigns." www.fec.gov/press/press2009/20090608Pres/4_PublicFundsPresCmpgs.pdf

for matching funds, only to regain it later. Similarly in 2004, Al Sharpton and Dennis Kucinich lost their eligibility early in the process and thus could not benefit from the multiplier effect that federal funds provide. The only strategy for a candidate who is fearful of falling short of the required percentage is not to enter a primary, a risky practice for non-front-runners early in the process, which contributes to the perception that they cannot win.

Minor-party candidates may also receive matching funds if they seek their party's nomination. In 2004, Ralph Nader received almost $900,000 in matching funds.

Although the matching fund provision provides opportunities for candidates who begin with less funding, it has not substantially reduced the advantage that nationally recognized candidates have in the private solicitation process. Moreover, the provision encourages all candidates to begin their fund-raising well before the election to qualify as soon as possible and have money available upfront. The catch is that candidates who accept matching funds have to abide by individual state and overall spending limits. In 2008, the state limits ranged from about $841,000 in the smallest states to almost $18.3 million for California; in 2012, they are expected to be about $885,000 in the smallest states to almost $19.7 million in California. The total spending limit, including fund-raising and compliance costs, was $56.7 million in 2008; in 2012, it will be approximately $60 million.

As the campaign progresses, candidates taking federal matching grants will bump up against the total spending ceiling. Since most nomination contests (2008 excluded) have been settled fairly early in the calendar year, the overall limits have not been as much of a problem as the individual state limits in Iowa and New Hampshire. The overall limit would have been a problem for McCain in 2000 had he stayed in the race against Bush. One of the reasons he didn't stay in the race in 2000 and declined matching funds in 2008 was because of those limits.

There's another problem. Even when the nomination is settled very early, money is needed by the prospective nominee to campaign in the months leading up to the national nominating convention for travel, staff, advertising, and fund-raising for the party and joint candidate–party committees. But the spending limits still apply for candidates who accept government funds. These limits explain why George W. Bush in 2000 and 2004, Howard Dean and John Kerry in 2004, and most of the principal candidates for their party's 2008 nomination (including John McCain) chose not to accept federal funds. Nor are they likely to do so in the future unless the grants are raised (and indexed to inflation) and the spending limits are substantially increased. Table 2.5 lists the limits since the Federal Election Campaign Act went into effect.

TABLE 2.5 | PRESIDENTIAL SPENDING LIMITS AND COLAS (COST OF LIVING ADJUSTMENTS) FOR THE DEMOCRATIC AND REPUBLICAN PARTIES, 1976–2012 (IN MILLIONS)

	1974	1976	1980	1984	1988	1992	1996	2000	2004	2008	2012*
Primary election limit†	$10	$10.9	$14.7	$20.2	$23.1	$27.6	$31.0	$33.8	$37.3	$41.0	$44.2
General election limit‡	20	21.8	29.4	40.4	46.1	55.2	61.8	67.6	74.6	84.1	88.5
Party convention limit§	2	2.2	4.4	8.1	9.2	11.0	12.4	13.5	14.6	16.2	17.5
Party general election limit	—	3.2	4.6	6.9	8.3	10.3	11.6	13.7	14.8	16.4	17.7

*Calculations based on 2011 data provided by the FEC in "Presidential Spending Limits if the Election Were Held in 2011," Federal Election Commission. fec.gov/pages/brochures/pubfund_limits_2011.

†Primary candidates receiving matching funds must comply with two types of spending limits: a national limit (listed in this table) and a separate limit for each state. The state limit is $200,000 or 164 multiplied by the state's voting-age population, whichever is greater. (Both amounts are adjusted for increases in the cost of living.)

‡Legal and accounting expenses to comply with the law are exempt from this limit. These funds may be raised through private contributions.

§This limit has been raised twice by legislation: once in 1979 and once in 1984.

Source: Federal Election Commission, *Annual Report, 1984* (June 1, 1985), pp. 8–9, updated by the author with data supplied by the Federal Election Commission.

Convention Grants

Federal funding also extends to the major parties for their national nominating conventions. The convention grant in 2008 was $16.3 million for the major parties and much less for minor parties that qualify for federal funding. In 2012, it is expected to be about $17.5 million. In addition to government grants, parties may also seek convention funding from the cities and states in which the event occurs as well as goods and services from the private sector. These supplements can be substantial. In 2008, the Democratic and Republican national committees raised a total of $118 million, $61 million for the Democrats and $57 million for the Republicans. Most of the money came from large organizations and private donors.[32]

General Election Funds

Once the major-party candidates have been officially nominated, they are eligible for a direct grant. In 2008, $84.1 million was given to Republican John McCain. Barack Obama refused to accept general election funds despite a pledge his campaign had made during the nomination period that he would accept them if his Republican opponent did as well. He was the first major-party candidate not to take federal funds.[33] Obama's decision was strategic; he knew he could raise much more money from private contributors even with the individual and group limits that the law established. And he did, raising $337 million for the general election. Although the Republican National Committee helped McCain to the tune of $150 million in coordinated and independent expenditures; Obama still had much more money to spend than his Republican opponent.

The advantage that successful private funding gives a presidential candidate has rendered the public financing provision for the general election irrelevant unless and until the amount given the major-party nominees is substantially raised and/or private contributions are permitted to supplement public funds. If the law is not changed, then the only candidates who are likely to accept public funds in the general election will be those who run as independent or minor-party candidates. Under the current law, minor-party nominees receive funding equal to their proportion of the popular vote provided it is at least 5 percent. However, they receive it after the election unless their party qualified in the previous election.

H. Ross Perot used his own money ($63 million) to run in 1992. He received 19 percent of the vote as the candidate of the Reform Party. Automatically eligible for federal funds in 1996 because of the size of the vote he received in 1992, Perot got $29 million; in 2000, the Reform Party nominee, Pat Buchanan, was eligible for $12.6 million from the campaign fund, but the small vote he received in that election made the Reform Party ineligible for federal funds in 2004. Green Party candidate Ralph Nader did not receive sufficient votes in 2000 or 2004 to qualify the party that nominated him for federal funding. He ran as an independent in 2008.

Table 2.6 | Revenues of the Major Party Candidates for the 2008 Nominations*

	Federal Matching Funds	Contributions From Individuals Minus Refunds	Other Revenues	Total†
Democrats				
Biden	$2,027,072	$7,767,364	$2,123,369	$11,917,805
Clinton	$0	$196,842,746	$27,016,479	$223,859,225
Dodd‡	$1,447,568	$8,889,713	$5,400,482	$15,737,763
Edwards	$12,882,864	$35,126,205	$149,599	$48,158,668
Gravel§	$100,000	$448,053	$3,502	$551,555
Kucinich	$1,070,521	$4,375,584	$33,755	$5,479,860
Obama**	$0	$657,117,793	$88,618,480	$745,736,273
Richardson	$0	$22,053,014	$346,737	$22,399,751
Republicans				
Brownback	$0	$3,530,942	$711,529	$4,242,471
Gilmore	$0	$349,736	$38,409	$388,145
Giuliani	$0	$55,008,874	$3,648,017	$58,656,891
Huckabee	$0	$15,991,901	$68,086	$16,059,987
Hunter	$453,527	$2,343,898	$77,274	$2,874,699
McCain	$0	$190,411,677	$29,179,374	$219,591,051
Paul	$0	$34,336,199	$198.704	$34,534,903
Romney	$0	$59,786,640	$45,369,912	$105,156,552
Tancredo§	$2,145,126	$3,979,701	$93,398	$6,218,225
T. Thompson	$0	$967,322	$245,932	$1,213,254
F. Thompson	$0	$23,202,419	$246,062	$23,448,481
Other				
Nader	$881,494	$3,102,020	$45,236	$4,028,750
Total Democrats	$17,528,025	$932,620,472	$123,692,402	$1,073,840,899
Total Republicans	$2,598,653	$389,909,310	$79,876,694	$472,384,657
Grand Total	$21,008,172	$1,325,631,802	$203,614,332	$1,550,254,306

*Figures rounded to the nearest whole dollar.

†Total includes other revenues such as loans, transfers from other committees, and PAC contributions.

‡Dodd received $1,961,742 in matching funds; however, his committee reported the receipt of $1,447,568.

§Gravel and Tancredo received an additional $115,966 and $83,775 in matching funds, respectively, in early 2009.

**Obama activity includes both primary and general election funds because he used a single committee for both elections.

Source: "2008 Presidential Campaign Financial Activity Summarized: Receipts Nearly Double 2004 Total," Federal Election Commision, June 8, 2009. www.fec.gov/press/press2009/20090608PresStat.shtml

BOX 2.2 | THE MONEY RACE FOR THE 2008 NOMINATION

The Democrats The money race for the 2008 presidential nominations began more than two years before the nomination when Democratic candidates began to map their initial strategies and assemble their fund-raising teams. They did not start their campaigns with the same amount of money, however. Some of them had funds left over from previous campaigns for federal office that they could use in the presidential quests: Hillary Rodham Clinton, $10 million; Chris Dodd, $4 million; Joe Biden, $2 million; and Barack Obama, $516,000.[i]

The candidates' leadership and advocacy PACs were also a source for initial staff expenses and travel before the official nomination campaign got underway in 2007. Clinton, Dodd, and Obama had made contributions from their PACs to fund the campaigns of other candidates for federal office with the hope that they could obtain the endorsements of the candidates whom they supported.

The first step in their money race was to establish finance committees and seek donations, the larger the better. Clinton had several advantages at the beginning of the contest. In addition to the funds that she transferred from her 2006 Senate account, her years and notoriety in Democratic politics and her husband's political connections gave her access to many of the leading Democratic fund-raisers, including people who had worked on Bill Clinton's campaigns. Moreoever, the perception that she was the leading candidate and, some believed, the inevitable nominee helped open the checkbooks of those who wanted to be associated with the winning team. Clinton was also helped by the support she received from Emily's List, an organization that helps women candidates raise money and gain support, and several major labor unions.

During the first quarter of 2007, Clinton raised $29.1 million, a relatively large amount so early in the race. What was more surprising, however, was that Obama raised $24.7 million. Edwards was third with $12.6 million. In the second quarter of that year, Obama actually raised $9.5 million more than Clinton, thereby putting people, especially the news media and dependable Democratic contributors, on notice that he could match Clinton's fund-raising. By the end of July, the Democratic money race had essentially become a contest between the Clinton and Obama campaigns. Each raised revenues of almost $98 million in 2007.[ii]

But Obama was in a more advantageous position. He had raised more money from small donors, whereas Clinton depended on those who gave the maximum amount. Initially, Obama too had turned to large donors to get started, gain visibility, and demonstrate his viability as a candidate, reinforcing the adage that it takes money to raise it. Once Obama proved that he could compete with Clinton, that her nomination was not inevitable as her campaign suggested, he then turned to the Internet and reached out to a broader base for support. (See Box 2.1 for how he did it.) The significance of his fund-raising effort is further magnified by the fact that he trailed Clinton by 20 to 30 percent in the pre-election polls during most of 2007.

Obama had another advantage. His campaign was much more disciplined in its spending. It relied on volunteers to canvass, identify potential supporters, and turn them out, particularly in states that held caucuses. In contrast, Clinton had fewer people on the ground and more of them were paid. *Newsweek* reported that the Clinton campaign spent lavishly on plush hotels, fancy food, and other luxuries.[iii]

Once the contests are held, it is the results that drive the money. Obama won the first caucus in Iowa. Clinton came in third, closely behind Edwards, who trailed Obama. The loss stunned the Clinton campaign. As stunning was the report she

BOX 2.2 THE MONEY RACE FOR THE 2008 NOMINATION *continued*

got from her chief delegate counter and political adviser, Harold Ickes: "The cupboard is empty."[iv] Were it not for the support she received in New Hampshire from union supporters and Emily's List, she might not have survived. But victory in New Hampshire gave her a reprieve, her fund-raising increased although she could not match Obama's prodigious efforts. The table below compares fund-raising over time for the two principal Democratic candidates (all amounts are in millions).

	Revenues	
	Obama	Clinton
Jan.–Sept. 2007	75.4	73.7
Oct.–Dec. 2007	22.1	24.0
Jan.–Feb. 2008	89.3	51.4
Mar.–May 2008	91.7	59.4
June–Aug. 2008	134.0	

Source: Michael Malbin, "Small Donors, Large Donors, and the Internet: Rethinking Public Financing for Presidential Elections after Obama," Campaign Finance Institute, April 22, 2009. www.cfinst.org/Press/PReleases/09-04-22/Small_Donors_Large_Donors_and_the_Internet_The_Case_for_Public_Financing_after_Obama.aspx

The Republicans There was no clear Republican front-runner for the nomination. The three best-known candidates—Mitt Romney, Rudolph Giuliani, and John McCain—established their fund-raising committees and began seeking donors. Romney made the headlines initially by scheduling a "Call Day" in early January 2007 in which he raised $6.5 million.[v] A wealthy man, Romney also contributed substantially to his own campaign. By the end of 2007, he had raised a little over $50 million from individuals in addition to the millions he had personally given to his campaign.

Giuliani was second in first year fund-raising with almost $56 million, and McCain was third with nearly $40 million in revenues. McCain had anticipated raising considerably more money in 2007 but was unable to collect donations that had been pledged to his campaign. After a while, he stopped asking people for money.

McCain had another problem, similar to Clinton's: he had overspent, anticipating larger revenues than he eventually received. By late spring–early summer of 2007, his campaign had literally run out of funds; it had become a hand-to-mouth operation, forcing McCain to cut back significantly, fire staff, including some of his principal advisers, and borrow $4 million just to keep his campaign afloat. The press began to write him off, making further fund-raising that much more difficult. The other Republican contenders had raised less, although Ron Paul had garnered headlines by receiving large amounts on two days that were symbolic to libertarians: $4.3 million on November 5, the date Guy Fawkes tried to blow up the English parliament, and $6 million on December 16, the 234th anniversary of the Boston Tea Party.

Even though there were significant financial inequities among the Republican candidates, once the caucuses and primaries got underway, it was their results, not

continued

BOX 2.2 THE MONEY RACE FOR THE 2008 NOMINATION *continued*

the bank accounts of the candidates that dictated the outcome. Romney's defeats in Iowa and New Hampshire undercut any perception his war chest alone would buy him the Republican presidential nomination. Similarly, Giuliani's failure to win a single primary in the early period doomed his candidacy. Huckabee's surprising win in Iowa gave him a boost, but one he could not take advantage of because of the rapid succession of Republican primaries that followed. McCain's win in New Hampshire had the opposite effect. It showed that he could win a compeititive election. Recognition and reputation subsequently boosted his chances in the large-state primaries that had winner-take-all voting. By March 4, the Republican race was over.

Listed below are the revenues for the Republican candidates for the 2008 nomination (all amounts are in the millions).

	Revenues				
	Romney	**Giuliani**	**McCain**	**Huckabee**	**Paul**
Jan.–Sept. 2007	$62.4	42.2	29.9	2.4	8.3
Oct.–Dec. 2007	27.1	13.9	9.5	6.7	20.0
Jan.–Feb. 2008	17.0	2.7	23.0	7.1	6.5

Source: Michael Malbin, "Small Donors, Large Donors, and the Internet: Rethinking Public Financing for Presidential Elections after Obama," Campaign Finance Institute, April 22, 2009. www.cfinst.org/Press/PReleases/09-04-22/Small_Donors_Large_Donors_and_the_Internet_The_Case_for_Public_Financing_after_Obama.aspx

Inequities in contribution size, the prevalence of large donors, and the campaign activities of outside groups work to reinforce the public perception that moneyed interests play a disproportionate role in determining the parties' nominees. In the 2007–2008 election cycle, however, unequal campaign resources did not determine the outcome of the Republican or Democratic races. McCain had and spent less money than Romney during the competitive phase of the Republican primaries, yet he won. Raising amounts equal to Clinton's helped Obama compete in the large states in which Clinton was thought to have an advantage. Although Obama spent more, he did not win in most of these states, but he did stay close. His large on-the-ground organization, composed primarily of volunteers, probably helped him as much, if not more, than the advertising he was able to purchase with his large war chest.

[i] "2008 Presidential Campaign Financial Activity Summarized: Receipts Nearly Double 2004 Total," Federal Election Commission, June 8, 2009. www.fec.gov/press/press2009/20090608PresStat.shtml

[ii] Michael Malbin, "Small Donors, Large Donors, and the Internet: Rethinking Public Financing for Presidential Elections after Obama," Campaign Finance Institute, April 2009, p. 12.

[iii] "How He Did It." *Newsweek*, November 5, 2008. www.newsweek.com/id/167582/ouput/print

[iv] Joshua Green, "The Front-Runner's Fall," *TheAtlantic.com* www.theatlantic.com/doc/print/200809/hillary-clinton-campaign

[v] Glen Johnson, "Romney Kicks Off Presidential Campaign with Fundraising Blitz," *Boston Globe*, January 9, 2007. www.bostonglobe.com/news/local/massachusetts/articles/2007/01/09/Romney_kicks_off

BOX 2.3 | The Money Race for the 2008 General Election

Obama The money race did not end with the nomination. Because Obama had decided not to accept federal funds, he had to continue to seek private donations with the same contribution limits in place of $2,300 per individual and $5,000 per group. In the summer, the campaign set a goal of adding 1.75 million contributors to its donor base of over 2 million and 5 million more e-mail addresses to the 7 million they had already collected.[i] Campaign manager David Plouffe assumed an additional $350 million could be raised from private donors.[ii] The law permitted the Democratic National Committee to spend an additional $19.1 million in coordination with the Obama campaign and other money independent of it. Democratically oriented PACs and nonprofits could also spend money on the campaign but could not by law coordinate that spending with the campaign.

The campaign almost achieved its fund-raising goal. Approximately $337 million was raised for the general election. Almost half of that money came in September, with contributions averaging less than $90 a person.[iii] The DNC and Democratically oriented groups spent another $60 million in support of Obama and $14 million in opposition to McCain.[iv] Obama thus had a significant spending advantage. It was evident in the final weeks of the campaign. He outspent McCain by margins of 3 to 1 in television advertising in the key competitive states.[v] He also had more field offices and more paid and unpaid volunteers in the field.

McCain The McCain campaign had little choice but to accept government funds for the general election. In addition to McCain's support of public funding and his sponsorship of the Bipartisan Campaign Reform Act, he did not have the organization, base of contributors, or the technology in place to rival Obama's private fund-raising. Accepting public funds was his only viable option. The plan was to supplement the $84.1 million he would receive upon his nomination by the Republican Party with support from the Republican National Committee and other state Republican organizations.

After his winning a majority of the Republican delegates in early March, McCain continued to raise money for his own campaign to cover his expenses in the five months before the Republican convention as well as solicit money for the party. He ended up with $27 million in unspent funds that he donated to the RNC ($18 million) and various state Republican parties ($9 million) with the expectation that they would spend it on his general election campaign. The problem was that his campaign could not control most of the spending by Republican state committees; moreover, only $19.1 million of the Republican National Committee's expenditures could be coordinated with the McCain campaign in the presidential election.

Republican Party committees and Republican-oriented groups decided how to spend most of their money: $78 million opposing Obama and only $6 million in support of McCain.[vi] Thus, McCain faced two major disadvantages in the general election. His campaign had less money, and it exercised less control over expenditures.

---

[i] David Plouffe, *The Audacity to Win.* (New York: Viking, 2009), pp. 254–255.

[ii] Ibid., p. 259.

[iii] Michael Luo, "Obama Raises More than $150 Million in September," *New York Times*, October 20, 2008. www.nytimes.com/2008/10/19/world/americas/19iht-19donate.17801557.html

[iv] Center for Responsive Politics. www.opensecrets.org/pres08/indexp.php

[v] "Obama Outspending McCain 3 to 1 on TV," Wisconsin Advertising Project, Oct. 31, 2008.

[vi] Center for Responsive Politics. www.opensecrets.org/pres08/indexp.php

CAMPAIGN SPENDING BY THE PRESIDENTIAL CANDIDATES

According to the Center for Responsive Politics, $1.3 billion was spent on the 2008 presidential campaign by the presidential candidates.[34] The largest single item on which money was spent was media. About 40 percent of total campaign expenditures was directed toward the production and airing of advertisements on radio, television, and the Internet, plus the cost of media consultants and their firms. (Consultants generally work on a percentage basis, with their firms getting a proportion of the costs of the advertising they place on local and national cable and broadcast media.)

Administrative expenses, such as salaries, travel, and office rentals, represented the next largest item, constituting about 30 percent of all costs. David Plouffe, Obama's campaign manager, stated that the Obama campaign capped the salaries of its top campaign aides at $12,000 per month, a hefty sum for most, but not for a small group of professionals whose reputation and expertise candidates desire and often vie with one another to obtain.[35]

Expenses directly related to campaigning, such as rallies, signs, buttons and bumper stickers, polling, focus groups, and candidate-directed research, get-out-the-vote activities, and direct mail not related to fund-raising constitute another 12 percent.The rest of the money is spent raising money, planning and conducting fund-raising events, hiring fund-raising consultants and telemarketers, and paying credit card fees, making contributions to other campaigns and party committees, and paying the interest on loans that the campaign may have incurred. Table 2.7 shows the Center for Responsive Politics' breakdown of expenses for the 2007–2008 presidential campaign.

Money is critical for all phases of the presidential campaign, but it acquires special importance in the first phase. Before the caucuses and primaries begin, the size of a campaign's war chest and its ability to attract donors is viewed as an indication of who's ahead by the press and political donors. For most candidates, the most important caucuses and primaries are the first ones, in Iowa and New Hampshire, two relatively small states with low spending limits for candidates who accept federal matching grants. These limits are the primary reason that most candidates do not take matching funds unless they have no other viable option.

There are various "tricks of the trade" that campaigns use to save money. It has become common practice for campaign workers to commute to the early states from neighboring ones, thus allowing the campaign to allocate only a portion of its expenses to the state in which the early contest will be held. Another tactic is to use national phone banks to canvas voters within these states. In 2008, the Obama campaign established virtual phone banks, with volunteers contacting potential voters and supporters from their own home computer or cells.[36] Similarly, cheaper and smaller television markets may be used to air commercials to reach specific targeted cities and localities.

Table 2.7 | Presidential Campaign Expenditures in 2008

Sector	Description	Total Expenditures
Administrative	salaries & benefits	$175,587,223
	travel	$167,308,386
	postage/shipping	$64,689,518
	rent/utilities	$57,066,097
	miscellaneous administrative	$51,866,260
	supplies, equipment, & furniture	$23,677,815
	administrative consultants	$5,591,669
	food/meetings	$2,091,938
Campaign Expenses	campaign events	$71,254,156
	polling/surveys/research	$44,941,085
	materials	$39,331,617
	campaign direct mail	$30,148,434
	political consultants	$25,770,845
	GOTV	$4,467,412
	miscellaneous campaign	$1,837,394
Contributions	parties (federal & non-federal)	$59,355,922
	contribution refunds	$56,977,701
	committees (federal & non-federal)	$1,080,867
	candidates (federal & non-federal)	$740,705
	miscellaneous contributions	$11,480
Fund-raising	fund-raising direct mail/telemarketing	$66,364,113
	fund-raising consultants	$20,155,664
	miscellaneous fund-raising	$14,034,583
	fund-raising events	$1,747,549
Media	broadcast media	$360,748,127
	miscellaneous media	$273,794,015
	Internet media	$43,605,647
	print media	$21,850,368
	media consultants	$11,477,888
Other	loan payments	$14,851,919
	charitable donations	$12,568,498
	miscellaneous	$1,042,220
Transfers	national party transfer	$32,251,482
	federal transfer	$32,168,060
	miscellaneous transfer	$7,500,000
Unknown	insufficient information	$1,309,254

Note: All the numbers on this page are for the 2008 election cycle and based on Federal Election Commission data released electronically on Thursday, July 16, 2009.

Source: Center for Responsive Politics, "Presidential Expenditures for 2008." www.opensecrets.org/pres08/expenditures

SUPPLEMENTARY CAMPAIGNS

In addition to the campaign run by the presidential candidates' organizations, party and nonparty groups are also active in presidential elections. As noted previously, the national party committee can coordinate a relatively small proportion of its spending with the campaigns of their presidential candidates. They can also spend independently on behalf of those candidates and against their opponents, as can PACs and other nonparty groups.[37]

The national party organizations tend to remain on the sidelines during the primaries and caucuses until these nomination contests have been decided. They do not make direct financial contributions to the various people seeking nomination, but they can and do help their potential nominee once a winner has emerged from the process. To do this, they need money, lots of it. Despite the prohibition placed on soft money solicitation beginning in 2002, national party committees have raised record amounts during the last two presidential election cycles. Table 2.8 lists the amount they raised in the past four presidential elections.

In addition to party spending, there is also spending by nonparty groups. The election law defines and legitimizes these groups. It permits them to get involved in the electoral process by contributing a limited amount of money to federal candidates, communicating in an unrestricted manner with their members, and mounting public appeals that are only constrained thirty days or less before a primary or caucus and sixty days or less before the general election.

During the 2007–2008 election cycle, political action committees raised a total of $1.2 billion, some of which they contributed directly to candidates, and the rest they spent independently on the campaign. Of this amount, about $100 million was spent on the presidential election, with labor unions supporting Obama and conservative advocacy groups supporting McCain. In addition, nonprofit groups that had been active in 2004 continued their involvement in 2008. These groups, referred to by the provision of the Internal Revenue Code in sections 527 and 501c, which permit their activity in federal elections, are distinctive from PACs in that there are no limits placed on the size of the contributions they can receive.[38] But they were not as active in 2008 as they were in 2004. Their expenditures totaled about $400 million in the 2007–2008 election cycle.[39] As with PACs, most of this spending was on the congressional races, not the presidential contest.

Individuals are also allowed to spend their own money in elections. Three people—Fred Eshelman, Sheldon Adelson, and George Soros—spent

TABLE 2.8 | NATIONAL PARTY REVENUES IN RECENT PRESIDENTIAL ELECTIONS (IN MILLIONS)

	1991–1992	1995–1996	1999–2000	2003–2004	2007–2008
Democrats	$163.3	221.6	275.2	678.8	763.3
Republicans	$264.9	416.5	465.8	782.4	792.9

Source: "Party Financial Activity Summarized for the 2008 Election Cycle: Party Support for Candidates Increases," Federal Election Commission, Press Release, May 28, 2009 (Revised August 5, 2009). www.fec.gov/press/press2009/05282009Party/20090528Party.shtml

$5 million or more in 2008, and a few others—Steven Bing and Gerald and Lilo Leeds—spent nearly that amount.[40]

FINANCIAL IRREGULARITIES IN CAMPAIGNS

Throughout the years, there have been numerous allegations about illegal campaign finance activities. Republicans claimed that a Democratic Party fund-raiser in a Buddhist temple in Los Angeles in 2000, one in which Vice President Gore participated, violated the law because the nonpartisan status of religious institutions as tax-exempt organizations precluded their use for partisan political purposes. Questions were also raised about the $5,000 contributions from monks who had taken vows of poverty and thus probably did not have much, if any, personal wealth to donate. None of the monks was prosecuted, however. The Democrats returned the money, but the accusation plagued the campaign.[41]

Short of illegalities, the need for money has led candidates to take funds from questionable sources and to reward those who can raise the most money. In 1996, the Clinton–Gore campaign and the Democratic Party were forced to return thousands of dollars donated by people with criminal ties and records and by foreign nationals who are not permitted by law to contribute to U.S. federal elections. In 2006, President Bush returned $6,000 his campaign received directly from lobbyist Jack Abramoff, his wife, and a friend after Abramoff admitted his guilt in business transactions, lobbying activities, and tax evasion.[42] The Obama campaign returned donations it received from lobbyists and PACs on principle. Obama had said that he would not accept funds from people and groups that try to influence government decisions. Questions were also raised about Obama donors making multiple contributions over the course of the campaign that in total exceeded the contribution limits. It was difficult for the campaign to keep track of aggregate totals during the period in September when he received about half of his donations for the general election.[43]

The use of government facilities for rewarding private contributors has also raised concerns. The White House served as a backdrop during the Clinton years; Vice President Cheney held a large fund-raising event on the grounds of his official residence at the Naval Observatory. It has become common practice for recent presidents to schedule public events before fund-raising activities in the same cities so that taxpayers will pick up the tab for the bulk of the president's travel expenses and the press can report on what the presidents said and did during the public phase of their travels.

A related issue is the special treatment that major contributors and fund-raisers receive. The Center for Responsive Politics, which charts the money flow and special treatment, reported that 40 percent of George W. Bush's $100,000+ fund-raisers in his 2000 campaign ended up on a presidential transition task force or with a government job during Bush's first term. Twenty-three became ambassadors, three cabinet secretaries, thirty-seven were on the teams that recommended people for federal appointments.[44] President Obama appointed twenty-four of his top fund-raisers, who had collected $10.9 million for the campaign, to ambassadorial positions.[45]

George W. Bush and Barack Obama are not the first and will not be the last presidents to appoint campaign staff, financial supporters, and party workers to top executive branch positions. The spoils system has deep roots in American politics that extend back to the beginnings of the party system in the Jefferson administration. The conundrum for a democratic election process, however, remains the same. Is it fair that those with the greater resources—money, expertise, and time—exercise more influence than others over the course of the election? Is it fair that money "buys" access in some cases and appears to have bought votes in others?[46]

MONEY AND ELECTORAL SUCCESS

The relationship between money and electoral success has spurred considerable debate in recent years and generated much anger from those who believe unequal resources undermine the democratic character of the U.S. electoral process. Is the conventional wisdom correct? Do those with more money have an advantage? Do they usually win? The simple answer is usually yes, but the longer answer is more complicated. First, who has or gets the money? Second, what difference does the money make in the election?

Two types of candidates tend to have disproportionate resources at their disposal: those who are personally wealthy and those who are well-known and well-connected public figures. Money can buy recognition, as it did for Ross Perot in 1992 and 1996, Steve Forbes in 1996 and 2000, and Mitt Romney in 2008; it gave them a chance that they might not otherwise have had. But obviously, money cannot, in and of itself, buy an electoral victory, as Perot, Forbes, and Romney found out. Similarly, party front-runners, such as Bill Clinton in 1996 and Hillary Clinton in 2008, can raise more money because they are perceived to be likely to win their party's nomination. That money, in turn, contributes to their likelihood for success, but again it does not guarantee it, as Hillary Clinton can attest.

Theoretically, campaign spending should have a greater impact on the nomination process than on the general election and at the beginning of the process rather than at the end. According to political scientists Michael Robinson, Clyde Wilcox, and Paul Marshall, money matters most when the candidates are least known to the voters, when they do not receive a lot of news coverage, and when paid advertising, which, of course, is expensive, can bring recognition and enhance images.[47] As the nomination process progresses and candidates become more easily recognized by the public, the expenditure of funds is not as critical to electoral success. What money buys initially are name recognition, organizational support, and campaign consultants; what it buys over the course of the campaign are media and a grassroots operation.

Have the candidates with the largest bankrolls generally been victorious in the general election? The answer again seems to be yes, although as in the nomination process, it is difficult to determine precisely whether money contributed to victory or simply flowed to the likely winner. Between 1860 and 1972, the winner outspent the loser twenty-one out of twenty-nine times. Republican candidates have spent more than their Democratic opponents in twenty-five out of twenty-nine elections during this period. The four times they did not, the Democrats won.

The correlation between money and electoral success has continued in the contemporary period even though the major-party candidates who accept federal funds are offered the same amount of money. Independent spending by party and nonparty groups can make a difference. In the 1980s, considerably more was spent on behalf of Republican nominees than on their Democratic opponents, and the GOP won each presidential election during this period. In the 1990s, the Democrats benefited from substantial expenditures by organized labor and the impact of the Perot campaign, although their total spending was still less than the Republicans'. George W. Bush was the financial as well as electoral victor in 2000; in 2004, however, the amount of money each side had was about equal and the results of the vote were very close. In 2008, Obama had a significant financial advantage and probably enlarged his general election victory by using his superior resources effectively. In Congress, the big spenders won 93 percent of House of Representatives races and 94 percent of Senate races.[48]

What do all these trends suggest? According to political scientist Larry Bartels, "campaign spending has had a significant electoral impact in presidential elections over the past half century [1952–2004]."[49] It has benefited the party that has spent the most, the Republicans. Bartels concludes that campaign spending increases the probability of voter support, particularly among the most affluent voters.[50]

The pattern of greater spending and electoral victories indicates that money contributes to success, potential success also attracts money. Having more funds is an advantage, but it does not explain all outcomes. The fact that heavily favored incumbent Richard Nixon outspent rival George McGovern more than 2 to 1 in 1972 does not explain McGovern's huge defeat, although it probably portended it. On the other hand, Hubert Humphrey's much narrower defeat by Nixon four years earlier was partially influenced by Humphrey spending less than $12 million, compared with more than $25 million spent by Nixon. The closer the election, the more the disparity in funds can make a difference.

SUMMARY

Campaign finance became an important aspect of presidential elections by the end of the nineteenth and the beginning of the twentieth centuries. In recent years, however, it has become even more important as campaign costs have escalated and legal restrictions have limited large gifts to candidates and their political parties. Expanded use of high technology and multiple channels of communication to reach the voters have been partially responsible for the large increase in expenditures and, in 2008, for the increase in revenues, particularly for the Obama campaign.

In the early-and mid-twentieth century, candidates of both major parties turned to large contributors for financial support. Their dependence on a relatively small number of large donors, combined with spiraling costs, created serious problems for a democratic selection process. The 1972 presidential election, with its high expenditures, "dirty tricks," and illegal campaign contributions, vividly illustrated these problems and generated public and congressional support for rectifying them.

In the 1970s, Congress enacted and amended the Federal Election Campaign Act to bring donors into the open, to limit the size of their contributions, and to provide government subsidies for the presidential election. These reforms were designed to make the presidential selection process less costly and more equitable. A Federal Election Commission was also established to monitor election activities, oversee compliance, and prosecute offenders.

But the legislation was only partially successful. It increased the importance of having a large base of contributors during the preconvention period but did not eliminate the impact of large donors and those who can raise large amounts for the parties' and candidates' efforts in the general election. For candidates who accepted federal funds, it limited the expenditures of individual campaigns in both the nomination process and the general election but did not reduce the amount of money spent on presidential elections. It produced greater equity by limiting contributions and expenditures and by providing federal subsidies but has not evened the playing field among the candidates during the nomination stage, although it did so for a short time during the general election. It has given greater opportunities to candidates who lack national recognition, but it has not lessened the advantages that well-known and well-funded candidates still have. It has benefited major-party candidates in the general election but also has contributed to fractionalization during the nomination process by providing financial incentives for candidates who might otherwise not have had opportunities to run to do so. It has reduced party leaders' direct control over the nomination process and over the conduct of the general election campaign, but it has also enhanced the strategic value of the national parties' fund-raising and grassroots organizing activities. It has encouraged the formation and involvement of nonparty groups, which supplement the campaigns of the major party candidates but cannot coordinate their efforts with the candidates and their parties.

Finally, the law has contributed to public knowledge of campaign finance by placing contributions and expenditures on the public record. Although it has forced campaigns to engage in additional bookkeeping and reporting procedures, it has generated a wealth of data: who gives how much to whom and when? The laws have also made those data available to the press, electorate, and other political candidates. The reporting and publicizing of campaign contributions and expenditures has generated more media scrutiny, more public awareness, greater activity by citizen watchdog groups, and, in the cases of possible violations, congressional investigations, and FEC sanctions.

The Bipartisan Campaign Reform Act, which banned soft money solicitation and distribution by the national parties, prohibited candidates from being named directly in issue advocacy ads thirty days or less before a primary and sixty days or less before the general election and raised the individual and party contribution limits, has not eliminated the problems that prompted the legislation: high costs, endless fund-raising, resource inequality, and perceived benefits for individuals and groups that raise and spend large amounts on behalf of the winning candidate.

Although the BCRA has reduced but not completely eliminated soft money from presidential campaigns and improved disclosure, it has not been the panacea its sponsors had hoped. Moreover, the failure of the law to index matching funds to inflation and to increase overall and individual state spending limits has rendered the law increasingly obsolete for major-party candidates who can raise money privately and thus spend more than they could if they accepted federal funds.

The Supreme Court's decision in the *Citizens United* case that corporations and, by inference, labor unions can spend as much as they desire on federal elections opens what some fear is a Pandora's box on election spending and what the public perceives as the benefits of that spending—undue influence over the results of the election and on the decisions of those elected to office. Although this development may be partially offset by online fund-raising from small donors, the financial floodgates have been opened and with them the questions of equity that were raised at the beginning of the chapter. Will the wealthy be benefited? Will motivational candidates, such as Barack Obama, be sought to mine the small-donor base? Will candidates of all political persuasions be tempted to make even more promises and create more unrealistic expectations to gain the additional support they need to win?

From a financial perspective, the 2008 presidential election was historic in several ways: in the amount of money raised and spent, especially by the winning candidate; in the proportion of small donors who contributed to Obama and other candidates and party committees; and in the use of the Internet as a cheap, quick, and reliable instrument for raising money, gaining volunteers, and building support. But the election also reinforced the perception that those with the largest war chests are advantaged and those who help the candidates raise the most money, whether it be online, by phone, or through personal contact, stand to benefit the most if their candidate wins. Some gain political appointments; some receive social favors; and most have more access and potential influence than the rest of the people.

WHERE ON THE WEB?

- **The Campaign Finance Institute**
  www.cfinst.org
  A nonprofit institute that collects and analyzes current information on campaign finance, reviews the impact of legislation on election giving and spending, and makes recommendations for legal reforms.
- **Center for Public Integrity**
  www.publicintegrity.org
  Evaluates the impact of public service, government accountability, and various ethical issues on democratic governance. Has also been concerned with campaign finance reform.

- **Center for Responsive Politics**
  www.opensecrets.org
  A nonpartisan, public interest group that is concerned with providing the public with information on the conduct of federal elections, particularly how money is raised and spent. Publishes alerts, press releases, and major studies on campaign finance.
- **Common Cause**
  www.commoncause.org
  Another public interest group that is concerned with large and unreported contributions and expenditures and has continually urged campaign finance reform.
- **Democracy 21**
  www.democracy21.org
  Still another public interest group interested in campaign finance reform, especially to reduce the influence of money on elections and government.
- **Federal Election Commission**
  www.fec.gov
  The first stop for any study of campaign finance, the FEC collects and disseminates data on contributions to and expenditures of candidates seeking federal office as well as money donated to and spent by parties, PACs, and other nonparty groups.
- **Public Campaign**
  www.publicampaign.org
  A public interest organization devoted to campaign reform to reduce the role of special interest money and large contributors in American politics.

EXERCISES

1. During the preelection period, see if you can identify the leadership PACs and other groups that potential candidates on the Republican and Democratic sides have created for their presidential campaigns. You can find these groups on the Web site of the Center for Responsive Politics (www.opensecrets.org). Some of them are also listed in the "Where on the Web?" section in Chapter 5. Note how much money groups have raised, from whom, and how they have spent it.
2. Compile a running summary of revenue and expenditures as filed with the FEC (www.fec.gov) by candidates who have officially declared themselves for their party's 2012 presidential nomination. Does the differential in their war chests explain their respective campaign activities and/or their position in the public opinion polls?
3. Note the impact of the BCRA on the candidates, parties, and nonparty groups in the 2011–2012 election cycle. Are the patterns evident during the 2008 nomination and general election apparent in 2012? Based on your answer, indicate whether you would or would not amend the BCRA. Would you change the public funding provision, and if so, how? Is there any way to limit campaign expenditures by profit-making corporations, trade and other associations, and labor unions?

SELECTED READINGS

Corrado, Anthony. "Party Finance in the Wake of BCRA: An Overview," in Michael J. Malbin, ed. *The Election after Reform: Money, Politics and the Bipartisan Campaign Reform Act.* Lanham, MD: Rowman and Littlefield, 2006.

Corrado, Anthony, Michael J. Malbin, Thomas E. Mann, and Norman J. Ornstein. *Reform in an Age of Networked Campaigns*. Washington, DC: Campaign Finance Institute, Brookings Institution, and the American Enterprise Institute, 2010. cfinst.org/Press/PReleases/10-01-14/Reform_in_an_Age_of_Networked_Campaigns.aspx

Haynes, Audrey A., Paul-Henri Gurian, and Stephen Nichols. "The Role of Candidate Spending in Presidential Nomination Campaigns." *Journal of Politics* (Feb. 1997): 213–235.

Magleby, David B., Anthony Corrado, and Kelly D. Patterson, eds. *Financing the 2004 Elections*. Washington, DC: Brookings Institution, 2006.

Malbin, Michael J., ed. *The Election after Reform: Money, Politics and the Bipartisan Campaign Reform Act*. Lanham, MD: Rowman and Littlefield, 2006.

Malbin, Michael J. "Small Donors, Large Donors and the Internet," Campaign Finance Institute (March 25, 2010). cfinst.org/Press/Releases_tags/10-03-25/Small_and_Large_Donors_to_National_Political_Parties_and_Candidates.aspx

Wayne, Stephen J. "The 2000 Presidential Election: Traveling the Hard and Soft Roads to the White House," in *The Interest Group Connection: Electioneering, Lobbying, and Policymaking*, 2nd ed., Paul S. Herrnson, Ronald Shaiko, and Clyde Wilcox, eds. Washington, DC: Congressional Quarterly, 2003.

Notes

1. "Presidential Fundraising and Spending, 1976–2008," Center for Responsive Politics. www.opensecrets.org/pres08/totals.php?cycle=2008.
2. Ibid.
3. Herbert E. Alexander, "Making Sense about Dollars in the 1980 Presidential Campaigns," in Michael J. Malbin, ed., *Money and Politics in the United States* (Washington, DC: American Enterprise Institute/Chatham House, 1984), p. 24.
4. Edward W. Chester, *Radio, Television, and American Politics* (New York: Sheed & Ward, 1969), p. 21.
5. Herbert E. Alexander, *Financing Politics: Money, Elections, and Political Reform*, 3rd ed. (Washington DC: Congressional Quarterly, 1984), pp. 11–12.
6. "Utilization of Selected Media, 1980–2007," *Statistical Abstract of the United States*, Table 1095. (Washington DC: Bureau of the Census, 2010). www.census.gov/compendia/statab/2010/tables/10s1095.pdf.
7. "Political Advertising in 2008," University of Wisconsin Advertising Project, March 17, 2010, p. 2. www.wiscadpeojwxt.wisc.edu/wiscads_report_031710.pdf.
8. Craig B. Homan and Luke P. McLoughlin, *Buying Time 2000: Television Advertising in the 2000 Federal Elections* (New York: Brennan Center for Justice, 2001), pp. 39–40. Michael M. Franz, Joel Rivlin, and Kenneth Goldstein, "Much More of the Same: Television Advertising Pre-and Post-BCRA," in Michael J. Malbin, ed., *The Election after Reform: Money, Politics and the Bipartisan Campaign Reform Act* (Lanham, MD: Rowman and Littlefield, 2006), p. 142. In 2008, about $400 million was spent on adverting during the nomination process itself. "Political Advertising in 2008," Wisconsin Advertising Project, March 17, 2010, p. 2. wiscadproject.wisc.edu/wiscads_report_031710.pdf.
9. Jasper B. Shannon, *Money and Politics* (New York: Random House, 1959), p. 35.
10. Herbert E. Alexander and Brian Haggerty, *Financing the 1984 Election* (Lexington, MA: Lexington Books, 1987), p. 148.
11. In 1972, the chief fund-raiser for the Nixon campaign, Maurice Stans, and Richard Nixon's private attorney, Herbert Kalmbach, collected contributions, some of them illegal, on behalf of the president. They exerted strong pressure on corporate

executives, despite the prohibition on corporate giving at that time. Secret contributions totaling millions of dollars were received, and three special secured funds were established to give the White House and the Committee to Reelect the President (known as CREEP) maximum discretion in campaign expenditures. It was from these funds that the "dirty tricks" of the 1972 campaign and the Watergate burglary were financed.

12. The 1971 act also limited the amount that could be spent on media advertising, but that limit was eliminated in 1974.
13. There was also a short but critical delay in the effective date for the disclosure provision of the other 1971 campaign finance act. Signed by the president on February 14, 1972, it was scheduled to take effect in sixty days. This delay precipitated a frantic attempt by both parties to tap major donors who wanted to remain anonymous. During this period, the Republicans collected an estimated $20 million, much of it pledged beforehand and some of it in forms that could not even be traced.
14. The FEC defined these activities broadly. It permitted parties to engage in a variety of public-oriented communications with one proviso: they could not expressly advocate the election of a specific candidate for federal office. Express advocacy included such words and expressions as "vote for," "support," and "elect." If these magic words were not included in the communication, then soft money could be used to pay for it.
15. It was not until 1992 that the FEC imposed reporting requirements on this soft money.
16. "Presidential Election Campaign Fund (PECF)," Federal Election Commission, (accessed February 23, 2011). www.fec.gov/press/bkgnd/fund.shtml.
17. The Court did strike down a provision of the law that prohibited minors from making contributions on the grounds that it violated their freedom of speech. It also held that a requirement that prevented the national parties from independent spending if they coordinated their campaign activities with their candidates was unconstitutional.
18. Even here there was controversy. The bill's sponsors objected to many of the regulations that the FEC issued, claiming that they undermined the objectives of the law. In September 2004 during the general election campaign, a district court sided with the critics of the FEC rules and voided some of them.
19. For an extended discussion of the FEC's rulings, see Anthony Corrado, "The Regulatory Environment: Uncertainty in the Wake of Change," in David Magleby, Anthony Corrado, and Kelley D. Patterson, eds., *Financing the 2004 Election* (Washington DC: Brookings Institution, 2006), pp. 48–53.
20. The Supreme Court had defined political organizations in its *Buckley v. Valeo* decision as a group controlled by a candidate or created for the purpose of nominating or electing a specific candidate. The groups claimed that their primary purpose was not the election of a specific candidate, so they did not have to file with the FEC nor were they subject to the soft money restrictions.
21. R. Jeffrey Smith, "FEC Fines 3 '527' Groups for Use of Large Donations in '04," *The Washington Post* (Dec. 14, 2006), p. A5. "FEC to Collect $750,000 Civil Penalty from Progress for America Fund," FEC, Feb. 28, 2007. www.fec.gov/press/press2007/20070228MUR.html.
22. According to the Campaign Finance Institute, two types of groups permitted to accept soft money under the IRS codes 501c and 527 spent about $400 million in the 2007–2008 election cycle. "Soft Money Political Spending by 501c Nonprofits Tripled in 2008," www.cfinst.org/Press/PReleases/09-02-25/Soft_Money_Political_Spending_by_Nonprofits_Tripled_in_2008.aspx.

23. *Citizens United v. Federal Election Commission,* 130 S. Ct.876 (2010).
24. Ibid.
25. Ibid.
26. Barack Obama, "State of the Union Address," January 27, 2010. www.whitehouse.gov.
27. "All CFI Funding Statistics Revised and Updated for the 2008 Presidential Primary and General Election Candidates," Campaign Finance Institute, January 8, 2010. www.campaignfinanceinstitute.org.
28. The Federal Election Commission has designated six categories of PACS: corporate, labor, trade/membership/health, nonconnected (not attached to an economic association), cooperative, and corporations without stock. The latter two are the smallest in number and spend the least amount. Corporate PACs are the most numerous and well endowed, followed by nonconnected PACs, trade/membership/health, and labor.
29. "2008 Presidential Campaign Financial Activity Summarized: Receipts Nearly Double 2004 Total," Federal Election Commission, June 8, 2009. www.fec.gov/press/press2009/20090608PresStat.shtml.
30. Aaron Blake, "Potential Presidential Candidates Ram Up their PACs," *Washington Post* (Dec. 3, 2010). voices.washingtonpost.com/thefix/eye-on-2012/romney-and-barbour-polling-20. Also, Fredreka Schouten, "GOP Fundraising Avoids Campaign Limits through PACs Ahead of 2012," *USA Today* (Dec. 30, 2010). www.usatoday.com/news/washington/2010-12-30-1Agropprez30_ST_N.htm?csp=34n.
31. The FEC sought to impose still another eligibility rule—how matching funds had been spent in the past. The commission denied matching funds to Lyndon LaRouche in 1992 on the grounds that his campaign had misused such funds in previous elections. LaRouche, who had been convicted and jailed for engaging in fraudulent fund-raising practices, appealed the FEC's decision and won.
32. "Heavy Hitters ($250,000 to $3 Million Donors) Supplied 80% of Private Financing for 2008 Party Conventions," Campaign Finance Institute, December 10, 2008. www.cfinst.org/Press/PReleases/08-12-10/Heavy_Hitters_Supplied_Bulk_of_Private . . .
33. Obama made a short video to explain his decision. In it, he said, "It's not an easy decision, especially because I support a robust system of public financing of elections. But the public financing of presidential elections as it exists today is broken, and we face opponents who've become masters at gaming this broken system." David Plouffe, *The Audacity to Win* (New York: Viking, 2009), p. 263.
34. "Presidential Fundraising and Spending, 1976–2008," Center for Responsive Politics. www.opensecrets.org/pres08/totals.php?cycle=2008.
35. Plouffe, *Audacity to Win*, p. 35.
36. Jose Antonio Vargas, "Obama Raised Half a Billion Online," *The Washington Post* (Nov. 20, 2008). www.bing.com/search?q=Jose+Antonio+Vargas,+%E2%80%9CObama+Raised+Half+a+Billion+Online&src=IE-Address.
37. The Supreme Court's decision in *Colorado Republican Federal Campaign Committee v. Federal Election Commission,* 518 U.S.604 (1996), voided a regulation by the FEC that prohibited parties from spending independently on the presidential contest if they also engaged in a coordinated campaign with their presidential candidate.
38. Even though 527 groups may accept unlimited campaign contributions, they still have to disclose the names of their contributors and the amount they gave. This disclosure provision, enacted by Congress in 2003, prompted the use of still another part of the Internal Revenue code, section 501c, to skirt that provision

entirely. The so-called 501c groups have less restrictive reporting requirements than 527s. They do not have to make their donors names and the size of their contributions public. Moreover, their campaign expenditures are tax deductible as long as they do not exceed 50 percent of the group's annual budget. The only requirement that 501c groups have is to make their annual tax returns public. Examples of 501c groups that were involved in recent presidential elections include the National Rifle Association, with a budget in the millions, and the Sierra Club, which also had a regular PAC and a 527 group.

39. "Soft Money Political Spending by 501(c) Nonprofits Tripled in 2008 Election," Campaign Finance Institute, February 25, 2009. www.cfinst.org/Press/PReleases/09-02-25/Soft_Money_Political_Spending_by_Nonprofits.
40. "Top Individual Contributors to 527 Organizations, 2008 Election Cycle," Center for Responsive Politics. www.opensecrets.org.
41. Beaulieu of America, a large carpet manufacturer, was not as fortunate as the Buddhist monks. Accused of funneling $36,000 in illegal contributions to Lamar Alexander's 1996 presidential campaign, the company entered into a plea-bargaining agreement with the government in which it agreed to pay a $1 million fine and civil penalties to be determined by the FEC. Kevin Sack, "Campaign Finance Case Costs a Carpet Company $1 Million," *New York Times* (Dec. 2, 1998), p. A23.
42. Abramoff was also a successful Pioneer in Bush's 2004 campaign, who once bragged, "Everyone in town is trying to be a Pioneer or Ranger. So far I've raised about $120,000, and I haven't even really started to make calls." David Firestone, "Bush Loyalists Compete for Spots on the President's A-Team by Raising Record Money for 2004," *New York Times* (July 21, 2003), p. A10. The money Abramoff raised was not returned or given to charity by the campaign.
43. Matthew Mosk, "Campaign Finance Gets New Scrutiny," *The Washington Post* (Sept. 26, 2008); www.washingtonpost.com/wp-dyn/content/article/2008/10/25/AR2008102502302.html?hpid=topnews. Matthew Mosk, "Obama Accepting Untraceable Donations," *The Washington Post* (Oct. 29, 2008), p. A2.
44. Thomas B. Edsall, Sarah Cohen, and James V. Grimaldi, "The Bush Money Machine: Pioneers Fill War Chest, then Capitalize," *The Washington Post* (May 16, 2004), pp. A1, A15–A16. See also Center for Responsive Politics, "George W. Bush," and "Embassy Row." www.opensecrets.org/bush/index and www.opensecrets.org/bush/ambassadors/index.
45. Michael Beckel, "Two Dozen Bankrollers-Turned-Ambassadors Bundled at Least $10 Million for Barack Obama," Center for Responsive Politics, November 18, 2009. www.opensecrets.org/news/2009/11/two-dozen-bankrollersturnedamb.html.
46. Abramoff provided members of Congress with dinners at his restaurant and with tickets to sporting events at his box at the Verizon Center in Washington, DC, paid for foreign travel, directly or indirectly hired spouses of members and their aides—all for help on legislative matters in which he was representing clients with an interest in the legislation.
47. Michael Robinson, Clyde Wilcox, and Paul Marshall, "The Presidency: Not for Sale," *Public Opinion* II (March/April 1989), p. 51.
48. "Money Wins Presidency and 9 of 10 Congressional Races in Priciest U.S. Election Ever," Center for Responsive Politics, Nov. 5, 2008. www.opensecrets.org/news/2008/11/money-wins-white-house-and.html.
49. Larry M. Bartels, *Unequal Democracy: The Political Economy of the New Gilded Age* (Princeton, NJ.: Princeton University Press, 2008), p. 120.
50. Ibid., pp. 120–122.

THE POLITICAL ENVIRONMENT

CHAPTER 3

INTRODUCTION

The nature of the electorate influences the content, images, and strategies of the campaign and affects the outcome of the election—an obvious conclusion to be sure, but one that is not always appreciated. Campaigns are not conducted in ignorance of the voters. Rather, they are calculated to appeal to the needs and desires, attitudes and opinions, and associations and interactions of the electorate.

Voters do not come to the election with completely open minds. They come with preexisting views. They do not see and hear the campaign in isolation. They observe it and absorb it as part of their daily lives. In other words, people's attitudes and associations affect their perceptions and influence their behavior. Preexisting views make it important for students of presidential elections to examine the formation of political attitudes and the patterns of social interaction.

Who votes and who does not? Why do people vote for certain candidates and not others? Do campaign appeals affect voting behavior? Are the responses of the electorate predictable? Political scientists have been interested in these questions for some time. Politicians have been interested in them for even longer. A great deal of social science research and political savvy has gone into finding the answers to these questions. Spurred by the development of sophisticated survey techniques, methods of data analysis, and experimetal research, political scientists, sociologists, and social psychologists have uncovered a wealth of information on how the public reacts and the electorate behaves during a campaign. They have examined correlations between demographic characteristics and voter turnout. They have explored psychological motivations, social influences, and political pressures that contribute to voting behavior. They are even beginning to do research on the genetic components of attitudes, participation, and voting. This chapter discusses some of their findings.

It is organized into three parts. The first looks at who votes. After describing the expansion of suffrage in the nineteenth and twentieth centuries, the section turns to recent voting trends in the twentieth and twenty-first centuries. Turnout is influenced by personal feelings and beliefs, especially partisanship; social factors such as age, education, and group associations; and situational variables such as the state of domestic and foreign affairs, the competitiveness of the election, the weather, and the efforts by candidate campaigns, parties, and nonparty groups to get out the vote. Turnout is also affected by state and national laws that govern elections, especially registration requirements, absentee and early voting, and the locations and hours that the polls are open. The impact of these variables, singularly and together, on the decision of whether or not to cast a ballot is the principal focus of this section.

The second and third parts of the chapter study influences on the vote. First, it examines the partisan basis of politics. How have political attitudes changed over the years, and how do they affect the ways people evaluate the candidates and their campaigns and shape their actual voting decisions? Models of voting behavior are presented and then used to help explain contemporary voting patterns.

Next, the chapter analyzes the social basis of politics. Here we look at the electorate's demography, its socioeconomic divisions, and the public's various beliefs and the values upon which those beliefs are based. Our objective is to discuss the relationship between electoral groups and their voting behavior. Primary emphasis is placed on the formation of party coalitions and their contemporary evolution. The chapter concludes with a description of the groups that comprise the Republican and Democratic electoral coalitions today.

TURNOUT

Who votes? In one sense, this is a simple question to resolve. Official election returns indicate the number of voters and the states, even the precincts, in which people voted. By easy calculation, the percentage of the voting-age population (VAP) that actually cast ballots for president can be determined: 50.0 percent (2000), 55.4 percent (2004), and 56.9 percent (2008).[1]

But there is a problem with these figures. They include people who are old enough to vote but may not be eligible to do so: noncitizens; most of the people who are currently incarcerated in penal institutions; in some states, ex-felons and ex-military who were dishonorably discharged from the armed forces; citizens who do not meet their state's residence requirements; and people who are not registered to vote (35 percent of the adult population in 2008).[2] If these people are excluded, then the percentage voting increases by about 4 to 5 percent.[3] Professor Michael McDonald, a political scientist who studies turnout figures, concluded that 60.1 percent of the voting-eligible population (VEP) actually did so in 2004 and 61.6 percent in 2008, a 1.5 percent increase.[4]

More people say they vote than actually do so. They realize that it is a responsibility of citizenship and do not like to admit that they have not voted. Pollsters anticipate inflated responses to the question, "Did you vote in the last election?" To get at a more accurate figure, they often ask questions about past voting practices, such as "By the way, where do people vote around here?" After the elections, survey researchers weigh the responses they receive on the basis of the official results, knowing full well that approximately 15 to 20 percent more people will claim that they voted than actually cast ballots.

VOTING IN AMERICAN ELECTIONS

Voting turnout in the United States has varied markedly over the years. A number of legal, social, and political factors have contributed to this variation. The next section documents these shifts and explains them within the context of the political environment of the times.

Turnout Before the Twentieth Century

The Constitution empowers the state legislatures to determine the time, place, and manner of holding elections for national office. Although it also gives Congress the authority to alter such regulations, Congress did not do so until after the Civil War. Thus, states were free to restrict suffrage, and most did. In some of them, property ownership was a requirement for exercising the franchise; in others, a particular religious belief was necessary. In most, it was essential to be white, male, and over twenty-one.[5]

Only about 11 percent of the adult population participated in the first national election. The percentage voting for president was even lower since most of the electors were designated by the state legislatures and not chosen directly by the people. Prior to 1824, voters remained a relatively small percentage of the eligible population, in the range of 20 to 25 percent. Without a tradition of participation in politics or a well-entrenched party system during this period, the general public deferred to the more politically prominent members of the society in choosing their state's elected officials.[6]

Turnout began to increase in the 1820s, spurred by a political reform movement known as Jacksonian Democracy. This movement advocated a greater role for the public in the electoral process. By the 1830s, most states had eliminated property and religious restrictions, thereby extending suffrage to approximately 80 percent of the adult white male population. Turnout expanded accordingly.[7] The rise of competitive, popular-based parties in the 1840s, along with campaigns directed at the entire electorate, boosted participation.

Professor Walter Dean Burnham estimated turnout in the range of 70 to 80 percent of eligible voters throughout the remainder of the nineteenth century, although these percentages may be misleading because of the coercive and sometimes fraudulent voting practices that occurred during the era of machine party politics, a period during which the parties ran the elections, provided the ballots (distinguished by color), oversaw the voting, mobilized their partisans, and got them to the polls early, and sometimes often.[8]

Reforms at the end of the nineteenth and beginning of the twentieth centuries, however, reduced some of the more flagrant attempts to influence election outcomes. States began to monitor the conduct of elections more closely and more impartially. They adopted the Australian ballot and instituted secret voting; no longer could party poll watchers determine people's votes by the color of the ballot they dropped into the box. Registration procedures were introduced to prevent nonresidents and noncitizens from voting. These reforms improved the integrity of the electoral process, but they also reduced the percentage of the population that voted.

Following the Civil War, the growth of one-party politics in the South and the removal of federal troops contributed to declining turnout in that region of the country. Despite the ratification of the Fifteenth Amendment in 1870, which removed race and color as qualifications for voting, the size of the southern electorate actually decreased after the Civil War. A series of restrictive state laws, such as poll taxes, literacy tests, and "private" primaries in which only whites could participate, plus the imposition of more restrictive residence requirements, substantially reduced the proportion of adults in the South who could vote.

Turnout During and After the Twentieth Century

Decreasing competition between the major parties in the North and West at the end of the nineteenth century had much the same effect. It reduced the percentage of the population that voted, as did the extension of suffrage to women in 1919. Although the size of the eligible electorate doubled in the 1920s, turnout declined because newly enfranchised citizens do not vote with the same regularity as do people who have been exercising the franchise for some time. In 1924, only 44 percent of the voting-aged population cast ballots. Within a period of thirty years, turnout had declined almost 40 percent.[9]

Although voter participation grew moderately during Franklin Roosevelt's presidency and the post–World War II era, it decreased again following the 1960 presidential election, an election in which 64 percent of the adult population voted. Part of the decline had to do with the expanding base of the electorate; part with growing voter disillusionment, heightened by the war in Vietnam, the Watergate scandal, and a series of lackluster presidential candidates; and part with the weakening of the major parties' grassroots organizations and their increased dependence on television for mobilizing the vote.

Beginning in the 1960s, suffrage rights were expanded. In 1961, the District of Columbia was granted three electoral votes, thereby extending to its residents the right to vote in presidential elections (Twenty-third Amendment); in 1964, the collection of a poll tax was prohibited in national elections

(Twenty-fourth Amendment); in 1971, the right to vote was extended to all citizens eighteen years of age and older (Twenty-sixth Amendment). Moreover, the Supreme Court and Congress began to eliminate the legal and institutional barriers to voting. In 1944, the Court outlawed the white-only primary.[10] In the mid-1960s, Congress passed the Civil Rights Act (1964) and the Voting Rights Act (1965). The latter banned literacy tests in federal elections for all citizens who had at least a sixth-grade education in a U.S. school. Federal officers were sent to facilitate registration in districts in which less than 50 percent of the population was registered to vote. Amendments to the Voting Rights Act have also reduced the residence requirement for presidential elections to a maximum of thirty days. In 2002, The Help Americans Vote Act, designed to improve the accuracy of registration lists and allow provisional voting in cases in which controversies over registration occurred at the time of voting, was enacted. The legislation also created the Election Assistance Commission to facilitate registration by providing people with information on where and how to vote.

These legal initiatives have broadened the opportunities for people, particularly minority ethnic and racial groups, to participate in the electoral process. However, it has taken years for the voting practices of these groups to catch up with their new voting opportunities. Table 3.1 indicates turnout numbers in recent presidential elections based on voting-age population (VAP).

COMPARATIVE TURNOUT IN WESTERN DEMOCRACIES

As the percentages in Table 3.1 reveal, turnout has been mediocre at best. A smaller percentage of U.S. citizens vote than in many other democratic countries. (See Table 3.2.)

Why is turnout in American elections lower than in many other democracies? Unlike some countries, the United States does not impose penalties on those who fail to register and vote, nor does it have a national system for automatic registration as do other democracies. Moreover, the day of the election is a workday in the United States, whereas in most other countries, it is Sunday or a holiday. Another factor that contributes to a lower turnout percentage in the United States is the winner-take-all system of voting, which discourages participation in noncompetitive electoral districts and states.

INFLUENCES ON TURNOUT

Why don't people vote? Does low turnout indicate voter satisfaction or alienation? Does it contribute to stability or create conditions for instability within the democratic political system? What party and which programs benefit and which suffer when so many people do not vote? The next part of the chapter answers these questions.

Legal Constraints

Some citizens have lost their right to vote. In 48 of the 50 states—Vermont and Maine are the exceptions—people who are incarcerated cannot vote.

TABLE 3.1 | SUFFRAGE AND TURNOUT IN THE TWENTIETH AND TWENTY-FIRST CENTURIES

Year	Voting-Age Population (VAP)	Turnout	Percent of the VAP
1900	40,753,000	13,974,188	35.0
1920	60,581,000	26,768,613	44.0
1932	75,768,000	39,732,000	52.4
1940	84,728,000	49,900,000	58.9
1952	99,929,000	61,551,000	61.6
1960	109,672,000	68,838,000	62.8
1964	114,090,000	70,645,000	61.9
1968	120,285,000	73,212,000	60.9
1972	140,777,000	77,719,000	55.5
1976	152,308,000	81,556,000	53.5
1980	164,595,000	86,515,000	52.6
1984	174,447,000	92,653,000	53.1
1988	182,600,000	91,602,291	50.2
1992	189,044,000	104,426,659	55.2
1996	196,507,000	96,277,564	49.1
2000	205,815,000	105,586,284	51.3
2004	215,694,000	122,295,345	56.7
2008	230,898,029	132,645,504	56.9

Sources: Population figures for 1900 and 1920 are based on estimates and early census figures that appear in Neal R. Peirce, *The People's President* (New York: Simon & Schuster, 1968), p. 206; copyright renewed © 1979 by Neal R. Peirce. Reprinted by permission of Yale University Press. Population figures from 1932 to 1984 are from the U.S. Department of Commerce, Bureau of the Census, *Statistical Abstract of the United States* (Washington, DC: Government Printing Office, 1987), p. 250. Figures from 1988 to 2004 were compiled from official election returns supplied by the Federal Election Commission (www.fec.gov); 2008 data from Michael P. McDonald, "2008 General Election Turnout Rates" (Updated March 13, 2010.). http://elections.gmu.edu/Turnout_2008G.html

Other states have laws that prohibit from voting those on parole or probation, convicted of a felony, or dishonorably discharged from the military. These restrictions, which excluded about 5.3 million people in 2008,[11] have disproportionately impacted African American males, disenfranchising about 13 percent of African American males.[12]

In addition, registration requirements have also inhibited voting. Congress tried to deal with this problem in 1993 by its enactment of the "Motor-Voter" bill, which requires states to permit registration by mail and provide registration forms at convenient statewide offices such as motor vehicle registries, military recruitment offices, and welfare services. Some smaller states, such as North Dakota, Montana, and Iowa, have even implemented election-day registration that allows residents to register and then vote at the same time and place.

TABLE 3.2 | INTERNATIONAL VOTER TURNOUT (IN PERCENTAGES)

Country	Year	Type of Election	Turnout of Eligible Voters
Argentina	2007	Parliamentary	73.1
Australia	2004	Parliamentary	95.2
Austria	2008	Parliamentary	81.7
Belgium	2008	Parliamentary	91.1
Brazil	2006	Parliamentary	83.3
Canada	2008	Parliamentary	59.5
France	2007	Parliamentary	60.4
	2007	Presidential	84.0*
Germany	2005	Parliamentary	77.7
Greece	2007	Parliamentary	74.1
India	2004	Parliamentary	57.8
Israel	2009	Parliamentary	64.7
Korea	2008	Parliamentary	46.0
	2007	Presidential	63.0
Mexico	2006	Parliamentary	58.9
	2006	Presidential	58.5
Pakistan	2008	Parliamentary	44.6
Poland	2008	Presidential	69.7
	2007	Parliamentary	53.9
Russia	2007	Parliamentary	63.7
South Africa	2009	Parliamentary	77.3
Spain	2008	Parliamentary	75.3
Switzerland	2007	Parliamentary	48.3
Turkey	2007	Parliamentary	84.2
Ukraine	2007	Parliamentary	62.0
United Kingdom	2010	Parliamentary	65.1
United States	2008	Presidential	61.6
	2010	Congressional	41.6

*Second round.

Sources: Institute for Democracy and Election Assistance. www.idea.int/vt UK Political Info.ukpolitical .info/Turnout45.htm; Michael P. McDonald, "2008 General Election Turnout Rates" (Updated March 13, 2010). http://elections.gmu.edu/Turnout_2008G.html; "2010 General Election Turnout Rates," (Updated January 28, 2011) http://elections.gmu.edu/Turnout_2010G.html

BOX 3.1 REGISTERING TO VOTE

It is easy to register to vote. All you have to do is go to the Web site of the Election Assistance Commission and download the National Voter Registration form: www.eac.gov/voter_resources/register_to_vote.aspx

The booklet containing the form also lists the location to which the form should be sent in each state.

You can also do any of the following to register:

- Contact your state's chief election official. In most states, it is the secretary of state; in some, it is the head of the board of elections; in a few, it may be the lieutenant governor.
- Go to your nearest department of motor vehicles, military recruitment, or public assistance office to obtain a copy of the registration form. Complete it, and give it to the appropriate person at the office where you obtained the form.
- Access the Web site of an organization called Rock-the-Vote at www.rockthevote.org, which will help facilitate your online registration.

After the Motor-Voter law took effect in 1995, the number of people registered to vote increased a little. Twenty-six million new registrants were added between 1996 and 2004, but 12.6 million people were removed from registration lists and millions of others were listed as inactive. Registration has increased significantly since then, however. The Election Assistance Commission reported an increase of 16.6 million between the 2004 and 2008 elections. There were at least 189 million people registered to vote 2008.[13] This increase exceeds the rate of population growth.[14]

The youngest group of eligible voters was expected to increase their electoral participation the most as a result of the Motor-Voter law. Although eighteen- to twenty-four-year-olds have traditionally had the lowest registration rates (in the range of 30 to 40 percent), they have much higher driving rates (85 percent have driver's licenses). By making registration available at the same time and place where people get or renew their driver's licenses, it was thought that the law would increase the number of registered voters in the lowest age cohort. It did in 2004 and 2008, but the youngest group of voters still has the lowest rate of turnout of all age groups. (See Table 3.4.)

Convenience Issues

In addition to the registration requirements of most states, the availability of absentee ballots and early voting—30 percent of the electorate voted early in 2008—are also factors that can affect turnout. The distribution of ballots by mail (Oregon requires mail voting), the extension of voting hours, more places to vote, and more voting booths facilitate voting and naturally enhance turnout. The bottom line is that the easier it is to vote, the more likely people will do so.

Geographic mobility can be an impediment to voting. Elections are conducted by state and local officials and official residence is the principal factor in determining where people vote. Going away to college makes voting more difficult. Students need to return home, obtain absentee ballots, or change their official residences. Moreover, many young people have not yet developed the habit of voting. Peer pressure to do so may be low as well because so many in this younger age group have not voted or even registered. Thus, it is the older generation with whom young people interact as they move into voting age—parents, teachers, community, and religious leaders—that exercises greater influence on who votes. Older voters provide the critical information and model civic behavior that affects the initial decision of many young people, whether or not to vote.

The act of voting, however, increases the likelihood of doing it again and again. Finding the correct location, getting to the polls, and figuring out how to use the machines or punch cards are no longer major obstacles once a person has voted. However, for people who have limited English language skills and for people with various mental and physical handicaps, voting can still be difficult. The bottom line, however, is that over time, voting becomes a habit, a ritual that citizens dutifully follow on most election days.[15]

Psychological and Political Attitudes

Personal feelings and beliefs are important in motivating people to vote.[16] Interest in the election, concern over the outcome, feelings of civic pride, and political efficacy (the belief that one's vote really counts) are factors that affect how regularly people vote.[17] A recent experimental study found that social pressure also contributed to voter turnout. In this study, people who received mail promising to publicize the fact that they voted to their family and community turned out at a higher level than those who did not receive the mailing.[18]

Naturally, those who feel more strongly about the election and who have the most interest in it are more likely to participate in the campaign and more likely to turn out on election day. Anger seems to be a greater motivater for voting than satisfaction with the candidates and their parties.[19] Engaging supporters and making them feel as if they were part of the campaign was a basic component of the Obama campaign strategy in 2008.

Since the mid-1960s, the proportion of people identifying themselves as Republicans and Democrats has declined while the percentage of Independents within the polity has gotten larger. Since party loyalties are a motivation for voting, the decline in partisan identification has contributed to lower turnout. Independents are less likely to vote than partisans.

Another factor that has reduced turnout is lower voter efficacy, the belief that one can make a difference and that voters can change the way government works or public officials behave. Political efficacy has declined since the late 1960s. This decline, combined with the weakening of partisan loyalties, has also contributed to lower turnout. According to Paul R. Abramson, John H. Aldrich, and David W. Rohde, three political scientists who have researched and written about voting since the 1980 election, the combined impact of this attitudinal change accounts for 78 percent of the decline in turnout during this period, with the decline in partisan identity more than twice as important as the decline in political efficacy.[20]

Nonetheless, for many, voting is a civic responsibility; for others, it is a matter a personal conviction; and as we have mentioned, it can even become a habit, one reason that turnout tends to increase with age. With advances in medicine, the point at which senior citizens stay informed and involved has been extended to their mid- to late seventies with correspondingly higher voting rates for people ages sixty-five and over.

Social and Economic Factors

Several social and economic variables correlate with turnout. They include education, income, and occupational status, which also correlate with one another. As people become more educated, as they move up the socioeconomic ladder, and as they gain jobs higher in status and income, they are more likely to vote.

Education has a larger impact than any other single social characteristic on voting.[21] The reason education is so important is that it provides people with the skills for processing and evaluating information; for perceiving differences among the parties, candidates, and issues; and for relating these differences to personal values and behavior. Education also increases a person's stake in the system, interest in the election, and concern over the outcome. Since the lesson that voting is a civic responsibility is usually learned in the classroom, schooling may also contribute to a more highly developed sense of responsibility about the importance of voting in a democracy.[22]

Given the relationship of education to turnout, why did the rate of turnout decline from the 1960s through most of the 1990s as the general level of education increased in the United States during this period? The answer is that the attitudinal factors of decreasing partisanship and efficacy countered the increase in education. Had educational levels not increased, turnout would have been even lower.[23] The larger number of younger voters who entered the electorate, the so-called "Generation Xers," voted at a lower rate than their elders did when their elders were the same age with the result that the proportion of the population that votes also decreased.[24]

Another contributing factor may be the growing gap between the rich and the poor. People with lower levels of income tend to have a lower sense of personal efficacy. They either do not see or are pessimistic about how the outcome of the election will affect them, so why vote?

Environmental Factors

In addition to legal, attitudinal, and social factors, the environment in which elections occur also affects the level of voter participation. Competition stimulates turnout. It does so directly because people believe that their vote can make a difference in the outcome. If the public perception is that the election is not likely to be a close one, then motivation for turning out to vote declines.

The candidates or issues can also affect the competitive climate. In 2004, Republican state officials purposely put initiatives opposing the marriage of same-sex partners on the ballot in eleven states. They believed that the people who felt most strongly about these issues, fundamentalist and evangelical Christians, would also be more likely to vote for George W. Bush if they voted at all, hence the reason for the ballot initiative bait.

To the extent that presidential strategies are targeted to the Electoral College, not to the general population, overall turnout will suffer in those states that the presidential campaign neglects because they are conceded to one side or the other. In 2004, turnout was up almost twice as much in the battleground states (8.3 percent) than in nonbattleground ones (4.7 percent).[25] In 2008, the same pattern emerged. Turnout in the ten battleground states averaged 65.9 percent VEP compared with 61.9 for the nonbattleground states.[26] Moreover, turnout increased the most in states in which Obama waged a strong challenge in 2008, states that had previously been considered safely Republican: North Carolina, Virginia, and Indiana; and it decreased in states that lost their battleground status in 2008: Maine, Minnesota, Oregon, Washington, and Wisconsin.[27]

Competition encourages more extensive mobilization efforts by the candidates. More people are contacted and personal contact increases voting. The recent gains in turnout have been associated with larger and more effective on-the-ground party and candidate mobilization efforts, as is evident from the increasing percentage of the population reporting that they have been contacted by at least one of the campaigns prior to voting: 24 percent in 1988, 1992, and 1996; 38 percent in 2000; 45 percent in 2004; and 43 percent in 2008.[28]

The weather on election day may be important. Three political scientists—Brad T. Gomez, Thomas G. Hansford, and George A. Krause—examined the impact of weather on turnout and found that rain reduces turnout by 1 percent per inch of precipitation. Snow also decreases participation, primarily in rural areas.[29]

Finally, situational variables help explain fluctuations in the vote. In 2004, the highly polarizing candidacy of George W. Bush, the controversy over the war in Iraq, and the domestic environment—the threat of terrorism and the spike in gas prices—energized both Republicans and Democrats and got them out to vote. In 2008, it was the increasing dissatisfaction of the electorate as the recession worsened. The magnetism of the candidates, Barack Obama for the Democrats and Sarah Palin for conservative Republicans, also helped drive up the vote. In short, the campaign and the environment matter as far as election turnout is concerned.

TURNOUT AND DEMOCRACY

What difference does it make that some people do not vote? A great deal!

Turnout affects perceptions of how well the democratic electoral system is functioning. Low turnout suggests that people may be alienated, lack faith in the candidates and parties, think that the government is and will remain unresponsive to their needs and interests, and most importantly, believe that they cannot achieve change through the electoral process.[30]

Low turnout also impacts representation and public policy decisions. "Who gets what" relates in large part to the influence of people and groups on election outcomes and government decisions. The connection between low economic status and not voting results in a class bias that undercuts the democratic character of the American political system by widening the participation gap between the haves and have-nots.[31] This gap has produced an electorate that is not representative of the population as a whole, an electorate that is better educated and has higher incomes than the general public. To the extent that government responds to the electorate rather than to the general population, government policies take on a "have" rather than "have-not" coloration.

This class bias in voting produces a tragic irony in American politics. Those who are most disadvantaged, who have the least education, and who need to change conditions the most, actually vote the least. Those who are the most advantaged, who benefit from existing conditions and presumably from the public policy that contributes to those conditions, vote more often.

TURNOUT AND PARTISANSHIP

Obviously, turnout has partisan implications as well. Since the Democratic Party draws more of its electoral support from those in the lower socioeconomic groups—people with less formal education and fewer professional opportunities—lower turnout has thus tended to hurt that party more than the GOP. (See Table 3.3 for demographic trends in turnout.)

The common wisdom is that, all things being equal, the larger the turnout, the better the Democrats will do. In 1960 and 1976, increases in turnout did favor the Democrats and resulted in two very close victories. The relatively high Democratic turnout in these two elections overcame the advantage the Republicans usually gain from having a larger proportion of their rank-and-file vote.[32] Similarly, in the 2000 presidential election, a late surge of support for Gore gave him a popular vote victory although he lost in the Electoral College. Republican strategists, surprised by the larger turnout the Gore campaign generated, studied the election day tactics, particularly the efforts of organized labor and the African American community to increase the Democratic vote in that election. Determined not to be outmaneuvered again, the Republicans devised a turnout strategy for 2004 in which potential Republican voters were targeted, canvassed, and contacted by local volunteers within seventy-two hours before the vote. The strategy was successful; Republican turnout increased more than Democratic turnout in 2004.

Obama's campaign advisers studied the Republican turnout effort in 2004 as they prepared for the 2008 campaign. They devised an even more sophisticated effort in which they used their Web site, Facebook, and other social networking sites to identify supporters. They then trained these supporters how to contact people, get them registered, and then out to vote—early if a state had early voting or on election day if it did not. The get-out-the-vote (GOTV) strategy was based on a huge number of volunteers and a lot of field offices.[33] The turnout strategy that the Republicans used in 2004 and the Democrats in 2008 also confirms the findings of political scientists that personal contact, strong feelings, and partisan allegiances are keys to maximizing turnout.[34]

TABLE 3.3 | TURNOUT IN PRESIDENTIAL ELECTIONS, 1980–2008 (TOTAL PERCENTAGE OF THE POPULATION WHO REPORTED THAT THEY VOTED)

	Year							
Population Characteristics	**2008**	**2004**	**2000**	**1996**	**1992**	**1988**	**1984**	**1980**
Race								
White	59.6	60.3	60.4	56.0	63.6	59.1	61.4	60.9
Black	60.8	56.3	54.1	50.6	54.0	51.5	55.8	50.5
Hispanic*	31.6	28.3	27.5	26.7	28.9	28.8	32.6	29.9
Gender								
Male	55.7	56.3	53.1	52.8	60.2	56.4	59.0	59.1
Female	60.4	60.1	56.2	55.5	62.3	58.3	60.8	59.4
Age								
18 to 24 years	44.3	41.9	32.3	32.4	42.8	36.2	40.8	39.9
25 to 44 years	51.9	52.2	49.8	49.2	58.3	54.0	58.4	58.7
45 to 65 years	65.0	66.6	64.1	64.4	70.0	67.9	69.8	69.3
65 years and over		68.9	69.9	67.0	70.1	68.8	67.7	65.1
65–74	70.1							
75 and over	65.8							
Race (South Percent Voted)								
White	57.7	61.7	58.2	57.4	64.9	60.4	63.0	62.4
Black	62.9	61.8	53.2	51.4	53.8	55.6	58.9	52.8

*Hispanics may be of any race.

Source: U.S. Census Bureau, Current Population Reports, "Voting and Registration," November 2008 (modified by author). www.census.gov/population/www/socdemo/voting.html

Not only does partisan orientation affect turnout but it also has a major impact on voting behavior. The next part of the chapter examines the role of political identity, the ebbs and flows of partisan feelings, and the impact of ideology on partisanship and voting behavior.

THE PARTISAN BASIS OF POLITICS

Why do people vote as they do? Considerable research has been conducted to answer this question. Initially, much of it has been done under the direction of the Center for Political Studies at the University of Michigan. Beginning in 1952, the center conducted nationwide surveys during presidential elections, surveys now called American National Election Studies (ANES).[35] To identify the major influences on voting behavior, a random sample of the electorate is interviewed before and after each election. Respondents are asked a series of questions designed to reveal their attitudes toward the parties, candidates, and issues. On the basis of their answers to these questions, researchers have amassed a wealth of data to explain the voting behavior of the U.S. electorate.

A Model of the U.S. Voter

One of the earliest and most influential theories of voting behavior based on the Michigan survey data was presented in a book entitled *The American Voter* (1960).[36] The model on which the theory is based assumes that individuals are influenced by their partisan attitudes and social relationships in addition to the political environment in which the election takes place. In fact, these attitudes and those relationships condition the impact of that environment on individual voting behavior. According to the theory, people develop attitudes early in life, largely as a consequence of interacting with their families, particularly their parents and other significant elders.[37] These attitudes, in turn, tend to be reinforced by neighborhood, school, and religious associations.

Psychologically, it is more pleasing to have beliefs and attitudes supported than challenged. Socially, it is more comfortable and safer to associate with "nice," like-minded people, people with similar cultural, educational, and religious experiences, than with others who do not share the same values, beliefs, and experiences. This desire to increase one's "comfort level" in social relationships explains why the environment for most people reinforces rather than challenges their values and beliefs most of the time.[38] Attitudes mature and harden over the years. The older people become, the less amenable they are to change. They are more set in their ways and their beliefs. Consequently, their behavior is more predictable.

Political attitudes are no exception to this general pattern of attitude formation and maintenance. They too are developed early in life, are reinforced by association, grow in intensity, and become more predictable with time.

Partisanship

Of all the factors that contribute to the development of a political attitude, identifying with a political party seems to be the most important. It affects how people see campaigns, how they evaluate candidates and issues, and how they vote on election day. Party identification operates as a conceptual framework, a mindset, a lens through which the campaign is understood and the candidates evaluated. Partisan allegiances provide cues for interpreting the issues, for judging the candidates, and for deciding whether or not to vote. If the decision is to vote, partisanship influences for whom the vote is cast. The stronger these attitudes, the more compelling the cues; conversely, the weaker the attitudes, the less likely they will affect perceptions during the campaign and influence voting.[39]

When identification with a party is weak or nonexistent, other factors, such as the personalities of the candidates and their issue positions, are correspondingly more important. In contrast to party identification, which is a long-term stabilizing factor but one that can be modified or even changed over time, candidate and issue orientations are shorter-term and more variable, often shifting from election to election.

Partisanship may be a factor even for those who do not identify with a political party. People who claim that they are Independent, that they vote for the best person regardless of party, or that they simply do not know whether they are Democratic or Republican may still display partisan voting tendencies.

Although partisan allegiances affect perceptions of the candidates and issues, perceptions of the candidates and issues over time can also affect allegiances toward the parties.[40] It is a two-way street in which people's perceptions can be reinforced or challenged by what happens during and after campaigns. To summarize, partisanship is stable but not static; it can vary in intensity.[41] It tends to be lower during bad times for the party in power and higher during good times.

Candidate and Issue Orientations

People form general impressions about candidates on the basis of what they know of the candidates' experiences, political leadership capabilities, and their personal character. For an incumbent president seeking reelection, policy decisions and actions in office that impact the conditions that people experience in their everyday lives provide much of the criteria for evaluating how well the incumbent has done. Even when an incumbent is not running, evaluations of the president affect assessments of the president's party and its presidential candidate. Reagan's positive evaluations in 1988 helped Republican George H. W. Bush, and George W. Bush's negative evaluations hurt Republican John McCain in 2008.[42] For the challengers, it is the potential for office as demonstrated by personal experience, knowledge, confidence, and assertiveness, plus a host of other leadership qualities, that help determine public perceptions of their qualifications.

Other characteristics, such as trustworthiness, integrity, empathy, and candor, may also be relevant. Much depends on the nature of the times. In the aftermath of a presidency besmirched by scandal or lacking in candor, integrity and honesty assume more importance than at other times when the problem has been weak or indecisive leadership. In 2008, the perception of Bush's adherence to a strong ideological perspective prompted Obama to emphasize his pragmatism, flexibility, and openness to new ideas.

Candidates' stands on the issues, however, seem less critical than do their partisan affiliation and their own potential for office or performance in it. The principal reason for downgrading the importance of issues is the low level of information and awareness that much of the electorate has. To be important, issues must be salient. They must attract attention; they must hit home. Without personal impact, they are unlikely to be primary motivating factors for voting. In addition, candidates must take sufficiently different positions on the issues for voters to decide which of those positions are most acceptable. To the extent that the candidates' issue positions are not known or are indistinguishable from one another, their respective personal images become a stronger influence.

Ironically, that portion of the electorate that can be more easily persuaded, weak partisans and Independents, tends to have the least information.[43] Conversely, the most committed also tend to be the most informed. They use their information to support their partisanship. The relationship between the degree of partisanship and the amount of information people possess has significant implications for a democratic society. The traditional view of a democracy holds that information and awareness are necessary to make an enlightened voting decision. However, the finding that those who have the most information are also the most committed, and that those who lack this commitment also lack the incentive to get more information, has upset some of the assumptions about the motivation for acquiring information and using it to vote intelligently.

A More Refined Theory of Voting

The model of voting behavior first presented in 1960 has engendered considerable controversy. Critics have charged that the theory presumes that most of the electorate is uninformed and votes habitually rather than rationally. One well-known political scientist, the late V. O. Key, even wrote a book dedicated to "the perverse and unorthodox argument . . . that voters are not fools."[44]

Key's contention was that most voters are not automatons and that most of their voting decisions are not solely or even primarily the product of their psychological dispositions and social pressures. Even though voters may have limited information, they use it to arrive at reasoned political judgments based in large part on their values, beliefs, and perceptions. They take into account their present situation, their beliefs about government, and their assessments of how the country is doing under its current leadership and will do in the future. In the words of political scientist, Samuel Popkin:

> They consider not only economic issues but family, residential, and consumer issues as well. They think not only of their immediate needs but also of their needs for insurance against future problems; not only about private good but also about collective goods.[45]

How do they do this? What criteria do they use in making judgments? Morris Fiorina, in his study *Retrospective Voting in American National Elections* (1981), tried to answer these questions. Utilizing a rational choice model adopted from economics, Fiorina argued that voting decisions are calculations people make on the basis of their accumulated political experience. They make these calculations by assessing the past performance of the parties and their elected officials in light of the promises they made and political events that have occurred. Fiorina called this a retrospective judgment.[46]

Retrospective judgments are not only important for influencing voting in a given election, they are also important for shaping partisan attitudes, which Fiorina defined as "a running tally of retrospective evaluations of party promises and performance."[47] In other words, the running tally is a summary judgment of how well the parties and their leaders have done and are doing. Over time, that judgment can change, which affects people's evaluations of the parties. How have these partisan attitudes evolved over the past several decades, and how have they impacted voting behavior?

SHIFTS IN PARTISANSHIP AND VOTING BEHAVIOR

The initial model of voter behavior was based on research conducted in the 1950s. During that decade, approximately three-fourths of the electorate identified with one of the major parties, half of them strongly. (See Table 3.4.) The rest of the electorate was, for the most part, uninterested, uninformed, and uninvolved. Nor did they hold strong ideological views.[48] The two major parties were heterogeneous, although they differed on economic issues, particularly about the role of government within the economy.

Nonetheless, during this period, the parties organized the presidential campaigns, raised most of the money for them, provided the skilled political operatives, and used their grassroots organizations to reach and turn out their supporters. Advertising was done primarily in newspapers and on radio; personal contact was deemed important.

The Weakening of Partisanship

Much has changed since then. Television and now the Internet have become primary communication links between candidates and the electorate. Public opinion polls are more accurate, dependable, and frequent. Not only have polls become a source of information about the views and preferences of the electorate but candidates now use them and focus groups to design and market their campaign appeals as well as test how their messages are being received.

Accompanying the communications revolution were significant social and economic changes as well as international developments. During the 1960s and continuing into the 1970s, the United States experienced an unsuccessful war in Southeast Asia and a civil rights movement at home. Both of these events divided the American electorate, particularly Democratic partisans. The Watergate scandal, culminating in President Nixon's resignation and his pardon by President Ford, adversely impacted the Republican Party, shrinking its base. Both major parties suffered as a result of these events. There was a drop-off in the percentage of the electorate who identified with a party and, concurrently, an increase in the proportion of self-proclaimed Independents. Not only did partisan identification decrease but party loyalties also became weaker.

As might have been expected from the weakening attachments to political parties, there was also an increase in split-ticket voting. The statement, "I vote for the best person, regardless of party," was often heard during this period.

As elections became more candidate-centered, candidate organizations competed with party committees for money, personnel, and political consultants. The candidates placed greater emphasis on personal imagery and the use of television advertising to project it. Media gurus began to replace grassroots organizers as key campaign staff. Not only were campaigns more candidate-focused but they also became more issue-oriented. Debates over social and economic policy became more common as clearer ideological differences began to emerge between the major parties on social issues in addition to the economic differences that existed since the 1930s. The Vietnam War also created divisions that carried over into the 1980s.

TABLE 3.4 | PARTY IDENTIFICATION, 1952–2008* (IN PERCENTAGES†)

Party Identification	1952	1956	1960	1964	1968	1972	1976	1980	1984	1988	1992	1996	2000	2004	2008
Total Democrat	57	50	52	61	55	52	52	52	48	47	50	52	50	49	51
Strong	22	21	20	27	20	15	15	18	17	17	18	18	19	17	19
Weak	25	23	25	25	25	26	25	23	20	18	18	19	15	16	15
Independent-Leaning Democrat	10	6	6	9	10	11	12	11	11	12	14	14	15	17	17
Independent	6	9	10	8	11	13	15	13	11	11	12	9	12	10	11
Independent§															
Independent-Leaning Republican	7	8	7	6	9	10	10	10	12	13	12	12	13	12	11
Weak	14	14	14	14	15	13	14	14	15	14	15	13	12	12	13
Strong	13	15	16	11	10	10	9	9	12	14	11	16	12	16	13
Total Republican	34	37	36	30	33	34	33	33	39	41	38	38	37	41	37
Apoliticals															
"Don't know"/other	4	4	3	1	1	1	1	2	2	2	1	1	1	0	0

*The survey question was "Generally speaking, do you usually think of yourself as a Republican, a Democrat, an Independent, or what?" If Republican or Democrat, "Would you call yourself a strong (R) (D) or a not very strong (R) (D)?" If Independent, "Do you think of yourself as closer to the Republican or Democratic Party?"

†Percentages may not equal 100 due to rounding.

§The people who fall into this category are those who declare themselves to be Independent, but in follow-up questions indicate that they may lean in a partisan direction.

Sources: "The ANES Guide to Public Opinion and Electoral Behavior," American National Election Studies (ANES), 1952–2004. www.electionstudies.org/nesguide/toptable/tab2a_1.htm; 2008 updated from ANES data.

In the short run, the Republicans benefited. Weakening support for the dominant party, the Democrats, and the greater stress put on personal images of the candidates allowed Republicans to run for office without hiding their political affiliation. The GOP's more conservative policies, and especially its opposition to preferential treatment for minorities, coincided with the views of many Americans, especially those living in the South. As the country prospered and the middle class grew, people became more conservative. They evidenced less sympathy for policies that trumpeted social, economic, and political equality, if not in theory, then in practice. They also became more leery of legislating social policy and of using government to promote that policy and redistribute resources within society.

The Democrats lost their status as the majority party by the end of the 1970s and their partisan plurality began to shrink in the mid-1980s. By the 1990s, the parties were at rough parity with one another. Although the Democrats still held a slight advantage in numbers of party identifiers, that advantage was offset by the higher Republican turnout. Electoral parity continued into the twenty-first century until disillusionment with the Bush administration increased the Democrats' partisan advantage. (See Table 3.4.)

But that increase has been short-lived. The persistence of a weak economy and large budget deficits and the inability of the Obama administration, in the short run, to reduce high unemployment and mortgage foreclosures and raise property values in its early years in office led to a decrease in the proportion of the population identifying itself as Democratic, a growth in the number of Independents, and steep losses for the Democrats in the 2010 midterm elections. (See Figure 3.1.)

Despite the shifts in partisan advantage and the growth in the proportion of the population that identifies itself as Independent, partisan orientation or

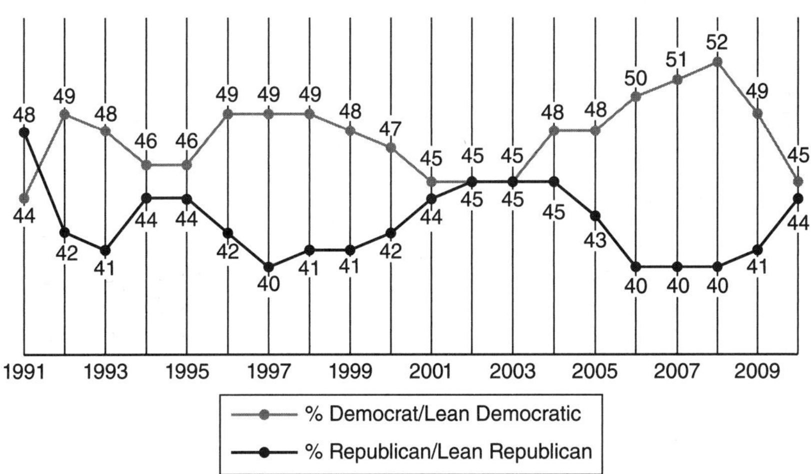

FIGURE 3.1 | PARTY IDENTIFICATION (INCLUDING INDEPENDENT LEANINGS) ANNUAL AVERAGES, GALLUP POLLS, 1991–2010

Source: Jeffrey M. Jones, "Democratic Party ID Drops in 2010, Tying 22-Year Low," January 5, 2011. Gallup.com/poll/145463/Democratic-Party-Drops-2010-Tying-Year-Low.aspx

leaning has remained a strong influence on voting behavior. If anything, that influence has increased for partisans as a consequence of the ideologicalization of the two major parties.

The Deepening of the Partisan Divide

As the policy differences between the major parties became clearer in the 1980s, two different governing philosophies emerged. They have been debated by political elites and increasingly by the American voters. The Republican blueprint was articulated by Ronald Reagan in his presidential campaigns and by his administration, Newt Gingrich in the House Republican's "Contract with America" in 1994, George W. Bush in his two terms as president, and Tea Party activists during the Obama administration. Conservative Republicans believe that the government has gotten too large, too expensive, and too invasive within the economic and domestic arenas. They believe that government should play a smaller and less regulatory role in the economic and social spheres while focusing instead on law and order and national security issues. In contrast, the Democrats believe that government is an important instrument for addressing social and economic inequities and for redistributing resources, for closing the gap between the rich and the poor. The New Deal and Great Society programs of Franklin D. Roosevelt and Lyndon B. Johnson embodied these beliefs. So has the legislative activism of the Obama administration, evident in the enactment of the Recovery and Reinvestment Act, health care reform, and the Frank-Dodd bill that increased regulation of the banking and investment industry.

The differences are less pronounced in foreign and national security policy. Democrats agreed with Republicans on the need for a strong defense during the Cold War. After the Cold War ended, the Democrats have been more reluctant than Republicans to use military force although they have supported the fight against domestic and international terrorism. In general, Democrats place greater emphasis on diplomacy, international organizations, and multilateral agreements in the conduct of U.S. foreign policy, whereas Republicans have been more willing to act unilaterally and use force to promote American national interests.

These diverging domestic and foreign policy perspectives have contributed to an aligning of partisan attitudes along ideological lines, with the Democrats the more liberal party and the Republicans the more conservative. The alignment of ideology with partisanship has made the two major parties more internally cohesive and externally distinct from one another.

Partisan cleavages within government have also become much more pronounced. There is more party-line voting in Congress, more partisan divisions over judicial appointments, more strident partisan rhetoric, and less civility in government. The number of moderates elected to Congress has declined. Conservative Southern Democrats, who frequently sided with the Republicans on budget and tax matters, were replaced by even more conservative Republicans, while moderate Republicans, especially from the Northeast, who sided with the Democrats and moderated their position on some social issues, have been replaced by liberal Democrats.

Not only has political polarization deeply divided elected officials but it has also divided the American electorate, although political scientists disagree on how deep and wide that division is. There are two schools of thought. One view, put forth by Professor Morris Fiorina and some of his colleagues at Stanford University, argues that the polarization is not nearly as extensive or as deep within the general population as it is among those in power.[49] The Fiorina school sees the public as much less ideological, less active, and less overtly partisan in its attitudes and beliefs, although they do concede that there has been a shifting of public issue positions along ideological lines. However, instead of identifying this shift as evidence of polarization, they see it as a "sorting" of issue opinions that may have been prompted by the clearer ideological choices put forth by candidates and elected officials to the public or by a natural alignment of the public's policy views with its partisan political predilections.[50]

In contrast, the Polarization school believes that the ideological divisions run deep within the body politic. They point to the persistence of partisan voting patterns and partisan presidential evaluations since the end of the 1980s and the increase in turnout and other forms of electoral activity.[51] If the public was not primed for such appeals, they argue, the turnout campaigns would not have been nearly as effective as they were in 2004 and 2008.[52]

The debate over the degree of social polarization in America has serious implications for politics and government. For the parties, it calls into question the extent to which they can accommodate the diversity of views and interests within the country as a whole. Can parties claim to be big tents, large enough to attract and welcome all those who choose to enter? At its core, the issue is the ability of the two-party system to sustain itself in an increasingly heterogeneous society.

For candidates, the dilemma is whether to moderate their policy views and appeal to those in the middle of the political spectrum by taking a centrist approach or direct their messages to core supporters who tend to be more ideological. With the most ideological partisans dominating the nomination processes of both parties, the pressure on candidates and elected officials is to reflect the beliefs of the activists who tend to be the most ideological.

For those in government, the issue is representational as well. To what extent do elected leaders represent the views of the body politic when articulating and pursuing ideological policy positions? To what extent should they remain true to their beliefs and to the core partisan supporters who nominated them, or should they be more willing to compromise on a range of policy issues for the sake of political accommodation? Put another way, is there a disconnect among those in government, the American electorate, and the population as a whole? Barack Obama campaigned on changing politics as usual, reducing the strident ideological rhetoric, and finding common ground. But he has found it difficult to achieve these goals as president.

In summary, partisan orientation remains a strong influence on how people evaluate candidates and issues and ultimately on how they vote. It is a relatively stable orientation, but one that can change over the years with events and circumstances and as new people enter and older ones leave the electorate. Today, partisanship has been reinforced by ideology and to some extent also by religious affiliation and activities,[53] topics we address in the next section when we examine the impact of social factors on partisanship, turnout, and voting behavior. Table 3.4 indicates partisan preferences of the American people since 1952.

THE SOCIAL BASIS OF POLITICS

When individuals develop attitudes and opinions, they are also influenced by the associations they have with others and by the groups with which they are affiliated. That social influences can affect voting behavior is a theory first postulated by Paul F. Lazarsfeld, Bernard R. Berelson, and others who examined the sociology of electoral politics more than sixty years ago in their groundbreaking studies *The People's Choice* and *Voting*.[54]

Although more attention has been devoted to the psychological influences on voting behavior since the publication of *The American Voter* in 1960, a more recent study by Paul Allen Beck and others lends support to the thesis that the social context in which elections occur matters. Beck and his associates found that intermediaries between the candidates and voters—individuals, media, and groups—provided information that contributed to voters' decisions. The intermediaries had most effect on those voters who were less tied to parties and, for the most part, were also less informed and interested in electoral politics. Coming into contact with others who had political information and enthusiasm for the parties, candidates, and/or issues brought the election to people who might otherwise have avoided it.[55]

As we have emphasized in this chapter, personal contact is important in turning out voters. Politicians have believed this proposition for a long time, and more recently experimental and field research by political scientists Donald P. Green and Alan Gerber has confirmed it, concluding: ". . . as a rule of thumb, one additional vote is produced for every fourteen people who are successfully contacted by canvassers."[56]

We now turn to these intermediaries and their influences on voting behavior, specifically to the demographic and social groups that are part of the major parties' electoral coalitions. Three factors, in particular, affect the extent to which groups contribute to the party's electoral base: their size, their turnout, and their loyalty to the party.

THE NEW DEAL REALIGNMENT

Political coalitions form during periods of partisan realignment. The last time a classic realignment occurred was in the 1930s. Largely as a consequence of the Great Depression, the Democrats emerged as the dominant party.[57] Their electoral coalition, held together by a common belief that the government should play a more active role in dealing with the nation's economic problems, supported Franklin Roosevelt's New Deal program. Those in more dire economic circumstances generally subscribed to this view; they had few other options. On the other hand, many of the owners and executives of still solvent businesses saw government intrusion into the free enterprise system as a threat to the capitalist system. They opposed much of Roosevelt's domestic legislation and remained Republican in attitude and vote.

The Democrats became the majority party during this period by expanding their base. Since the Civil War and the withdrawal of federal troops, the Democrats had enjoyed solid support in the South. White Protestants living in rural areas dominated the southern electorate; African Americans were largely excluded. Only in the election of 1928, when Al Smith, the Catholic governor of New York, ran as the Democratic candidate was there a sizable southern vote for a Republican candidate at the presidential level. As a Catholic and an opponent of prohibition, Smith was unacceptable to many southern, white Protestants.

Catholics also voted Democratic even before the 1930s. Living primarily in the urban centers of the North, they became an increasingly important component of the Democrats' electoral coalition as their numbers grew in the population. Facing difficult economic circumstances, social discrimination, and, for many, language barriers, Catholic immigrants turned to big-city bosses for help; what they were expected to give in return was their support for the boss and the candidates that he and his party organization supported. In 1928, for the first time, a majority of the cities in the country voted Democratic. Catholic support for Smith and the Democratic Party figured prominently in this vote.

The harsh economic realities of the Great Depression enabled Roosevelt to expand Democratic support in urban areas even further, especially among those in the lower socioeconomic strata. Outside the South, Roosevelt's political coalition was differentiated along class lines. It attracted people with less education and income and those who were unemployed, underemployed, or had lower-paying jobs. Organized labor, in particular, became reliably Democratic. In addition to establishing a broad-based, blue-collar, working-class coalition, Roosevelt also lured specific racial and ethnic groups, such as African Americans and Jewish Americans, from their former Republican roots. African Americans who lived outside of the South voted increasingly Democratic for economic reasons, whereas Jewish Americans supported Roosevelt's liberal domestic programs and his anti-Nazi foreign policy. Neither of these groups provided the Democratic Party of the 1930s with a large number of votes, but their long-term allegiances to that party has given the Democrats a secure and dependable base among these racial and religious minority groups.

In contrast, during the same period, the Republican Party shrank. Not only were Republicans unable to attract new groups, they were unable to prevent the defection of people whose economic plight made the Democratic program more appealing. Although the Republicans did retain the support of the business and professional classes, which grew after World War II, their working-class base eroded. Republican strength remained concentrated in the Northeast, particularly in the rural areas.

EVOLVING POLITICAL COALITIONS: 1950S–1970S

The coalitions that were restructured during the 1930s and 1940s held together for another twenty years. During this period, African Americans and Jewish Americans increased their identification with and support of the Democratic Party and its candidates. Although Catholics, for the most part, stayed

Democratic, their vote fluctuated more at the presidential level. Catholic support for John Kennedy, a Catholic, reached a high of 78 percent of the total Catholic vote in 1960. The Democrats retained majority Catholic support through the 1970s. Protestants remained Republican with the exception of less-educated, lower-income fundamentalist and evangelical groups that voted Democratic, largely for economic reasons. Concentrated in the South and border states, these fundamentalist and evangelical Christians voted overwhelmingly for Jimmy Carter, a born-again Christian, in 1976.

Prior to the 1980s, there were no major partisan distinctions in gender preferences although some cleavages among different age cohorts were evident. Younger voters, attracted by the liberal policies of Democratic candidates and older Americans who had benefited from these policies, particularly Social Security, gave the Democrats more support, while newly affluent, more conservative voters became increasingly Republican.

Socioeconomic Shifts

The changes that did take place in the 1950s and early 1960s emanated primarily from the growth of a larger and more populous middle class and its movement from the cities to the suburbs. In the short run, the nation's postwar prosperity did not result in a complete partisan realignment. People who gained in economic and social status did not, as a general rule, discard their partisan loyalties unless and until they objected to some of the social changes that were occurring during this period: Democratically initiated civil rights legislation followed by affirmative action policies, Supreme Court decisions on abortion and school prayer, and the movement by feminists for greater equality in the workplace. Over time, however, rising economic prosperity made the Republicans' policy positions more attractive to a growing and more prosperous middle class. Coincidentally, the Democrats' labor base began to shrink. In 1952, organized labor represented about 25 percent of the American electorate. Today, it constitutes less than 13 percent.

Regional Shifts

More dramatic than this economic erosion of the Democrats' electoral coalition was the defection of Southern Democrats, a group that had been solidly Democratic since the end of the Civil War. The political attitudes and partisan allegiances of whites in the South began to change as a consequence of the national Democratic Party's support of civil rights. Harry Truman's order to integrate the military and his backing of the 1948 Democratic Convention platform's civil rights plank led to a walkout of southern delegates at the party's nominating convention, the third-party candidacy of Strom Thurmond, and a decline in the Democratic presidential vote in the South. In 1948, Harry Truman won 52 percent of the southern vote, compared with Roosevelt's 69 percent four years earlier. Although Adlai Stevenson and John Kennedy carried the South by reduced margins, the southern white Protestant vote for president went Republican for the first time in 1960. And it has continued, for the most part, to do so. However, the enfranchisement of African Americans in the South following the enactment of the Voting Rights Act of 1965 has made the southern vote less homogeneous. The Republicans also gained strength in the Southwest with the movement of population to this area of the country; in contrast, the coastal areas in the Northeast and on the Pacific Coast were becoming more Democratic.

PARTY PARITY AND THE REALIGNMENT OF ELECTORAL COALITIONS: 1980–PRESENT

The 1980s saw the end of Democratic dominance and the growth of the Republican Party to near parity with the Democrats.

The Republicans

President Ronald Reagan gave voice and structure to a rejuvenated conservative Republican coalition. The composition of this coalition includes southern whites, Protestant fundamentalists and evangelicals, and other economic and national security conservatives already aligned with the Republican Party. The coalition is disproportionately white, male, and increasingly middle-aged. Women who are part of the coalition tend to be married and older than women who consider themselves Democratic.

SOUTHERN WHITES Since the 1980s, southern whites have continued to shift their political allegiances from the Democrats to the GOP. They have given Republican presidential candidates a majority vote in seven of the last eight elections. In fact, they have been the most Republican area of the country, more apt to vote Republican at the national level than any other region. In the 1994 midterm elections, Republican congressional candidates won a majority of the southern vote for the first time since Reconstruction. In subsequent elections, the Republicans maintained their congressional southern majority.

Even though the Democrats nominated a presidential and vice presidential candidate from the South in 1992 and 1996 (Bill Clinton and Al Gore), the white vote they received from the South was less than the white vote they received from other regions of the country, and that trend has continued. Although Barack Obama did make inroads in the South in 2008 and won the electoral vote of three southern states (Florida, North Carolina, and Virginia), he did so primarily with the help of a large, unified African American vote and a growing Hispanic vote from that region.

Whites in other parts of the country have also become more Republican. Since 1964, a plurality of whites had voted for the Republican presidential candidate until 2008, when McCain and Obama split the white vote. The tendency of whites to vote Republican and other racial groups in the United States to vote Democratic has produced a large racial divide within American politics.

PROTESTANT FUNDAMENTALISTS AND EVANGELICALS Another major shift from the Democrats' electoral coalition to the Republicans' has been among orthodox religious believers who have been attracted to the Republican Party by its support of traditional family values. Beginning in the 1980s, Protestant fundamentalist and evangelical churches became better organized and more involved in national politics. Establishing organizations such as the Moral Majority, Christian Coalition, the Family Research Council, and a host of antiabortion groups, Protestant fundamentalists and evangelicals have become active within the Republican Party's nomination process and a dependable component of its electoral coalition.

People who attended mainline Protestant churches, however, did not become as unified as their fundamentalist and evangelical brethren on the social issues that the Republican Party advocated. As a consequence, they have been somewhat less supportive of Republican candidates than Christian fundamentalist groups. Much depends on the theological and ideological orientation of the churches and the activities of their members. Those people who have the greatest involvement, who attend church services most regularly, who subscribe to more literal readings and interpretations of the Bible, are more likely to vote Republican. Those whose theological views are more nuanced, who are less engaged in church-related activities, and who attend services less regularly tend to be more moderate in their social outlook and less Republican in their political behavior.[58]

The "traditionalist–modernist" distinction within the Protestant religious community extends to other religions as well, to Catholics who subscribe to the Church's doctrine and regularly attend Mass and even to orthodox Jews. The key variable predicting voting behavior is the regularity of religious worship. People who attend services regularly are more apt to vote Republican than those who attend less regularly or not at all.

The sectarian–secular divide, evident for the past three decades, is applicable to white America. It does not extend to racial minority groups whose allegiances to the Democratic Party are more deeply rooted in that party's economic and social policy positions than they are in its attitude toward religious values and practices.

MEN AND MARRIED WOMEN A gender gap has also been apparent since the 1980s. Males have been more attracted to the Republican Party and women to the Democratic Party. The gap in the voting behavior of the two groups had been in the range of 4 to 8 percent until 1996, when it rose to 11 percent and remained at about that level in 2000. It was reduced in 2004 but grew again in 2008 despite the nomination of a woman, Sarah Palin, as the Republican vice presidential nominee.[59] The gender gap is larger among whites than non-whites and larger among those with more formal education than less. It is also greater among those who are unmarried than those who are married and those without children than those with them.[60]

AGE The Roosevelt Democrats are being replaced by generations whose experiences with government are less positive than people who came of voting age during the 1930s and 1940s. As a consequence, middle-aged and older Americans today are more receptive to Republican appeals for less government in the economic and social sectors but a strong government role in national security. The 2004 presidential election was the first since the 1930s in which the over sixty-five vote went Republican at the presidential level; the election of 2008 was the second.

How then can the contemporary Republican electoral coalition be described? Beginning in the 1980s and continuing into the twenty-first century, the Republican coalition has become whiter, more middle class, more rural, more male, more religious, and more conservative. The party has become more homogeneous. Its base has shrunk since the 1980s. Republicans have maintained their regional support in the South and Rocky Mountain areas and have lost support in the Northeast, the Pacific Coast, and those states in the Southwest in which the Hispanic population is growing the most rapidly.

The Democrats

The Democrats' electoral coalition has frayed from its New Deal days; Democrats no longer constitute the majority and their coalition has also decreased in size, but it remains more diverse in composition than the Republicans'. The Democrats have a party in which ethnic and racial minorities and, increasingly, women, younger people, and secularists constitute core constituencies. Democrats still receive overwhelming support from those with the lowest incomes and those who live in the cities. However, the relatively small size of the latter two groups within the electorate makes them a less important voting bloc than they used to be.

RACIAL AND ETHNIC MINORITIES The Democratic electoral coalition has retained and even increased its support among African Americans and Hispanics. Today, at least 90 percent of African Americans consider themselves Democrats compared to the late 1950s when only about 75 percent did.[61] With their increased loyalty to the Democrats and their election turnout now equal to whites',[62] African Americans have become a larger and more important component in the Democrats' core constituency. The flip side of this increase in support has been that the party's positions on economic and social issues, particularly on civil rights and welfare benefits, have alienated some white working-class voters whose allegiance to the Democrats has declined over the past several decades.[63]

Hispanic voters have become another increasingly important component of the Democrats' electoral coalition. With the exception of Cuban Americans concentrated in South Florida, a majority of Hispanic voters identify with the Democratic Party, and two-thirds of them tend to vote for its candidates on a regular basis. The growth of the Hispanic population in the United States and increases in Hispanic turnout have rendered this group increasingly important to the Democrats' electoral coalition.

COASTAL RESIDENTS The Northeast has become more Democratic but not primarily as a consequence of population movement. The Republican Party's increasing ideological rigidity, particularly its social agenda, has alienated some of old-line moderate Republicans from this area. New Hampshire, the last bastion of GOP strength, went Democratic at the presidential level in 2004 and stayed that way in 2008. The mid-Atlantic and Pacific Coast states have also become more Democratic. Competition between the parties tends to be greatest in the Midwest, an area in which many of the battleground states critical to winning an Electoral College majority are located.

SECULARS The movement of Protestant fundamentalists to the Republican Party has left the Democrats with a more secular base. With the exception of the Jewish community, which has remained in the Democrats' electoral coalition, and Muslims, who have more recently reacted to the domestic security measures and foreign policies of the Bush administration by voting Democratic, the party lacks the strong religious base it had in previous eras.

Catholic support has declined particularly among the older-line Catholic groups, primarily Irish and Italian. Despite the fact that John Kerry, a Catholic, was on the Democratic ticket in the 2004 presidential election, the Catholic vote almost evenly divided between Kerry and Bush. Had it not been for the expansion of the Hispanic population, the drop in Catholic support for the Democrats would have been even greater. Again, the more traditional the religious beliefs and practices of Catholics, the less likely they are to vote Democratic. Similarly, people who are not affiliated with a religious institution or who are not practicing their religious beliefs and heritage are much more likely to consider themselves Democrats.

GENDER ORIENTATION Partisan voting trends are also evident on the basis of sexual orientation. According to the exit polls in recent elections, more than 70 percent of those who indicated that they were homosexual or lesbian voted Democratic. However, only a relatively small percentage of voters, about 4 percent, admit to being gay.

In summary, the Democrats are a party of racial, ethnic, and religious minorities; women, particularly unmarried women; those in the younger-aged groups; people who are most and least educated; and those living in metropolitan areas, primarily on the East and West coasts, and in areas in which minority groups are concentrated. Gallup Poll data on group voting patterns in the presidential election since 1996 are presented in Table 3.5.

What conclusions can we draw about the social basis of politics today? It is clear that the old party coalitions have evolved. The class distinction evident during the New Deal era has faded, although income levels, and to a lesser extent education levels, continue to distinguish partisan voting behavior, as do race, gender, gender orientation, and religion and religious activity. Population shifts are also affecting partisan voting patterns and the Electoral College map.

TABLE 3.5 | VOTE BY GROUPS IN PRESIDENTIAL ELECTIONS, 1996–2008 (IN PERCENTAGES)

	1996			2000			2004		2008	
	Clinton	Dole	Perot	Gore	Bush	Nader	Kerry	Bush	Obama	McCain
NATIONAL	50.0	41.0	9.0	48.7	48.6	2.7	48.5	51.5	53.0	46.0
Sex										
Men	45	44	11	45	52	3	44	56	50	50
Women	54	39	7	53	45	2	52	48	57	43
Race										
White (incl. Hispanics)	46	45	9	43	55	3	44	56	45	55
Non-white	82	12	6	87	9	4	83	17	90	10
Non-Hispanic white	—	—	—	42	56	2	43	57	44	56
Non-white (incl. Hispanics)	—	—	—	80	17	3	78	22	86	14
Black	—	—	—	95	3	2	93	7	99	1
Age										
Under 30 years	54	30	16	47	47	6	60	40	61	39
30–49 years	49	41	10	45	53	2	43	57	53	47
50–64 years old	—	—	—	50	48	2	48	52	54	46
65 years and older	—	—	—	56	42	2	52	48	46	54

continued

TABLE 3.5 | VOTE BY GROUPS IN PRESIDENTIAL ELECTIONS, 1996–2008 (IN PERCENTAGES) *continued*

	1996			2000			2004		2008	
	Clinton	**Dole**	**Perot**	**Gore**	**Bush**	**Nader**	**Kerry**	**Bush**	**Obama**	**McCain**
NATIONAL	50.0	41.0	9.0	48.7	48.6	2.7	48.5	51.5	53.0	46.0
Education										
Grade School	58	27	15	55	42	3	69	31	67	33
High School	52	34	14	52	46	2	54	46	47	53
College	47	45	8	46	51	3	48	52	55	45
Post-Grad	—	—	—	53	43	4	53	47	65	35
Region										
East	60	31	9	55	42	3	58	42	57	43
Midwest	46	45	9	48	49	3	48	52	53	47
South	44	46	10	45	54	1	43	57	50	50
West	51	43	6	48	47	5	48	52	55	45
Politics										
Republicans	10	85	5	7	92	1	5	95	7	93
Democrats	90	6	4	89	10	2	93	7	93	7
Independents	48	33	19	44	49	7	52	48	51	49
Ideology										
Conservative	—	—	—	27	71	2	20	80	23	77
Moderate	—	—	—	57	41	2	63	37	63	37
Liberal	—	—	—	84	9	7	88	12	94	6

Religion										
Protestants	44	50	6	42	55	3	38	62	47	53
Catholics	55	35	10	52	46	2	52	48	53	47
Attend Weekly	—	—	—	41	56	2	37	63	45	55
Attend Monthly	—	—	—	47	51	2	45	55	51	49
Seldom/Never Attend	—	—	—	52	41	7	60	40	62	38
Marital Status										
Married	—	—	—	40	57	2	40	60	44	56
Not Married	—	—	—	59	36	3	60	40	65	35
Married Men	—	—	—	37	59	3	39	61	42	58
Married Women	—	—	—	41	56	2	42	58	47	53
Unmarried Men	—	—	—	49	42	5	55	45	63	37
Unmarried Women	—	—	—	66	31	2	64	36	66	34
Labor Union										
Union families	—	—	—	68	31	2	67	33	64	36

National figures are based on actual election outcomes, repercentaged to exclude minor third-party candidates.

Demographic data are based on Gallup Poll final preelection surveys, repercentaged to exclude "no opinions" and support for minor third-party candidates; results are then weighted to conform with actual election results.

Source: Gallup Poll, "Election Polls: Vote by Groups" http://www.gallup.com/poll/112132/Election-Polls-Vote-Groups-2008.aspx. Used with permission.

SUMMARY

The electorate is not neutral. People do not come to campaigns with completely open minds. Rather, they come with preexisting attitudes and accumulated experiences that color their perceptions and affect their judgments, much as stimuli from the campaign affect those attitudes and experiences.

Of the political beliefs people possess, partisanship has the strongest impact on turnout and voting behavior. It provides a perspective for evaluating the campaign and for deciding whether and how to vote. It is also a motive for being informed, for getting involved, and for voting.

Toward the end of the 1960s, there was a decline in the proportion of the population that identified with a political party. This decline, a product of disillusionment with both major parties, contributed to lower voter turnout. It also increased the importance of short-term factors on voting behavior. During this period, more people identified themselves as Independent; there was more candidate and issue voting; and, as a consequence, more split-ticket ballots.

The use of television as the primary channel through which candidates and parties communicated to the electorate, the weakening of the major parties' grassroots organizations, and the creation of separate candidate and party organizations required by the Federal Election Campaign Act all worked to reduce the influence of the parties on voting behavior. By the 1980s, however, that influence had returned even though the proportion of the population identifying themselves as political partisans declined.

The increase in party voting encouraged both parties to reach out to their partisans for support, with the result that turnout in the 2004 and 2008 presidential elections increased. Using the latest computer and Internet technologies, the Republicans in 2004 and the Democrats in 2008 succeeded in activating their bases. The result has been a more participatory electorate in which more people have given more money, volunteered for campaign activities, and helped produce higher voting turnout in presidential elections.

Since the 1980s, the parties have also become more ideological, with the Republicans more conservative and the Democrats still liberal. This ideologicalization has divided the electorate and deeply divided the government. How wide and deep these divisions are within the body politic is less clear, although the growth in the proportion of self-identified Independents suggests that many people may be "turned off" by the extreme beliefs and behavior of party leaders and elected officials. During this period, the parties have moved closer to electoral parity. That parity has been reflected in relatively close elections with frequent shifts in the control of the White House and Congress.

Group ties to the parties have shifted as well. The Democratic Party has lost the support of a majority of southern whites, non-Hispanic Catholics, and Protestant fundamentalists and evangelicals. The Democratic labor base shrunk as union laborers declined as a proportion of the population. Racial minorities, however, such as African Americans and Hispanics, have increased their loyalty to the Democrats. Jewish Americans, though a declining portion of the population, have retained their Democratic allegiances. Women have become much more supportive of Democratic candidates, as have people with secular views. The party has improved its proportion of the vote in the Northeast, Pacific Coast, and more recently, the Southwest—the latter a result of Hispanic immigration.

The Republicans have made inroads among the growing middle- and upper-middle classes, older people who came of age after the New Deal, and people with sectarian beliefs who are most active within their religious communities. The Republicans' emphasis on family and traditional values has attracted more support from married heterosexuals but less from people who are single, particularly young people. White men also became more Republican in outlook and voting behavior. In addition to the South, the GOP has maintained its support in the Mountain states and is competitive in the Midwest.

The changes within the political environment have important implications for presidential politics. They have produced a more ideologically based party system, but they have also alienated moderate voters who find it difficult to identify with the policies and candidates of either major party. They have also produced a more divided government in which Republicans and Democrats find it difficult to work together, much less agree, on national public policy. The extent to which these trends will continue may depend on the perceived state of the economy and the nation's security. The greater the level of dissatisfaction, the more opposition there is likely to be to those in positions of power; conversely, when conditions improve, the party in power benefits.

WHERE ON THE WEB?

- **Democratic National Committee**
  www.democrats.org
  Provides information on Democratic Party history, rules, conventions, and campaigns with links to Democratic youth and state party affiliates.
- **Green Party**
  www.gp.org
  Information on the Green Party, its rules, conventions, and candidates.
- **League of Women Voters**
  www.lwv.org
  A nonpartisan organization, it provides information on candidates, their positions, and how to register and vote.
- **Reform Party**
  www.reformparty.org
  Information on the Reform Party, its rules, conventions, and candidates.
- **Republican National Committee**
  www.rnc.org
  Information on Republican Party history, rules, conventions, and campaigns with links to Republican youth and state party affiliates.
- **Rock-the-Vote**
  www.rockthevote.com
  An organization whose goal is to encourage young people to register and vote by providing a registration form online, as well as details about how to obtain an absentee ballot.

- **Project Vote Smart**
  www.vote-smart.org
  An organization that provides a wealth of information on candidates and their issue positions and evaluates their performance in office.
- **VOTE 411.org**
  www.dnet.org
  A public interest site sponsored by the education fund of the League of Women Voters where you can find out candidate positions on the issues as well as connect to grassroots groups involved in a variety of salient issues.

EXERCISES

1. If you are a U.S. citizen, eighteen years of age or older, and haven't already done so, register to vote by accessing the Election Assistance Commission's Web site at www.eac.gov and downloading the national voter registration form, completing it, and sending it to your state election officials. Alternately, access Rock-the-Vote at www.rockthevote.com and provide that organization with information to begin the registration process.
2. Indicate all the services that the major parties provide to their candidates in the general election by accessing their Web sites and going through their menu of services. Which of these services do you think will be most helpful to the presidential candidates in the coming election?
3. Go to the Web sites of the candidates who are running for president in the next election to determine what they are doing to mobilize supporters in their campaigns. On the basis of what you can determine from their Web sites, which candidates seem to have the most comprehensive and creative turnout campaigns? Which of them do you think will be able to turn out the most supporters on election day?
4. Describe the composition of the major parties' electoral coalitions. On the basis of your description, locate interest groups that represent groups of supporters. Access the Web sites of these groups and note what they have done or plan to do to mobilize their supporters in the election.

SELECTED READINGS

Abramson, Paul R., John H. Aldrich, and David W. Rohde. *Change and Continuity in the 2008 Elections*. Washington, DC: CQ Press, 2010.

Black, Earl, and Merle Black. *The Vital South: How Presidents Are Elected.* Cambridge, MA: Harvard University Press, 1992.

Burnham, Walter D. "The Turnout Problem" in *Elections American Style*, edited by A. James Reichley. Washington, DC: Brookings Institution, 1987, 97–133.

Campbell, Angus, Philip E. Converse, Warren E. Miller, and Donald E. Stokes. *The American Voter*. New York: Wiley, 1960.

Fiorina, Morris, Samuel J. Abrams, and Jeremy C. Pope. *Culture War? The Myth of a Polarized America*. New York: Longman, 2006.

Gerber, Alan S., Donald P. Green, and Christopher W. Larimer, "Social Pressure and Voter Turnout: Evidence from a Large-Scale Field Experiment,"*American Political Science Review*, 102 (Feb. 2008): 33–48.

Green, Donald P., and Alan S. Gerber. *Get Out the Vote! How to Increase Voter Turnout*. Washington, DC: Brookings Institution, 2004.

Green, Donald P., Bradley Palmquist, and Eric Schickler. *Partisan Hearts and Minds: Political Parties and the Social Identities of Voters.* New Haven: Yale University Press, 2002.

Highton, Benjamin. "Voter Registration and Turnout in the United States," *Perspectives on Politics*, 2 (September 2004): 507–515.

Holbrook, Thomas M., and Scott D. McClurg. "The Mobilization of Core Supporters: Campaigns, Turnout, and Electoral Composition in United States Presidential Campaigns," *American Journal of Political Science*, 49 (October 2005): 689–703.

Jacobson, Gary C. "The Effects of the George W. Bush Presidency on Partisan Attitudes," *Presidential Studies Quarterly*, 39 (June 2009): 172–206.

Keith, Bruce E., David B. Magleby, Candice Nelson, and Elizabeth Orr. *The Myth of the Independent Voter*. Berkeley: University of California Press, 1992.

Leege, David, and Lyman A. Kellstedt. *Rediscovering the Religious Factor in American Politics*. New York: M. E. Sharpe, 1993.

Lewis-Beck, Michael S., William G. Jacoby, Helmut Norpoth, and Herbert F. Weisberg. *The American Voter Revisited*. Ann Arbor: University of Michigan Press, 2008.

Lyons, William, and Robert Alexander. "A Tale of Two Electorates: Generational Replacement and the Decline of Voting in Presidential Elections." *Journal of Politics*, 62 (Nov. 2000): 1014–1034.

Martinez, Michael D., and Jeff Gill. "The Effects of Turnout on Partisan Outcomes in U.S. Presidential Elections, 1960–2000," *Journal of Politics*, 67 (November 2005): 1248–1274.

Miller, Warren E. "Party Identification, Realignment, and Party Voting: Back to the Basics," *American Political Science Review*, 85 (June 1991): 557–570.

Nagler, Jonathan. "The Effect of Registration Laws and Education on U.S. Voter Turnout," *American Political Science Review*, 85 (December 1991): 1395–1405.

Nie, Norman H., Sidney Verba, and John R. Petrocik. *The Changing American Voter*. Cambridge, MA: Harvard University Press, 1976.

Nivola, Pietro S., and David W. Brady, eds. *Red and Blue Nation? Characteristics and Causes of America's Polarized Politics*. Washington, DC: Brookings Institution, 2006.

Patterson, Thomas E. *The Vanishing Voter*. New York: Knopf, 2002.

Popkin, Samuel L. *The Reasoning Voter: Communication and Persuasion in Presidential Campaigns*. Chicago: University of Chicago Press, 1991.

Stanley, Harold W., and Richard G. Niemi. "Partisanship, Party Coalitions, and Group Support, 1952–2004," *Presidential Studies Quarterly*, 36 (June 2006): 172–188.

Tate, Katherine. *From Protest to Politics: The New Black Voters in American Elections*. Cambridge, MA: Harvard University Press, 1994.

Wattenberg, Martin P. *The Decline of American Political Parties: 1952–1996*. Cambridge, MA: Harvard University Press, 1998.

Wolfinger, Raymond E., and Steven J. Rosenstone. *Who Votes?* New Haven: Yale University Press, 1980.

NOTES

1. Michael P. McDonald, "2008 General Election Turnout Rates" (Updated: March 13, 2010). elections.gmu.edu/Turnout_2008G.html.
2. "Voting and Registration in the Election of November 2008," U.S. Census Bureau, Current Population Reports, P 20-252, 2010. www.census.gov/compendia/statab/2011/tables/11s0418.pdf.

3. Michael P. McDonald and Samuel L. Popkin, "The Myth of the Vanishing Voter," *American Political Science Review,* 95 (Dec. 2001), pp. 963–974; Samuel L. Popkin and Michael McDonald, "Turnout's Not as Bad as You Think," *The Washington Post,* (Nov. 5, 2000), pp. B1, B2; Michael P. McDonald, "The Return of the Voter: Voter Turnout in the 2008 Presidential Election," *The Forum,* 6 issue 4, article4 (2008). www.bepress.com/forum/vol6/iss4/art4.
See also Michael P. McDonald, "2008 General Election Turnout Rates" (Updated: March 13, 2010). elections.gmu.edu/Turnout_2008G.html.
4. The gap between the voting-age population and the voting-eligible population has increased over the last fifty years. There are more immigrants, legal and illegal, in the United States today. There are also more people who are or have been incarcerated and as a consequence have lost their right to vote on a temporary or permanent basis. See Michael P. McDonald, "Up, Up and Away! Voter Participation in the 2004 Presidential Election," *The Forum, II* (Post Election) (2004). www.bepress.com/ forum/vol2/iss4.; Michael P. McDonald, "The Return of the Voter," *The Forum* 6 (2008), pp. 1–10. See also Michael P. McDonald, "2008 General Election Turnout Rates" (Updated: March 13, 2010). elections.gmu .edu/Turnout_2008G.html.
5. Although some states initially permitted all landowners to vote, including women, by 1807, every state limited voting to men. Michael X. Delli Carpini and Ester R. Fuchs, "The Year of the Woman: Candidates, Voters, and the 1992 Election," *Political Science Quarterly,* 108 (Spring 1993), p. 30.
6. Ronald P. Formisane, "Deferential-Participant Politics: The Early Republic's Political Culture, 1789," *American Political Science Review,* 68 (June 1974), pp. 473–487.
7. Delli Carpini and Fuchs, "The Year of the Woman," p. 30.
8. Despite these allegations, Walter Dean Burnham still maintains that the high turnout percentages were real, "not artifacts of either census error or universal ballot stuffing." (p. 117). Walter Dean Burnham, "The Turnout Problem," in A. James Reichley, ed., *Elections American Style* (Washington, DC: Brookings Institution, 1987), pp. 112–116.
9. Peter F. Nardulli, Jon K. Dalager, and Donald E. Greco, "Voter Turnout in U.S. Presidential Elections: An Historical View and Some Speculation," *PS: Political Science and Politics* (Sept. 1996), p. 480.
10. In the case of *Smith v. Allwright,* 321 U.S. 649 (1944), the Supreme Court declared the white primary to be unconstitutional. In its opinion, the Court rejected the argument that parties were private associations and thus could restrict participation in their selection process.
11. "Felony Disenfranchisement Laws in the United States," The Sentencing Project. www.sentencingproject.org/doc/publications/fd_bs_fdlawsinusJan2011.pdf.
12. Ibid.
13. "The Impact of the National Voter Registration Act of 1993 on the Administration of Elections for Federal Office, 2007–2008." A Report to the 111th Congress, June 30, 2009, Election Assistance Commission. www.eac.gov.
14. "National Voter Registration Act Studies." Election Assistance Commission. www.eac.gov/research/national_voter_registration_act_studies.aspx.
15. Eric Plutzer, "Becoming a Habitual Voter: Inertia, Resources, and Growth in Young Adulthood," *American Political Science Review*, 96 (March 2002), pp. 41–56.
16. There has been considerable political science research on the development of political attitudes and the behavior that follows from them. Initially, this research

focused on political socialization; in recent years, there have been new studies on genetics, how heredity factors influence voting and political participation. See James H. Fowler, Laura A. Baker, and Christopher T. Dawes, "Genetic Variation in Political Participation," *American Political Science Review,* 102 (May 2008): 233–248. In another study, James H. Fowler and Christopher T. Dawes, found two genes that predict voter turnout. James H. Fowler and Christopher T. Dawes, "Two Genes Predict Voter Turnout," *Journal of Politics,* 70 (July 2008), pp. 579–591.

17. Angus Campbell, Philip E. Converse, Warren E. Miller, and Donald E. Stokes, *The American Voter* (New York: Wiley, 1960), p. 102.
18. Alan S. Gerber, Donald P. Green, and Christopher W. Larimer, "Social Pressures and Voter Turnout: Evidence from a Large-Scale Field Experiment," *American Political Science Review*, 102 (Feb. 2008): 233–248.
19. Nicholas A. Valentine, Ted Brader, Eric W. Groenendyk, Krysha Gregorowicz, and Vincent L. Hutchings, "Election Night's Alright for Fighting: The Role of Emotions In Political Participation," *Journal of Politics,*73 (Jan. 2011): 156–170.
20. Paul R. Abramson, John H. Aldrich, and David W. Rohde, *Change and Continuity in the 2008 Elections,*(Washington DC: CQ Press, 2010), p. 107. The data that the authors analyze to reach this conclusion comes from the American National Election Studies (ANES) time series survey that has been administered before and after elections since 1952. It pertains to the white electorate.
21. Raymond E. Wolfinger and Steven J. Rosenstone, *Who Votes?* (New Haven: Yale University Press, 1980), pp. 13–26; Rachel Milstein Sondheimer and Donald P. Green, "Using Experiments to Estimate the Effects of Education on Voter Turnout," *American Journal of Political Science,* 54 (Jan. 2010): 174–189.
22. Wolfinger and Rosenstone, *Who Votes* Ibid., pp. 18–20, 35–36.
23. Estimates range from 16 to 19 percent for the decline in turnout if educational levels had not increased. Abramson, Aldrich, and Rohde, *Change and Continuity in 2008,* p. 103; Steven J. Rosenstone and John Mark Hansen, *Mobilization, Participation, and Democracy in America* (New York: Macmillan, 1993), pp. 214–215.
24. Why the drop in turnout among the young? Younger people may not have perceived the national government as relevant to them as their parents and grandparents saw the government when they were young. Until the terrorist attacks of September 11, 2001, there was not an event of the magnitude of the Great Depression and World War II that demonstrated the importance of government or events such as the Vietnam War and race relations that illustrated the dangers of government to people who found these experiences disconcerting.
25. McDonald, *Up, Up and Away!* p. 2.
26. McDonald, "The Return of the Voter," *The Forum* 6 (2008), p. 1.
27. Ibid., p. 2.
28. McDonald attributes the decline in 2008 to the Republicans' strategy of conserving their limited resources by contacting only "low-to-moderate propensity voters." They assumed that those with a higher propensity would vote. Ibid., p. 2.
29. Brad T. Gomez, Thomas G. Hansford, and George A. Krause, "The Republicans Should Pray for Rain: Weather, Turnout, and Voting in U.S. Presidential Elections," *Journal of Politics* 69 (August 2007), pp. 649–663.
30. On the other hand, low turnout can also indicate a level of satisfaction since citizens are more likely to vote when they are angry than when they are content.
31. Another related factor is the increasing percentage of single people and single parents in the voting-age population over the past fifty years. For a variety of

reasons, from time constraints to lower income levels, single adults do not turn out to vote as regularly as do married adults.

32. Michael D. Martinez and Jeff Gill, "The Effects of Turnout on Partisan Outcomes in U.S. Presidential Elections 1960–2000," *Journal of Politics,* 67 (Nov. 2005), pp. 1248–1274.
33. Jon Carson, the National Field Director for the Obama campaign, described the field office component as his "Starbucks strategy": "We wanted offices everywhere because, despite all the focus on the online network, the truth of the matter was where we had offices and volunteers were working together with staff, we got work done." Kathleen Hall Jamieson, ed., *Electing the President 2008: The Insider's View* (Philadelphia: University of Pennsylvania Press, 2009), p. 43.
34. Donald P. Green and Alan S. Gerber, *Get Out the Vote! How to Increase Voter Turnout.* (Washington, DC: Brookings Institution, 2004).
35. Actually, a small interview/reinterview survey was conducted in 1948, but the results were never published. In contrast to the emphasis on political attitudes of the large-scale interview projects in the 1950s, the project in 1948 had a sociological orientation.
36. Campbell, Converse, Miller, and Stokes, *The American Voter.*
37. Most political science research has been directed toward the effect of environmental factors on attitude formation, factors such as parents, schools, religious institutions, and peer and adult relationships. More recently, however, the research in genetics suggests that there may be a link between the genes people inherit and the beliefs and attitudes they formulate. Since genes help explain physical appearance, they may also contribute to psychological dispositions and orientations, intelligence, and even political attitudes. See John R. Alford, Carolyn L. Funk, and John R. Hibbing, "Are Political Orientations Genetically Transmitted?" *American Political Science Review,* 99 (May 2005), pp. 153–167.
38. Campbell, Converse, Miller, and Stokes, *The American Voter,* pp. 146–152.
39. Ibid., pp. 133–136. In examining the concept of party identification, Michigan analysts have stressed two dimensions: direction and strength. Others, however, have criticized the Michigan model for overemphasizing party and underemphasizing other factors, such as social class, political ideology, and issue positions. For a thoughtful critique, see Jerrold G. Rusk, "The Michigan Election Studies: A Critical Evaluation." Paper presented at the annual meeting of the American Political Science Association, New York (Sept. 3–6, 1981).
40. See Benjamin Highton and Cindy D. Kam, "The Long-Term Dynamics of Partisanship and Issue Orientations," *Journal of Politics*, 73 (Jan. 2011): 202–215.
41. Janet M. Box-Steffensmeier and Renee M. Smith, "The Dynamic of Aggregate Partisanship," *American Political Science Review* (Sept. 1996), pp. 567–580; Ronald B. Rapoport, "Partisanship Change in a Candidate-Centered Era," *Journal of Politics* (Feb. 1997), pp. 185–199.
42. Aware of the public's view of President Bush, McCain tried to distance himself from the administration by emphasizing that he was an independent thinker, a maverick; Obama's theme was also change.
43. Campbell, Converse, Miller, and Stokes, *The American Voter,* pp. 143, 547. Independents who lean in a partisan direction tend to be better informed than those who do not. These independent leaners have many of the characteristics of party identifiers, including loyalty to the party's candidates. They do not, however, identify themselves as Republicans or Democrats.
44. Key studied the behavior of three groups of voters between 1936 and 1960: switchers, stand-patters, and new voters. He found those who switched their

votes to be interested in and influenced by their own evaluation of policy, personality, and performance. In this sense, Key believed that they exercised an intelligent judgment when voting. V.O. Key, Jr., *The Responsible Electorate* (Cambridge, MA: Harvard University Press, 1966), p. 7.

45. Samuel L. Popkin, *The Reasoning Voter* (Chicago: University of Chicago Press, 1991), p. 43.
46. Morris P. Fiorina, *Retrospective Voting in American National Elections* (New Haven: Yale University Press, 1981), pp. 65–83.
47. Ibid., p. 84.
48. Philip E. Converse, "The Nature of Belief Systems in Mass Publics," in David E. Apter, ed., *Ideology and Discontent* (New York: Free Press, 1964), pp. 206–261.
49. Morris Fiorina, Samuel J. Abrams, and Jeremy C. Pope, *Culture War? The Myth of a Polarized America* (New York: Longman, 2006).
50. Morris P. Fiorina and Matthew S. Levendusky, "Disconnected: The Political Class versus the People," in Peitro S. Nivola and David W. Brady, eds., *Red and Blue Nation? Characteristics and Causes of America's Polarized Politics* (Washington, DC: Brookings Institution, 2006), pp. 49–71; pp. 95–111.
51. According to data in recent American National Election Studies, the level of participation in elections has increased. More people have given money; contacted more friends, neighbors, or acquaintances; attended rallies or other campaign events; and volunteered to work for candidates than in the past. The expansion of turnout in 2004 by both parties, and in 2008 by the Democrats, illustrates this increased activity. American National Election Studies. www.electionstudies.org/nesguide/gd-index.htm#6.
52. See Alan I. Abramowitz, "Disconnected or Joined at the Hip?" in Nivola and Brady, *Red and Blue Nation?* pp. 72–85, and Gary C. Jacobson, "Comment," Ibid. pp. 85–95.
53. A candidate's religion can affect partisan voting behavior. David E. Campbell, John C. Green, and Geoffrey C. Layman, "The Party Faithful: Partisan Images, Candidate Religion, and the Electoral Impact of Party Identification," *American Journal of Political Science*, 55 (Jan. 2011): 42–58.
54. Paul F. Lazarsfeld, Bernard R. Berelson, and Hazel Gaudet, *The People's Choice: How the Voter Makes Up His Mind in a Presidential Campaign* (New York: Columbia University Press, 1948); Bernard R. Berelson, Paul F. Lazarsfeld, and William N. McPhee, *Voting: A Study of Opinion Formation in a Presidential Campaign* (Chicago: University of Chicago Press, 1954).
55. Paul Allen Beck, Russell J. Dalton, Steven Greene, and Robert Huckfeldt, "The Social Calculus of Voting: Interpersonal, Media, and Organizational Influences on Presidential Choices," *American Political Science Review*, 96 (March 2002), pp. 67–69.
56. Green and Gerber, *Get Out the Vote*, p. 34.
57. This description of the New Deal realignment is based primarily on the discussion in Everett Carll Ladd, Jr., with Charles D. Hadley, *Transformations of the American Party System* (New York: Norton, 1975), pp. 31–87.
58. David Leege C. and Lyman A. Kellstedt, eds., *Rediscovering the Religious Factor in American Politics* (Armonk, NY: M. E. Sharpe. 1993); John C. Green, "The American Religious Landscape and Political Attitudes: A Baseline for 2004," Ray C. Bliss Institute of Applied Politics, University of Akron. www.uakron.edu/bliss/docs/Religious_Landscape_2004.pdf.
59. The choice of Palin was intended to appeal to women who had supported Hillary Clinton and were disappointed that she did not win the Democratic nomination,

according to Nicolle Wallace, a senior adviser to the McCain–Palin campaign. Jamieson, *Electing the President*, p. 13.

60. Abramson, Aldrich, and Rohde, *Change and Continuity in 2008,* pp. 120–121.
61. Lyman A. Kellstedt, John C. Green, James L. Guth, and Corwin E. Schmidt, "Religious Voting Blocs in the 1992 Election: Year of the Evangelical?" *Sociology of Religion, 55* (1994), pp. 307–326; Robert B. Fowler and Allen D. Hertzke, *Religion and Politics in America: Faith, Culture, and Strategic Choice* (Boulder, CO: Westview Press, 1995).
62. The turnout of African Americans was actually higher than white turnout in 2008.
63. For an extended discussion of the impact of race on the Democratic Party, see Robert Huckfeldt and Carol Weitzel Kohfeld, *Race and the Decline of Class in American Politics* (Urbana: University of Illinois Press, 1989).

The Nomination

PART

4 CHAPTER PARTY RULES AND THEIR IMPACT: THE LEGAL ENVIRONMENT

INTRODUCTION

Presidential nominees are selected by the delegates who attend their party's national nominating convention. The manner in which these delegates are chosen, however, influences the choice of nominees and also affects the influence of the state and its party leadership.

State law determines the procedures for delegate selection. Today, these procedures also have to conform to the general guidelines and rules established by the national parties. Prior to the 1970s, they did not. Under the old system, statutes passed by a state legislature reflected the needs and desires of state party leaders. Naturally, these laws were designed to buttress that leadership and extend its clout.

Although primary elections were held, many of them were advisory; the actual selection of the delegates was left to caucuses, conventions, or committees, which were more easily controlled by party officials. The selection of favorite-son candidates, tapped by state party leaders, prevented meaningful contests in many states. There were also impediments to delegates getting on the ballot: high fees, lengthy petitions, and early filing dates. Winner-take-all provisions gave a great advantage to candidates backed by the party organization, as did rules requiring delegates to vote as a unit.

Popular participation in the selection of convention delegates has been a relatively recent phenomenon in the history of national nominating conventions. It began in the 1970s when the Democratic Party adopted a series of reforms that affected the period during which delegates could be selected, the procedures for choosing them, and ultimately their behavior at the party's national nominating convention. Although these Democratic rules limited the states' discretion, they did not result in uniform voting practices in primaries and caucuses. Considerable variation still exists in how delegates are chosen, how the vote is apportioned, and who participates in the selection.

This chapter explores these rules and their consequences for the nomination process. It is organized into three sections: the first details the changes in party rules; the second considers the legal challenges to these rules and the Supreme Court's decisions on them; the third section examines the impact of the rules changes on the parties and their electorates.

REFORMING THE NOMINATION PROCESS: DEMOCRATIC PARTY RULE CHANGES

The catalyst for the changes in the delegate selection rules was the tumultuous Democratic convention of 1968, a convention in which Senator Hubert Humphrey won the nomination without actively campaigning in the party's primaries. Yet the primaries of that year were very important. They had become the vehicle by which Democrats could protest the Johnson administration's conduct of the war in Vietnam. Senator Eugene McCarthy, the first of the antiwar candidates, had challenged Lyndon Johnson in the New Hampshire primary. To the surprise of many political observers, McCarthy received 42.4 percent of the vote, almost as much as the president, who got 49.5 percent.[1]

Four days after McCarthy's unexpectedly strong showing, Senator Robert Kennedy, brother of the late president and a political rival of Johnson, declared his candidacy for the nation's highest office. With protests against the war mounting across the country and divisions within the Democratic Party intensifying, Johnson bowed out, declaring that he did not want the nation's involvement in Southeast Asia to become a divisive political issue.

Johnson's withdrawal cleared the way for Hubert Humphrey, the vice president, to run. Humphrey, however, waited almost a month to announce his candidacy. His late entrance into the Democratic nomination process intentionally precluded a primary campaign since filing deadlines had expired in most of the states. Like Johnson, Humphrey did not want to become the focal point of antiwar opposition, nor did he have a grassroots organization to match McCarthy's and Kennedy's. What he did have was the support of most national and state Democratic leaders, including the president.

The last big-state primary in 1968 was California's. In it, Kennedy scored a significant win, but during the celebration that followed, he was assassinated. His death left McCarthy as the principal antiestablishment, antiwar candidate, but he was far short of a convention majority. Despite the last-minute entrance of Senator George McGovern, who hoped to rally Kennedy delegates to his candidacy, Humphrey easily won the nomination.

To make matters worse for those who opposed Humphrey and the administration's war efforts, an amendment to the party platform calling for an unconditional end to the bombing of North Vietnam was defeated. McCarthy and Kennedy delegates felt victimized by the nomination process and the resulting Humphrey victory. They were angry. Compounding the divisions within the convention were demonstrations outside of it. Thousands of youthful protesters, calling for an end to the war, congregated in the streets of Chicago. To maintain order, the police, under direction from Mayor Richard Daley, used strong-arm tactics to disperse the crowds. Clashes between police and protesters followed. Television news crews filmed these confrontations, and the networks showed them during their convention coverage. The spectacle of police beating demonstrators further inflamed emotions and led to calls for party reform, not only from those who attended the convention but also from those who watched it on television.

To try to unify a divided party, Humphrey and his supporters agreed to the demands of dissident delegates to establish a commission to study procedures for electing and seating convention delegates and to propose ways of improving the selection process. Initially chaired by Senator George McGovern, the commission recommended a series of reforms aimed at encouraging greater rank-and-file participation during the nomination stage and the choosing of convention delegates who were more representative of the party's electorate. They also desired the process to be timely, to occur in the year of the general election, and to be accessible to a wider range of candidates.

To achieve these objectives, the commission proposed that delegate selection be a *fair reflection* of Democratic sentiment within the state and, implicitly, less closely tied to the wishes of state party leaders. Rules were approved by the party to make it easier for individuals to run as delegates, to limit the size of the districts from which they could be chosen, and to require that the number of delegates elected be proportional to the popular vote that they, or the candidates to whom they were pledged, received. A requirement that delegates be chosen no earlier than the calendar year of the election was also established.

Additionally, Democrats tried to prevent Independents and, especially, partisans of other parties, from participating in the selection of Democratic delegates. The difficulty, however, was to determine who was a Democrat since some states did not require or even permit registration by party. When implementing this rule, the national party adopted a very liberal interpretation of Democratic affiliation. People who identified themselves as Democrats at the time of voting, or those requesting Democratic ballots, were considered to be Democrats for the purpose of participating in the primaries. This process of identification effectively permitted crossover voting, allowing Republicans or Independents to cross over and vote in the Democratic primaries in some states. The only primaries that the Democratic rules effectively prohibited were those that were open, primaries in which voters were given the ballots of both major parties, discard one, and vote the other.

In addition to translating public preferences into delegate selection, another major objective of the reforms was to equalize representation in the delegations themselves. Three groups in particular—African Americans, women, and people under thirty—had protested their underrepresentation on party councils and at the conventions. Their representatives and others sympathetic to their plight pressed the party for more equitable representation. The reform commission reacted to these pressures by proposing a rule requiring that all states represent these particular groups in reasonable relationship to their presence in the state population. Failure to do so was viewed as *prima facie* evidence of discrimination. In point of fact, the party had established quotas. Considerable opposition developed to the application of this rule during the 1972 nomination process, and it was subsequently modified to require only that states implement affirmative action plans for those groups that had been subject to past discrimination.[2]

Still another goal of the reforms, to involve more Democrats in the selection process, was achieved not only by the fair reflection rule but also by making primaries the preferred method of delegate selection. To avoid a challenge to the composition of their delegation, states switched to primaries in which delegates were elected directly by the people.[3] Caucuses in which party regulars selected the delegates were still permitted, but they, too, were redesigned to encourage greater rank-and-file participation. No longer could state party leaders vote a large number of proxies for the delegates of their choice. Caucuses had to be publicly announced with adequate time given for campaigning. Moreover, they had to be conducted in stages, and three-fourths of the delegates had to be chosen in districts no larger than those for members of Congress.

The rules changes, which were approved by the Democratic National Committee, achieved some of these initial objectives. Turnout increased; representation of the Democratic electorate at the party's convention improved; more candidates sought the nomination; and two candidates not associated with the national Democratic Party leadership, George McGovern (1972) and Jimmy Carter (1976), won their party's nomination.

Problems remained, however. Rank-and-file participation in the primaries was not as large as anticipated; the states that held their contest early received disproportionate candidate and media attention, had higher turnouts, and exercised more influence. It took longer than in the past to determine a winner, which, in turn, extended divisions within the party that became harder to heal for the general election. The amount of money needed to run for the nomination increased substantially. In addition, divisions between the winning candidate and the national party organization were becoming increasingly evident. These included divisions between the policy priorities and even issue positions of the nominee and the platform of the party, the organization of the nominee and that of the party, and the delegates selected to go to the national convention and party leaders who were not selected.

Finally, and most importantly, even though the Democrats constituted a partisan majority in the 1970s, they lost two of three presidential elections by large amounts after the reforms were implemented and had difficulty governing when they were in power from 1977 to 1980. From the perspective of the party leadership, the new delegate selection rules needed to be modified.

There were three principal problems. The first was the disproportionate influence of the early states on the outcome of the nomination. The second was the continuing unequal representation of the partisan electorate in delegate selection and convention participation. The third problem was the declining influence of party leaders on the presidential nominating process and the fraying connection between the presidential nominee and other elected national party officials.

FIXING THE CALENDAR

The nomination calendar was becoming unbalanced. The attention given to the states that held their nomination contests early in the year by the candidates and the press created an incentive for other states to move the date of their primary or caucus forward, and they have done so. Over the years, the nomination schedule has become more and more front-loaded and compressed. In 1996, almost two-thirds of all the Democratic convention delegates were chosen by the end of March; in 2000 and 2004, two-thirds were chosen by mid-March; in 2008, almost 60 percent were chosen by the first Tuesday in February and more than 80 percent by the first Tuesday in March.

There are several problems associated with a front-loaded primary process. As states move their presidential nomination earlier and earlier, they have separated presidential selection from other state nominations, thereby increasing election costs and potentially damaging party unity. The partisan electorate has suffered as well. The sequential nature of the nomination process facilitates public learning more than a compressed process does. In recent nominations, by the time people turn their attention to the presidential nomination campaign, the field of candidates has been narrowed and much of the issue debate has already occurred. Moreover, once a front-runner emerges with a sizable delegate lead, turnout declines, thereby reducing the proportion of partisans who participate and have a voice in the selection of the party's standard-bearer.

A front-loaded nomination process reinforces and magnifies resource inequality. It allows the candidates who have the most money, those with national reputations, to wage media-oriented, multistate campaigns, forcing others to focus their efforts on one or a few of the early states. And even if lesser-known, less-well-funded candidates are successful, they have less time to take advantage of their good fortune to raise additional funds in a highly compressed nomination calendar. The front-loaded schedule forces all candidates to begin running a year or two before the nomination in order to raise the money and gain the visibility they need to compete.

To encourage greater participation of rank-and-file partisans, achieve better representation of all groups within the party, and provide more opportunities for a larger field of candidates, the Democrats have tried to impose a "window" during which primaries and caucuses may be held; they have also instituted a bonus delegate system to reward states that hold their caucuses and primaries later in the spring.

Initially, the Democrats allowed states to hold their presidential nominations from the second Tuesday in March to the second Tuesday in June. Pressured to begin earlier, the window was extended forward the first Tuesday in March in 2004 and the first Tuesday in February in 2008. Even though the competition between Barack Obama and Hillary Rodham Clinton lasted for the duration of the nomination period, a Democratic Change Commission recommended after the 2008 election that the official starting date for 2012 revert back to the first Tuesday in March, a change that the Democratic National Committee has approved.

What to do with those states, such as Iowa and New Hampshire, whose laws require them to hold their contests before others has been a perennial issue since the rules changes went into effect.[4] Believing that the national party could not conduct its own selection process in these states, the Democrats decided that the best they could do was grant Iowa and New Hampshire exceptions to the regulations that imposed the calendar on the other states. However, complaints within the party that these two states were unrepresentative of rank-and-file Democrats and that they skewed the selection process led the party to revisit the issue of who goes first prior to the 2008 nomination process. To improve the representation of the party's rank and file, Democrats decided to allow Nevada with its growing Hispanic population to hold its caucus after Iowa's, and South Carolina with a large number of African Americans to hold its primary after New Hampshire's.

When Michigan and Florida also decided to hold their primaries early in 2008, thereby violating the Democratic nomination calendar, the party pressured candidates not to campaign in these states and initially indicated that they would not seat delegates chosen in these elections. After the nomination was decided, however, Michigan and Florida were given half their delegate votes back in an effort to unify the party for the general election but still penalize the states for violating party rules.

In addition to imposing sanctions, the party also tried to encourage states to hold their nomination contests later by offering them more convention delegates if they did so—the later the date, the more delegates they would receive.[5] However, only ten states took advantage of this opportunity; a total of fifty-four bonus delegates were awarded to them in 2008, with North Carolina gaining the most, twenty-four. The bonus system remains in effect for 2012.

Improving Representation

A second problem concerns the fair reflection principle and its application. The formulas states initially used in converting the popular vote into delegate support did not always reflect the wishes of most partisan voters. And when it did, the results did not always work to the party's advantage.

Straight proportional voting theoretically extended the nomination process, adversely affecting the party and its nominees in the general election; it diffused power, reducing the collective influence of state party officials, two reasons why states initially modified the Democrats' proportional voting rule. For the candidates, proportional voting sometimes discouraged them from investing resources in districts that were highly competitive and from which they could gain only minimal advantage; it encouraged them to concentrate on less-competitive districts in which they enjoyed the most support. This strategy resulted in lower turnout in the caucuses and primaries, which in turn, led to lower turnout of partisans in the general election.

The issue of proportionality came to a head in the 1980s when Democratic front-runners Walter Mondale (1984) and Michael Dukakis (1988) each received a larger proportion of the delegates than the popular vote. Jesse Jackson, another candidate in those elections, in contrast, won less. His complaints led the party to prohibit state discretion in applying the fair reflection rule. Today, candidates receive delegates in the Democratic primaries strictly in proportion to the vote they receive within electoral districts, provided they get at least 15 percent of the total. This percentage, referred to as a *threshold*, was designed to discourage frivolous candidates from running and keeping the party divided for an extended period.

Democratic rules also specify that no more than 25 percent of the delegates can be selected on a state-wide basis. The rest are chosen in districts that can be no larger than congressional districts. The allocation of at-large and district delegates is based on the population and the Democratic vote in the last three presidential elections. This allocation formula advantages the most Democratic areas, which tend to be districts with large proportions of minority voters. Barack Obama designed a strategy to take advantage of higher concentrations of Democratic delegates in urban districts that increased the number of convention delegates he received.

Another representational problem with which the Democrats had to contend initially was the selection of more men than women as delegates. To rectify the balance and achieve gender equality, the Democrats now require the elected delegates to consist of equal proportions of men and women.

Despite the changes designed to reflect partisan voting preferences during the nomination process more accurately, inequities still exist. Hillary Rodham Clinton received a higher proportion of the popular vote in the 2008 Democratic primaries (including Florida and Michigan)—48 percent—than the proportion of pledged delegates she received from these states—39 percent. In the caucus states, the discrepancy between the vote and the delegates was much less: Obama won 63 percent of the popular vote in the caucuses and 65 percent of the pledged delegates from those states.

Still concerned about the representativeness of the caucus process, the Democratic Change Commission recommended that caucus states adopt a "Best Practices" program which would help them plan, organize, and staff their caucuses in such a manner that they would "maximize the opportunity for full participation for all Democratic voters." This recommendation was adopted by the Democratic National Committee for the 2012 nomination process, but the vagueness of the rule still gives caucus states considerable discretion in designing and conducting their caucuses. Box 4.1 describes how the Iowa caucus works.

BOX 4.1 | The Iowa Caucus: How It Works

STAGES

Step 1: Caucuses are held in nearly 1,800 precincts within the state to choose approximately 2,500 delegates to 99 county conventions.

Step 2: One month later, conventions are held in counties to elect delegates to the five congressional district conventions.

Step 3: Conventions are held in congressional districts to elect district-level delegates to national party conventions. The same delegates also attend the state convention.

Step 4: State conventions elect at-large delegates to the national party convention.

Democrats also select their state party and elected official delegates.

PROCEDURES FOR THE FIRST-ROUND PRECINCT CAUCUSES

Democrats: Only registered Democrats who live in the precinct and can vote may participate. Attendees are asked to join preference groups for candidates. A group must consist of at least 15 percent of those present to be viable. Nonviable groups are dissolved, and people in these groups are free to join other viable groups. Much lobbying occurs at this stage of the meeting. Delegates are allocated to candidates strictly on the basis of each group's proportion to the caucus as a whole.

Republicans: Attendees, who must be eligible to vote but do not have to be registered as Republicans, cast a presidential preference vote by secret ballot, which is tabulated on a statewide basis. Delegates to the county conventions are then selected by whatever method the caucus chooses—either by direct election or proportionally on the basis of a straw vote.

Empowering the Leadership

The third unintended consequence of the Democratic rule changes that the party revisited was the decreasing number of party leaders and elected officials who were chosen as delegates. Unhappy about their loss of influence over the presidential selection process as well as their decreasing visibility and notoriety at the nominating conventions, state and national party leaders convinced the party to establish a new category of delegates.[6]

To facilitate closer ties between the nominees and the party, the Democrats established a category of add-on delegates to be composed of political leaders and elected officials (PLEOs). Included in this group were all members of the Democratic National Committee, all Democratic governors and members of Congress, plus a number of other national, state, and local officials. These PLEOs were to be unpledged. It was thought that this group of distinguished Democrats might be in a position to hold the balance of power if the primaries did not produce a winner, a situation that has not occurred since the rules were changed.[7] Although these superdelegates, as they were called, have not been in a position to broker a divided convention, they have had an impact on delegate selection by their endorsement of candidates. These endorsements, which have tended to help frontrunners, led to the criticism that the PLEOs made the Democratic selection process more elitist and less democratic. The fear that the superdelegates could reverse the results of a popular-based nomination process was expressed by Obama's campaign and its supporters in 2008. Hillary Clinton, the Democratic front-runner, initially received the endorsements of a majority of the superdelegates, who were eager to back the prospective nominee. Barack Obama's early victories and his growing lead in the number of pledged delegates created a potential problem for the superdelegates who had endorsed Clinton as well as for the democratic character of the party's nomination process. The problem did not materialize, however, because the superdelegates, politicians and political leaders, were sensitive to the preferences of voters of their states. Thus, as Obama neared a majority of convention delegates, party leaders and elected officials jumped on his bandwagon.

Nonetheless, the possibility of superdelegates upsetting the electoral results of the caucuses and primaries prompted the Democratic Change Commission to recommend that superdelegates no longer be unpledged. The commission established a new category of pledged superdelegates, eliminated the unpledged ones, and added the superdelegates to their respective state's delegations.

Technically, all Democratic delegates can still vote for whom they want at the national convention because in 1980 the Democrats adopted a rule that allows delegates to vote their consciences rather than simply redeem their campaign pledges. However, the requirement that people indicate in writing their presidential preference before they are put on candidate slates in the caucuses and primaries makes it highly unlikely that many of them will change their minds at the convention, unless the candidate to whom they are pledged encourages them to do so. In 2008, 19.3 percent of the delegates who attended the Democratic convention were superdelegates.

REPUBLICAN RULES

Although the Republicans initially did not change their rules as quickly or as extensively as the Democrats, they still were affected by the Democratic rules changes. Since state legislatures enact laws governing party nominations, and since the Democrats controlled many of these legislatures in the 1970s and 1980s when laws were changed to conform to the new Democratic rules, some of the reforms were literally forced on the Republicans by the states. Subsequently, the Republicans did make changes of their own to eliminate discrimination and prevent a small group from controlling the nomination process. Nonetheless, it has been the philosophy of the GOP to give states discretion to determine their own rules and procedures for delegate selection and then abide by them at the national level.

It is the Republican convention that formally approves the rules for choosing delegates for the next Republican convention. This practice has effectively prevented rules changes between conventions. In 2008, however, the rules adopted by the Republican National Convention authorized the creation of a Republican Temporary Delegate Selection Committee to examine the calendar and process for delegate selection and to make recommendations to the Republican National Committee, which was given authority to adopt new recommendations without amendment and by virtue of a two-thirds vote.

On August 5, 2010, the RNC approved new rules that established a revised calendar for Republican primaries and caucuses. That calendar designates the first Tuesday in March as the official opening date when any state can hold its caucus or primary. However, the new rules also granted exceptions to Iowa, New Hampshire, Nevada, and South Carolina, which were permitted to start one month earlier, beginning the first Tuesday in February. Any state that violates these rules and holds its nomination before the designated period automatically loses half of its allocated convention delegates, a penalty that was imposed on six states in 2008. Like the Democrats, the Republicans have also set up a bonus system that gives additional delegates to states that hold their nomination later in the calendar year, but thus far, there have been few takers.[8]

Another change, which the Republicans will implement in 2012, is a proportional selection rule for any state that holds its caucus or primary in March. This change was intended to discourage early winner-take-all primaries that advantage Republican front-runners and effectively shorten the selection process. In 1988, George H. W. Bush won 59 percent of the popular vote in states holding some type of winner-take-all voting on Super Tuesday but won 97 percent of the delegates from those states, giving him an almost insurmountable lead over his principal opponent, Robert Dole. Similarly in 2008, John McCain received 38 percent of the Republican vote in states holding winner-take-all primaries on or before February 5, the first Tuesday of the month. He won 81 percent of the delegates from those states (578 out of 712), thereby effectively determining the outcome of the Republican nomination, although it took him until March 4 to win the requisite number of delegates to secure his victory. The new regulation for proportional voting in Republican primaries does not apply to states that hold their nomination after March or the four that are allowed to do so before March.

Whereas the Democrats prescribe a minimum threshold to receive delegate support, the Republicans do not. Their threshold varies from state to state. Nor do Republicans have special categories of delegates for party leaders and elected officials, although Republican state and national leaders have traditionally attended their party's conventions in greater proportion than their Democratic counterparts. The GOP also does not have a requirement for gender equality. Since the 1980s, the proportion of women at Republican conventions has ranged from 29 percent to 44 percent.

A summary of delegate selection rules for the 2012 nomination appears in Table 4.1.

TABLE 4.1 | DELEGATE SELECTION RULES

	Democrats	Republicans
Rank-and-file participation	Open to all voters who want to participate as Democrats.	No national rule.*
Apportionment of delegates within states	75 percent of base delegation elected at congressional district level or lower; 25 percent elected at large on a proportional basis.	No national rule; may be chosen at large.
Apportionment of delegates to states	Democratic delegate counts are determined by the jurisdiction's presidential vote in 2000, 2004, and 2008, along with the jurisdiction's electoral vote allocation based on 2010 census.	Republican delegate counts are based on the number of Republicans elected to the state legislatures, governors, and to the U.S. House and Senate through December 31, 2011.
Allocation of delegates	By proportional vote in both caucuses and primaries.	By proportional vote for primaries and caucuses held in March.
Party leaders and elected officials	DNC members, Democratic members of the U.S. House and Senate, Democratic governors, and distinguished party leaders are all allocated proportionally according to the state-wide vote.	None.
Composition of delegations	Equal gender division; no discrimination; affirmative action plan required with goals and timetables for specified groups (African Americans, Native Americans, and Asian/Pacific Americans).	No gender rule but each state is asked to try to achieve equal gender representation; "positive action" to achieve broadest possible participation required.
Time frame	Prewindow for Iowa, Nevada, New Hampshire, and South Carolina opens February 1, 2012; all others may hold caucuses and primaries on or after the first Tuesday in March.	Prewindow for Iowa, Nevada, New Hampshire, and South Carolina opens February 1, 2012; all others may hold caucuses and primaries on or after the first Tuesday in March.
Threshold	15 percent.	No national rule.
Delegate voting	May vote their conscience.	No national rule.
Enforcement and penalties	Automatic reduction in state delegation size for violation of time frames, allocation, or threshold rules.	Reduction of delegation size by one-half for violating time frame and proportional voting rules.

*Republican national rules prescribe that selection procedures accord with the laws of the state.

THE LEGALITY OF PARTY RULES

As previously mentioned, party reforms, to be effective, must be enacted into law. Most states have complied with the new rules. A few have not, sometimes resulting in confrontation between these states and the national party. When New Hampshire and Iowa refused to move the dates of their respective primary and caucuses into the Democrats' window period in 1984, the national party backed down. But previously, when Illinois chose its 1972 delegates in a manner that conflicted with new Democratic rules, the party sought to impose its rules on the state.

In addition to the political controversy that was engendered in that case, the conflict between the Democratic National Committee and Illinois also presented an important legal question: Which body—the national party or the state—has the higher authority on delegate selection? In its landmark decision *Cousins v. Wigoda*, 419 U.S. 477 (1975), the Supreme Court sided with the national party. The Court stated that political parties were private organizations with rights of association protected by the Constitution. Moreover, choosing presidential candidates was a national experience that states could not abridge unless there were compelling constitutional reasons to do so. Although states could establish their own primary laws, the party could determine the criteria for representation at its national convention.

Crossover voting in open primaries prompted still another court challenge between the rights of parties to prescribe rules for delegate selection and the rights of states to establish their own election laws. Democratic rules prohibit open primaries. Four states had conducted this type of election in 1976. Three voluntarily changed their law; a fourth, Wisconsin, did not. It permitted voters who participated in the primary to request the ballot of either party. The national party's Compliance Review Commission ordered the state party to design an alternative process. It refused. The case went to court. Citing the precedent of *Cousins v. Wigoda*, the Supreme Court held in the case of *Democratic Party of the U.S. v. Wisconsin ex. rel. La Follette*, 450 U.S. 107 (1981), that a state had no right to interfere with the party's delegate selection process unless it demonstrated a compelling reason to do so. It ruled that Wisconsin had not demonstrated such a reason; hence, the Democratic Party could refuse to seat delegates who were selected in a manner that violated its rules.[9]

In the case of *California Democratic Party v. Jones*, 530 U.S. 567 (2000), the Supreme Court reiterated its judgment by invalidating California's "blanket" primary system, which voters had approved in a 1996 ballot initiative. The initiative required state officials to provide a uniform ballot in which voters, regardless of their partisan affiliation, could vote for any candidate of any party for any elected position. Naturally, the parties were upset by the possibility that their nominees could be determined by people who did not consider themselves partisans of their party. Four California state parties, including the Democrats and Republicans, went to court to challenge the constitutionality of the initiative, claiming that it violated their First Amendment right to freedom of association. The Supreme Court agreed. Its majority opinion held that the blanket primary system represented "a clear and present danger" to the parties and was therefore unconstitutional.

Although these Court decisions have given the political parties the legal authority to design and enforce their own rules, the practicality of doing so is another matter. Other than going to court if a state refuses to change its election law, a party, particularly a national party, has only two viable options: require the state party to conduct its own delegate selection process in conformity to national rules and penalize it if it does not do so, or grant the state party an exemption so that it can abide by the law of the state.

The rule for allocating a specific number of delegates to the states has also generated legal controversy, but in this case, within the Republican Party. The formula that the Republicans use contains a bonus for states that voted Republican in the previous presidential election (see Table 4.2).[10] Opponents of this rule contend that it discriminates against the large states because bonuses are allocated regardless of size. Moreover, they argue that the large states are apt to be more competitive and thus less likely to receive a bonus. Particularly hard hit are states in the Northeast and on the Pacific Coast, which have gone Democratic in recent elections. The Ripon Society, a moderate Republican organization, has twice challenged the constitutionality of this apportionment rule, but it has not been successful. The Democratic apportionment formula, which results in larger conventions than the Republicans, has also been subject to some controversy, but not in recent years.[11]

THE IMPACT OF THE RULES CHANGES

The reforms to the nomination process have produced some of their desired effects. They have opened up the process by allowing more people to participate. They have increased minority representation at the conventions. And they have weakened the ability of party leaders to dictate the delegates and their voting behavior, but party elites still enjoy disproportionate influence in the process.

TURNOUT

One objective of the reforms was to involve more of the party's rank and file in the delegate selection process. This goal has been partially achieved. In 1968, before the reforms, only 12 million people participated in primaries, approximately 11 percent of the voting-age population (VAP). In 1972, the first nomination contest held after the changes were made, that number rose to 22 million. For the next three decades, turnout rose and fell depending on the level of competition within the major parties and the number of weeks or months it took to effectively determine a winner. In 2004, only the Democrats had a competitive nomination and it was settled early. Less than 10 percent of eligible voters, 16.3 million people, participated.[12] In 2008, it was another story. With competitive contests in both parties, almost 58 million—approximately one quarter of the voting age population—participated (37.2 million in the Democratic nomination process and 20.8 million in the Republican one).[13]

Table 4.2 | Turnout of Eligible Voters in the 2008 Presidential Primaries

Date	State	Turnout
Jan. 8	New Hampshire	53.6
Jan. 15	Michigan	20.0
Jan. 19	Florida	34.0
Jan. 19/26	South Carolina	30.3
Feb. 5	Alabama	32.2
	Arizona	24.2
	Arkansas	26.8
	California	40.0
	Connecticut	20.5
	Delaware	23.8
	Georgia	32.0
	Illinois	33.8
	Massachusetts	38.2
	Missouri	33.0
	New Jersey	29.2
	New York	19.5
	Oklahoma	29.1
	Tennessee	26.1
	Utah	24.7
Feb. 9	Louisiana	17.7
Feb. 12	District of Columbia	30.1
	Maryland	31.5
	Virginia	26.9
Feb. 19	Washington*	30.6
	Wisconsin	37.1
March 4	Ohio	42.4
	Rhode Island	28.4
	Texas	28.4
	Vermont	40.7
March 11	Mississippi	27.5
April 22	Pennsylvania	34.0
May 6	Indiana	37.3
	North Carolina	32.8
May 13	West Virginia	32.5

continued

TABLE 4.2 | TURNOUT OF ELIGIBLE VOTERS IN THE 2008 PRESIDENTIAL PRIMARIES *continued*

Date	State	Turnout
May 20	Kentucky	29.2
	Oregon	43.3
May 27	Idaho	17.7
June 3	Montana	38.7
	South Dakota	28.4

*Democratic primary is a nonbinding, preference vote.

Source: Michael McDonald, "2008 Presidential Nomination Contest Turnout Rates," October 8, 2008. http://elections.gmu.edu/Turnout_2008P.html

The level of participation in presidential nominations varies with the type of election. It has always been greater in primaries than in caucuses. In Iowa, which traditionally holds the first caucus, only 6.1 percent participated in 2004 when only the Democrats had a contested race; in 2008, with competition in both parties, 16.1 percent of eligible voters came to the caucuses: 108,000 (5 percent) Republicans and 239,000 (11.1 percent) Democrats.

Primary turnout is much larger than that of caucuses, especially for the early contests. New Hampshire, which has the first primary, usually has the highest percentage of voters participating. In 2008, 53.6 percent of those eligible voted in the New Hampshire primary: about 24 percent for Republican candidates and 29 percent for Democrats. The key to primary turnout is the date and competitiveness of the election. Table 4.2 indicates levels of turnout in 2008. That year the Republican race was decided on March 4 while the Democratic contest continued until the end.

Not only does turnout vary among states, it also varies among population groups within the states. People who are better educated, have higher incomes, and are older vote more often than do younger, less-educated, and poorer people. In general, the lower the turnout, the greater the demographic differences between voters and nonvoters. Although this pattern of participation has persisted in recent elections, the success of the Jesse Jackson campaigns in 1984 and 1988 in attracting minority voters and, to a much lesser extent, the campaign of Pat Robertson in 1988, which appealed to white, evangelical Protestants, muted some of the differences that had existed between primary voters and their party's electorate in these elections. In 2008, the Obama campaign increased the turnout of African Americans in the Democratic nomination process.

There have also been claims that primary voters tend to be more ideologically extreme in their political beliefs than the average party voter, with Democrats being more liberal and Republicans more conservative than their party as a whole. Strong empirical evidence has not been found to support this contention, although studies have shown southern Democrats that participate in their party's primary tend to be more moderate than the southern electorate as a whole.[14] For most of the country, primary voters do not appear to be more ideologically extreme than people who vote in the general election, but convention delegates who represent them do.[15]

Finally, higher turnout in the nomination process benefits the parties because it encourages more partisans to participate. It also informs and energizes the party's electorate, thereby priming it for the general election. The long gap between the primaries and the beginning of the general election campaign, however, reduces that priming effect.

REPRESENTATION

Another goal of the reforms was to improve the representative character of the nomination process both with respect to the electorate that participated in the caucuses and primaries and the delegates who represented them at the national nominating conventions.

Prior to the reforms, the people who voted in the nomination contests were not representative of their party's rank and file. Part of the rationale for the Democratic rules changes for 2008, which added one caucus after Iowa (Nevada) and one primary after New Hampshire (South Carolina), was to better represent Hispanics and African Americans, two groups that constitute major components of the Democrats' electoral coalition. African Americans, 20 to 25 percent of the Democratic vote in recent presidential elections, made up 55 percent of that party's electorate in South Carolina and 15 percent in Nevada.[16] Hispanics also made up 15 percent of the participants in Nevada's Democratic caucuses.[17]

The front-loading by larger states in 2008, although certainly not prescribed nor encouraged by party rules, actually improved representation among Democrats since the large states that held their contests on February 5 (California, Illinois, New Jersey, and New York) are demographically more reflective of rank-and-file Democrats than are many of the smaller states that traditionally held their nomination contests toward the beginning of the process.

Large-state front-loading combined with winner-take-all voting had the opposite effect for the Republicans. Early primaries in states that usually went Democratic gave Independents and moderate Republicans a larger voice than they otherwise would have had in the GOP's delegate selection process, helping the more moderate John McCain and hurting his more conservative opponents.

In theory, the more representative the nomination electorate, the more likely that the party's standard-bearers and its platform will reflect the wishes of its rank and file. One of the criticisms of the reforms that the major parties initiated in the 1970s was that they gave organized groups and party activists greater opportunities to affect the outcome of the nominations. That did not happen in 2008. The nomination winners had been critical of the influence special interests exert on American politics and government. Although Obama refused to accept PAC contributions, McCain did; both received nonparty group endorsements. The demographic makeup of each party's convention delegates still have not accurately reflected its rank and file, much less the general electorate. The Democrats better represent women and minorities than do the Republicans, but these two groups also constitute a much larger proportion of the Democrats' electoral coalition.

Ideologically, Democratic delegates have overrepresented liberals and moderates within their party's electoral coalition; Republican delegates have overrepresented conservatives. Regular churchgoers were overrepresented at both major party conventions, although the greater religiosity of the Republican delegates was also indicative of voters in that party's electoral coalition. Interestingly, delegates at both nominating conventions in 2008 believed that economic issues would be more important to voters than did the general public in mid-August.[18]

PARTY ORGANIZATION AND LEADERSHIP

Although increasing turnout and improving representation have been two desired effects of the reforms, weakening the state party organizations and their leadership has not. Yet this development seems to have resulted from the reforms as well. By promoting internal democracy, the primaries initially created divisions within party organizations that already had been weakened by new modes of campaigning, the loss of patronage opportunities, and the growth of social services provided by state and local governments. Moreover, the rules changes have encouraged the proliferation of candidates, which in turn has led to the creation of separate electoral organizations that can rival the regular party organization and weaken its organizational capacity to affect the presidential electoral process.

Party leaders can still use their influence with their state legislatures to help determine the date on which the nomination contest will be held and the rules that govern it; they can also use their organization to support a particular candidate, but they can no longer dictate the composition of their state delegation and their votes at the national nominating convention. Leaders also can work with interest group leaders, party donors, and partisan-oriented media to endorse candidates and mobilize support for them during the nomination. Referred to as party elites, the leaders and their activist supporters band together to pursue a range of overlapping and disparate policy goals.[19] The influence of these elites is greatest in the first stage of the contest, the so-called invisible primary, when their endorsements and resources effectively narrow the field, identify the front-runners, gain media attention for them, and shape public opinion, as reflected in the prenomination polls.

Do partisan divisions, created and inflated by the nomination process, adversely affect the party's chance in the general election? Some political scientists have argued that they do.[20] They claim that the longer and more divisive the nomination process, the more likely that it will hurt the party's nominee in the general election.

Yet the election of Bill Clinton in 1992 and of Barack Obama in 2008, both after extended nomination battles, suggests that there is more that unifies partisans in the general election than divides them. The passage of time, the healing efforts of the winning candidates, and shared political beliefs and perspectives of the candidate and their fellow partisans can overcome a divisive nomination, particularly one that focuses more on personal than policy differences. Other factors, such as the electoral environment, the quality of the candidates, and situational factors such as the recessions of 1992 and 2008, seem to have a much greater impact on the general election than does the residue from the nomination process.[21]

WINNERS AND LOSERS

Rules changes are never neutral. They usually benefit one group at the expense of another. Similarly, they tend to help certain candidates and hurt others. That is why candidates have tried to influence the rules and why the rules themselves have been changed so frequently. Candidate organizations and interest groups have put continuous pressure on state and national parties to modify the calendar and rules to increase their own clout in the selection process.

Clearly, the prohibition of discrimination, the requirement for affirmative action, and the rule requiring an equal number of men and women in state delegations have improved the representation of women and minorities for the Democrats. For candidates seeking their party's nomination, this change has required that slates of delegates supporting a candidate be demographically balanced to ensure that many groups are included.

The openness of the process and the greater participation by the party's rank and file have encouraged those who have not been party regulars to become involved and have created opportunities for outsiders to seek their party's nomination. Businessman Steve Forbes (1996 and 2000), ministers Jesse Jackson (1984) and Pat Robertson (1988), columnist Pat Buchanan (1992, 1996, and 2000), and former senators Paul Tsongas (1992) and Bill Bradley (2000), and to some extent even governors Michael Dukakis (1988), Bill Clinton (1992), and Howard Dean (2004), let alone three-year Senator Barack Obama (2008), have literally come out of political nowhere to run for their party's nomination. On the other hand, the more the process concentrates the number of primaries at the beginning of the delegate selection process, the more those who have access to the largest amounts of money, the most political endorsements, and the organizational support from governors and other party and interest group leaders are likely to benefit.

All of this has affected the candidates' quests for the nomination and their ability to govern if elected. It has extended campaigning and made it more arduous, more expensive, and it has made governing more difficult, especially at the beginning of a new administration. It has created incentives for candidates to promise more than they can deliver. Thus, the quest for the nomination and what it takes to win may ultimately weaken a newly elected president by hyping performance expectations and then generating discontent when these expectations cannot be realized. Ronald Reagan, Bill Clinton, and Barack Obama each faced this problem in the first years of their presidencies.

SUMMARY

The delegate selection process has changed dramatically over the past forty years. Originally dominated by state party leaders, it has become more open to the party's rank and file as a consequence of the reforms initiated by the Democratic Party. These reforms, designed to broaden the base of public participation, improve the representation of the party's rank and file, and give its partisan electorate more influence over the selection of their party's nominees, have affected the Republicans as well, even though the GOP does not mandate national guidelines for its state parties as restrictive as the Democrats'. Supreme Court decisions that give the national parties the authority to dictate rules, and public pressure to reflect popular sentiment and improve representation have led to a greater number of primaries and more delegates selected in them for both major parties.

Turnout has increased although the proportion of the partisan electorate that participates varies from one nomination to another. The date of the contest, the level of intraparty competition, the amount of money spent, and other candidate-related factors help explain these variations. But the democratic bottom line is that even in highly contested nominations, many fewer people follow the campaigns and vote in them than in the general election.

Representation has improved but inequities persist. Partisan activists continue to exercise disproportionate influence. This influence has contributed to the ideologicalization of the major parties; it has increased their internal cohesiveness and external distinctiveness, alienating moderates and shrinking rather than broadening their electoral base.

WHERE ON THE WEB?

- **The Center for Voting and Democracy**
  www.fairvote.org
  An organization devoted to promoting a more democratic electoral process and publicizing plans to improve it.
- **Democratic National Committee**
  www.democrats.org
  Information on Democratic Party history, rules, convention, and campaigns with links to Democratic youth and state party affiliates.
- **Green Party**
  www.gp.org
  Information on Green Party candidates, the party's platform, press releases, and state party affiliates.
- **The Green Papers**
  www.thegreenpapers.com/P12
  A Web site that provides detailed information on the nomination processes and the general election. Contains reports on the changes the parties have approved for 2012.

  http://www.thegreenpapers.com/P12/2009-12-30-DNC-Change-Commission.phtml
  http://www.thegreenpapers.com/P12/2010-08-06-RNC-Temporary_Delegate_Selection_Committee.phtml

- **Republican National Committee**
  www.rnc.org
  Information on Republican Party history, rules, convention, and campaigns with links to Republican youth and state party affiliates.
- **Wikipedia**
  en.wikipedia.org/wiki/United_States_presidential_primary
  An online encyclopedia.

EXERCISES

1. Party officials in Iowa and New Hampshire strongly objected to the changes in the Democratic caucus and primary schedule for 2008. Describe the arguments for and against a few small states, such as Iowa and New Hampshire, being allowed to hold their nomination contests before the rest of the states. Have these states contributed to or detracted from a democratic presidential nomination process?
2. Have the Democratic and Republican party nomination reforms improved or hurt the democratic character of the parties and of presidential elections? What changes would you suggest to make the nomination process even more democratic?
3. Devise what you consider fair and equitable rules for the major parties for the selection of their presidential nominees.

SELECTED READINGS

Altschuler, Bruce E. "Selecting Presidential Nominees by National Primary: An Idea Whose Time Has Come?" *The Forum*, 5 (4): Article 5 (2008). www.bepress.com/forum/vol/iss4/art5

Atkeson, Lonna Rae. "Divisive Primaries and General Election Outcomes: Another Look at Presidential Campaigns." *American Journal of Political Science*, 42 (1998): 257–261.

Bartels, Larry M. *Presidential Primaries and the Dynamics of Public Choice.* Princeton, NJ: Princeton University Press, 1988.

Cook, Rhodes. *Race for the Presidency: Winning the 2008 Nomination.* Washington, DC: CQ Press, 2008.

Day, Christine L., Charles D. Hadley, and Harold W. Stanley. "The Inevitable Unanticipated Consequences of Political Reform: The 2004 Presidential Nomination Process," in William Crotty, ed., *A Defining Moment.* Armonk, NY: M. E. Sharpe, 2005, pp. 74–86.

Geer, John G. *Nominating Presidents: An Evaluation of Voters and Primaries.* New York: Greenwood, 1989.

Kamarck, Elaine C. *Primary Politics: How Presidential Candidates Have Shaped the Modern Nomination System.* Washington, DC: Brookings Institution, 2009.

Kaufman, Karen M., James G. Gimpel, and Adam H. Hoffman. "A Promise Fulfilled? Open Primaries and Representation," Journal of Politics, 65 (2003): 457–476.

Mayer, William G., and Andrew E. Busch. *The Front-Loading Problem in Presidential Nominations.* Washington, DC: Brookings Institution, 2004.

______________. "Reforming the Reforms Revisited," in Steven S. Smith and Melanie J. Springer, eds., *Reforming the Presidential Nomination Process.* Washington, DC: Brookings Institution, 2009.

Norrander, Barbara. "Ideological Representativeness of Presidential Primary Voters." *American Journal of Political Science*, 33 (Aug. 1989): 570–587.

____________. *The Imperfect Primary.* New York: Routledge, 2010.

Polsby, Nelson W. *The Consequences of Party Reform.* New York: Oxford University Press, 1983.

Shafer, Byron E. *Quiet Revolution: The Struggle for the Democratic Party and the Shaping of Post-Reform Politics.* New York: Russell Sage Foundation, 1983.

Tolbert, Caroline, and Peverill Squire, eds. "Reforming the Presidential Nomination Process." *PS: Political Science and Politics,* 42 (Jan. 2009): 27–79.

Wayne, Stephen J. "When Democracy Works: The 2008 Presidential Nominations," in William J. Crotty, ed., *Winning the Presidency.* Boulder, CO: Paradigm Publishers, 2009, pp. 48–69.

NOTES

1. McCarthy's name was on the ballot, but the president's name was not. The regular Democratic organization in New Hampshire had to conduct a campaign to have Democrats write in Johnson's name.
2. The groups that were initially singled out were Native Americans, African Americans, and youth. Subsequently, the list of affected groups has been altered by the addition of Hispanics, Asian/Pacific Americans, and women, and by the deletion of youth. In 1992, the party also added those with physical disabilities to the groups protected against discrimination.
3. Some states still hold a presidential preference vote with a separate election of delegates by a convention. Others connect the presidential vote and delegate selection on an at-large or district basis. By voting for a particular candidate or delegates pledged to that candidate (or both), voters may register their presidential choice and delegate selection at the same time and by the same vote. The number of these primaries has increased as a consequence of the rules changes.
4. Iowa and New Hampshire both have laws that require their contests to be, respectively, the first caucus and primary. They obviously gain advantages by doing so. The candidates come and visit with voters often. The news media also arrive in force to cover the beginnings of the next campaign. There is an economic gain as well. New Hampshire estimates that it took in $264 million from its 2000 primaries ("First in the Nation: The New Hampshire Primary; What It Means to the State and the Nation," published by the State of New Hampshire, 2000, p. 4).
5. The Democratic Party commission recommended that the calendar be divided into four stages. The states that held their nomination contests during the first stage, the two-week period beginning with the first Tuesday in March, would receive additional delegates equal to 15 percent of their total number of pledged delegates; if they held their election during stage two, the three-week period beginning the third Tuesday in March, they would receive an additional 20 percent; if their selection date was in the third stage, the three-week period that begins the second Tuesday in April, they would be allocated an additional 30 percent; if they held it after that and before the end of the Democratic nomination process, the second Tuesday in June, they would be entitled to an additional 40 percent.
6. Jimmy Carter's difficulties with the Democratic Congress during his presidency were also cited as evidence of the need for closer cooperation between congressional party leaders and their presidential standard-bearer. These PLEOs were designed to facilitate such cooperation.

7. Additionally, the party also provided for the selection of pledged add-on delegates equal to 15 percent of the state's base delegation in order to give representation to a larger number of state party leaders.
8. Prior to the 2000 Republican convention, a commission recommended the implementation of a population-based nominating system in which states would be placed in one of four groups, based on their population size rather than geographic location, and then would conduct their primary election or the first stage of their caucus selection on the same day. The group containing the least-populated states would go first, and the one with the most populated states would go last, with the dates on which the four groups would hold their contests spaced approximately one month apart.

   Opposition to the plan quickly developed from the large states, fearful that the nominee would be effectively determined before they had a chance to vote. Concerns were also expressed about the added costs to the candidates if they had to compete for four months, as well as the wear and tear they would encounter. Not wanting the issue to divide the 2000 convention and interfere with his launch for the presidency, George W. Bush opposed the recommendation. The Republican Rules Committee, controlled by Bush delegates, decided not to propose the change to the convention.
9. In another decision by the Supreme Court, also involving open primaries, the power of parties (in this case, state parties) to establish rules for nominating candidates was affirmed. In December 1986, the Supreme Court, in the case of *Tashjian v. Republican Party of Connecticut*, 479 U.S. 208 (1986), voided a Connecticut law that prohibited open primaries. Republicans, in the minority at the time in Connecticut, had favored such a primary as a means of attracting independent voters. Unable to get the Democratic-controlled legislature to change the law, the state Republican Party went to court, arguing that the statute violated its First Amendment rights of freedom of association. In a 5-to-4 ruling, the Supreme Court agreed and struck down the legislation.
10. The formula Republicans use to determine the size of each state delegation is complex. It consists of three criteria: statehood (six delegates), House districts (three per district), and support for Republican candidates elected within the previous four years (one for a Republican governor, one for each Republican senator, one if the Republicans won at least half of the congressional districts in one of the past two congressional elections, and a bonus of four and one-half delegates plus 60 percent of the electoral vote if the state voted for the Republican presidential candidate in the previous election).
11. Under the plan used since 1968 and modified in 1976, the Democrats have allotted 50 percent of each state delegation on the basis of the state's electoral vote and 50 percent on the basis of its average Democratic vote in the past three presidential elections. The rule for apportionment was challenged in 1971 on the grounds that it did not conform to the "one-person, one-vote" principle, but a court of appeals asserted that it did not violate the equal protection clause of the Fourteenth Amendment.
12. Curtis Gans, "2004 Primary Turnout Low." www.american.edu/ccps/files/Files/csae030904.pdf; Linda L. Fowler, Constantine J. Spiliotes, and Lynn VaVreck, "The Role of Issue Advocacy Groups in the New Hampshire Primary," in David B. Magleby, ed. *Getting Inside the Outside Campaign* (Provo, UT: Brigham Young University, 2000), p. 31.
13. Michael McDonald, "Presidential Turnout Rates,1948–2008." elections.gmu.edu/voter_turnout.

14. Earl Black and Merle Black, *The Vital South: How Presidents Are Elected* (Cambridge, MA: Harvard University Press, 1992), p. 268.
15. Barbara Norrander, "Ideological Representativeness of Presidential Primary Voters," *American Journal of Political Science*, 33 (Aug. 1989), pp. 570–587.
16. Jon Cohen and Jennifer Agiesta, "Black Vote Was Vital, Not the Whole Story," *The Washington Post* (Jan. 27, 2008). www.washingtonpost.com/wp-dyn/content/article/2008/01/26/AR2008012602741.html; "The Entrance Polls: Why Clinton Won Nevada," *Politico* (Jan. 8, 2008). www.politico.com/news/stories/0108/7994.
17. Susan Minushkin and Mark Hugo Lopez, "The Hispanic Vote in the 2008 Democratic Presidential Primaries," Pew Hispanic Center (Feb. 21, 2008). pewhispanic.org/reports/86.pdf.
18. New York Times/CBS News Poll, "2008 Republican National Delegate Survey," (July 23–Aug. 26, 2008). www.nytimes.com/2008/09/01/us/politics/01poll.html?_r=1.
19. Marty Cohen, David Carol, Hans Noel, and John Zaller, *The Party Decides: Presidential Nominations Before and After Reform* (Chicago: University of Chicago Press, 2008), p. 232.
20. James I. Lengle, "Divisive Presidential Primaries and the Party Electoral Prospects, 1932–1976," *American Politics Quarterly*, 8 (1980), pp. 261–277; James I. Lengle, Diana Owen, and Molly Sonner, "Divisive Nomination Campaigns and Democratic Party Electoral Prospects," *Journal of Politics*, 57 (1995), pp. 370–383.
21. Lonna Rae Atkeson, "Divisive Primaries and General Election Outcomes: Another Look at Presidential Campaigns," *American Journal of Political Science*, 42 (Jan. 1998), pp. 256–271.

Campaigning for the Nomination

CHAPTER 5

INTRODUCTION

Rules changes, finance laws, and press coverage have affected the strategies and tactics of the candidates. Today, entering primaries is essential for everyone, even an incumbent who is challenged by a fellow partisan. No longer can a front-runner safely sit on the sidelines and wait for the call. The winds of a draft may be hard to resist but, more often than not, it is the candidate who is manning the bellows.

In the past, candidates carefully chose the primaries they entered and concentrated their efforts where they thought they would run best. Today, they have much less discretion, particularly at the beginning of the process, when press coverage is essential. Before 1972, it was considered wise to wait for an opportune moment in the spring of the presidential election year before announcing one's candidacy. Today, planning for a nomination run starts years in advance. Candidates usually establish exploratory committees following the midterm election. These committees help potential candidates test the waters. The money they raise during the preelection stage of the nomination process helps them pay for travel, staff, fund-raising, and other expenses such as designing a Web site, building a donor base, hiring campaign consultants, and appealing to party and interest group leaders for endorsements and organizational support.

BASIC STRATEGIC GUIDELINES

Every nomination campaign has to make a number of strategic decisions: when to begin the quest for the nomination and what type of organization to create; how to raise the necessary funds and to whom to turn to do so; how and where to spend resources; on what issues to focus; to which groups to target specific appeals and how to project a presidential image when doing so; how to obtain sufficient and favorable news coverage and when to supplement that coverage with paid advertising and coordinated social networking; how to criticize one's opponents yet be in a position to gain their support after winning the nomination; and finally, how to position the campaign after becoming the preordained nominee in the period before the national nominating conventions.

PLAN FAR AHEAD

Creating an organization, devising a strategy, and raising the amount of money necessary to conduct a national campaign all takes time. These needs have prompted potential aspirants for their party's nomination to set up exploratory committees, leadership PACs, and other precampaign organizations; hire personnel; contract with political consultants; raise money; and visit Iowa and New Hampshire and the other early states more than two years before the caucuses and primaries will be held.[1] In the words of Howard Wolfson, Hillary Clinton's communications director, "You have to move early because the process starts early, and if you are not announcing in the early time, you are going to lose out."[2]

Some candidates have announced their intentions of running years in advance. George McGovern did so in January 1971; similarly, long-shot Jimmy Carter began his quest in 1974, almost two years before the 1976 Democratic convention. By the end of 2006, eleven Democratic and Republican candidates had either officially declared their candidacy or set up exploratory committees to evaluate their chances for their party's 2008 nomination. One potential candidate, Fred Thompson, had not. When he finally hired a campaign chairman, Bill Lacy, in July 2007, it was almost too late. Lacy noted, "When I got to the campaign, I knew there was trouble. There was no campaign plan, there was no strategy and no polling had been done. There was some personnel in place, some extremely good although our communications shop . . . had zero experience in political campaigns . . . so we had to make changes."[3]

Start up began more slowly for the Republicans interested in obtaining their party's 2012 nomination. Unlike previous GOP nomination campaigns, prospective candidates did their initial organizing and fundraising out of the focus of news media attention. The conservative PAC annual meeting held in February 2011 was the first major political event that attracted GOP hopefuls.

Even incumbent presidents plan for their renomination well in advance of the election year. President Clinton did so in the winter of 1994, following his party's defeat in the midterm elections. However, the president never formally announced his candidacy in order to convey the impression that his actions and decisions during this period were motivated solely by the demands of the presidency, not by his desire to remain in office for another term. President George W. Bush, anxious to avoid his father's belated and unsuccessful quest for reelection, began planning his campaign from almost the moment he was declared the winner of the 2000 election.[4] President Barack Obama, also attentive to reelection, began raising money and positioning himself for 2012 in the aftermath of the midterm elections in which he campaigned actively for Democrats. He enunciated his prospective campaign theme, "win the future," in his 2011 State of the Union address. Obama's chief political strategist, David Axelrod, press secretary, Robert Gibbs, and deputy chief of staff, Jim Messina, resigned from their positions in the Obama White House at the end of the president's second year in office to return to Chicago to plan for the president's reelection campaign.

CONCENTRATE EFFORTS IN THE EARLY CONTESTS

Doing well in the initial caucuses and primaries, raising money, gaining visibility, and organizing the campaign and staffing it with political professionals are the principal aims of most candidates today. The early contests are particularly important for lesser-known aspirants, less for the number of delegates they can win than for the amount of publicity they can get, the number of people they can meet, and the momentum they can generate. For them, it is necessary to get to the top tier. Chris Dodd's campaign manager in 2008 put it this way: "Our initial goal was to be seen as the fourth in the race. . . . We thought we would do that in the first quarter [of 2007] by having raised more money, by having built a stronger organization, by having a tighter narrative, all the basic things. . . . If we did that, . . . the press would then pay more attention to Senator Dodd."[5]

Personal contact is very important in this period because it informs and motivates potential contributors, staff, and volunteers down the road. The small states provide these "living-room" opportunities that are lacking in multistate media campaigns.

Iowa

By tradition, the first official selection of delegates occurs in Iowa. Jimmy Carter (1976), George H. W. Bush (1980), Gary Hart (1984), John Kerry (2004), Mike Huckabee (2008), and Barack Obama (2008) got great boosts from their unexpectedly good showings in this state. Conversely, Republicans Ronald Reagan (1980), George H. W. Bush (1988), Robert Dole (1996), and Mitt Romney (2008) were hurt by their disappointing performances as were Democrats Howard Dean (2004) and Hillary Rodham Clinton (2008). In 2000, Iowa simply confirmed the front-runners' status that George W. Bush and Al Gore enjoyed over their rivals.

Winning in Iowa can enhance the fortunes of a lesser-known candidate equally as well as losing will call the status of a front-runner into question. Obama's victory in 2008 demonstrated his broad appeal in a state with a relatively small percentage of African Americans. It also indicated that Hillary Clinton's nomination by the Democrats was not inevitable.

Sometimes even coming in second boosts a candidacy. It did for Gary Hart in 1984. Although Hart received only 16.5 percent of the Democratic vote compared with front-runner Walter Mondale's 48.9 percent, Hart's second-place finish was unexpected; Mondale's first place finish was not. As a consequence, Hart shared the media spotlight with Mondale but profited from more laudatory coverage.

John Edwards did not benefit nearly as much from his second-place finishes in Iowa in 2004 or 2008. Kerry's victory in 2004 launched his candidacy while Howard Dean's poor showing and his antics on election night doomed his. Trying to encourage his disappointed workers and supporters, Dean gave a passionate speech ending with a yell that looked to television viewers as if he had lost control of himself. Kerry's victory and Dean's scream were newsworthy and dominated the headlines; Edwards's relatively strong performance did not. Media coverage repeated itself in 2008. Even though Edwards came in second ahead of Hillary Clinton, Obama's win and Clinton's defeat were the storylines, not Edwards' second place. Moreover, the fact that Edwards was known to Iowa voters, campaigned vigorously in that state, and still did not win contributed to his political obituary.

Lesser-known candidates have trouble surviving an Iowa defeat, which usually ends their campaign, as it did for Richardson, Biden, and Dodd in 2008. Front-runners have more options. With larger war chests, greater organizational support, and more public recognition and political endorsements, they can survive an Iowa defeat provided they do well in the New Hampshire primary. Republicans Reagan (1980), Bush (1988), and Dole (1996) lost Iowa yet went on to win their party's nomination. Hillary Clinton was also able to wage a strong fight for the 2008 Democratic nomination despite a third-place finish in Iowa.

The financial boost that an early victory brings has been reduced by the compressed and front-loaded nomination calendar. In 1976, Jimmy Carter benefited from a large surge in campaign contributions following his unexpected wins in Iowa and, a month later, in New Hampshire. In contrast, Mike Huckabee, the surprise Republican winner in Iowa in 2008, had only four days to parlay success in Iowa into resources for New Hampshire. Huckabee came in a distant third in the Granite State, thereby losing the momentum he had gained from Iowa.

Iowa "winners" face another problem. Not only do expectations of their future performance increase, making a subsequent defeat that much more disheartening, but media coverage also tends to become more critical. The press has an interest in keeping the race as competitive and newsworthy as long as possible.

New Hampshire

After Iowa, attention turns to New Hampshire, traditionally the first state to hold a presidential primary in which the state's entire electorate participates.[6] Candidates who do surprisingly well in this primary have benefited enormously. Eugene McCarthy (1968), George McGovern (1972), Jimmy Carter (1976), Gary Hart (1984), Bill Clinton (1992), Pat Buchanan (1996), and John McCain (2000 and 2008) all gained visibility and credibility from their New Hampshire performances, although none had a majority of the vote. Bill Clinton actually came in second with 25 percent of the vote in 1992, 8 percent less than former Massachusetts Senator Paul Tsongas.

Clinton's relatively strong showing, however, in the light of allegations of marital infidelity and draft dodging made his performance more impressive in the eyes of the news media than Tsongas's expected win. Tsongas was not considered to be a viable candidate; Clinton was. Similarly, John McCain's impressive victory in 2000 over front-runner George W. Bush by 18 percent elevated him overnight from just another candidate to a serious contender. His victory in 2008, though smaller, revived his sagging campaign for which the press had written a premature obituary in the fall of 2007. Hillary Clinton's win in New Hampshire in 2008 also saved her sagging campaign, energizing her supporters and generating badly needed contributions.

Like Iowa, New Hampshire also receives extensive media attention. Together, these two states usually account for the bulk of prenomination television coverage on the national news. For this reason alone, most candidates have no choice but to enter the first presidential caucus and primary, even though a double loss in Iowa and New Hampshire will normally doom their candidacies. Mitt Romney's campaign stayed alive by winning the Michigan primary, which occurred one week after New Hampshire in 2008. His subsequent losses in South Carolina, Florida, and thirteen of the fifteen Republican primaries held on Super Tuesday ended his bid in 2008.

RAISE AND SPEND BIG BUCKS EARLY

Having a solid financial base at the outset of the nomination process provides a significant strategic advantage. It allows a presidential campaign to plan ahead, to decide where to establish its field organizations and how much media advertising to buy, as well as where and on which groups to focus that advertising. It is no coincidence that those candidates who raise and spend the most money tend to win their party's nomination, but not always.[7] Romney had the largest war chest for the 2008 Republican nomination, but did not receive the most votes, dropping out after McCain's wins on Super Tuesday.

The impact of early money is particularly significant for candidates who do not begin the quest for their party's nomination with a national reputation, candidates such as Michael Dukakis in 1988, Bill Clinton in 1992, Howard Dean and John Edwards in 2004, and Mitt Romney and Barack Obama in 2008. The ability to raise relatively large amounts of money early, particularly in comparison with one's rivals, gives a candidate an edge in gaining media recognition, building organizational support, raising even more money, and discouraging potential rivals from entering the race.

In fact, the amount of money raised is frequently viewed by the press as a harbinger of future success or failure in the primaries. Howard Dean's campaign is a good illustration. Dean raised more money than did any of his Democratic rivals in 2003, almost $40 million, much of it from small donations. The press took notice. He rose in the polls. By November, he was the acknowledged Democratic front-runner. Similarly, Hillary Rodham Clinton and Barack Obama's fundraising in the first quarter of 2007 reinforced their poll status as the leading Democratic candidates for the party's 2008 presidential nomination.

Early money is considered important for several reasons. It buys recognition for those who need it. Steve Forbes bought that recognition in 1996 with the expenditure of more than $42 million, much of it his own money. Mitt Romney needed it in 2008. Not wanting to be known as a Mormon from Massachusetts, particularly in a state such as Iowa that has a strong Christian fundamentalist Republican base, Romney spent money to increase his name recognition in a way he hoped would be more beneficial to his candidacy.[8] But as noted previously, public recognition also brings increased scrutiny from the news media and increased criticism from the other candidates.

Early money can buy viability. The press evaluates the candidates in part on the basis of how much money they can raise and how willing people are to contribute. Thus, a few days after Romney filed papers to create a presidential exploratory committee, his campaign raised $6.5 million in a single day, thereby gaining headlines and credibility as a viable presidential candidate. Candidates who cannot raise much money are not usually taken seriously by the news media and by other potential contributors, even if they are well known.

Another important reason for having money up front is that it gives a candidate the opportunity to hire an expert staff and develop a deep field organization in the early primary states. In the event of an early mishap, such an organization can come to the rescue, as it did in South Carolina for George W. Bush after his defeat in New Hampshire in 2000. Front-loading also forces the candidates to spend more money earlier and earlier.

Two principal consequences follow from the need for early money: the financial campaign in the years before the nomination, the so-called *invisible primary*, has assumed greater importance than in the past, and non-front-runners are disadvantaged even more than they were previously unless they are independently wealthy. The odds against a little-known outsider using Iowa, New Hampshire, and the other early states to obtain the resources necessary to compete seriously for the nomination have increased in recent years.

GAIN MEDIA ATTENTION

Candidates cannot win if they are not known. Gaining visibility is most important at the beginning of the nomination process when the electorate starts to pay some attention to the contests that loom ahead. Since lesser-known aspirants are not as likely to have large war chests, unless they are independently wealthy or have substantial sums left over from previous campaigns, they need free media. Their problem is that coverage and public recognition go hand in hand. Better-known candidates get more coverage precisely because they are better known and thus considered more likely to do well. It is not news when a long shot loses; it is news when a front-runner does. On the other hand, when a long shot does well in raising money, gaining endorsements, drawing crowds, and winning straw votes and especially delegates, the press follows the story of the "conquering hero."

Free Media

What can non-front-runners do to gain more coverage? They can stage events, release a stream of seemingly endless faxes and videos to local media outlets and place them on popular sites on the Internet, leak unfavorable information about their opponents, and solicit invitations to appear on talk/entertainment programs on radio and television. Here's how Pat Buchanan's 1996 campaign manager described a typical media-oriented day in Iowa before that state held the first nominating caucus:

> Gregg [Mueller, the press secretary] and Pat would get up at about five in the morning, get some coffee, get in the minivan, and go from one TV station to the other, in the local market, wherever they had morning shows, and they would do a live segment on every morning television show.
>
> Then they'd come back to the hotel, read through the newspapers and at 10 A.M., we'd go out and do our theme event for the day—drive whatever our message was, get out a press release, which we faxed out everywhere and let that, hopefully, resonate into the newspapers.
>
> At noon, we'd go back to the television stations, if they would have us, or else we'd drive into a new market . . . all the time that they would be driving the van, Greg would have Pat on the cell phone doing radio interviews. . . . Buchanan would literally go from one station to the other to the other, go back to the hotel, maybe take a nap in the afternoon, then you go out at 5 P.M. and you do the evening TV stations. If you literally saturated the local TV market, you try to get to the next one. You try to maximize the amount of time you could get on TV in a state while you were there.[9]

Participating in debates against their political opponents has become a necessity, even though the large number of candidates makes it more difficult for any one of them to stand out. During the 2007–2008 nomination campaign, there were twenty-one debates among the Democratic contenders and sixteen among the Republicans. Although debates among party candidates spark local interest and educate the partisan electorate, they rarely receive much national media coverage. The first televised debate in the 2008 nomination cycle occurred on April 26, 2007 for the Democrats and on May 3, 2007 for the Republicans. Most were carried by only one broadcast or cable network. Few people watched them. Is it any wonder that prenomination debates do not have much national impact unless, of course, one of the candidates makes a major faux pas or claim that is deemed newsworthy?

In general, there has been a decline in the amount of time given to election news on the broadcast networks and an even larger decline in the number of candidate stories that appeared on the evening news shows.[10] On the other hand, the 24/7 cable networks have increased candidate coverage, as have the Web sites of the major news networks. With campaign news sources more dispersed, candidates must pay close attention to what viewers are watching. Increasingly, they must design and present their own messages via paid advertising. Free media is not sufficient nor is receiving favorable coverage automatic.

Paid Media

Advertisements remain one of the most effective ways to communicate with voters. Studies have shown that people tend to retain more information from candidate commercials than they do from the broadcast networks' evening news.[11] As a result, campaigns continue to spend the bulk of their revenues on political advertisements. Box 5.1 provides a summary of the 2007–2008 nomination advertising campaign.

BOX 5.1 | CANDIDATE ADVERTISING IN THE 2007–2008 NOMINATION PROCESS

Barack Obama and Mitt Romney ran the most ads during the 2008 nomination process because they had the most money to do so. Obama's advantage was most apparent in the large industrial states that held their contests on and after March 5, 2008; Romney's advantage was in the early states, especially Iowa and New Hampshire.[i] He began his on-the-air campaign in April 2007. His advertising costs exceeded those of all the other Republican candidates combined but still were less than half of what Obama spent. Despite spending advantages, neither Romney nor Obama won in the states in which they concentrated their ads, although they might have lost those states by more had they not advertised as much. The following table indicates advertising expenditures for the 2008 presidential primaries.

TABLE 5.1 | TOTAL ADVERTISING SPENDING BY CANDIDATES FOR THE 2008 PRESIDENTIAL PRIMARIES

	Airings	Estimated Spending ($)
Democrats		
Biden	3,165	1,799,000
Clinton	80,505	46,027,000
Dodd	4,028	1,777,000
Edwards	14,732	8,283,000
Kucinich	27	6,000
Lamagna	4	5,000
Obama	139,006	74,823,000
Richardson	5,936	4,234,000
Total	247,403	136,954,000
Republicans		
Cort	15	6,000
Giuliani	7,127	5,777,000
Huckabee	8,400	3,569,000
Hunter	114	68,000
McCain	16,413	11,084,000
Paul	7,220	3,161,000
Romney	36,841	31,658,000
Tancredo	99	158,000
Thompson	4,032	2,224,000
Total	80,261	57,705,000
Total (All Candidates)	327,664	$194,659,000

Source: TNS Media Intelligence/CMAG with analysis by the Wisconsin Advertising Project, June 2, 2008. wiscadproject.wisc.edu/wiscads_pressrelease_060208.pdf

BOX 5.1 | CANDIDATE ADVERTISING IN THE 2007–2008 NOMINATION PROCESS *continued*

Romney used his early advertising to introduce himself, his conservative values, and salient policy positions to Republican voters. Obama also began with biographical commercials in which he emphasized his campaign themes of policy and political change. Clinton emphasized her experience in government. Obama narrated most of his ads; Clinton did not.

Ads by the Democratic candidates highlighted domestic issues such as health, education, and the economy (jobs and trade) and personal qualities, such as leadership and experience. Republican ads emphasized moral values, immigration, and taxes as well as attributes of leadership, trust, and honesty. Despite the controversy over the war in Iraq, it was not a focus of candidate advertising during the 2008 nominations.[ii]

There were 301 different candidate ads in the 2008 nomination process with a substantial portion targeted to voters in Iowa and New Hampshire. Much of the advertising was confrontational, more than in previous nominations. Sixty-one percent of the Democratic ads were negative compared to 43 percent for the Republicans. Clinton ran more negative ads than Obama.[iii] Her most newsworthy ad began with an announcer saying, "It's 3 A.M., and your children are safe and asleep, but there's a phone in the White House, and it's ringing." The ominous ring continues throughout the ad as the announcer reminds would be voters that they live in a dangerous world. At the end of the ad, the announcer asks the question, "Who do you want answering the phone?" as a picture of Mrs. Clinton, wearing eyeglasses, picks it up.

[i]"Battle of the Ads," *The New York Times*, April 29, 2008. www.nytimes.com/imagespages/2008/04/29/us/20080429

[ii]Darrell M. West, "A Report on the 2008 Presidential Nomination Ads: Ads More Negative than Previous Years," Brookings Institution, July 2, 2008. www.brookings.edu/papers/2008/0603_campaignads_west.aspx

[iii]Ibid.

DEVELOP A DEEP AND WIDE ORGANIZATION AND POLICY MESSAGE

The major task of any organization is to mobilize voters and build electoral coalitions among core partisan groups.[12] Media coverage is necessary but not sufficient. Having an organization in the field is deemed especially important in caucus states in order to get supporters and sympathizers to the precinct meetings, which are less well known than the voting places at which people cast their primary ballots and also vote in the general election. In both caucuses and primaries, telephone banks must be established, door-to-door canvassing employed, and appropriate material posted or e-mailed or hand delivered. It is also necessary to create the impression of broad public support and generate excitement. Such activities involve a large grassroots effort.

Eugene McCarthy, George McGovern, and to a lesser extent, Bill Bradley, recruited thousands of college students to ring doorbells, distribute literature, and get supporters out to vote in 1968, 1972, and 2000. Jimmy Carter had his

"Peanut Brigade," a group of Georgians who followed him from state to state in 1976. Jesse Jackson effectively used African American churches to recruit volunteers and raise money for his presidential campaigns in 1984 and 1988, while Pat Robertson in 1988 depended on the 3 million people who signed petitions urging him to run for president.

One of Howard Dean's biggest disappointments in 2004 was his campaign's failure to create an efficient grassroots operation from the 500,000 people who provided their e-mail addresses or blogged on his Web site. The Dean volunteers who came to Iowa lacked political savvy and organizing skills. Their dress and manner branded them as outsiders, reducing their ability to persuade Iowans of the merits and viability of Dean's candidacy.[13]

The Obama team learned from the Dean experience. They used the Internet to identify volunteers and then trained them in campaign organizing. According to Jon Carson, a field director for Obama:

> What the online efforts allowed us to do is grab . . . people quickly . . . we were able to go into Texas with three and a half weeks to go, had a quarter of a million volunteers signed up, with phone numbers, e-mail addresses. They had been using our social networks to form themselves into teams.[14]

The campaign set up training sessions of three to four days duration for volunteers who had never worked in political campaigns. At Camp Obama, they were taught the fundamentals of political networking, event organizing, storytelling, and personal contact by phone and in person, as well as given maps, addresses, and numbers to call.

In addition to the activity generated by campaigns, nonparty organizations, such as labor unions and advocacy groups, also play a role in presidential nominations. Pro-life, pro-gun, even pro-tobacco groups helped George W. Bush defeat John McCain in the 2000 South Carolina primary. Conservative Christian groups aided Mike Huckabee in Iowa and several southern primaries in 2008. Emily's List, a group that helps elect women candidates, got out the vote for Hillary Clinton in the 2008 New Hampshire primary. Both Clinton and Obama received support from different labor unions in their quests for the 2008 Democratic nomination.

MONITOR PUBLIC OPINION

With intentions clear, money in hand, events planned and scheduled, and an organization in place, it is necessary to monitor public sentiment, appeal to it, and try to manipulate it, all at the same time. To achieve these goals, state polls and focus groups are considered essential. However, they did not become part and parcel of the nomination process until the middle of the twentieth century.

Republican Thomas E. Dewey was the first to have private polling data available to him when he tried unsuccessfully to obtain the Republican nomination in 1940. John F. Kennedy was the first candidate to engage a pollster in his quest for the nomination. Preconvention surveys conducted by Louis Harris in 1960 indicated that Hubert Humphrey, Kennedy's principal rival, was potentially vulnerable in West Virginia and Wisconsin. On the basis of this information, the Kennedy campaign decided to concentrate time, effort, and money in these predominantly Protestant states. Victories in both helped demonstrate Kennedy's broad appeal, thereby improving his chances for the nomination.

Today, all major presidential candidates commission their own polls. These proprietary surveys provide critical information about the beliefs and attitudes of voters, their initial and ongoing perceptions of the candidates, and the kinds of appeals that are apt to be most effective. Bill Clinton used polls to great advantage in 1992 to develop and target an economic appeal and to respond to allegations about his personal character. He used them even more in 1995 and 1996 to reposition himself and launch his reelection bid following the Democrats' debacle in the 1994 midterm elections.

Although there are a lot of public polls commissioned by news organizations, polls that focus on particular information needs that campaigns have, such as whether a particular appeal is having the desired effect, are more useful. Similarly, state polls have more value than national ones when running for the nomination. But polls are expensive and a campaign may not be able to afford them. After her victory in the New Hampshire primary, Clinton was out of money and could not commission the polls that her campaign needed to plan its strategy after Super Tuesday. It operated on "best estimates" for much of the remainder of the campaign.[15]

The use of focus groups to gauge the public's reaction to words and phrases as well as to evaluate the potential impact of candidate appeals has become an increasingly valuable tool for speechwriters and media consultants. In his book *The Audacity to Win*, David Plouffe, Obama's campaign manager, wrote:

> Focus groups conducted by a professional moderator (not a pollster) and feedback from the field were two of our most important assets; we wanted to listen to voters every way we could to see how they processed arguments throughout the campaign. We did not use them to make policy decisions. We used them to gauge how the arguments in the campaign were being received and digested.[16]

Almost all campaign advertising is pretested by such groups to gauge likely reactions to it. Adjustments may be made before the ad is actually aired, if it is aired at all. A negative response by the focus group may kill the ad entirely. Dick Morris, the political strategist behind Clinton's reelection campaign, described how he and his aides crafted the president's media advertising:

> We prepared several different rough versions of the ads, called animatics, which [pollster] Mark Penn would arrange to test at fifteen shopping malls around the nation. After the Republicans began to attack us in their own ads, Penn tested the opposition ad and our reply at the same time to measure their relative impact. Penn's staffers would set themselves up in a mall and invite shoppers one by one to fill out a short questionnaire about Clinton, Dole, and their own political views. Then they would show the voters the ad we wanted to test. Afterward the shopper would fill in the same questionnaire and Penn would measure any changes in opinion.

> Based on the mall tests, we decided which ad to run and whether to combine it with elements from ads that did not do as well. We worked for hours to make the ad fit thirty seconds. Then we'd send the script to Doug Sosnik, the White House political director, who gave it to the president for his OK.[17]

Such procedures have now become standard.

Although polls and focus groups can and do directly affect a candidate's strategy, tactics, and fund-raising, their impact on the general public is less direct and much less pronounced. Despite the fears expressed by politicians, there are few empirical data to suggest that polls published in newspapers and on their Web sites and announced on news programs generate a *bandwagon effect*, a momentum for a candidate that causes others to jump on board. There is, however, some evidence of a relationship among the candidate's standing in the polls, success in the primaries, and winning the nomination. What is unclear is whether the public opinion leaders win because they are more popular or whether they are more popular initially because they are better known and ultimately because they look like winners.

Design and Target a Distinctive Personal Image and Policy Message

The information obtained from polls and focus groups is used to create and sharpen leadership images and to target these images to sympathetic voters. In designing an appeal, candidates must first establish their credentials, then articulate a general approach, and finally discuss specific policy problems and solutions. For lesser-known candidates, the initial emphasis must be on themselves: who they are and what their experience is, especially their qualifications for the presidency.

Thus, the first and essential tasks are to gain name recognition, project a leadership image, and develop a distinctive policy appeal. The more candidates seeking the nomination, the more difficult it is to differentiate them from one another, particularly in debates in which they have only a few minutes to talk. In 2008, Obama emphasized change, Clinton experience, and Edwards a popularist appeal. Ron Paul, who advocated a libertarian policy agenda and opposed the war in Iraq, distinguished himself from the other Republicans, but his views failed to receive much support from the GOP base. John McCain began the campaign with a reputation as a maverick, not an advantage in seeking support from Republican activists. On the other hand, Mike Huckabee, who was not well known before the campaign began, was able to convey his earnestness and social values, which helped him with the base.

In general, the candidates' issue positions and image projections do reach voters. The Annenberg Public Policy Center at the University of Pennsylvania, which has studied policy agendas and image projections in recent presidential elections, found that people gain greater awareness and knowledge of the candidates and their positions as the nomination process advances, particularly in states in which the candidates actively campaign.[18] In 2008, the public followed the nomination campaign more closely than they did in 2004, although a later report from the Annenberg Center indicated that people still had a lot to learn about the candidates' issue positions.[19]

Annenberg researchers also examined the impact on the electorate of political endorsements and campaign attacks. They concluded that endorsements and attacks can inform voters and, in some cases, influence their behavior on election day, although most people are not aware of endorsements, and when they are, deny that they influence their vote.[20]

Negative attacks, particularly those that become items in the news, also can have an effect. In the 2000 nomination campaign, ads criticizing McCain for voting against breast cancer research and against environmental legislation took their toll on his candidacy. In 2008, talk radio host Rush Limbaugh cast doubt among listeners about McCain's conservative credentials.[21] Four years earlier, an avalanche of negative commercials by the Gephardt and Dean campaigns against each other in Iowa turned off undecided voters and made it difficult for both candidates to extend their base of support.

In short, the campaign matters. Candidate appeals and attacks, particularly those that are reinforced by items in the news and commentary on the campaign, can inform, inflame, and influence the electorate.

MAKE EFFECTIVE USE OF COMMUNICATION TECHNOLOGIES

In addition to advertising, other communication channels are used to reach voters. One of the distinctive aspects of nomination campaigns since the beginning of the 1990s has been the propensity of candidates to circumvent the national networks entirely for less expensive local media. Campaigns design products and events for expanded local news. Products include videotapes; opposition research, usually anonymously leaked; tailored interviews with local anchors; and made-for-television events. Computer-targeted telephone calls, candidate Web sites, and popular blogs are also used to reach out to voters.

The potential of political cyberspace is enormous. In January 2007, Senator Hillary Rodham Clinton announced her candidacy on her Web site; Obama used the Internet to indicate that he would not accept government funds for the general election; he announced his vice presidential choice of Joe Biden to his e-mail subscribers first before putting out a press release. The Internet is cheap, quick, and increasingly accessible. The Obama campaign used it in 2008 to identify supporters, energize volunteers, solicit contributions, provide information, register eligible voters, and get them to polls. (See Chapter 8 for a discussion of Obama's use of the Internet.)

In 2000, John McCain collected over $7 million in donations from Web site appeals, much of it after his surprisingly strong showing in New Hampshire.[22] In 2004, Dean received the bulk of his $40 million online. Obama raised over $200 million from Internet donations during the 2008 nomination process.[23]

Campaigning on the Internet is not without its problems, however. Squatters have registered Web addresses and then demand large sums from the campaigns to give them up. Parody sites and linkages have mushroomed in recent years. Unsubstantiated rumors circulate widely and rapidly on the Web.

Security has also become a problem as Web sites become targets of political opponents and hackers who want to damage candidates by invading their sites.

Nonetheless, the Internet offers campaigns many compelling opportunities. It has become a vehicle for reaching the younger generation, whose online sophistication generally exceeds their political knowledge and activity. It is a way to convert passive observers into more active participants and a means by which candidates can communicate directly with their online electorate and, most importantly, do so without press distortion. Speeches and rallies can be carried live or made readily available to users; ads can be viewed in their entirety; and reactions can be solicited and suggestions encouraged.

Candidates can also use their sites to maintain a campaign archive for the news media as well as a screen on which to alert the press to new and potentially newsworthy happenings and events. Communicating this information to the news media is very important since most major news outlets maintain their own Web sites and must keep them current.[24]

NOMINATION STRATEGIES

Timing, finance, organization, and communications affect the quest for delegates. They help shape the candidates' strategies and tactics for the nomination. Generally speaking, there have been two successful contemporary prototypical strategies, one for front-runners and another for lesser-known aspirants.

Ronald Reagan's preconvention campaign in 1980 is a good example of the front-runner approach. Reagan raised and spent much of his money in the early primaries and caucuses. His tightly run, top-down campaign built in-depth organizations in key states, obtained the support of many state officials, and benefited from a large staff of professionals and volunteers. George W. Bush and Al Gore followed similar strategies in 2000 as did Hillary Clinton in 2008, although, in her case, unsuccessfully.

Jimmy Carter and Barack Obama had no choice but to adopt a non-front-runner strategy. In 1976, Carter was relatively unknown to most of the electorate; he also began with little money. He had to build a campaign from the ground up. He did so in Iowa, New Hampshire, and Florida, defeating candidates who had better recognition and financial support. Similarly, Obama began without Clinton's reputation and resource base. His victories in Iowa and South Carolina helped establish his credibility as a viable candidate who could win the Democratic Party's presidential nomination.

FRONT-RUNNER STRATEGIES

Front-runners begin with reputation, resources, and national credentials. What they need to do is stay in front and enlarge their lead. Their strategy is simple and straightforward—take advantage of the advantages they already have: recognition as the potential nominee, the political influence that recognition conveys, and superior resources in the form of money, staff, endorsements, press coverage, volunteers, and the ability to wage a multistate campaign.

Front-runners use these resources to discourage challengers, acquire as many delegates as quickly as possible, and build an insurmountable lead.

A front-runner's advantages are most potent at the beginning of the nomination process when the perceived gap with the other candidates is widest. The front-loading of the primaries provides an additional benefit because it makes it more difficult for lesser-known competitors to use an early win to gain momentum. Thus, most front-runners try to deliver a knockout blow in the early rounds when their challengers are least able to compete with them. Scott Reed, Robert Dole's 1996 campaign manager, describes how this scheduling helps the front-runner:

> [I]f we were well funded and well organized, we'd be able to take advantage of the condensed period. We also recognized that even if we did stumble early in New Hampshire or Iowa—and we recognized in early January that we might—it would be very difficult for somebody else to capitalize with the next six, seven, or eight primaries happening so quickly. We were the only campaign that had gone out and registered actual delegates to run in all the other states; the other campaigns had missed a few states here and there.[25]

Walter Mondale pursued a front-runner strategy in 1984, as did Democrats Al Gore in 2000, John Kerry in 2004, and Hillary Rodham Clinton in 2008. All Republican front-runners, beginning with Ronald Reagan in 1980, adopted this approach as well. Democrats Michael Dukakis and Bill Clinton used variations of this strategy in 1988 and 1992: spending heavily up front, employing large professional staffs, and seeking (and receiving) political endorsements. These resources produced early payoffs—delegate leads that encouraged most of their opponents to drop out and gave them, as front-runners, a hedge against any future losses down the road.

For those who are unchallenged, the nomination strategy is obviously different. They can use their position to relaunch their presidential campaign, as Reagan did in 1984, Clinton in 1996, Bush in 2004, and Obama in 2012. The key here is to have sufficient resources (money, staff, and endorsements) at the beginning of the nomination cycle to discourage challengers and have sufficient flexibility to respond to critics.

Non-Front-Runner Strategies

Non-front-runners lack the resources for victory. Their objectives must be to build an organization, solicit the resources, and gain news media attention. The most effective way to achieve these objectives is for candidates to run hard and fast at the outset: enter the early contests, do well, get noticed, and win pledged delegates—all to demonstrate their viability as serious contenders capable of winning the nomination and being elected president of the United States.

There are two types of non-front-running candidates: those who have an outside chance to win (serious candidates) and those who don't, but compete

BOX 5.2 | FRONT-RUNNER STRATEGIES: SUCCESSES AND FAILURES

George W. Bush (2004)

George W. Bush's political advisers began planning his reelection campaign from the moment he was declared the victor in the 2000 election. Their announced goal was to raise $200 million even though Bush did not anticipate a challenge. Raising large sums of money in advance of the caucuses and primaries is the best way to discourage challengers. Bill Clinton used a similar approach in 1996. George H. W. Bush did not in 1992 and as a consequence, his candidacy was weakened.

Incumbents use the money they raise to staff their reelection team, establish an ongoing research operation and a policy agenda, conduct surveys and focus groups, and develop and air campaign advertisements prior to the convention, commercials that will be directed against their general election challenger once that person wins enough delegates to become the *de facto* opponent. Having money up front also gives them the flexibility to respond to criticism by other party candidates.

Bush's large war chest and extensive endorsements from elected Republican leaders allowed his campaign to go into action the moment his Democratic opponent became clear. The president's reelection campaign aired its first anti-Kerry ads in early March 2004, at the time when Kerry had become the consensus Democratic candidate and was even in the preelection polls with the president.

The objective of the initial phase of the Bush advertising campaign was to drive up Kerry's negatives by criticizing his voting record in the Senate. Bush's advisers also used that record to illustrate the stereotype by which the Republicans hoped to define Kerry, a consummate politician, a man without strong personal beliefs who went with the popular view of the moment. This stereotype was intended to draw a vivid and unmistakable contrast with Bush, who was projected by his advertisements as a strong leader; a man of conviction, courage, compassion, and consistency; and a person of faith, who knew what had to be done and would do it.

John Kerry (2004)

John Kerry was also a successful front-runner. But in the fall of 2007 it looked like he would not be. Kerry had been the early favorite. A wealthy man himself, he also had access to money. A strong campaigner, he had been elected to the Senate for three terms; in his previous election, he had come from behind to defeat the then sitting governor of Massachusetts, William Weld. Kerry had contemplated running for president for several years and formed his exploratory committee at the end of 2002; two months later, he hired a well-known, Democratic political consulting firm; and in 2003, he began raising money. In September of that year, he officially announced his candidacy and began his campaign.

Kerry's speeches and manner suggested that he was running for president, not for the Democratic nomination. He focused on Bush, not on the other Democratic candidates. He directed his appeal to a broad cross section of Democrats, not to a particular constituency within the party. Careful not to alienate anyone, Kerry hedged on his policy positions, seemed distant and aloof, and talked but didn't listen. His early speeches were not followed by question-and-answer periods. As a consequence, he excited few Democrats even though most conceded that he was their party's strongest candidate. Being the front-runner had raised expectations about Kerry's position in the polls, his fund-raising totals, and his capacity to energize Democrats, expectations that he was unable initially to realize. Once Dean began to capture the attention, money, and enthusiasm of party activists, Kerry's star began to fall.

BOX 5.2 | Front-Runner Strategies: Successes and Failures *continued*

More and more, the 2004 Democratic nomination process seemed to be a rerun of 1972's when the candidacy of Maine Senator Edmund Muskie, the presumptive favorite to win the 1972 Democratic nomination, imploded in New Hampshire. Kerry fell in the polls during the summer and fall preceding the election year. His campaign seemed to be dead in the water by November 2003. Radical surgery was necessary if his candidacy were to survive. Kerry fired his campaign manager and replaced him with Mary Beth Cahill, a longtime senior aide to Senator Ted Kennedy. He tried to become more personal, shortening his speeches, interacting more with his audience, and staying to answer questions. He mortgaged his house in Massachusetts for $6.4 million dollars and lent the money to his campaign so that he could stay on the air in Iowa and New Hampshire. And he got unexpected outside help.

Jim Rassman, a navy veteran who had served with Kerry in Vietnam, showed up at one of the candidate's rallies in Iowa and testified that Lt. Kerry had saved his life. He said, "I'm not a politician . . . I'm a registered Republican . . . I owe this man my life . . . He's going to get my vote."[i] It was an emotional moment; Kerry embraced him; their reunion brought credibility to Kerry's military service and to his heroism and the decorations that he received for it. It solidified his relationship with the veterans who were supporting his campaign in Iowa, and most importantly, it added the human dimension that had been missing from Kerry's campaign up to that point. Rassman's appearance and endorsement brought Kerry down to earth; it made him look real and gave credibility to his presidential qualifications.

The next six weeks evidenced a shift in public opinion toward Kerry. The results of the Iowa primary suggested that the Massachusetts' senator had successfully turned the corner. The results in New Hampshire reinforced that judgment. Kerry would soon emerge as the consensus candidate, the person who Democrats believed to have the best chance of defeating George W. Bush in the general election.

Hillary Clinton (2008)

Clinton ran a carefully calculated and scripted campaign, focusing on the large states that had a strong Democratic base. She relied on many of the advisers and fund-raisers who had worked in her husband's presidential campaigns. Seeking to maximize her front-runner's advantage, she raised a lot of money quickly, as her husband had done in 1996 to discourage a quality challenger. She also transferred $10 million in unspent funds from her 2006 Senate campaign. Gaining endorsements from well-known Democrats, Clinton lead Obama by about 25 percent in the public opinion polls throughout 2007 and seemed well on her way to winning the Democratic nomination. Clinton's strategy was to use her financial resources to score an early knockout. Victories in the initial contests would reinforce the "inevitability" theme of her nomination. She directed her appeal to rank-and-file Democrats, especially to women, minorities, and labor.

The Clinton game plan was to play it safe, make no mistakes, and take centrist positions on the issues. She refused to apologize for her 2002 Senate vote to give the president authority to use force in Iraq, which she claimed was the correct decision based on the information that was available to members of Congress at that time. She also supported a congressional resolution that categorized the Iranian Revolutionary Guard as a terrorist organization. Her opponents hammered her on these

continued

BOX 5.2

Front-Runner Strategies: Successes and Failures *continued*

votes; they pointed to her high negatives as an indication that she was not electable in a general election.

Clinton's negative perception in the eyes of the public discouraged her from initially going negative against her Democratic opponents. Mark Penn, her chief strategist, had urged her in a campaign memo that he wrote 2007 to embrace her American values and criticize Obama's "lack of American roots."[ii]

> Every speech should contain the line you were born in the middle of America to the middle class in the middle of the last century. And talk about the . . . deeply American values you grew up with, learned as a child and that drive you today. Values of fairness, compassion, responsibility, giving back.[iii]

Clinton did not take Penn's advice.

Obama's prodigious fund-raising, Edwards's populist appeal, and the news media's penchant for subjecting the front-runner to the most critical scrutiny raised questions about the inevitability of her nomination, particularly after Obama's win in Iowa and Edwards's second-place finish. After her disappointing showing in Iowa, Clinton became more aggressive and less staged. She showed more of her personality. An incident in New Hampshire in which she showed emotion from the pressures of the campaign revealed a human dimension that had been missing from her carefully scripted candidacy.[iv] Women voters responded by shifting support to her in the days preceding the New Hampshire primary. Clinton won with 39 percent of New Hampshire's vote compared to Obama's 36 percent, Edwards's 17 percent, and Richardson's 5 percent. However, the delegate split was even, with Clinton and Obama each winning nine delegates from that state. Her victory gave her campaign a much needed boost and helped to renew her spirits.

But "the cupboard is bare" according to one of her senior advisers, Harold Ickes.[v] Her campaign had gone through $100 million in about a year. Nor could she match Obama's fund-raising in the early months of 2008. Clinton had to lend her campaign $5 million just to stay on the air in the big primaries that were to follow on Super Tuesday, February 5. After New Hampshire, the Democratic nomination campaign moved into Nevada, a caucus state in which Clinton won more popular votes but fewer pledged convention delegates. In the next contest, the South Carolina primary, Obama scored a huge victory giving him the momentum going into Super Tuesday when eight Democratic caucuses and sixteen primaries were scheduled.

Obama's prodigious fund-raising, his effective grassroots operations, and his strategy to run a fifty-state nominating campaign began to pay off. Lack of money and on-the-ground organization forced Clinton to focus her efforts on the larger states of California, New York, and New Jersey and the states around them. She won the big states. However, her popular vote exceeded the proportion of the delegates she received. She failed to focus as many resources on the delegate-rich districts in these states as did Obama, many of which had concentrations of African American voters. Clinton also did not compete with Obama in most of the caucus states and lost in all but one of them on Super Tuesday. When the results of that delegate selection process on Super Tuesday were tallied, Clinton trailed Obama by about fifty pledged delegates.

February proved to be Clinton's worst month. After Super Tuesday, February 2, 2008, she lost the five caucuses and five primaries held in that month, swelling Obama's pledged delegate lead to around 150. She also was falling further behind in

BOX 5.2 | FRONT-RUNNER STRATEGIES: SUCCESSES AND FAILURES *continued*

the money race, raising about $53 million (through February) compared to Obama's $91 million. To stay competitive, she had to lend her campaign more money. Clearly, her early knockout strategy had failed.

In February, the Clinton campaign began to unravel internally. Dissent within the campaign organization erupted. Mutual recriminations were voiced by her advisers against each other and leaked to the news media. She fired her campaign manager.[vi] Her campaign was on the ropes. Moreover, she had to win the remaining large states (Texas, Ohio, Indiana, and Pennsylvania) by a sizable percentage just to catch up. Behind in pledged delegates, her focus turned to the unpledged super delegates. Despite receiving more early endorsements from this group than Obama, Clinton was unable to maintain the support of these delegates. As politicians, they reflected their states' choice and generally sided with a majority of the pledged delegates from their respective states. Clinton won the popular vote in Texas, Ohio, and Pennsylvania but the Democrats' proportional voting rule made it virtually impossible for her to close the pledged delegate gap.

The front-runner had been overtaken by a more skillful campaign, led by a charismatic candidate with a more popular message and a more energetic base of supporters.

---

[i]Patrick Devlin, "Contrasts in Presidential Primary Campaign Commercials of 2004," Paper presented at Georgetown University, November 2004, p. 26.

[ii]Joshua Green, "The Front-Runner's Fall." *The Atlantic.com* www.theatlantic.com/magazine/print/2008/09/the-front-runner-8217-s-fall/6944\

[iii]Ibid.

[iv]On the evening preceding the New Hampshire primary, Clinton was asked how she was doing. She seemed to choke up as she noted how important the election was to the country. Her show of emotion resonated with voters, particularly women.

[v]Harold Ickes, senior aide to Clinton, was charged with overseeing campaign spending. He is quoted in Green, "The Front-Runner's Fall." www.theatlantic.com/magazine/print/2008/09/the-front-runner-8217-s-fall/6944\

[vi]Ibid.

anyway just to hammer home an ideological orientation or issue position (pulpit candidates). Howard Dean (2004), Mitt Romney (2008), and Barack Obama (2008) fit into the first category; Reverend Jesse Jackson (1984) and Ron Paul (2008) fit into the second.

Serious Contenders

George McGovern and Jimmy Carter used the reforms in the Democratic nomination process, particularly the spread of caucuses and primaries over a three-month period, as stepping-stones to the nomination. Carter's quest in 1976 became the model that others tried, with less success, to follow. Hamilton Jordan, Carter's campaign manager, who designed this basic game plan two years before the election, described the initial assumptions upon which Carter's strategy was based:

> The prospect of a crowded field coupled with the new proportional representation rule does not permit much flexibility in the early primaries.

> No serious candidate will have the luxury of picking or choosing among the early primaries. To pursue such a strategy would cost that candidate delegate votes and increase the possibility of being lost in the crowd. I think that we have to assume that everybody will be running in the first five or six primaries.
>
> A crowded field enhances the possibility of several inconclusive primaries with four or five candidates separated by only a few percentage points. Such a muddled picture will not continue for long as the press will begin to make "winners" of some and "losers" of others. The intense press coverage, which naturally focuses on the early primaries plus the decent time intervals, which separate the March and mid-April primaries, dictate a serious effort in all of the first five primaries. Our "public" strategy would probably be that Florida was the first and real test of the Carter campaign and that New Hampshire would just be a warm-up. In fact, a strong, surprise showing in New Hampshire should be our goal which would have tremendous impact on successive primaries.[26]

Jordan's plan worked. Dubbed the person to beat after his victories in the Iowa caucus and New Hampshire primary, Carter, with his defeat of George Wallace in Florida, overcame a disappointing fourth place in Massachusetts a week earlier and became the acknowledged front-runner. The Carter effort in 1976 became the strategic plan for George H. W. Bush in 1980, Gary Hart in 1984, John McCain in 2000, and most of the Democratic candidates (other than Hillary Clinton) in 2004 and 2008.

Doing well in the early caucuses and primaries is important but no longer has the payoff it had for Carter. The front-loading of the selection process has reduced the "bump" that Iowa and New Hampshire can give to a victorious non-front-runner. Yet, candidates have few other options to increase their name recognition and demonstrate their electability at the beginning of the nomination process.

The benefits of an early win are enormous for non-front-runners. Their victory, no matter how slight, confounds the odds, surprises the news media, embarrasses the front-runner, and energizes the non-front-runner's candidacy. Media coverage expands; fund-raising is made easier; volunteers join the organization; endorsements become more likely; and momentum can be generated, at least in the short run.

On the other hand, early losses for non-front-runners doom their candidacy, either immediately or in short order. In 2008, Democratic candidates Joe Biden and Christopher Dodd withdrew after doing poorly in Iowa; Bill Richardson dropped out after losing in the New Hampshire primary. John Edwards lasted longer; he ended his campaign after a disappointing performance in the state in which he had grown up and needed to win, South Carolina. On the Republican side, the end came after it was evident that McCain had a majority of the convention delegates.

Pulpit Candidates

In most contemporary nominations, there have been fringe candidates who have no realistic chance of winning their party's nomination. They run to bring attention to an issue or ideological orientation that they believe their

BOX 5.3 | NON-FRONT-RUNNER STRATEGIES: FAILURES AND SUCCESSES

Howard Dean (2004)

For political pundits, campaign operatives, and the news media, the big news of the 2003–2004 Democratic nomination process was the rise and fall of Howard Dean. When Dean announced his presidential ambitions in the fall of 2001, few took him seriously. How could a political unknown from a small, rural state have a realistic chance of winning the Democratic Party's presidential nomination? It was not 1976, when a poisonous political climate in Washington (the Watergate scandal and President Gerald Ford's pardon of Richard Nixon) and an extended Democratic primary process allowed Georgia Governor Jimmy Carter to parlay early and surprising victories in Iowa, New Hampshire, and Florida into a nomination victory.

Nor did Dean fit the mode of successful Democratic presidential candidates. He did not come from a southern state as Carter and Clinton did. He was not associated with the moderate wing of his party as both ex-presidents were. In fact, his support of a bill to grant civil unions to same-sex adults in Vermont was seen as a major liability for a presidential candidate in the general election in 2004. He did not have a lot of wealthy backers, a national political organization, or even much public recognition. Few people had ever heard of him as he began his quest.[i] How, then, did he become the Democratic front-runner, and why did his campaign collapse so quickly?

Dean's rise to prominence was a result of his innovative campaign appeal and a successful strategy to build a base of core supporters by using the Internet. Recalling the idealism of the 1960s, Dean talked about empowering people who felt alienated by the policies and practices of the Bush administration; and he categorically opposed the war in Iraq. Dean's clear-cut opposition to that war in Iraq contrasted sharply with the support that most of the other Democratic contenders had given the president in their votes for a resolution supporting the use of force, if necessary, and for appropriations to fund the military action.

Dean used the Internet effectively to solicit funds, to involve those who accessed his Web site in the activities of his campaign, and to provide them with information to convince others to join the cause. Live and recorded speeches, advertisements, and even responses to criticisms of Dean made by opposing candidates or the news media were available on his Web site. Dean raised more money than any of the other Democratic candidates in the year prior to the election, and he did so from small donors. His broad-based financial support suggested that he was tapping into a large segment of the Democratic base and possibly beyond it, reaching and energizing young people. That political perception gave credence to his campaign.

The Dean campaign maintained an ongoing conversation with people who frequented his Web site. The campaign requested comments and suggestions from those who accessed the site and posted them on the blog, which became an ongoing political forum. Campaign officials, including manager Joe Trippi, spent hours communicating with people who had asked questions and made recommendations. By the end of 2003, the names of 500,000 subscribers were in the campaign's data bank, ready to be mobilized for the caucus and primary campaigns.[ii]

Dean's rhetoric, fund-raising, and Internet operations were newsworthy. They attracted the attention of the reporters who evaluate the candidates in the year before the election on the basis of the money they raise, the recognition they gain, the distinctiveness of their campaign, their standing in the polls, the endorsements they get, and the seriousness with which they are viewed by their opponents within their party

continued

BOX 5.3 | NON-FRONT-RUNNER STRATEGIES: FAILURES AND SUCCESSES *continued*

and by the other party. Dean scored well in all these categories. That he exceeded initial expectations was also newsworthy. He became the front-runner in the fall of 2003. Al Gore and several labor unions endorsed him in December 2003; these endorsements from political insiders, however, raised questions about Dean's status as an outsider and anti-establishment fighter.

Being number one also meant being the number one target. Dean did not fare well under the microscope of news media and attacks by his political opponents. His words and actions during the period in which he was the governor of Vermont were used against him. As governor, he had once called Medicare "a bureaucratic disaster" and cautioned against creating a national health system modeled on it; as candidate, he advocated strengthening and expanding the benefits of the Medicare program. As governor, he had disparaged the Iowa caucus, saying that it was "controlled by special interests;" as candidate, he appealed to Iowans for their votes. When Dean left the governorship, he ordered many of his files closed for ten years; as candidate, he railed against the secrecy of the Bush White House and the president's failure to disclose his National Guard records in Texas and Alabama. After the capture of Saddam Hussein, Dean asserted that America was no safer than before the Iraqi dictator was apprehended, a claim that most Americans rejected.

Dean's campaign comments were highlighted as evidence that he lacked the temperament, thoughtfulness, and truthfulness to be president. He was rebuked for implying that his brother (who had been missing and believed dead since he traveled to Southeast Asia in 1974) had served in the military when he had not done so, rebuked for stating that U.S. policy in the Middle East was unbalanced and unfair, and rebuked for the comment "I still want to be the candidate for guys with Confederate flags in their pickup trucks," a comment that some interpreted as racist. Dean's opponents asked: Was he ready for prime time? Could he be elected if he were the Democratic nominee?

Dean's temperament, particularly the anger and emotion he displayed, also raised questions about his mental balance and emotional stability. His "screaming" speech to supporters after his disappointing finish in the Iowa caucuses, played and replayed by the news media, became the target of late-night comics. Had he snapped under the pressure? Would he do so in the White House?

The Dean campaign also suffered from internal staff strife.[iii] The knockout strategy, which the campaign adopted after Dean emerged as the Democratic front-runner, also boomeranged. The plan, designed in the fall of 2003, was to utilize the campaign's financial advantages and Dean's high standing in the polls to score a one-two knockout punch in Iowa and New Hampshire, and thereby make it unlikely that any candidate could overtake him. To achieve this goal, the campaign spent heavily from June 2003 to January 2004, so heavily in fact that it began the election year with a $1.2 million debt.

Dean had squandered his financial lead by advertising before Democrats were tuned to the contest, expanding his staff too quickly, and decentralizing the campaign's decision-making structure too much. Nor did his Web supporters congeal into an effective grassroots force. One hand seemed to be working against the other.[iv] And his performance in Iowa and New Hampshire provided little incentive for supporters to dig more deeply into their pockets. His campaign collapsed around him. After losing in Michigan and Wisconsin, states that he believed he had a chance to win, he ended his quest for the Democratic Party's presidential nomination, and a month later endorsed Kerry.

Non-Front-Runner Strategies: Failures and Successes *continued*

Barack Obama (2008)

The people who ran the Obama 2008 campaign learned from Dean's mistakes. Preliminary planning for Obama's presidential campaign began in 2006, right after the midterm elections. David Axelrod and David Plouffe, the political consultants who had managed Obama's 2004 Senate campaign, met with him in November 2006 to explore the possibilities of a presidential run in 2008. At the meeting, Obama indicated that he was interested, but had not definitely decided to do so. His biggest concerns were Clinton's large lead in the polls and the effect of a presidential campaign on his family. It was not until January 2007, after returning from Hawaii from a short vacation, that he decided to throw his hat into the ring.

Intense campaign planning began after he made his decision. David Plouffe, designated as campaign manager, and David Axelrod, its chief strategist, wanted the organization to be small and highly focused on critical needs: personnel, money, communications, and scheduling and advance. Special units, reporting directly to Plouffe, were established to handle relations with Democratic Party leaders and elected officials, volunteers, information technology, and strategic operations.[v]

Winning the Iowa caucus was the campaign's initial strategic goal. Iowa was important for three reasons: to demonstrate that Obama, an African American, could win in a predominantly white state; to show that Hillary Clinton's nomination was not inevitable; and to prove that an army of volunteers could be identified, organized, and mobilized, using the Internet as a primary vehicle of communications. Since Clinton had the endorsements of many prominent state and national party leaders, labor union officials, and the sympathy of much of the Democrats' rank-and-file voters, Plouffe concluded that the only way Obama could win in Iowa and other states was to enlarge the Democratic electorate by attracting new voters.

With the caucus a year away, the campaign literally set up shop in Iowa along with most of the other Democratic candidates, except for Clinton, who did not want to do so for fear of jeopardizing her fund-raising and reelection as a senator from New York. Obama visited Iowa forty-four times and stayed there a total of eighty-nine days.[vi] During his visits he held up to six events a day. His campaign flooded the state with volunteers who went to every high school, college, and university to inform students about Obama, recruit in-state volunteers, and generate excitement about his candidacy. Major events in Iowa were geared to attracting Democratic activists as well as new voters. Tickets were distributed online and at events so that the campaign could collect information on attendees and communicate with them after the event. E-mail addresses, cell phone numbers, and zip codes were fed into the campaign's data bank and used to gain volunteers, staff events, and help to register and turn out voters.[vii]

Obama loved the crowds and drew energy from them. His stump speeches, which he refined in the early months of the campaign, inspired and motivated many of those in attendance to work on his behalf. Social networking increased the reach of the campaign. To convert the volunteers into a viable grassroots organization, the Obama camp set up three- to four-day training sessions at which volunteers, many of whom had never worked in a political campaign, were given instruction on how to identify potential supporters, mobilize them, and interact with voters. Personal contact by phone or preferably by door-to-door visits was encouraged. The payoff was evident at caucus night when almost twice as many Democrats turned

continued

NON-FRONT-RUNNER STRATEGIES: FAILURES AND SUCCESSES *continued*

out than in the party's 2004 presidential caucus. Obama won 37.6 percent of the vote compared Edwards's 29.7 percent and Clinton's 29.5 percent.

Although his strategy produced a growing base of support in Iowa, Obama had not yet commanded national attention. Thus his victory in the first caucus surprised many of those who had not been following the campaign that closely. In the first nation-wide poll following Iowa, Obama surged ahead of Clinton after trailing her by about 25 percent throughout 2007. Obama had ended 2007 even with Clinton in fund-raising, but had several advantages going into election year. He had a larger donor base but had received smaller average contributions, so he could go back to that base for more money. A larger proportion of Clinton's contributors had given the maximum amount. With his victory in Iowa, revenues shot up. In January and February of 2008, Obama took in revenues of $90.5 million, almost equal to the amount he received in all of the previous year and almost double the money Clinton received during the first two months of the election year. His campaign was also more frugal in spending than Clinton's.[viii]

The victory in Iowa raised expectations for Obama, but the New Hampshire primary, scheduled five days later, presented additional problems for the grassroots component of his campaign.[ix] Moreover, it is harder to enlarge the electorate as much in a primary as in a caucus, particularly in a state that traditionally has a high rate of voting. Clinton had a stronger base in New Hampshire, one that included state party leaders, labor unions, and Emily's List, an organization devoted to the election of women candidates. Moreover, Obama was competing against McCain for the votes of Independents.[x]

Clinton beat Obama by 3 percent of the popular vote in New Hampshire, but they divided the delegates evenly, undercutting the significance of her victory. Following New Hampshire, the Democratic contest turned to the Nevada caucus, in which Clinton won the popular vote by 6 percent, but the delegates were again divided with Obama eventually getting a majority.

South Carolina, the last primary before Super Tuesday when twenty-three states were to hold their primaries or start their caucus selection process, was critical for Obama. With Clinton expected to do well in the large states on Super Tuesday, Obama needed a victory in South Carolina to regain momentum after New Hampshire and Nevada. His campaign had been active in the state, visiting barber shops, beauty salons, and college and university campuses. Its goal, to maximize the votes of African Americans and whites under 40, was successful, resulting in an unexpectedly large win for Obama. He received 55 percent of the popular vote and twenty-five of the state's forty-five delegates, giving him momentum going into Super Tuesday.

To counter Clinton's advantage in the large populous states, Obama used his growing war chest to advertise extensively in these states; he also competed in *all* of the smaller caucus states. Clinton contested only one of them, Colorado. Obama's strategy proved more successful. Although Clinton won the large states and Obama the small states, Obama received a total of fifteen more delegates than Clinton. He had survived Super Tuesday and was in position to extend his delegate lead in February against a Clinton campaign that was becoming increasingly disorganized and underfinanced. By the first Tuesday in March, when Democrats in Ohio and Texas were to vote, Obama held a 150 pledged delegate lead.

BOX 5.3 | Non-Front-Runner Strategies: Failures and Successes *continued*

At this point the press's campaign narrative began to change from its emphasis on popular vote to one that emphasized pledged delegates. David Plouffe had helped this narrative along by convincing the *New York Times* to count delegates in caucus states on the basis of the vote in the first stage of the caucus process even though the actual delegates would not be chosen until state conventions later in the spring. Plouffe pointed out to Adam Nagourney, the chief political correspondent of the *New York Times*, that the initial caucus vote almost always reflected the final allocation of delegates chosen at state conventions because of the pledges the delegates take before they were elected.[xi]

Even though Clinton won the Ohio, Texas, and Rhode Island primaries on March 4, the date on which 85 percent of the Democratic delegates had been selected, she had reduced the Obama delegate lead by only 6. Clinton's only realistic hope to win the nomination was to gain the support of most of the 852 unpledged superdelegates, a group that constituted 19 percent of the convention. As previously mentioned, Clinton had begun the race with considerably more support from this group than Obama had.

Both campaigns communicated regularly with these "supers." As Obama built a lead among the pledged delegates, his campaign launched a public relations effort to convince the superdelegates not to reverse the judgment of the people who had already voted. In his book *The Audacity to Win,* Plouffe wrote, "we assumed that if we did well at the polls, the supers would follow, and if we stumbled early, it wouldn't matter."[xii] And he was right. The superdelegates began to fall into the Obama camp, reflecting the choice of voters in their states. In some cases, the "supers" had to repudiate an earlier endorsement they had made for Clinton.

Although the Democratic campaign continued until all the primaries and caucuses were completed, Obama never relinquished his delegate lead. His campaign had designed and executed a successful strategy. The use of the Internet as a communications tool to identify volunteers, solicit contributions, and mobilize supporters contributed substantially to that success. Although there were unexpected bumps along the way—Clinton's New Hampshire victory, the incendiary remarks of Obama's minister the Rev. Jeremiah Wright, and a few careless ad lib comments by Obama—they did not matter in the end. He won the most delegates and with them, the Democratic Party's presidential nomination.

John McCain

2000

In 2000, John McCain had challenged George W. Bush and other Republicans for that party's nomination. Lacking the financial and organizational support that Bush had, McCain skipped the Iowa caucus and turned his attention to New Hampshire. He spent months traveling through the state with a small staff on a bus dubbed *The Straight Talk Express*. McCain won 48 percent of the New Hampshire vote compared to Bush's 30 percent and 13 percent for publisher Steve Forbes.

The senator's unexpectedly large victory put Bush on the defensive, hastened the departure of other Republican candidates, and added $7 million to McCain's coffers. But it also raised expectations for McCain in the next contest, South Carolina, a state

continued

BOX 5.3

NON-FRONT-RUNNER STRATEGIES: FAILURES AND SUCCESSES *continued*

in which Bush enjoyed the backing of the Republican establishment, the Christian Coalition, and pro-tobacco groups whom McCain had alienated by his antismoking crusade. These groups went after McCain personally and politically, focusing on his Senate record, his loyalty to the Republican Party, and even rumors about his private life. Operating at the grassroots level, the anti-McCain groups contacted millions of voters by phone and mail, raising questions about McCain's religious convictions, his moral turpitude, and his stands on abortion, school prayer, and civil rights.

Initially, the senator responded to these attacks with attacks of his own. However, when the press made negative campaigning an issue, McCain abruptly pulled his negative ads. He pledged not to go negative even though the pro-Bush groups continued their anti-McCain campaign. In the end, Bush won handily; McCain's New Hampshire bubble had burst, and his momentum slowed appreciably.

The 2000 primaries then moved to more friendly territory for McCain, Michigan and his home state of Arizona, states in which religious conservatives were not nearly as strong as in South Carolina. Although the Republican establishment in both states endorsed Bush, and conservative antiabortion and antitax groups mounted grassroots campaigns against him, McCain was able to overcome this opposition by appealing to independent and Democratic voters. He won both contests, at which point his candidacy looked viable, raising money and appealing to a cross section of voters. Public opinion polls actually showed McCain running better than George W. Bush against the likely Democratic nominee, Al Gore.

The next three contests, the Washington and Virginia primaries and the caucus in North Dakota, proved disappointing to McCain and essentially undercut the boost that he had received from his Arizona and Michigan victories. Facing on-the-ground opposition again, state rules that prohibited crossover voting by Independents and Democrats, and a resurgent Bush campaign, McCain lost in each of these states. A failed tactical gamble sealed his fate in Virginia. Speaking to voters in the southern part of the state, an area known for its religious fundamentalism, McCain denounced two of Virginia's most prominent fundamentalist ministers, Jerry Falwell and Pat Robertson, as "agents of intolerance" and "forces of evil," comments that united the Christian fundamentalists and brought out an unusually large vote against McCain.[xiii]

The next week was Super Tuesday, a date on which twelve Republican primaries and two first-round caucuses were to be held. McCain could not match Bush's money or organization. Although he won four out of the five New England primaries, he lost everywhere else, including the delegate-rich states of California, Ohio, and New York. With his opponent's delegate lead all but insurmountable, having come within $1 million of his spending limit because he had been forced to accept federal funds and Bush had not, the race was essentially over. McCain announced he would reevaluate his campaign. He went home to Arizona.

The lessons for 2008 were clear. McCain had not established sufficient credibility among Republicans. He had alienated fundamentalist Christians, a core constituency within the party. He lacked the support of most Republican state party leaders; he did not have a genuine grassroots movement in states in which only Republicans could participate in the caucuses and primaries. He did not start his campaign early enough, did not raise sufficient funds, did not accept criticism easily, and did not consult sufficiently with campaign professionals. His independence, so appealing to

BOX 5.3 | Non-Front-Runner Strategies: Failures and Successes *continued*

the general public, had backfired with core Republicans; his dependence on federal matching funds limited his competitiveness over the long haul. Moreover, his appeal to independent and Democratic voters, an asset in the general election, proved to be a mixed blessing at best, and a detriment at worst, in the primaries. Clearly, McCain had much to change in his statements and actions as a senator, in his personal image and policy appeal as a candidate, and in his campaign strategy and tactics if he was ever going to be a serious contender for the Republican presidential nomination.

2008

As the 2008 nomination approached, McCain showed his solidarity with Protestant fundamentalists on social issues. He gave a 2006 commencement address at Liberty University and campaigned extensively for Republican candidates in the midterm elections of that year. Meeting with Republican leaders and benefactors, he emphasized his conservatism and his loyalty to basic Republican principles. Although he had criticized the way the Bush administration was conducting the war in Iraq, he backed the president's surge of troops there. These actions, along with McCain personal notoriety, put him in the front-runner's position as the 2007–2008 election cycle began.

The McCain campaign initially adopted a front-runner's strategy. In the words of Rick Davis who became his campaign manager:

> The campaign at the get-go was, to some degree, a reaction to the campaign in 2000. We ran a totally different campaign in 2000 and it lost. . . . The win quotient was probably the strongest motivator for our design and strategy. Therefore, we looked at the Bush successes in both 2000 and 2004. We believed bigger was better.[xiv]

The campaign began early in 2007 with appearances at Republican events, appeals to party leaders, and fund-raising as the initial focus. Unfortunately for McCain, Republican losses in the 2006 midterm elections marred his fund-raising and party mobilization efforts. Moreover, his history of independence, his support of immigration reform, and his de-emphasis of social issues also generated concerns about his conservative values. The financial and political support he anticipated from Republicans did not materialize.

By the summer of 2007, the press was reporting that McCain's campaign was suffering from internal divisions, insufficient revenue, and an incoherent strategic plan. Top aides were let go; McCain had to borrow $4 million in November just to keep his campaign a float.[xv] A new strategic plan, one that was more consistent with McCain's independent style and personal character, was adopted. It was decided to skip Iowa, which has a large, socially conservative Republican base; McCain did not want to end up in the middle or at the bottom of the pack of Republicans running in the first caucus. He climbed back aboard the *Straight Talk Express* and headed to New Hampshire. Iowa was no longer in the cards. McCain also began to reposition himself as a centrist Republican to the right of former New York mayor and presidential candidate Rudolph Giuliani and to the left of the other Republicans who were running for the nomination. The campaign was largely dependent on volunteers, some of whom had been active in McCain's previous presidential effort.

continued

NON-FRONT-RUNNER STRATEGIES: FAILURES AND SUCCESSES *continued*

The decision not to compete in Iowa worked to McCain's political advantage. Mitt Romney's loss in that state, after vastly outspending his opponents, raised questions about his viability as a Republican candidate. Giuliani's poor showing and his campaign's decision to pull out of New Hampshire helped McCain attract moderate Republicans in that state and in subsequent primaries. Even Obama's victory in Iowa indirectly helped McCain. According to Plouffe, Obama's meteoric rise in public opinion polls contributed to the vote McCain received from Independents who may have thought that McCain needed their vote more than Obama did.[xvi]

Although McCain won only 37.1 percent of the vote in New Hampshire, substantially less than in 2000, to 31.6 percent for Romney and 11.2 percent for Mike Huckabee, his victory reversed his fortunes, inflicted a second straight loss on Romney, and undercut Mike Huckabee's boost from his surprising victory in Iowa. McCain lost the next primary to Romney in Michigan, a state in which Romney's father had served as governor. The Republican campaign then shifted to South Carolina. Unlike 2000, McCain had secured the support of party leaders in that state with the help of his close friend and colleague Senator Lindsay Graham. He beat Huckabee, a former governor of Arkansas, by 3 percent of the vote and won nineteen of the state's twenty-four delegates.

Florida was the next big Republican primary. It was a do-or-die state for Giuliani, who had not done well in the previous Republican contests. Prior to his victory in New Hampshire, McCain had only one paid staffer in Florida but a strong organization of volunteers. He received an infusion of contributions following his wins in New Hampshire and South Carolina and used it to mount a large media effort in Florida in the final 10 days of the campaign. Although the vote was primarily divided among four Republican candidates, McCain was the plurality winner with 36 percent. But Florida was the first of the large Republican winner-take-all states, and McCain's vote, only 5 percent more than Romney's, gave him all of Florida's fifty-four delegates and momentum going into Super Tuesday. Giuliani's withdrawal and his quick endorsement of McCain, along with the endorsement of California Governor Arnold Schwarzenegger, added to that momentum.

There were twenty-one Republican contests on February 5, Super Tuesday. McCain won nine of them compared to Romney's seven and Huckabee's five. However, McCain won all the big states—California, Illinois, Missouri, New Jersey, and New York—that allocated most of their delegates to the popular-vote winner. Thus he added 511 delegates to the 95 he had already won, while Romney only picked up 176 and Huckabee 147. In the February primaries, McCain added to his delegate lead. By March 4, he had won a majority of GOP convention delegates. The race was over.

Mitt Romney (2008)

Mitt Romney was another non-front-runner who began the 2008 campaign for the Republican nomination with high hopes and abundant resources. He had been governor of Massachusetts, played an instrumental role in saving the Salt Lake City winter Olympic games, and came from a prominent Republican family. His father, a popular governor of Michigan, had run for president in 1968. However, it was not Romney's past but his prodigious fund-raising that brought him media attention and a political boost. His own personal wealth added to the resources he had available to mount a strong nomination campaign.

BOX 5.3

Non-Front-Runner Strategies: Failures and Successes *continued*

Romney was not without political liabilities, however. His "real" positions on social issues, his religion, and perceptions of inauthenticity plagued him throughout his campaign. As a candidate for governor of Massachusetts, he said that he would not overturn that state's liberal law on abortion; as candidate for the Republican nomination, he said he was pro-life. His Mormon religion was viewed by some fundamentalist Christians, who were part of the GOP base, as a heresy. To overcome that issue, Romney spent months in Iowa trying to restructure his image and articulate his conservative policy credentials.[xvii] But to many, his physical appearance and structured language seemed unreal, contrived.

Romney used his financial advantage to flood the early states, particularly Iowa and New Hampshire, with advertising, yet it seemed to have little effect. Despite his large expenditure of funds, he came in second in both states. Although he gained a brief reprieve by winning the Michigan primary, he lost in South Carolina, Florida, and all the large states, except for Massachusetts, on Super Tuesday. He stayed close to McCain in the popular vote but lost all the large winner-take-all states. After McCain won enough delegates to secure the Republican nomination, Romney dropped out, effectively ending the Republican race.

---

[i]In surveys conducted over the summer of 2003, the Pew Research Center for the People and the Press found substantial but decreasing portions of the population (63 percent in early July, 54 percent in August, and 43 percent in September) who had *not* heard of Howard Dean. See "The 2004 Political Landscape," the Pew Research Center for the People and the Press, question 27.

[ii]Brian Faler, "Dean Leaves Legacy of Online Campaign," *The Washington Post* (Feb. 20, 2004), p. A12; and Brian Faler, "Add 'Blog' to the Campaign Lexicon," *The Washington Post* (Nov. 15, 2003), p. A4.

[iii]Joe Trippi, a political consultant who had become the campaign manager, and Kate O'Connor, Dean's longtime aide, did not get along well, nor was Trippi able to exercise tight control over campaign operations. Critics pointed to the campaign manager's poor administrative skills, his abrasive manner, and his tendency to talk but not listen. Moreover, Trippi did not have a close personal relationship with Dean. After the disappointing showing in Iowa, Trippi left the campaign and Dean named a new campaign manager, but by then, it was too late. Dan Balz and Jonathan Finer, "Dean Staff Shake-Up Long Coming," *The Washington Post* (Jan. 30, 2004), p. A7.

[iv]Glen Justice and Jodi Wilgoren, "Figures Detail Dean's Slide from Solvent to Struggling," *The New York Times* (Feb. 2, 2004), p. A18.

[v]David Plouffe, *The Audacity to Win* (New York: Viking, 2009), p. 30.

[vi]"Democracy in Action: Race for the White House, 2008," www.gwu.edu/~action/2008/ia08/iavisits08d.html

[vii]Plouffe, *Audacity*, p. 48.

[viii]Ibid., pp. 34–35.

[ix]Although Obama had visited New Hampshire often, his grassroots operation was smaller than in Iowa. www.gwu.edu/~action/2008/nh08/nhvisits08d.html

[x]David Plouffe writes that the Obama campaign received numerous reports of Independents telling them, "Your guy is going to win. I think McCain is the best Republican, it will give us a good choice. But don't worry, I'm voting Obama in November." Plouffe, *Audacity*, p. 153.

[xi]Ibid., pp. 183–184.

[xii]Ibid., p. 183.

[xiii]Alison Mitchell, "Birth and Death of the 'Straight-Talk Express'," *The New York Times* (March 11, 2000), p. A8.

[xiv]Rick Davis as quoted in Kennedy Institute, *Campaign for President: the Managers Look at 2008* (Landam, MD.: Rowman and Littlefield, 2010), pp. 5–6.

[xv]McCain used anticipated government matching funds as collateral for the loan. He had failed as a celebrity candidate, as the Republican heir apparent.

[xvi]Plouffe, *Audacity*, p. 153.

[xvii]Beth Myers in *Campaign for President: 2008*, p. 73.

party is neglecting. For them, campaigning in full public view is an end in itself. They use the campaign as a pulpit. These candidates include Rev. Jesse Jackson (1984 and 1988), Rev. Pat Robertson (1988), Pat Buchanan (1992, 1996, and 2000), Carol Mosley Braun (2004), Rev. Al Sharpton (2004), Dennis Kucinich (2004 and 2008), and Ron Paul (2008).

Pulpit candidates cannot afford large staffs, high-priced consultants, or much, if any, paid media. They depend on volunteers, free media, and events to which all the candidates are invited. They run because they want a podium to promote particular points of view, to draw attention to themselves and their causes, and/or to represent the communities that they believe are not being adequately represented by establishment candidates.

In 2004, Carol Moseley-Braun did not want the Democratic Party to take its large female constituency for granted. She thought it important that there be a woman candidate. The biggest applause line in her abbreviated campaign was "Take the men-only sign off the White House door." But Moseley-Braun could not campaign for long. She lacked the stature to raise sufficient funds, even among women. Her war chest of less than $600,000 was the smallest of all the Democrats. She dropped out before the Iowa caucus.

Rev. Al Sharpton had greater name recognition than Mosley-Braun. He had been at the forefront of various social protests. He gave voice to many of the concerns of those at the lower end of the socioeconomic scale. A critic of the war in Iraq and the administration's probusiness economic and social policies, he presented the other side, often with great wit, during the debates among the Democratic candidates. His campaign helped energize the African American community after its disappointment in the Electoral College outcome of the 2000 presidential election.

Dennis Kucinich, a liberal member of Congress and former mayor of Cleveland, was also an outspoken critic of Bush's Iraq policy, his use of executive power, his unilateral approach to foreign and domestic policy making, and restrictions placed on Americans' civil rights and political liberties in the name of fighting terrorism. But his campaigns lacked money, organization, and visibility. He stayed in the 2004 race but had little effect on it. In 2008, he was forced to drop out early when his congressional seat was challenged.

Initially, Congressman Ron Paul did not want to run for president. He did not like government and couldn't imagine himself as head of it. Persuaded by aides who supported a libertarian policy agenda, Paul entered the Republican nomination process. Without much public recognition and resources, his strategy was to try to attract Republicans who were dissatisfied with the Bush administration and libertarians who had few inroads into the political process. According to his campaign manager Lew Moore, "at some point it [the campaign] caught on fire on the Internet and we were able to start raising money. We were able to start building an organization through Meetup. Before the end of the campaign, we had seventy-five thousand people in Meetup groups and we raised thirty-five million dollars."[27]

The money, much of it raised on two special days for libertarians, the anniversary of the Boston Tea Party and Guy Fawkes Day,[28] caught the news media's attention, but it didn't convert into much public support or delegate votes. Moreover, Paul's criticism of the Bush administration's interventionist foreign policy did not sit well with strong national security advocates, primarily Republicans, who supported the war in Iraq and other administration initiatives. Paul got his podium, but little else.

SUMMARY

In running for their party's nomination, candidates have to make a number of important strategic decisions. These include when to begin, how to organize, where to concentrate their early focus, how to raise money and on what to spend it, how to gain the necessary news media coverage, monitor public opinion, and design and target a distinctive appeal and simultaneously create an authentic leadership image. Making effective use of modern communication technologies is essential.

Tactical decisions on how to mobilize and allocate sufficient resources to build and maintain delegate support depend on the particular circumstances of individual candidates, the environment in which the state nomination contest occurs, and the time frame required for tactics to have an impact. The new technologies of the late twentieth and early twenty-first centuries have extended the reach but shortened the candidate's reaction time. Computers are now used to map and track political advertising and test it with focus groups; targeted appeals are calibrated to arouse particular emotions in selective political communities; and interactive campaigning on the Internet is now standard. The use of these technologies requires expertise and financial resources—another reason for having a large war chest early in the campaign. In general, there have been two successful prototypes for winning the nomination: the out-front, big-bucks, challenge-me-if-you-dare approach of the leading candidates and the come-from-the-pack approach of the non-front-runners.

Front-runners have to maintain their position as likely nominees. That position brings recognition, money, and political endorsements. These resources, in turn, provide front-runners with more flexibility at the outset, but it also requires them to wage a broad-based campaign since they would be criticized for not doing so. They also need to stay in the news, which their participation in multistate caucuses and primaries ensure. Their aim is an early knockout. If successful, such a strategy will end the nomination process toward the beginning of it; if they are not successful, then they face the initial danger of not meeting expectations and eventually running out of gas.

In contrast, non-front-runners need stepping stones to the nomination. Their initial goal must be to establish themselves as viable candidates. At the outset, the key is recognition. Over the long haul, it is momentum. Recognition is bestowed by the news media on those who do well in the early caucuses and primaries; momentum is achieved through a series of prenomination victories that demonstrate electability. Together, recognition and momentum compensate for what the non-front-runners lack in reputation and popular appeal. That is why non-front-runners must concentrate their time, efforts, and resources on the first few contests. They have no choice: winning will provide them with opportunities; losing will confirm their secondary status.

In the end, the ability to generate a popular appeal among the party's electorate is likely to be decisive. Only one person in each party can amass a majority of the delegates, and that is the individual who can build a broad-based coalition. Although specific groups may be targeted, if the overall constituency is too narrow, the nomination cannot be won. That is why most candidates tend to broaden and moderate their appeal over the course of the nomination process.

WHERE ON THE WEB?

The Nomination Campaign

- **Democracy in Action**
  www.P2012.org
  A Web site maintained by Eric M. Appleman. Contains pertinent and up-to-date information on the current or next campaign with links to other sources.
- **4President.org**
  www.4president.org
  Contains information on candidates, their Web sites, and commercials. Also maintains a blog on the campaign and election.
- **Gallup Poll**
  www.gallup.com
  Check this site for up-to-date polling data and analyses.
- **National Journal**
  www.nationaljournal.com
  There are many news sources for following the presidential primaries and caucuses; the *National Journal's* site is one of the best.
- **New York Times**
  www.nytimes.com
  The New York Times prides itself on being a paper of record. You will find much information on the policy positions and speeches of the candidates in this newspaper as well as the latest delegate count and prenomination polls.
- **Politico**
  www.politico.com
  A daily news site that focuses on national and state politics and government.
- **Politics1**
  www.politics1.com
  An online guide to current politics with links to other relevant sites for the presidential election.
- **Polling Report**
  www.pollingreport.com
  Summarizes public polls on the election.
- **The Daily Beast**
  www.thedailybeast.com
  Another Web site that reports and blogs on politics and government.

Exercises

1. Check the official and unofficial Web sites of the candidates. Use the information from these Web sites to compare and contrast their positions on the most controversial issues in the campaign. Then compare the personal images that they have tried to project. On the basis of these comparisons, whom do you support and why?
2. Follow the news of the nomination campaign from the perspective of a major newspaper, television network, and print or online magazine. Is the coverage of different media and of the different candidates essentially the same? From which source did you learn the most about strategy and tactics? From which did you learn the most about the candidates themselves?
3. Analyze the nomination campaign on the basis of the candidates' basic appeals, strategies, and tactics. Use Internet sources from the candidates, the news media, and public interest Web sites to obtain the information you need for your analysis.

Selected Readings

Burden, Barry. "The Nominations: Technology, Money, and Transferable Momentum," in Michael Nelson, ed., *The Election of 2004*. Washington, DC: CQ Press, 2005, pp. 18–41.

Green, Joshua. "The Front-Runner's Fall," *The Atlantic*, Sept. 2008. www.theatlantic.com/magazine/print/2008/09/the-front-runner-8217-s-fall/6944.

Heilemann, John, and Mark Halperin. *Game Change*. New York: HarperCollins, 2010.

Jamieson, Kathleen Hall, ed. *Electing the President, 2008: The Insider's View.* Philadelphia: University of Pennsylvania Press, 2009.

Kennedy Institute of Politics. *Campaign for President: The Managers Look at 2008.* Landam, MD: Rowman & Littlefield, 2009.

Magleby, David B. *Getting Inside the Outside Campaign*. Provo, UT: Brigham Young University, 2000.

Mayer, William G. "The Basic Dynamics of the Contemporary Nomination Process: An Expanded View," in William G. Mayer, ed., *The Making of the Presidential Candidates 2000*. Lanham, MD: Rowman & Littlefield, 2004, pp. 83–132.

Norrander, Barbara. "Democratic Marathon, Republican Sprint: The 2008 Presidential Nominations," in Janet M. Box-Steffensmeier and Steven E. Schier, eds., *The American Elections of 2008*. Lanham, MD: Rowman & Littlefield, 2009, pp. 33–53.

Plouffe, David. *The Audacity to Win*. New York: Viking, 2009.

Simien, Evelyn M. "Clinton and Obama: The Impact of Race and Sex on the 2008 Democratic Presidential Primaries," in William J. Crotty, ed., *Winning the Presidency.* Boulder, CO: Paradigm Publishers, 2009, pp. 123–134.

Stokes, Ashli Quesinberry. "Clinton, Post-Feminism, and Rhetorical Reception on the Campaign Trail," in Robert E. Denton, Jr., ed., *The 2008 Presidential Campaign.* Lanham, MD: Rowman & Littlefield, 2009, pp. 127–147.

Notes

1. When Rudolph Giuliani finally decided to run for the Republican presidential nomination in early February 2007, he found that most of the key GOP political consultants had already been hired by other candidates. According to his director for strategy, Brent Seaborn, Giuliani, had difficulty finding competent staff for his campaign. Kennedy Institute of Politics at Harvard University, *Campaign for President: the Managers Look at 2008* (Lanham, MD: Rowman & Littlefield, 2009), p. 13.

2. Howard Wolson quoted in Ibid., p. 45.
3. Bill Lacy, Campaign Chair for Fred Thompson, quoted in Ibid., p. 10.
4. In his first three years in office, Bush took 40 percent of his domestic trips from the White House to states he won or lost by 6 percent of the vote or less. Kathryn Dunn Tenpass and Anthony Corrado, "Permanent Campaign Brushes Aside Tradition," *Arizona Daily Star* (March 30, 2004). www.brookings.edu
5. Sheryl Cohen, Campaign Manager for Chris Dodd, quoted in *Campaign for President 2008,* p. 38.
6. New Hampshire brags that its primary has been the first in the nation since 1920. "First in the Nation," in *The New Hampshire Primary: What It Means to the State and the Nation* (published by the State of New Hampshire, 2000), p. 26.
7. Professor Barbara Norrander notes that in nomination contests between 1976 and 1988 some of the biggest spenders on the Republican side have also been the biggest losers. Barbara Norrander, "Nomination Choices: Caucus and Primary Outcomes, 1976–1988," *American Journal of Political Science,* 37 (May 1993), p. 361.
8. Beth Myers, Campaign Manager for Mitt Romney, *Campaign for President 2008,* p. 73.
9. Terrence Jeffrey, Buchanan's Campaign Manager, Kennedy Institute, *Campaign for President: The Managers Look at '96.* (Hollis, NH: Hollis Publishing Company, 1997), pp. 7–8.
10. "Election Watch '08: The Road to the Conventions," *Media Monitor,* 22 (Summer 2008). www.cmpa.com.
11. Thomas E. Patterson and Robert D. McClure, *The Unseeing Eye* (New York: Putnam, 1976), p. 58.
12. Dante J. Scala notes that the Democratic candidates who have been most successful in New Hampshire are those whose campaigns built such partisan coalitions. Dante J. Scala, "Rereading the Tea Leaves: New Hampshire as a Barometer of Presidential Primary Success," *PS: Political Science and Politics,* 36 (April 2003), pp. 187–192. John Kerry and Hillary Clinton also emphasized their partisan base in New Hampshire.
13. Craig Allen Smith, "Candidate Strategies in the 2004 Presidential Campaign: Instrumental Choices Faced by the Incumbent and His Challengers," in Robert E. Denton, Jr., ed., *The 2004 Presidential Campaign: A Communication Perspective* (Lanham, MD: Rowman & Littlefield, 2005), p. 141.
14. Jon Carson, Obama's Field Director, quoted in Kathleen Hall Jamieson, ed., *Electing the President, 2008: The Insiders' View* (Phildelphia: University of Pennsylvania Press, 2009), p. 42.
15. Joshua Green, "The Front-Runner's Fall," *The Atlantic* www.theatlantic.com/magazine/print/2008/09/the-front-runner-8217-s-fall/6944\.
16. David Plouffe, *The Audacity to Win* (New York: Viking, 2009), p. 86.
17. Dick Morris, *Behind the Oval Office* (New York: Random House, 1997), pp. 146–147.
18. Annenberg Center, "The Primary Campaign," (March 27, 2000); "About One Third of Super-Tuesday Democratic Voters Say They Know Enough to Make an Informed Choice." Annenberg Public Policy Center of the University of Pennsylvania. www.annenbergpublicpolicycenter.org/naes/2004_03_knowledge-dem-candidates-supertuesday_02–27_pr.

19. "Americans Following Presidential Campaign More Closely Than in 2004, Annenberg Data Show," www.annenbergpublicpolicycenter.org; "Public has Much to Learn about Presidential Candidates' Issue Positions, National Annenberg Election Survey Shows," Annenberg Public Policy Center (Sept. 26, 2008). www.annenbergpublicpolicycenter.org.
20. "Endorsements Don't Sway the Public—With a Few Exceptions," Annenberg Public Policy Center (March 5, 2008). www.annenbergpublicpolicycenter.org.
21. "Rush Limbaugh Succeeded in Defining John McCain's Credential, New National Annenberg Election Survey finds," Annenberg Public Policy Center (Feb. 8, 2008). www.annenbergpublicpolicycenter.org
22. Neil Munro, "The New Wired Politics," *National Journal* (April 22, 2000), p. 1260.
23. Plouffe, *Audacity*, p. 237.
24. According to a survey conducted by the Pew Research Center for the People and the Press, 11 percent of the population reported the Internet as their primary source of news about the 2000 election campaign, 21 percent about the 2004 campaign, and 40 percent about the 2008 election. "Internet Overtakes Newspapers as News Outlet," Pew Research Center for the People and the Press (Dec. 23, 2008). pewresearch.org/pubs/1066/internet-overtakes-newspapers-as-news-source.
25. Scott Reed quoted in Kennedy Institute, *Campaign for President: The Managers Look at '96*. (Hollis, NH: Hollis Publishing Company, 1997), p. 24.
26. Hamilton Jordan, "Memorandum to Jimmy Carter, August 4, 1974," in Martin Schram, *Running for President 1976* (New York: Stein & Day, 1977), pp. 379–380.
27. Lew Moore, Campaign Manager for Ron Paul, quoted in *Campaign for President 2008*, p. 22.
28. Libertarians celebrate Guy Fawkes Day, the day when a group of rebels, including Fawkes, planned to blow up the English Parliament. Fawkes was captured, tried, and executed.

6 CHAPTER

Spring and Summer Interregnum: Consolidating Victory and Posturing for the Election

INTRODUCTION

Caucuses and primaries start earlier, and conventions occur later, leaving a period of four to five months from the time the nomination may be effectively determined to the time when the nominee is officially "crowned" as the party's standard-bearer. This interregnum is important for the prospective nominees and their parties. The nominees need to repair any damage that the competitive nomination process inflicted on their image, policy stands, and electoral coalition. The parties need to reenergize, reunify, and refocus their efforts on the forthcoming campaign. And they both need to keep the public focused on the forthcoming election and the merits of their candidacies and their policy positions.

THE NONCOMPETITIVE PHASE OF THE NOMINATION CAMPAIGN

Even after becoming the preordained nominee, it is necessary for a candidate to continue the campaign until the convention to raise money, unify the party, project a strong and desirable leadership image, and keep the public interested and informed about the forthcoming election.

Repairing the Damage

In a competitive nomination, the more negative the campaign, the more likely that the nominee's personal image will have been tarnished, policy positions questioned, and divisions within the party widened. Each of these election-oriented problems requires attention and a public campaign to overcome them.

Candidates may have to reintroduce themselves to the voters to regain the electorate's attention and to remove or at least reduce the negative stereotypes by which their partisan opponents, other party candidates, and the news media and late-night comics have characterized them. Biographical ads, reinforced by information given to the press, and convention speeches given by distinguished party leaders can alter a less-than-desirable image that remains after a bitter nomination campaign.

Bill Clinton faced this problem after winning the Democratic nomination in 1992. Savaged first by press allegations of womanizing, draft dodging, and smoking marijuana, and later by criticism of his centrist policy positions by his liberal opponent, former California Governor Jerry Brown, Clinton needed to recast his presidential image. To do so, his campaign designed a series of commercials that detailed the hardships and struggles that this poor boy from Arkansas encountered growing up and ultimately surmounted in his rise to political prominence. The ads, combined with talk-show appearances in which the candidate reminisced about his upbringing, gradually muted Clinton's negative image.

Al Gore faced a different type of image problem in the spring of 2000. He needed to establish his own leadership credentials by moving out of Clinton's shadow. The primaries had not enabled him to do so fully, in part because his opponent, Bill Bradley, had proven to be a weak challenger, and in part because Clinton remained a very active and visible president. To gain stature, Gore needed to stand on his own or be credited with some of the economic successes of the Clinton years. He chose initially to emphasize his independence, thereby distancing himself from the president and making it harder to claim credit for the administration's accomplishments in the general election.

In 2004, John Kerry faced a different task. Not as well known as Gore, he had to present his qualifications to the American people. Most importantly, he had to define himself, knowing that Bush's reelection committee would do so as well and in much less flattering terms. He also needed money. His campaign had spent most of the funds he had raised to win the Democratic nomination, whereas the president's reelection committee was flush with cash. Kerry had little choice but to concentrate much of his time and energy during the spring on fund-raising while the Bush campaign unleashed attacks against him, beginning in early March 2004. During this period, the Kerry campaign depended on the advertising by outside, nonparty groups to defend his candidacy and attack Bush. However, he could not coordinate his particular advertising needs with these groups because federal law prohibits such consultation. Unfortunately for Kerry, the ads by nonparty groups did not do what his campaign would have liked them to do—define Kerry in positive terms.[1] Instead, they criticized Bush, who already had high negatives among Democrats. Thus, the early definitions of Kerry were provided primarily by the Bush campaign, much to Kerry's disadvantage.

Bringing his opponent down to size was the first objective of Bush's anti-Kerry campaign; setting the foundation for the president's reelection efforts was the second. Almost immediately, the Bush campaign aired negative Kerry commercials that presented the Massachusetts senator as a flip-flopper who regularly voted on both sides of controversial issues. The Kerry campaign did not respond directly to these allegations. Instead, it took time to reorganize, raise money, and tailor the message that it was going to present to the American people: the John Kerry story, his career, his knowledge of the issues, his policy positions, and his character. Cumulatively, these ads comprised a biography that Kerry's campaign staff thought was more compelling than disjointed refutations of the various charges the Republicans were directing at him. By not directly confronting the flip-flopper accusation, however, Kerry inadvertently let the charges stick in the public's mind. His personal negatives increased; his standing in the polls declined; and he lost much of the luster that he had gained by winning the Democratic primaries. Bush's anti-Kerry message made it more difficult for the Democratic challenger to project his own image of strong leadership.

Obama faced a different challenge in 2008. The length of the Democratic nomination process, which continued through the first week of June, gave him less time to refashion his image, unify the party, and plan for the convention and his general election campaign. His staff was exhausted; he had money but needed to raise more for the general election.[2] Obama met secretly with his Democratic opponent, Hillary Clinton, two days after the last primaries were held on the first Tuesday in June. They each agreed to appoint committees to begin the healing process and encourage Clinton's volunteers and donors to work for the Obama campaign in the general election. Clinton's role (and that of her husband) at the convention and during the election campaign was to be clarified. Finally, her large campaign debt had to be paid; Clinton needed Obama's help to do so, and he agreed to try.

In addition to working out problems that the competition with Clinton had generated, Obama had to demonstrate his capacity to lead and his knowledge of world affairs in the period leading up to the Democratic convention. A trip abroad, which candidates usually take after winning enough delegates to get their party's nomination, was planned to show Obama as a world leader, respected by the heads of other governments and well received by their respective publics. The eight-day itinerary included Britain, France, and Germany in

Europe and Israel and Iraq in the Middle East. The trip got extensive coverage in the news media. All three anchors of the broadcast evening news reported from the countries Obama was visiting. Their reports featured his meetings with heads of government and U.S. military commanders and troops in Iraq. In Berlin, an exuberant public rally attended by over 200,000 people, heard the prospective Democratic nominee outline his international policy objectives and consultative processes in which he said he would engage.

The attention Obama received from his trip abroad was substantially greater than that which McCain received from his. Obama's coverage literally left the McCain trip in the dark and out of the news. In response to this predicament, McCain's media consultants designed and aired a clever political commercial that compared Obama's celebrity status to that of Britney Spears and Paris Hilton, both of whom were briefly pictured in a thirty-second spot that showed Obama addressing the Berlin crowd that was shouting his name. The intent was to paint the Democratic candidate as a celebrity but at the same time question his leadership credentials. The narrator in the ad said:

> He's the biggest celebrity in the world.
> But, is he ready to lead?
> With gas prices soaring, Barack Obama says no to offshore drilling.
> And, says he'll raise taxes on electricity.
> Higher taxes, more foreign oil, that's the real Obama.
> Britney Spears, Paris Hilton . . . Barack Obama?

The press reinforced the ad's message by replaying it as a news item.[3] The "celebrity" ad had the effect of diminishing some of the bounce Obama received from the trip; it even caused his campaign to limit the number of big rally events planned before the Democratic convention, a decision that his manager later regretted.[4] The ad presented a contrast between the nominees and reintroduced the criticism that Clinton had voiced about Obama during the Democratic campaign—that his message and manner were more style than substance.

Although the ad helped McCain, it also pointed to his problems. He was not as exciting as Obama and could not energize crowds as his Democratic opponent could. In trying to establish the most favorable contrast with his Democratic opponent, McCain's campaign presented their candidate as experienced and serious.

McCain also had to reestablish his image as maverick after campaigning as a conservative Republican; he had to reinforce his heroic stature as a seven-year prisoner-of-war survivor of the war in Vietnam. The problem here was complicated by McCain's difficulty in staying in the news after he had effectively won the GOP nomination on March 4, 2008. He could not personally compete with the exciting Democratic race and, later, with Obama's trip abroad. McCain also needed time to raise money for the Republican National Committee, which planned to supplement his presidential campaign, as well as gain funds for his own campaign to pay for its administration, travel, and advertising expenses prior to the Republican convention, which was scheduled for the first week in September.

A third problem that McCain had was distancing himself from an increasingly unpopular president of his own party. The campaign plan, according to manager Rick Davis, was for McCain to visit the White House and Republican National Committee the day after he had won a majority of the delegates and not go near the White House again.[5] The financial crisis in September, however, brought him and his Democratic opponent back to the White House to participate in the meetings that led to the administration's proposal to bail out the large, failing investment and insurance firms, a proposal that both candidates supported.

REPOSITIONING AND REPRIORITIZING THE ISSUES

In addition to readjusting and refining their presidential images, nominees often have to reposition themselves after moving toward their party's ideological core during the contested phase of the nomination campaign. Traditionally, the spring interregnum allows them time to soften and broaden their policy appeal by moving back toward the center and reprioritizing issues for the general election. Repositioning and reprioritizing can be tricky business, however, since the news media and opposition party are sure to point out the policy inconsistencies, and in doing so, raise questions about the candidates' credibility and dependability to follow through on campaign promises if elected.

With economic and international matters equally salient at the beginning of 2004, the Bush and Kerry campaigns emphasized different policy areas. Kerry stressed the country's economic problems, particularly its loss of jobs to other countries in which the cost of labor was cheaper. He promised to make economic growth and job creation priorities of his administration. He also spoke of the need for expanded health care coverage. By focusing on economic and social issues, Kerry hoped to take advantage of the public's predisposition to believe that Democrats deal more effectively with domestic issues than do the Republicans.

George W. Bush adopted different strategies in 2000 and 2004 when prioritizing and presenting his policy proposals. Forced to appeal to the conservative Republicans to win the GOP nomination in 2000, Bush then moderated his stands, softened his rhetoric, and moved toward the policy center in the general election. He accentuated the positive, stressing his compassion and issues such as education, housing, Medicare, and Social Security—issues that had special appeal to Democrats, and especially to women voters, and which would help mute the impression left by the competition with McCain that he was a hard-core conservative. By taking moderate stands on social issues, Bush was following the same strategy that Clinton used so successfully in 1995–1996 when he emphasized the Republican policy agenda but took more centrist positions than did their congressional leadership.[6]

In 2004, however, Bush campaigned for president as if he were running for the Republican nomination. His conservative orientation was consistent with the policies of his administration, although he did place greater emphasis on domestic issues in the 2004 campaign than he was able to do as president after the terrorist attacks of September 11, 2001. Bush's conservative policy emphasis in 2004 was an acknowledgement of the highly polarized political environment in the United States. Republican strategists operated on the basis of three assumptions: that the country was evenly divided between Republicans and Democrats; that most partisans had already made up their minds for whom to vote; and that the proportion of independent or swing voters had shrunk to a very small percentage of the population. Bush's advisers believed that they stood a better chance of winning by motivating their base rather than persuading the relatively few undecided voters.[7]

In 2008, with public dissatisfaction rising, the issue was change and the leadership needed to achieve it. McCain stressed his independence and experience; he also pointed to his family values and voiced support for continuing the Bush tax cuts, which he had opposed as a senator. In contrast, Obama drew a sharp distinction between the economic policies of the Bush administrations and his policies, which he said would benefit the middle class. With the exception of the trip abroad, Obama maintained his focus on the priorities and policies he articulated during the nomination campaign, emphasizing policy and political change.

Healing Partisan Discord

A third task that usually follows a competitive nomination battle and occurs before the convention is reaching out to partisans who supported other candidates for the party's nomination. The sooner such an effort is undertaken the better, since the news media will continue to highlight rifts within the party as potential problems for the campaign.

Both candidates in 2008 faced unification issues with their base. McCain's maverick appeal did not sit well with Republican activists who desired a candidate who advocated and prioritized their socially conservative values and beliefs. Although McCain said he was a Reagan conservative during the nomination campaign, his emphasis on his own independence and the need for policy change did not sit well with social conservatives. His choice of Sarah Palin as his running mate did, however. Her nomination as vice presidential candidate energized the Republican base, so much so that McCain began to appear at her rallies.

Obama's problem was to gain the support of women who had backed Hillary Clinton. The campaign was confident that it could do so.[8] Although Obama emphasized his agreement with Clinton on most domestic issues, it was her convention speech and subsequent campaigning for Obama that ended the bitterness and brought her supporters into the Democratic fold.

The Prelude to the Conventions

Considerable planning and much hype go into the convention buildup. Media attention turns to the vice presidential selection, usually the only unknown item left before the big show. That choice is the presidential nominee's. The last time that a convention actually selected the vice presidential nominee rather than ratified the person whom the winning presidential candidate designated was in 1956 when Adlai Stevenson, the Democratic candidate, professed no choice between Senators John F. Kennedy and Estes Kefauver, both of whom were vying for the vice presidential nomination. The convention chose Kefauver.

Picking the Vice Presidential Nominees

The selection of the vice presidential nominee is one of the most important decisions that the prospective nominee must make. It is a character judgment that reflects directly on the presidential nominee. Picking an experienced, well-respected person who might have been or perhaps could become a candidate for the presidency some time in the future usually suggests a willingness to delegate power as well as share some decisional responsibility. Another factor is the political benefit that the vice presidential nominee brings to the ticket. In the past, the vice presidential nominee has been selected primarily to provide geographic or ideological balance. Occasionally, demographic variables, such as gender and age, are also considered.

Bill Clinton broke with tradition in 1992 when he chose a fellow southerner and moderate, Al Gore, to reinforce the New Democrat image that Clinton wanted to project to the American people. George W. Bush's selection of Dick Cheney—a former White House chief of staff, representative from Wyoming, member of the Republican House leadership, and defense secretary in his father's administration—brought experience, particularly in national security affairs, expertise that Bush initially lacked as a state governor. The choice of a governing mate more than a running mate also broke with tradition and suggested an enhanced vice presidency in a Bush administration.

There had been speculation and even a campaign launched by Hillary Clinton's supporters to urge Obama to choose her for the number-two spot in 2008. Such a choice would have quickly unified the party, but it would also have put a person who had been highly critical of Obama on the ticket, and if successful, another Clinton and potential presidential rival in the White House. Obama did not want to encourage the kind of press coverage that focused on internal rivalry between the president and vice president during the last two years of Bill Clinton's administration, nor did he want the former president in or near the White House. Instead, Obama chose Joe Biden. He saw Biden as supplementing the experience he lacked in foreign policy. Biden had served for thirty-six years in the Senate, and for the last decade as chair or ranking member of the Senate Foreign Relations Committee. He was also popular with the Democratic base, especially organized labor. Coming from Delaware, he also balanced the ticket geographically.[9]

McCain chose Sarah Palin because he needed a "game changer," according to Nicolle Wallace, a senior adviser to the campaign.[10] He also needed to appeal to women, both disaffected Clinton supporters as well as other women who seemed more sympathetic to the Democratic Party. With her reputation as a reform governor, Palin would complement McCain's record of independence and his opposition to special interest politics.

Because so much media attention is directed toward the vice presidential selection, nominees and their advisers try to keep their decisions secret for as long as they can. They want to create a situation in which the announcement can be made with as much hoopla and favorable commentary as possible. McCain had a third objective, to turn attention from Obama and the Democratic convention to himself and the Republican convention that had been scheduled to begin the week after Democrats met—thus, the timing of his announcement on the day after the Democratic convention had concluded.

Rick Davis, McCain's campaign manager, explains the need for secrecy: "the trick for us was to be able to do it in some degree of secrecy, in order for it not to spill out and then get tangled up in the Democratic convention—because you are not going to compete with Barack Obama on a Thursday night with a hundred thousand people in a stadium."[11] Palin was flown out of Alaska by private plane in the middle of the night to meet with McCain, his wife, and a few top aides in Arizona and then flown to a "very dingy hotel in Youngstown, Ohio." Nicole Wallace, a senior adviser to McCain, added: "Our joke was they will never suspect we're here. The campaign staff would never stay in a place like this."[12] Obama's announcement of his vice president was made via text message to campaign supporters in the early morning hours a few days before the Democratic convention.

The preoccupation with surprise, however, has often precluded adequate screening of the candidates for fear that the news media will find out the identity of the prospective choice before the presidential candidate announces it. The worst-case scenario of this charade occurred in 1972 when George McGovern selected Thomas Eagleton, a senator from Missouri, as his running mate. Although McGovern had spoken with the Democratic governor of the state, the senator himself, and the Missouri press, he had not been informed of Eagleton's hospitalization for depression and the shock treatments he received for it at the Mayo Clinic.[13] When this information was revealed by the news media, McGovern was caught in a dilemma—he could admit he made a mistake and drop Eagleton from the ticket, looking weak and perhaps mean-spirited in the process, or he could indicate that it wasn't a mistake and stick with him. Initially, McGovern chose the latter strategy. However, when medical authorities suggested that the malady was serious and too risky for a person who might become president, McGovern was forced to drop him and select another person.

George H. W. Bush faced a similar dilemma in 1988. Although he had chosen Indiana Senator Dan Quayle, in part because he wanted a person who could appeal to the next generation of voters, Bush was unaware of Quayle's mediocre record as a student or his family's help in getting him an appointment in the Indiana National Guard, which lessened the possibility of active-duty service during the Vietnam War. Bush, who had been accused of being a "wimp," felt he could not back off when the going got tough. He stayed with Quayle and won.

In the case of Sarah Palin, the problem was inadequate briefing following her convention speech, which had been drafted by McCain's speechwriters and delivered well by Palin. In her first television interview following the Republican convention, however, Palin did not seem to know the Bush doctrine in foreign affairs; in a subsequent interview she seemed confused over the bailout of Wall Street investment firms, large banks, and the insurance giant AIG. Pundits questioned her understanding of world affairs while Tina Fey, a comedian, mocked her intelligence on *Saturday Night Live*.

Overseeing Convention Planning
In addition to the vice presidential selection, the prospective nominee also must oversee the planning for the national nominating convention. One objective of this planning is to avoid any problems, especially factional divisions that carry over from the primaries or are generated by a dispute over policy. A unified convention is viewed as the most successful way to launch a presidential campaign. Candidates and their handlers go to great lengths to orchestrate public events leading up to the convention. Nothing is left to chance.

Thus, George W. Bush let it be known in 2000 that he opposed changes to the traditional positions the party took in its platform so as not to alienate any group in the Republicans' core constituency and chose a running mate who was acceptable to all major party factions. Bush wanted an upbeat, people-oriented convention that emphasized positive imagery. In 2004, he wanted to use the convention to launch his presidential campaign, present his second-term agenda, and continue his and Republican criticism of the Democratic nominee.

Obama and McCain had similar objectives in 2008. They wanted to minimize internal dissent. Hillary Clinton was given a prominent convention role to facilitate this objective; she also made the motion to make the nomination unanimous. On the Republican side, McCain's senior aides nixed his desire to pick his close friend and former Democratic vice presidential candidate Joe Lieberman as his running mate. They believed that such a nomination would have divided the convention, resulted in considerable internal opposition, and could have been defeated.[14] Harmony is the name of the game for contemporary nominating conventions.

NATIONAL NOMINATING CONVENTIONS

National nominating conventions were at one time important decision-making bodies. They were used to decide on the party's nominees, platforms, and rules and procedures, as well as to provide a podium for launching presidential campaigns. They also became an arena for settling internal party disputes, unifying the delegates, and getting ready for the general election campaign. Today, however, they are not nearly as important and certainly not as newsworthy. They are theater, orchestrated for television. Conventions are designed to present a picture of a cohesive and energized party that enthusiastically supports its nominees and its platform and optimistically launches its presidential campaign.

THE POLITICS OF CONVENTIONS PAST

Early conventions were brokered by party leaders who exercised considerable influence over the selection and actions of their state delegations. The leaders debated among themselves, formed coalitions, and fought for particular candidates and over credentials, rules, and platform planks. These internal disputes occurred within committees that were charged with credentialing the delegates, establishing the rules by which the convention would be governed, and drafting the platform on which the party would stand in the general election.

Twice in the twentieth century, Republican conventions were the scene of major credential challenges that ultimately determined the nominees. William Howard Taft's victory over Theodore Roosevelt in 1912 and Dwight Eisenhower's victory over Robert Taft in 1952 followed from convention decisions to seat certain delegates and reject others.[15] Rules fights have also been surrogate disputes over the selection of the nominees. Until 1936, the Democrats operated under a rule that required a two-thirds vote for winning the nomination. James K. Polk's selection in 1844 was a consequence of Martin Van Buren's failure to obtain the support of two-thirds of the convention, although Van Buren had a majority. The two-thirds rule in effect permitted a minority of the delegates to veto a person they opposed.

In general, most convention rules are accepted without controversy. The most recent rules controversy occurred at the 1980 Democratic convention. At issue was a proposed requirement that delegates vote for the candidate to whom they were publicly pledged at the time they were chosen. Trailing Jimmy Carter by about 600 delegates, Ted Kennedy, who had previously supported this requirement, urged an open convention in which delegates could vote their consciences rather than merely exercise their commitments. Naturally, the Carter organization favored the pledged delegate rule and lobbied strenuously and successfully for it. Subsequently, the Democrats modified the rule. Today, delegates must reflect in good conscience the sentiments of those who elected them and the candidates to whom they were pledged.[16]

The Democrats had a major policy dispute in 1948 that led to a walkout of delegates from several southern states. At issue was the party's stance in support of civil rights, a stand that the delegates from the southern states opposed. When they were unable to get the convention to change its position, several of the southern delegations left the convention and backed the States' Rights candidacy of Strom Thurmond for president. In 1964, Republican delegates fought over proposed amendments opposing extremism and favoring a stronger position on civil rights, amendments that delegates supporting Barry Goldwater defeated. The 1968 Democratic convention witnessed an emotional four-hour debate on U.S. policy in Vietnam. Although the convention voted to sustain the majority's position, which had the approval of President Johnson, the discussion, carried on television, reinforced the image of a divided party to millions of home viewers.

Before the choice of the nominee was dictated by the results of the caucuses and primaries, the delegates had to make that decision themselves by voting on the convention floor. Sometimes agreeing on a nominee took several votes. In 1924, Democratic delegates cast 103 ballots before they agreed on John W. Davis and Charles W. Bryan as their nominees; in 1932, they took four roll calls before obtaining the two-thirds vote they needed to nominate Franklin Roosevelt. After the two-thirds rule was changed to a simple majority, the Democratic conventions had much less difficulty agreeing on its nominees. In fact, the only other Democratic convention that took more than one ballot was in 1952 when it took three votes to nominate Adlai Stevenson. In 1940, Republican Wendell Willkie was selected on the eighth ballot, breaking a deadlock among Thomas Dewey, Arthur Vandenberg, and Willkie himself. Eight years later, Dewey was nominated on the third ballot.

Today, a first-ballot nomination is preordained by the results of the caucuses and primaries. There are few disputes that make it to the convention floor since the winning candidate controls a majority of the delegates and wants a unified convention.

CONTEMPORARY CONVENTIONS

Modern conventions are made-for-television productions. They are designed and organized by convention planners months before they are scheduled. And there is much to plan and orchestrate. They are large events, held over four days, involving thousands of delegates, media representatives, and support staff. Their cost runs into the millions of dollars.

The Delegates

The number of participants in contemporary conventions runs into the thousands. In 2008, the Republicans had 2,380 delegates and the Democrats had 4,419. The 2012 conventions will be of similar size.

The demographic composition of the delegates tends to reflect their electoral constituencies. When the candidates for the nomination compose their slates of delegates, they try to balance them so as to achieve broad representation. Democratic rules require an even gender division. Republican rules do not. In 2008, only about one-third of the Republican delegates were women. More Democratic delegates were unmarried (38 percent compared to 20 percent for the Republicans) and more were under the age of 40 (19 percent compared to 12 percent for the GOP).

Ethnic and racial minorities comprise a large part of the Democrats' electoral base. Almost 37 percent of the Democratic delegates in 2008 were minorities compared to only 9 percent for the Republicans. On the other hand, the Republicans, who usually benefit from the vote of active-duty military and veterans, had a larger percentage of veterans (23 percent) than did the Democrats (14 percent). The demographic breakdown of convention delegates is indicated in Table 6.1.

From an attitudinal perspective, delegates reflected their party's ideological orientation, with 43 percent of Democratic delegates identifying themselves as liberal and 63 percent of Republican delegates identifying themselves as conservative (see Table 6.2). On issues that divided the country, issues such as health care, illegal immigration, abortion, gay marriage, and gun control, the delegates reflected their party's position to a greater extent than did partisans and to a much greater extent than did the general public (see Table 6.2).

Location and Cost

Although the convention is planned by representatives of the winning candidates, preliminary decisions, such as where to hold it and who should run it, are made by the party's national committee, usually on the recommendation of its chair and appropriate convention committees. An incumbent president normally exercises considerable influence over many of these decisions: the choice of a convention city, the selection of temporary and permanent convention officials, and the designation of the principal speakers.

In choosing a site, many factors are considered: the size, configuration, and condition of the convention hall, transportation to and from it, financial

Table 6.1 | The Representative Character of the 2008 Convention Delegates

	Democratic		Republican		All
	Delegates	Voters	Delegates	Voters	Voters
Gender					
Male	51	42	68	44	46
Female	49	58	32	56	54
Race					
White	65	72	93	93	83
African American	23	23	2	2	12
Asian	3	3	2	2	2
Hispanic Origin/ Descent	11	9	5	10	8
Education					
High School or Less	5	42	4	32	37
Some College	12	28	15	29	30
College	26	17	31	28	21
Postgraduate	55	13	50	11	12
Masters	22		18		
Ph.D.	5		4		
JD/LLB	19		17		
Family Income					
Under $50,000	10	44	5	31	39
$50,000–75,000	17	21	22	22	23
Over $75,000	70	26	66	39	31
Over $100,000	34		30		
Over $200,000	20		24		
Union Membership					
Yes	24	10	5		10
No	76	89	95		90
Religious Attendance					
Weekly	23	24	43	38	30
Almost Weekly	13	10	19	14	10
Once/Twice a Month	19	13	15	9	11
A Few Times a Year	30	33	16	25	29
Never	13	20	4	14	20

continued

TABLE 6.1 | THE REPRESENTATIVE CHARACTER OF THE 2008 CONVENTION DELEGATES *continued*

	Democratic		Republican		All Voters
	Delegates	**Voters**	**Delegates**	**Voters**	
Religious Preference					
Protestant	43	52	57	61	55
Catholic	26	23	30	25	24
Jewish	9	5	3	1	3
Other	8	9	5	4	7

Source: The New York Times/CBS News National Delegate Surveys, conducted July 16–August 17, 2008 (Democrats) and July 23–August 26, 2008 (Republicans). graphics8.nytimes.com/packages/pdf/politics/demdel20080824.pdf

TABLE 6.2 | IDEOLOGICAL AND ISSUE DIFFERENCES BETWEEN DEMOCRATS AND REPUBLICAN DELEGATES AND PARTISANS IN 2008

	Delegates		Partisans		All Voters
	Dem.	**Rep.**	**Dem.**	**Rep.**	
Ideology					
Liberal	43	1	48	8	26
Moderate	50	33	34	30	36
Conservative	3	63	16	61	36
Issues					
Health Care					
More important to provide health care even if it means raising taxes	94	7	90	40	67
More important to hold down taxes even if it means Americans do not have health care	3	77	7	53	27
Illegal Immigration					
Illegal immigrants should be allowed to stay in jobs and eventually apply for citizenship	68	22	50	26	40

TABLE 6.2 | IDEOLOGICAL AND ISSUE DIFFERENCES BETWEEN DEMOCRATS AND REPUBLICAN DELEGATES AND PARTISANS IN 2008 *continued*

	Delegates		Partisans		All Voters
	Dem.	Rep.	Dem.	Rep.	
Illegal immigrants should be allowed to stay as guest workers but not allowed to apply for citizenship	18	38	24	29	26
Illegal immigrants should be required to leave their jobs and the United States	6	29	23	43	31
Abortion					
Abortion should be generally available to those who want it	70	9	43	20	33
Abortion should be available under stricter limits	20	38	39	41	40
Abortion should not be permitted	3	43	16	37	24
Same-Sex Unions					
Gay couples should be allowed to marry legally	55	6	49	11	34
Gay couples should be allowed to form civil unions	35	43	19	28	24
There should be no legal recognition of gay marriage or unions	5	46	29	57	39
Gun Control Laws					
Should be stricter	62	8	70	32	52
Should be less strict	4	38	3	17	11
Should be kept the way they are	29	49	24	49	36

Source: The New York Times/CBS News National Delegate Surveys, conducted July 16–August 17, 2008 (Democrats) and July 23–August 26, 2008 (Republicans). www.cbsnews.com/htdocs/pdf/RNCDelegates_issues.pdf

inducements, the political climate, the geographic area, and the cultural ambiance of the city itself. For example, when detailing its logistic requirements for the party's 2008 convention, the Democrats asked cities bidding for the convention for 17,000 hotel rooms, 125 air-conditioned buses, and control over the convention site for a three-month period preceding and following the meetings. Security is also a factor.

Conventions are very costly. The federal government provides a grant to the major parties to hold their annual meetings and pays a major portion of security expenses. In 2008, the government grant totaled $16.4 million, but that was only a drop in the bucket to what the conventions actually cost. Local authorities contribute to nonadministrative costs, construction, transportation, and security. The rest comes from private donations. The Democrats raised $61 million for their convention in Denver, and the Republicans $57 million for theirs in Minneapolis–St. Paul in 2008.[17] They both will raise millions again in 2012.

Most of the money comes from large contributors who are given a variety of convention-related perks ranging from deluxe hotel suites, to box seats at the convention, to invitations to meet with the candidates and party leaders, to tickets to the receptions and other events. Major corporations and associations, whose lobbyists are frequently in attendance, provide transportation, food, and entertainment. It is a big party for the delegates, party leaders and elected officials, and the generous donors. The delegates also spend a lot of money, which is a principal reason that cities bid to hold the meetings. For example, spending on or at the 2008 Republican convention in Minneapolis–St. Paul totaled $170 million; the average delegate spent $1,600.[18] The cities chosen to host the 2012 conventions are Charlotte, North Carolina, for the Democrats and Tampa, Florida, for the Republicans.

Timing

The period during which conventions are held and the time at which speeches, roll calls, and reports occur are also important. Parties want to attract as large an audience as possible. Conventions have to be scheduled so as not to compete with other major events, such as the summer Olympics or the traditional Labor Day holiday. Holding a convention last is a financial advantage for candidates who accept federal funds for the general election because it shortens the period during which these funds can be spent. For candidates who fund their general election campaign with private funds, the scheduling is less important because fund-raising for the presidential election begins the moment the nomination battle is settled.

Candidates want to use the convention as a springboard to their general election campaign. Scheduling the convention at or near the end of the summer permits the campaign to follow without much interruption; holding it early may not. Thus, the Republicans chose to set their 2012 convention dates for August 27–30 while the Democrats chose September 3–7.

Conventions have become faster paced and more varied than in the past, primarily to keep their viewing audience's attention as long as possible. From the standpoint of the parties' convention planners, the more cogent the message and the more entertaining the proceedings, the more likely the convention will have a positive impact on the voters. Modern-day conventions entertain, inform, and provide opportunities for party leaders to gain media attention; present the policy positions for which the party stands in its platform; and anoint their presidential and vice presidential candidates by formally nominating them. Ritual surrounds each of these functions.

Speeches

Conventions are full of speeches. Some of political oratory has been very powerful, occasionally eloquent, and almost always emotive, designed to "turn on" the delegates and their partisan brethren who are watching. The substance of the oratory is also readily predictable. The speakers trumpet the achievements of their party, eulogizing their leaders and criticizing, often harshly, their opponents. They also reinforce and validate the ideology and policy positions associated with their party by attributing the country's prosperity to these policies and its problems to their opponents'.

In past conventions, there used to be a keynote address, which occurred early in the convention and was intended to unify the delegates, smoothing over any divisions that may have emerged during the preconvention campaign, and arouse the delegates, partisans, and the general public for the forthcoming election.[19] That tradition continues at Democratic conventions. In 2004, it was Barack Obama's well-received keynote address that gave him national recognition and initiated blogs encouraging him to run for president. Senator Mark Warner from Virginia was the Democratic keynoter in 2008.

Although recent Republican conventions have not featured a keynote address, they have invited well-known Democrats, dissatisfied with their party's selection, to speak on behalf of the Republican nominees. In 2004, former Georgia Governor Zell Miller, who had nominated Clinton for the Democrats in 1992, gave a hard-hitting address in which he lit into the Democratic Party "for its warped way of thinking" and Kerry for having weakened the military by his votes as a Senator.[20] In 2008, former Democratic senator and 2000 vice presidential nominee Joe Lieberman spoke in support of his friend and fellow senator, John McCain, whom he praised as a great leader and independent thinker. Lieberman said that McCain was far more experienced and qualified for the presidency than his Democratic opponent, Barack Obama.

Most of the conventions are scripted. Speeches are usually written or approved by the top advisers for the nominee. Usually each of the four days of the meetings has an overall theme; the speakers are chosen and their speeches written with this theme in mind. In 1984, Governor Mario Cuomo of New York sounded such a theme in his keynote address. Describing the United States as a tale of two cities, he chided the Reagan administration for pursuing policies that benefited the rich at the expense of the poor. In a folksy and humorous address at the 1988 Democratic convention, Ann Richards, then treasurer of Texas, ridiculed George H. W. Bush for being aloof, insensitive, and uncaring. She concluded sarcastically, "He can't help it. He was born with a silver foot in his mouth."[21] Richards's comment so irritated George W. Bush, that he resolved to run against her for governor, a race that he won, and later for president. Box 6.1 lists the themes and major speakers at the 2008 Democratic and Republican nominating conventions.

Amid the oratory of both conventions, delegates are shown movies, hear bands, and are given plenty of opportunity to applaud the speakers and shout

BOX 6.1 | **2008 CONVENTION THEMES AND SPEAKERS**

Day 1	Day 2	Day 3	Day 4
The Democratic Convention			
One Nation	**Renewing America's Promise**	**Securing America's Future**	**Change We Can Believe In**
Maya Soetoro-Ng [Obama's sister] Caroline Kennedy Ted Kennedy	Hillary Clinton Mark Warner	John Kerry Bill Clinton Joe Biden John Edwards	Al Gore Tim Kaine Bill Richardson Barack Obama
The Republican Convention			
Serving a Greater Cause Than Self	**Service**	**Reform**	**Country First**
George W. Bush Dick Cheney (Postponed because of Hurricane Gustav; George Bush delivered his speech via satellite the next day from Washington, DC.)	Joe Lieberman Fred Thompson	Rudy Giuliani Mitt Romney Mike Huckabee Sarah Palin	Cindy McCain John McCain

their support. Within contemporary conventions, there are few unscripted events. Speakers who are deemed potentially controversial are frequently scheduled early in the day's festivities before the broadcast networks began their prime-time telecasts. Unpopular presidents and former presidents may fit into this category.

In 2008, the Republicans had to schedule an address by President George W. Bush, whose job approval ratings were around 29 percent prior to the Republican convention. McCain and his fellow Republicans had wanted to distance themselves from the unpopular Bush administration. Tradition required, however, that the sitting president address the delegates, and by doing so, the national viewing audience. Bush and his wife were to speak on the first night and then depart for the White House. However, with a severe hurricane threatening the Southeast and the memories of the government's inadequate response to Katrina still vivid, McCain canceled the public events of the first day and Bush remained in the White House. His speech was broadcast by satellite early in the evening proceedings the next day.

In recent conventions, the Democrats have had the same problem with ex-President Carter. Unpopular during his presidency and controversial thereafter, the Democrats have tried to limit Carter's public visibility by scheduling him for short appearances early in the evening when the viewing audience is smaller.

Much of the convention is ritual and is carefully orchestrated to prevent embarrassing incidents. Despite the planning, occasional unexpected events occur, which are usually highlighted by the news media. In 1956 after Vice President Richard Nixon was to be unanimously renominated by the Republicans, a delegate from Nebraska grabbed the microphone during the roll call of states and said he had a nomination to make. "Who?" said Joseph Martin, chair of the convention, surprised at this deviation from the script. "Joe Smith," the delegate replied. Martin did not permit the name of Joe Smith to be placed in nomination, although the Democrats were later to contend that any Joe Smith would have been better than Nixon.

It has become customary in recent conventions for the nominees' wives to speak, usually introducing their spouse. Elizabeth Dole and Hillary Clinton did so in 1996 and Laura Bush and Tipper Gore in 2000. Teresa Heinz Kerry and Laura Bush spoke earlier in the proceedings in 2004, as did Michele Obama in 2008. Cindy McCain introduced her husband on the last night of the 2008 Republican convention.

In recent conventions, the vice presidential candidate is nominated and gives an acceptance address on the third night, a practice that both parties followed in 2008. The speech, intended to energize the party's base, recounts the positive images and deeds of the nominee's party and criticizes those of the opposition. Traditionally, the speech also attacks the opposing presidential candidate. Democrat Joe Biden stuck to script when he criticized the Bush administration's failed policies, tied McCain to those policies, and emphasized the need for policy change, the theme of the Obama campaign. Republican Sarah Palin, who was less well known, introduced herself to the delegates and viewing audience and lampooned Barack Obama, questioning his experience and his accomplishments in public office. She ended by praising McCain's heroism and character.

The final night is devoted to the acceptance addresses by the presidential candidates, which are usually preceded by a biographical video. It is the highlight of the convention and the beginning of the presidential campaign. The custom of the presidential standard-bearer giving an acceptance speech began in 1932 with Franklin Roosevelt. Before that time, conventions designated committees to inform the presidential and vice presidential nominees of their selection. Journeying to the candidate's home, the committees would announce the choice in a public ceremony. The nominee, in turn, would accept in a speech stating his positions on the major issues of the day. The last major-party candidate to be told of the nomination in this fashion was Republican Wendell Willkie in 1940. Today, acceptance speeches are both a call to the faithful and an address to the country. They articulate the principal themes for the general election and the priorities the nominee attaches to them. They also provide insight into the qualifications of the party's presidential candidate.

Harry Truman's speech to the Democratic convention in 1948 is frequently cited as one that helped to fire up the party. Truman chided the Republicans for obstructing and ultimately rejecting many of his legislative proposals and then adopting a party platform that called for some of the same social and economic goals. He electrified the Democratic convention by challenging the Republicans to live up to their convention promises and called a special session of Congress to enact those promises. When the Republican-controlled Congress failed to do so, Truman was able to pin on them a "do-nothing" label and make that label the basic theme of his successful presidential campaign.

In 1984, Democratic candidate Walter Mondale made a mammoth political blunder in his acceptance speech. Warning the delegates about the U.S. budget deficit that had increased dramatically during Reagan's first term, Democrat Mondale said that he would do something about it if he were elected president: "Let's tell the truth. Mr. Reagan will raise taxes, and so will I. He won't tell you. I just did." Democratic delegates cheered his candor, directness, and boldness; the public did not. He and his party were saddled with the tax issue throughout the *entire* campaign.

The 2004 acceptance addresses continued the practice of reiterating themes, emphasizing priorities, and illustrating character. To emphasize his own military service in Vietnam and his patriotism, John Kerry began his remarks by saying, "I'm John Kerry, and I'm reporting for duty." He saluted, surrounded by Vietnam veterans, and the delegates roared. His emphasis on his Vietnam experience proved in retrospect to be a mixed blessing, however, after a Republican group, Swift Boat Veterans for Truth, disputed his record of service in Vietnam and pointed to his antiwar protests after leaving active duty. President Bush trumpeted his administration's achievements in education, Medicare, and the war on terrorism in his 2004 acceptance speech. He reiterated his domestic policies of simplifying the tax code and making his first-term tax cuts permanent, increasing job training, partially privatizing Social Security, and remaining vigilant in the war on terrorism.

In 2008, the Democrats desired to highlight the event and take advantage of their candidate's rhetorical skills and inspirational oratory by staging his acceptance address at a football stadium that could accommodate thousands more people than the convention hall. Speaking to an enthusiastic crowd of 75,000 delegates and invited guests at Denver's INVESCO field and to thousands of others who watched the event on television or the Internet, Obama tied McCain to Bush and the Republicans, spoke about the American dream, the challenges facing the country, and the need for political and policy change and his determination to achieve it. He said:

> America, we cannot turn back. Not with so much work to be done. Not with so many children to educate, and so many veterans to care for. Not with an economy to fix and cities to rebuild and farms to save. Not with so many families to protect and so many lives to mend. America, we cannot turn back. We cannot walk alone. At this moment, in this election, we must pledge once more to march into the future. Let us keep that promise—that American promise—and in the words of Scripture hold firmly, without wavering, to the hope that we confess.[22]

The Republicans stayed with convention tradition. Fearing that McCain's address might be anticlimactic after the enthusiasm generated by Sarah Palin's speech the night before, Republican planners built a special stage for McCain that moved him closer to his audience. The design was intended to emphasize the town meetings at which the candidate was familiar and where he did well. McCain reinforced the theme of change, referring to himself as a maverick, contrasting his policy positions to Obama's, emphasizing his experience in foreign affairs, and ending with the story about his own mistreatment and forced confession as a prisoner of war in Vietnam. He noted:

> I was in solitary confinement when my captors offered to release me. I knew why. If I went home, they would use it as propaganda to demoralize my fellow prisoners. Our Code said we could only go home in the order of our capture, and there were men who had been shot down before me. I thought about it . . . But I turned it down. . . . after I turned down their offer, they worked me over harder than they ever had before. For a long time. And they broke me.
>
> When they brought me back to my cell, I was hurt and ashamed, and I didn't know how I could face my fellow prisoners. The good man in the cell next door, my friend, Bob Craner, saved me. Through taps on a wall he told me I had fought as hard as I could. No man can always stand alone. And then he told me to get back up and fight again for our country and for the men I had the honor to serve with. Because every day they fought for me.[23]

It was a very emotional moment. He called on others to stand up with him and fight for their country.

Platform

In addition to the speeches, conventions must approve the party's platform, which is a statement of the party's principal positions and agenda for the fall campaign. Contrary to popular belief, platforms are important even though few people read them in their entirety or know what is in them. They are important because they help shape the agenda for the government if the party is successful and wins control of Congress and the presidency.

Political scientists have found that elected officials of both parties have a relatively good record of redeeming their campaign promises and platform planks. Although party platforms contain high-sounding rhetoric and lofty goals, they also have fairly specific policy pledges. Of these, the majority have been proposed as laws or implemented as executive actions if the party's candidates are successful.[24] Party leaders in government follow through on their platform's promises because they believe in them personally, they want to maintain the cohesion of their electoral coalition, and many of them have been on the committee that drafted the platform or testified before it. In most cases, the successful presidential candidate's delegates will constitute a majority of the committee drafting the platform and thus ensure that the nominee's priorities and policy positions are consistent with the party's. Not to do so would give the opposition a divisive issue that could be used in the campaign to divide partisan supporters.

Party platforms also differ from one another, more now than in the past. In an examination of the Democratic and Republican platforms between 1944 and 1976, political scientist Gerald Pomper found that most of the differences were evident in the planks incorporated by one party but not by the other.[25] Contemporary platforms have become more detailed and policy specific. Drafted with the party's electoral coalition in mind, they tend to have something for every relevant group. They also reflect the ideological differences that have come to divide Democrats and Republicans in recent decades. Box 6.2 contrasts the

BOX 6.2 | Excerpts from the 2008 Republican and Democratic Platforms

Republicans	Democrats
War in Iraq Our success in Iraq will deny al Qaeda a safe haven, limit Iranian influence in the Middle East, strengthen moderate forces there, and give us a strategic ally in the struggle against extremism. . . . That outcome is too critical to our own national security to be jeopardized by artificial or politically inspired timetables that neither reflect conditions on the ground nor respect the essential advice of our military commanders.	To renew American leadership in the world, we must first bring the Iraq war to a responsible end. Our men and women in uniform have performed admirably while sacrificing immeasurably. Our civilian leaders have failed them. Iraq was a diversion from the fight against the terrorists who struck us on 9-11, and incompetent prosecution of the war by civilian leaders compounded the strategic blunder of choosing to wage it in the first place.
War in Afghanistan We must prevail in Afghanistan to prevent the reemergence of the Taliban or an al Qaeda sanctuary in that country. A nationwide counterinsurgency strategy led by a unified commander is an essential prerequisite to success. Additional forces are also necessary, both from NATO countries and through a doubling in size of the Afghan army. The international community must work with the Afghan government to better address the problems of illegal drugs, governance, and corruption.	Our troops are performing heroically in Afghanistan, but as countless military commanders and the Chairman of the Joint Chiefs of Staff acknowledge, we lack the resources to finish the job because of our commitment to Iraq. We will finally make the fight against Al Qaeda and the Taliban the top priority that it should be. We will send at least two additional combat brigades to Afghanistan, and use this commitment to seek greater contributions—with fewer restrictions—from our NATO allies.
War on Terrorism Along with unrelenting vigilance to prevent bioterrorism and other WMD-related attacks, we must regularly exercise our ability to quickly respond if one were to occur. We must continue to remove barriers to cooperation and information sharing. Modernized 9-1-1 services must be made universally available and be adequately funded. We must be able to thwart cyber attacks that could cripple our economy, monitor terrorist activities while respecting Americans' civil liberties, and protect against military and industrial espionage and sabotage. All this requires experienced leadership.	Here at home, we will strengthen our security and protect the critical infrastructure on which the entire world depends. We will fully fund and implement the recommendations of the bipartisan 9-11 Commission. We will spend homeland security dollars on the basis of risk. This means investing more resources to defend mass transit, closing the gaps in our aviation security by screening all cargo on passenger airliners and checking all passengers against a reliable and comprehensive watch list, and upgrading plant security and port security by ensuring that cargo is screened for radiation.

BOX 6.2 | Excerpts from the 2008 Republican and Democratic Platforms *continued*

Republicans	Democrats
Economy Economic freedom expands the prosperity pie; government can only divide it up. That is why Republicans advocate lower taxes, reasonable regulation, and smaller, smarter government. That agenda translates to more opportunity for more people.	Our free market was never meant to be a free license to take whatever you can get, however you can get it. That is why we have put in place rules of the road to make competition fair, open, and honest. We have done this not to stifle—but rather to advance—prosperity and liberty.
Taxes The most important distinction between Republicans and the leadership of today's Democratic Party concerning taxes is not just that we believe you should keep more of what you earn. That's true, but there is a more fundamental distinction. It concerns the purpose of taxation. We believe government should tax only to raise money for its essential functions. Today's Democratic Party views the tax code as a tool for social engineering. They use it to control our behavior, steer our choices, and change the way we live our lives. The Republican Party will put a stop to both social engineering and corporate handouts by simplifying tax policy, eliminating special deals, and putting those saved dollars back into the taxpayers' pockets.	We must reform our tax code. It's thousands of pages long, a monstrosity that high-priced lobbyists have rigged with page after page of special interest loopholes and tax shelters. We will shut down the corporate loopholes and tax havens and use the money so that we can provide an immediate middle-class tax cut that will offer relief to workers and their families. We will not increase taxes on any family earning under $250,000 and we will offer additional tax cuts for middle-class families. For families making more than $250,000, we'll ask them to give back a portion of the Bush tax cuts to invest in health care and other key priorities.
Education We advocate policies and methods that are proven and effective: building on the basics, especially phonics; ending social promotion; merit pay for good teachers; classroom discipline; parental involvement; and strong leadership by principals. We reject a one-size-fits-all approach and support parental options, including home schooling, and local innovations such as schools or classes for boys only or for girls only and alternative and innovative school schedules. We recognize and appreciate the importance of innovative education environments, particularly homeschooling, for stimulating academic achievement.	The Democratic Party firmly believes that graduation from a quality public school and the opportunity to succeed in college must be the birthright of every child—not the privilege of the few. We must prepare all our students with the 21st century skills they need to succeed by progressing to a new era of mutual responsibility in education. We will also meet our commitment to special education and to students who are English Language Learners. We support full funding of the Individuals with Disabilities Education Act. We also support transitional bilingual education and will help

continued

BOX 6.2 | Excerpts from the 2008 Republican and Democratic Platforms *continued*

Republicans	Democrats
We oppose over-reaching judicial decisions which deny children access to such environments. We support state efforts to build coordination between elementary and secondary education and higher education such as K–16 councils and dual credit programs. To ensure that all students will have access to the mainstream of American life, we support the English First approach and oppose divisive programs that limit students' future potential. All students must be literate in English, our common language, to participate in the promise of America.	Limited English Proficient students get ahead by supporting and funding English Language Learner classes. We support teaching students second languages, as well as contributing through education to the revitalization of American Indian languages.
Health Care Republicans believe the key to real reform is to give control of the health care system to patients and their health care providers, not bureaucrats in government or business. . . . It is not enough to offer only increased access to a system that costs too much and does not work for millions of Americans. The Republican goal is more ambitious: Better health care for lower cost. The American people rejected Democrats' attempted government takeover of health care in 1993, and they remain skeptical of politicians who would send us down that road. Republicans support the private practice of medicine and oppose socialized medicine in the form of a government-run universal health care system.	We believe that covering all is not just a moral imperative, but is necessary to making our health system workable and affordable. Doing so would end cost-shifting from the uninsured, promote prevention and wellness, stop insurance discrimination, help eliminate health care disparities, and achieve savings through competition, choice, innovation, and higher quality care. While there are different approaches within the Democratic Party about how best to achieve the commitment of covering every American, with everyone in and no one left out, we stand united to achieve this fundamental objective through the legislative process.
Social Security We are committed to putting Social Security on a sound fiscal basis. . . . Under the current system, younger workers will not be able to depend on Social Security as part of their retirement plan. We believe the solution should give	We will make it a priority to secure for hardworking families the part of the American Dream that includes a secure and healthy retirement. Individuals, employers, and government must all play a role.

EXCERPTS FROM THE 2008 REPUBLICAN AND DEMOCRATIC PLATFORMS *continued*

REPUBLICANS	DEMOCRATS
workers control over, and a fair return on, their contributions. No changes in the system should adversely affect any current or near retiree. Comprehensive reform should include the opportunity to freely choose to create your own personal investment accounts which are distinct from and supplemental to the overall Social Security system.	We will adopt measures to preserve and protect existing public and private pension plans.
Environment As part of a global climate change strategy, Republicans support technology-driven, market-based solutions that will decrease emissions, reduce excess greenhouse gasses in the atmosphere, increase energy efficiency, mitigate the impact of climate change where it occurs, and maximize any ancillary benefits climate change might offer for the economy.	We will lead to defeat the epochal, man-made threat to the planet: climate change. Without dramatic changes, rising sea levels will flood coastal regions around the world. Warmer temperatures and declining rainfall will reduce crop yields, increasing conflict, famine, disease, and poverty. Never again will we sit on the sidelines, or stand in the way of collective action to tackle this global challenge. Getting our own house in order is only a first step. We will invest in efficient and clean technologies at home while using our assistance policies and export promotions to help developing countries preserve biodiversity, curb deforestation, and leapfrog the carbon-energy-intensive stage of development.
Immigration The rule of law means guaranteeing to law enforcement the tools and coordination to deport criminal aliens without delay—and correcting court decisions that have made deportation so difficult. It means enforcing the law against those who overstay their visas, rather than letting millions flout the generosity that gave them temporary entry. It means imposing maximum penalties on those who smuggle illegal aliens into the U.S., both for their lawbreaking and for their cruel exploitation.	For the millions living here illegally but otherwise playing by the rules, we must require them to come out of the shadows and get right with the law. We support a system that requires undocumented immigrants who are in good standing to pay a fine, pay taxes, learn English, and go to the back of the line for the opportunity to become full Americans.

continued

EXCERPTS FROM THE 2008 REPUBLICAN AND DEMOCRATIC PLATFORMS *continued*

REPUBLICANS	DEMOCRATS
We oppose amnesty. The rule of law suffers if government policies encourage or reward illegal activity. The American people's rejection of en masse legalizations is especially appropriate given the federal government's past failures to enforce the law.	
Abortion	
Faithful to the first guarantee of the Declaration of Independence, we assert the inherent dignity and sanctity of all human life and affirm that the unborn child has a fundamental individual right to life which cannot be infringed. We support a human life amendment to the Constitution, and we endorse legislation to make clear that the Fourteenth Amendment's protections apply to unborn children. We oppose using public revenues to promote or perform abortion and will not fund organizations which advocate it.	The Democratic Party strongly and unequivocally supports *Roe v. Wade* and a woman's right to choose a safe and legal abortion, regardless of ability to pay, and we oppose any and all efforts to weaken or undermine that right. The Democratic Party also strongly supports access to comprehensive affordable family planning services and age-appropriate sex education which empower people to make informed choices and live healthy lives.
Guns	
We uphold the right of individual Americans to own firearms, a right which antedated the Constitution and was solemnly confirmed by the Second Amendment. We applaud the Supreme Court's decision in Heller affirming that right, and we assert the individual responsibility to safely use and store firearms. We call on the next president to appoint judges who will similarly respect the Constitution. Gun ownership is responsible citizenship, enabling Americans to defend themselves, their property, and communities.	We recognize that the right to bear arms is an important part of the American tradition, and we will preserve Americans' Second Amendment right to own and use firearms. We believe that the right to own firearms is subject to reasonable regulation, but we know that what works in Chicago may not work in Cheyenne. We can work together to enact and enforce commonsense laws and improvements—like closing the gun show loophole, improving our background check system, and reinstating the assault weapons ban, so that guns do not fall into the hands of terrorists or criminals.

Excerpts from the 2008 Republican and Democratic Platforms *continued*

Republicans	Democrats
Marriage Republicans have been at the forefront of protecting traditional marriage laws, both in the states and in Congress. A Republican Congress enacted the Defense of Marriage Act, affirming the right of states not to recognize same-sex "marriages" licensed in other states. Unbelievably, the Democratic Party has now pledged to repeal the Defense of Marriage Act, which would subject every state to the redefinition of marriage by a judge without ever allowing the people to vote on the matter. We also urge Congress to use its Article III, Section 2 power to prevent activist federal judges from imposing upon the rest of the nation the judicial activism in Massachusetts and California.	We support the full inclusion of all families, including same-sex couples, in the life of our nation, and support equal responsibility, benefits, and protections. We will enact a comprehensive bipartisan employment non-discrimination act. We oppose the Defense of Marriage Act and all attempts to use this issue to divide us.

Source: Adapted from the 2008 Republican and Democratic Party platforms, which are available at the Web site of the American Presidency Project at the University of California at Santa Barbara. www.presidency.ucsb.edu/ws/index.php?pid=78545 www.presidency.ucsb.edu/ws/index.php?pid=78283

2008 Republican and Democratic Party platforms on several of the most salient contemporary issues.

News Media Coverage of Political Conventions

Political conventions used to be major newsworthy events. Radio began covering national conventions in 1924 and television in 1956. Because conventions in the 1950s were interesting, unpredictable events in which important political decisions were made, they attracted a large audience, one that increased rapidly as the number of households having television sets expanded. During the 1950s and 1960s, about 25 percent of the potential viewers watched the conventions, with the numbers swelling to 50 percent during the most significant part of the meetings.

The sizable audience made conventions important for fledgling television news organizations, which were beginning to rival newspapers for news reporting. Initially, the three major networks provided almost gavel-to-gavel coverage. They focused on the official events, that is, what went on at the podium. Commentary was kept to a minimum. The changes in the delegate selection process that began in the 1970s had a major impact on the amount and type of television coverage as well as the size of the viewing audience. As the decision-making capabilities of conventions declined, their newsworthiness decreased, as did the proportion of households that tuned in and the amount of time spent watching them.

With the exception of the public broadcasting system (PBS), the major broadcast networks (ABC, CBS, and NBC) subsequently reduced their coverage. In 1992, they covered each of the conventions for a total of fifteen hours; in 1996, they reduced that coverage to twelve hours; in 2000, they covered eight and a half hours; and in 2004 and 2008, it was about one hour per night.

Although coverage on the major broadcast networks has declined, cable news, C-Span, public television, and the Web sites of major news organizations have picked up the slack. The audience for 2008 was larger than in 2004. According to the Nielsen company, which monitors the size of the viewing audience, two-thirds of American households, about 120 million people, watched part of at least one of the conventions, with the acceptance speeches of the presidential candidates getting the largest audience.[26] In 2008, Sarah Palin's vice presidential acceptance address also had a sizable television audience.

Viewership has varied with partisanship. Partisans watch their party's convention more than do Independents and people who identify with other parties. The composition of the viewing audience is also disproportionately older and more educated than the population as a whole.[27]

Since conventions are less newsworthy—a primary reason why a smaller proportion of Americans watches them—the reporters who cover the conventions have to search for news. Television cameras constantly scan the floor for dramatic events and human-interest stories. Delegates are pictured talking, eating, sleeping, parading, even watching the convention on television. Interviews with prominent party leaders and elected officials, rank-and-file delegates, and family and friends of the candidate are interspersed with the speeches, convention movies, and, of course, the breaks for advertising. To provide a balanced presentation, supporters and opponents are frequently juxtaposed. To maintain the audience's attention, the interviews are kept short, usually focusing on reactions to actual or potential political problems. There are also endless commentaries, prognoses, and forecasts of how the convention is likely to affect the electorate and their voting decisions.

Coverage inside the convention is supplemented by coverage outside the hall. Knowing this, groups come to the convention city to air grievances and to protest. The most violent of these political demonstrations occurred in 1968 in Chicago, the city in which the Democratic Party was meeting. Thousands of people, many of them students, marched through the streets and parks protesting U.S. military involvement in the Vietnam War. Police set up barricades, blocking, beating, and arresting many of the protestors. Claiming that the events were newsworthy, the broadcast networks broke away from their convention coverage to report on these activities and show tapes of the bloody confrontation between police and protestors. Critics charged that the presence of television cameras incited the demonstrators and that coverage was disproportional and distracted from the proceedings. In response, one network, CBS, reported that it had devoted only thirty-two minutes to these events out of its thirty-eight hours of convention coverage.[28] At subsequent conventions, protests have occurred but have not received as much attention from the mainstream press. Even though there were some demonstrators during the 2004 and 2008 conventions, they received minimal attention and did not disrupt convention proceedings. Only alternative radio gave them substantial coverage.

The news media's orientation, which highlights conflict, drama, and human interest, obviously clashes with the party leadership's desire to present a united and enthusiastic front to launch their presidential campaigns. The clash between these two conflicting goals has resulted in a classic struggle for control between the news media and politicians. The convention managers have been more successful in orchestrating their meetings to achieve their objectives, which is a principal reason for the decline in broadcast news coverage. Both major parties also have convention Web sites and blogs to extend their influence and reach a broader cross section of people.

When the conventions are over, however, they are rarely mentioned in the reporting of the campaign, although clips of their highlights, especially from the acceptance speeches of the nominees, reappear in television advertising. Nonetheless, the national party conventions still receive a bigger audience than any other election event except for the debates between the major party presidential and vice presidential candidates.

Minor-Party Conventions

Although the major parties get limited coverage on most of the broadcast networks, minor-party conventions get almost no coverage, not even on cable news networks. The absence of competition within most of these parties combined with the improbability of their candidates winning the election or even affecting its outcome explain the low visibility given to these events. The one exception was the Reform Party's conventions in 1996 and 2000, which received some attention from the cable news and public affairs networks. The broadcast networks covered these conventions only as items on their news shows. H. Ross Perot, the party's founder and financial backer, had much to do with getting coverage in 1996, whereas the attraction in 2000 was the battle between supporters and opponents of Pat Buchanan, the former Republican who left that party to run as the Reform candidate.

In 1996, the Reform Party held a two-stage convention. At the first stage of the nomination process, Perot and his opponent, former Governor Richard D. Lamm of Colorado, were given an opportunity to address the assembled delegates. During the next week, partisans voted by regular mail or e-mail and the results were announced at the second convention, which also provided an opportunity for the winning candidate, Perot, to announce his vice presidential selection and make his acceptance speech.

In 2000, there was also a mail ballot as well as a convention vote, but it was the organizational battle over Buchanan's candidacy in the months leading up to the convention that attracted media attention. The hardball tactics that Buchanan's supporters employed to oust state party officials who opposed his candidacy created deep divisions within the party and ultimately led to a walkout by delegates hostile to Buchanan. These angry delegates proceeded to hold their own convention, nominate their own candidates, and claim the Reform Party label as their own, while Buchanan's backers nominated him as their Reform Party candidate. The dispute ended up in the courts, which had to decide which of these two sets of candidates should be listed as the Reform nominees for 2000. Similarly, the Federal Election

Commission had to determine which of them was entitled to the $12.6 million the party was to receive on the basis of Perot's 1996 vote. The commission chose Buchanan.

The other minor party that received some national coverage in 2000 was the Green Party, which nominated consumer advocate and anticorporate crusader Ralph Nader. Holding its convention in June before those of the Republicans and Democrats, the Green Party gained coverage by virtue of Nader's reputation as an outspoken critic of corporate America and special interest politics as well as the results of early polls that indicated his candidacy could make a difference in the outcome of the Bush–Gore contest. In other words, Nader provided the party with visibility, and the party gave him a pulpit from which to articulate his beliefs. Nader did not receive the Green Party nomination four years later. He ran as an Independent then and in 2008.

ASSESSING CONTEMPORARY CONVENTIONS' IMPACT ON VIEWERS AND VOTERS

Do national nominating conventions have an impact on the election? Most observers believe that they do. Why else would the major parties devote so much time, money, and effort to these events? Why else would party leaders and academics concerned with civic education bemoan the reduction of convention coverage by the broadcast networks? Why else would the parties conduct focus groups, consult poll data, and even tally hits on their convention Web sites and monitor e-mail responses? And why else would people watch them when they know the identity of the nominees, have a general sense of the parties' political stands, and probably have heard portions of the successful nominees' campaign speeches during the nomination process? Political scientists also believe that conventions matter. They have hypothesized that there is a relationship between convention unity and electoral success. Convention planners believe this hypothesis as well and do everything they can to promote unity during the four-day meetings.

In the short run, conventions almost always boost the popularity of their nominees and decrease that of their general election opponents. This boost is referred to as the convention "bounce," which tends to average about a 5 to 6 percent gain in the public opinion polls. The only recent nominees who did not get a bounce from their conventions were George McGovern in 1972 and John Kerry in 2004. Kerry actually dropped 1 percent in the polls (2 percent among likely voters); in contrast, his opponent, George W. Bush received a 2-percent bounce in 2004. Table 6.3 indicates the bounces that nominating conventions since 1960 have given their party's nominees. Bounces, however, can be short-lived, as President George H. W. Bush discovered in 1992, Robert Dole in 1996, George W. Bush in 2000, and John McCain in 2008.

The importance of conventions for the nominees is that they allow them to define themselves before a large audience. Thus, candidates such as George H. W. Bush and Al Gore, both vice presidents who were seen largely in the shadow of the more charismatic presidents with whom they served, finally had the opportunity to shine alone, and they did, albeit briefly. Others who were

Table 6.3 | Convention Bounces, 1968–2008

	Candidates (winner)	Last Poll Before First Convention	Poll After First Convention (Challenger/Party)	Bounce for Challenger/Party	Last Poll Before Second Convention	Poll After Second Convention (Incumbent/Party)	Bounce for Incumbent/Party
1968	Nixon (R)	40	45	+5	NA	43	–
	Humphrey (D)	38	29	–	NA	31	+7
	Wallace (AI)	16	18	–	NA	19	–
1972	Nixon (R)	53	56	–	57	64	+7
	McGovern (D)	37	37	0	31	30	–
1976	Carter (D)	53	62	+9	57	50	–
	Ford (R)	36	29	–	32	37	+5
1980	Reagan (R)	37	45	+8	45	38	–
	Carter (D)	34	29	–	29	39	+10
	Anderson (I)	21	14	–	14	13	–
1984	Reagan (R)	53	46	–	52	56	+4
	Mondale (D)	39	48	+9	41	37	–
1988	Bush (R)	41	37	–	42	48	+6
	Dukakis (D)	47	54	+7	49	44	–
1992	Clinton (D)	40	56	+16	56	52	–
	Bush (R)	48	34	–	37	42	+5

continued

TABLE 6.3 | CONVENTION BOUNCES, 1968–2008 *continued*

	Candidates (winner)	Last Poll Before First Convention	Poll After First Convention (Challenger/ Party)	Bounce for Challenger/ Party	Last Poll Before Second Convention	Poll After Second Convention (Incumbent/Party)	Bounce for Incumbent/ Party
1996	Clinton (D)	52	48	–	50	55	+5
	Dole (R)	30	41	+11	38	34	–
	Perot	12	7	–	7	6	–
2000	Gore (D)	39	37	–	39	47	+8
	Bush (R)	50	54	+4	55	46	–
2004	Kerry (D)	49	48	−1	48	48	–
	Bush (R)	45	48	–	47	49	+2
2008	Obama (D)	45	49	+4	49	44	–
	McCain (R)	44	43	–	43	49	+6

Source: Gallup Poll data; David W. Moore, "Bush Bounce Keeps Going," Gallup Poll, September 17, 2004. Gallup Daily: "McCain's Bounce Gives Him 5-Point Lead," September 8, 2008. www.gallup.com/poll/110110/Gallup-Daily-McCains-Bounce-Gives-Him-5point-Lead. Used with permission.

not as well known at the time, such as Sarah Palin in 2008, used the conventions to introduce themselves to the American electorate.

The long-term impact is more difficult to measure. Nonetheless, political scientists have suggested three major effects of conventions on voters: (1) the conventions heighten interest, thereby increasing turnout; (2) they arouse latent feelings, thereby raising partisan awareness; (3) they color perceptions, thereby affecting personal judgments of the candidates and their stands on issues.[29] Surveys taken before, during, and after conventions attest to increased public interest and information that results from the conventions and the news about them.[30] Convention watchers tend to make their voting decisions earlier in the campaign.[31] Whether they make those decisions because they watch the convention or whether they watch the convention because they are more partisan and politically aware and have made or are making their voting decisions is unclear, however.

In brief, conventions can have a powerful psychological impact on those who watch them for extended periods of time. They make viewers more inclined to follow the campaign after the convention is over and vote for their party's candidates. Conventions usually energize partisans. They can also have an organizational effect, fostering cooperation among the different and frequently competing groups within the party, encouraging them to submerge their differences and work toward a common goal.

CHARACTERISTICS OF THE NOMINEES

In theory, many are qualified to be nominated for the presidency. The Constitution prescribes only three formal criteria: a minimum age of thirty-five, a fourteen-year residence in the United States, and native-born status. Naturalized citizens are not eligible for the office.

In practice, a number of informal qualifications have limited the pool of potential candidates. Successful nominees have usually been well known and active in politics and have held high government positions. Of all the positions from which to seek the presidential nomination, the presidency is clearly the best. Only five incumbent presidents (three of whom were vice presidents who became president through the normal succession process) have failed in their quest for the nomination.

Over the years, there have been a variety of paths to the White House. When the congressional caucus system was in operation, the position of secretary of state was regarded as a stepping-stone to the nomination if the incumbent chose not to seek another term. When national conventions replaced the congressional caucus, the Senate became the incubator for most successful presidential candidates. After the Civil War, governors emerged as the most likely contenders, particularly for the party that did not control the White House. Governors of large states possess a political base, a prestigious executive position, and leverage by virtue of their control over their delegations. They also are not forced to take stands on as many controversial national issues as members of Congress must do during their terms in office and do not get as much critical coverage in the national news media as do

Washington-based politicians.[32] Today, the vice presidency is also seen as a stepping-stone to the presidential nomination.

There are other informal criteria, although they have less to do with qualifications for office than with public attitudes about religion, race, and gender. Prior to John F. Kennedy's election in 1960, no Catholic had been elected, although in 1928 the Democrats nominated Governor Alfred E. Smith of New York, a Catholic, who did not win. Prior to Joseph Lieberman's selection as Al Gore's running mate in 2000, no Jewish American had been nominated for that position. The selection of Barack Obama as the Democratic standard-bearer in 2008 marked the first time an African American candidate had been chosen to lead his party. The gender barrier fell for vice presidential nominations in 1984 when the Democrats chose Geraldine Ferraro and in 2008 when the Republicans selected Sarah Palin. Hillary Rodham Clinton's nearly successful quest for the Democratic presidential nomination in 2008 suggests that gender may no longer be a barrier to presidential nominations.

Public attitudes are changing. The American people are becoming more open to candidates that mirror the country's diversity, although contemporary surveys do indicate that belief in God and heterosexuality may still be criteria that candidates need to evidence.[33] Health, age, marital status, and personal behavior may still be relevant. After Alabama governor George Wallace was disabled by a would-be assassin's bullet in 1972, even his own supporters began to question his ability to cope with the rigors of the office. As noted previously, Senator Thomas Eagleton was forced to withdraw as the Democratic vice presidential nominee in 1972 when his past psychological illness became public knowledge. Before George W. Bush announced Dick Cheney's selection as his running mate, he had his father, former President George H. W. Bush, inquire about Cheney's medical condition. Cheney had suffered three heart attacks in the 1980s, but his Houston doctors described his health as excellent. Republican John McCain had been treated for skin cancer on at least two occasions, but neither that treatment nor his age of 72 seemed to be factors that affected voting behavior in 2008.[34]

Family ties have also affected nominations and elections, as the father–son relationships of the Adamses and the Bushes and the marriage between Bill and Hillary Clinton demonstrate. Only two bachelors have been elected president, James Buchanan and Grover Cleveland.[35] During the 1884 campaign, Cleveland was accused of fathering an illegitimate child and was taunted by his opponents with the jingle,"Ma, Ma, Where's my Pa? Gone to the White House, Ha! Ha! Ha!" Cleveland admitted responsibility for the child, even though he could not be certain he was the father.

Until 1980, no person who was divorced had ever been elected. Andrew Jackson, however, married a divorced woman, or at least a woman he thought was divorced. As it turned out, she had not been granted the final court papers legally dissolving her previous marriage. When this information became public during the 1828 campaign, Jackson's opponents asked rhetorically, "Do we want a whore in the White House?"[36] Jackson and Cleveland both won. That a candidate has been divorced and remarried seems to have little impact or even gain much notoriety today, but whether being divorced and remarried more than one time as Rudy Giuliani and Newt Gingrich were, would have an impact remains to be seen.

Adultery may be another matter. Senator Edward Kennedy's marital problems and his driving accident on Chappaquiddick Island, off the coast of Massachusetts, in which a young woman riding with the senator was drowned, were serious impediments to his presidential candidacy in 1980. Gary Hart's alleged "womanizing" forced his withdrawal in 1988 and made his reentry into Democratic presidential politics problematic. On the other hand, Bill Clinton was elected despite the allegations of Gennifer Flowers that she had a long-term relationship with him while he was governor of Arkansas. Clinton, however, feared that he would not have been renominated and reelected if the Monica Lewinsky affair had become public before the 1996 Democratic convention and general election campaign.

Nonetheless, Bill Clinton's nomination in 1992, despite the allegations of marital infidelity, marijuana smoking, and draft dodging, and in 1996, despite a pending sexual harassment suit by an Arkansas employee and the ongoing Whitewater investigation, as well as George W. Bush's self-admitted binge drinking as a younger man, suggest that the electorate is more concerned about contemporary behavior than it is with previous relationships and actions of the distant past.

SUMMARY

With the end of the competitive stage of the caucuses and primaries coming months before the nominating conventions, victorious candidates have to continue campaigning even though their nomination seems to be a certainty. During this interregnum, which in 2008 lasted almost six months for McCain and two for Obama, the would-be nominees must consolidate their base, unify their party, and gain the support and endorsements of their nomination opponents. In addition, they may have to raise money to pay off debts, their own and their primary opponents', continue their campaign, help the party, and, if they do not accept federal funds, build a war chest for the general election. They also have to design their election strategy, developing and testing the themes they want to articulate, the policy stands they want to emphasize, and the personal images they desire to project. Moreover, they have to stay in the news, avoid mistakes, and build their campaign organization. There is little rest for the weary.

As the nomination process now preordains the party's presidential candidate and control of the committees that set the rules, review the credentials, and draft the platform, the national nominating conventions have become more scripted than spontaneous, more glamour than substance, and more entertaining than newsworthy. They have become theatre designed to energize the participants, attract viewers, emphasize certain policy goals and positions, create or reinforce leadership images, and launch the presidential campaign.

The parties still see their conventions as important events that provide a favorable environment for beginning their fall campaigns. From the perspective of convention planners, the goals are to generate and illustrate partisan unity and enthusiasm for the nominees, inform and energize the partisans who watch, and provide media exposure for the politicians who attend—exposure that may help them in their reelection campaigns and also will be salve for their egos. From the perspective of the party, the goals are to raise the spirits and hopes of its workers, both delegates and the partisans at home; obtain even more donations; mobilize the faithful; and educate the public. From the perspective of the nominees, the goals are to demonstrate their broad-based policy appeals and strong leadership images.

The press that covers the convention has different objectives. Not oblivious to their public service function, they still need to maximize their viewing audience by reporting the convention as news, as well as presenting it as the party's public relations spectacular. To do this, they must find and report newsworthy events, especially those that are dramatic, divisive, and unexpected; provide analysis; and engage in endless prognosis about what it all means for the election and for the next government. The commercial broadcast networks seem to be giving up this task, leaving most of the coverage to the public broadcasting system, C-Span, and the cable news networks.

Although contemporary conventions are more theatrics than politics and more rhetoric than action, they continue to attract public attention, although a smaller proportion of the electorate sees or hears them today than two or three decades ago. For those who watch them, inadvertently or deliberately, conventions do increase awareness and shape perceptions of the candidates, parties, and their respective issue positions.

The impact of conventions varies with the attitudes and predispositions of those who watch or read about them. For partisans, conventions reinforce allegiances, making party identifiers more likely to vote and work for their party's nominees. For those less oriented toward a particular party, conventions deepen interest in the campaign and knowledge about the candidates, which enables them to make a more informed voting decision.

The changes in the nominating process have also enlarged the field of candidates. Times have changed; the electorate, reflecting the mores of the society, has become more accepting of candidates who mirror the country's diversity today. More people have a realistic chance of being nominated by their party for president.

WHERE ON THE WEB?

The political parties are obviously a good source of information about their nominating conventions. Here again are the sites for the major parties and the Green and Reform parties.

- **Democratic National Committee**
  www.dnc.org
- **Green Party**
  www.gp.org
- **Reform Party**
  www.reformparty.org
- **Republican National Committee**
  www.rnc.org

EXERCISES

1. Compare the Democratic and Republican conventions on the basis of their schedules, the tenor of their televised speeches, and their video presentations. Which did you find more interesting and why?
2. Compare the acceptance speeches of the major-party candidates for the presidential and vice presidential nominations. On the basis of your comparison, indicate to what extent these speeches previewed the principal appeals of the candidates in the general election. Compare these appeals to those of the minor-party candidates.
3. To what extent do the major-party platforms today reflect the increasing ideological content of contemporary politics? Are there any major areas in which the major parties take similar stands and/or use similar rhetoric today? You can access the last party platform at the Web sites of the major parties' national committees.
4. Contrast the major-party platforms with those of two third parties, one on the left of the political spectrum and one on the right. Would you categorize the major parties as centrist? Are they still within the mainstream of American public opinion?
5. Looking back toward the previous presidential campaign, indicate which parts of the winning party's platform and promises of the winning candidate were enacted into law and which planks and promises were not. Were there any promises or platform planks that the winners ignored?
6. Examine the inauguration address of the newly elected president and any other major addresses made within the first 100 days in office to see which of the party's platform positions are highlighted and which are not. On the basis of your analysis, do you think that platforms are important agenda-setters for the new administration?

SELECTED READINGS

Adler, Wendy Zeligson. "The Conventions on Prime Time," in *The Homestretch: New Politics,* Martha FitzSimon and Edward C. Pease, eds. New York: The Freedom Forum Media Studies Center, 1992, pp. 55–57.

Davis, James W. *National Conventions in an Age of Party Reform.* Westport, CT: Greenwood Press, 1983.

Holloway, Rachel L. "Political Conventions of 2004: A Study in Character and Contrast," in *The 2004 Presidential Campaign: A Communication Perspective,* Robert E. Denton, Jr., ed. Lanham, MD: Rowman & Littlefield, 2005, pp. 29–73.

Maisel, L. Sandy. "The Platform-Writing Process." *Political Science Quarterly,* 108 (Winter 1993–1994): 671–698.

Panagopoulos, Costas, ed. *Rewiring Politics: Presidential Nominating Conventions in the Media Age.* Baton Rouge, LA: Louisiana State University Press, 2007.

Pavlik, John V. "Insider's Guide to Coverage of the Conventions and the Fall Campaign," in *The Homestretch: New Politics,* Martha FitzSimon and Edward C. Pease, eds., pp. 40–54.

Shafer, Byron E. *Bifurcated Politics: Evolution and Reform in the National Party Convention.* Cambridge, MA: Harvard University Press, 1988.

Smith, Larry David, and Dan Nimmo. *Cordial Concurrence: Orchestrating National Party Conventions in the Telepolitical Age.* New York: Praeger, 1991.

NOTES

1. Erik Smith, president of the Media Fund, one of the nonparty groups that wanted to help Kerry, explained the fund's predicament:

   > We were by three or four weeks out in front of the Kerry campaign. We felt that we were better prepared, certainly at that point, to do the negative track. We did not know enough about how the Kerry campaign was going to develop and what their message was going to be and what they wanted or what they were doing or saying to be able help in that endeavor at all. We felt that we were better suited for the negative message, which we embraced and did. We did that for . . . eight weeks. The hope was that through our actions, we would show very clearly what we were setting out to do.

   Campaign for President: The Managers Look at 2004 (Lanham, MD: Rowman & Littlefield, 2006), p. 223.
2. Obama could use money designated for the nomination during the period preceding the Democratic convention but not money designated for the general election. Since he had decided to rely on private funds for the presidential election, his campaign had to begin raising general election money immediately after the Democratic primaries ended, much of it from the same donor base that contributed to Obama during the Democratic caucus and primary period.
3. It also prompted a humorous reply ad from Hilton, one that was favorable to Obama.
4. David Plouffe in *Electing the President 2008: The Insider's View,* Kathleen Hall Jamieson, ed. (Philadelphia, PA: University of Pennsylvania Press, 2009), p. 36.
5. Rick Davis in *Campaign for President: The Managers Look at 2008,* The Institute of Politics at the John F. Kennedy School of Government at Harvard University, ed. (Lanham, MD: Rowman & Littlefield, 2009), p. 88.
6. Alison Mitchell, "Bush Strategy Recalls Clinton on the Trail in '96." *The New York Times* (April 18, 2000), p. A18.
7. Matthew Dowd in *Campaign for President: The Managers Look at 2004,* p. 100.
8. Joel Benenson in *Campaign for President: The Managers Look at 2008,* p. 194. The McCain campaign conceded that women who supported Clinton would probably vote for the Democratic candidate in the general election. Steve Schmidt in Jamieson, *Electing the President 2008*, p. 59.
9. David Plouffe in *Campaign for President: The Managers Look at 2008*, p. 155.
10. Nicole Wallace in Jamieson, *Electing the President 2008*, p. 27.
11. Rick Davis quoted in *Campaign for President: The Managers Look at 2008*, p. 91.
12. Nicole Wallace quoted in Jamieson, *Electing the President 2008*, p. 14.
13. George McGovern, conversation with author.
14. Steve Schmidt in Jamieson, *Electing the President 2008*, p. 30.
15. In both cases, grassroots challenges to old-line party leaders generated competing delegate claims. The convention in 1912 rejected these challengers and seated the regular party delegates, producing a walkout by Roosevelt's supporters and giving the nomination to Taft. Forty years later, the delegates denied the nomination to Taft's son by recognizing the credentials of delegates pledged to Eisenhower and rejecting those supporting Senator Taft. There was no delegate walkout in 1952.
16. During the 1976 Republican convention, the Reagan organization proposed a rules change that would have required Gerald Ford to name his choice for vice president before the convention's vote for president, as his opponent, Ronald Reagan had done. Ford's supporters strongly opposed and subsequently beat this

amendment. As a consequence, there was no way for Reagan to shake the remaining delegates loose from Ford's coalition.

17. "Heavy Hitters ($250,000 to $3 Million Donors) Supplied 80% of Private Financing for 2008 Party Conventions, Recent Filings Show," Campaign Finance Institute, December 10, 2008.
18. "Report by Minnesota Public Radio," www.minnesota.publicradio.org/display/web/2009/08/28/rnc-impact.
19. The keynoter for the party that does not control the White House usually sounds a litany of failures and suggests that the country needs new leadership. Naturally, the keynoter for the party in office reverses the blame and praise. Noting the accomplishments of the administration and its unfinished business, the speaker urges a continuation of the party's effective leadership and policy successes.
20. Zell Miller, "Speech at the Republican Convention," September 1, 2004. www.cnn.com/2004/ALLPOLITICS/09/01/gop.miller.transcript/index.html (accessed July 20, 2006).
21. Ann Richards, "Address to the Democratic Convention in Atlanta, Georgia, on July 19, 1988," as quoted in *Congressional Quarterly,* 46 (July 23, 1988): p. 2024.
22. Barack Obama, "Address Accepting the Presidential Nomination at the Democratic National Convention in Denver: 'The American Promise,'" August 28, 2008. www.presidency.ucsb.edu/ws/index/.php?pid=78284.
23. John McCain, "Address Accepting the Presidential Nomination at the Republican National Convention in Minneapolis–St. Paul," September 4, 2008. www.presidency.ucsb.edu/ws/index/.php?pid=78576.
24. Gerald M. Pomper, "Control and Influence in American Politics," *American Behavioral Scientist,* 13 (Nov./Dec. 1969): pp. 223–228; Gerald M. Pomper with Susan S. Lederman, *Elections in America* (New York: Longman, 1980), p. 161; Jeff Fishel, *Promises and Performance* (Washington, DC: CQ Press, 1994), pp. 38, 42–43.
25. Pomper, "Control and Influence," p. 161.
26. "Nielsen Examines TV Viewers to the Political Conventions," September 2008. blog.nielsen.com/nielsonwire/wp-content/uploads/2008/092008_conventions_tvr-final.
27. "Support for the Presidential Ticket and Identification with Party Predicted Convention Speech Viewing," National Annenberg Election Survey, September 12, 2008. www.annenbergpublicpolicycenter.org.
28. "Republicans Orchestrate a Three-Night TV Special," *Broadcasting* (August 28, 1972), p. 12.
29. Thomas E. Patterson, *The Mass Media Election* (New York: Praeger, 1980), pp. 72–74.
30. A survey taken by the Shorenstein Center during the week of the 2004 Democratic convention found that 40 percent of those surveyed said that they had learned a great deal or quite a bit compared to 23 percent who indicated that they had not learned much or anything about John Kerry from the convention. "Americans Say Conventions Important," *Vanishing Voter* (Aug. 5, 2004). www.vanishingvoter.org/Releases/release080504.shtml. These findings parallel those by the Annenberg Center that knowledge increases for those who watch the proceedings, particularly the candidate's acceptance speeches. "Despite Limited Convention Coverage, Public Learned About Campaign from Democrats, Annenberg Data Show," Annenberg Center for Public Policy (Aug. 29, 2004).
31. Patterson, *Mass Media Election,* p. 103.

32. The House of Representatives has not been a primary source of nominees. Only one sitting member of the House, James A. Garfield, has ever been elected president, and he was chosen on the thirty-fifth ballot. In recent nominations, there have been House candidates, but they have not done well. Most lack national visibility, even those who have been in office for many years.
33. Gallup polls taken during the 2007–2008 election cycle raise questions about whether candidates who are Hispanic or Asian or a candidate who is a Mormon could be elected. See Jeffrey M. Jones, "U.S. Ready for a Female President," October 3, 2006. www.gallup.com/content/ ?ci=24832&pg=1; Fox News/ Opinion Dynamics Poll, February 27–28, 2007 as reported in the Polling Report. www.pollingreport.com.
34. Contemporary presidential and vice presidential candidates are expected to release detailed medical reports to demonstrate that they are in good health and capable of performing the duties of president and vice president.
35. Historian Thomas A. Bailey reports that James Buchanan was once greeted by a banner carried by a group of women that read, "Opposition to Old Bachelors." *Presidential Greatness* (New York: Appleton-Century Crofts, 1966), p. 74.
36. Ibid.

The Presidential Campaign

PART 

7 CHAPTER ORGANIZATION, STRATEGY, AND TACTICS

INTRODUCTION

Elections have been held in the United States since 1789; campaigning by parties for their nominees began soon thereafter. It was not until the end of the nineteenth century, however, that presidential candidates actively participated in the campaigns. Personal solicitation was viewed as demeaning and unbecoming of the dignity and stature of the presidency.

Election paraphernalia, distributed by the parties, first appeared in the 1820s; by 1828, there was extensive public debate about the candidates. Andrew Jackson and, to a lesser extent, John Quincy Adams generated considerable commentary and controversy. Jackson's supporters lauded him as a hero, a man of the people, "a new or second Washington"; his critics referred to him as "King Andrew the first," alleging that he was immoral, tyrannical, and brutal.[1] Adams was also subjected to personal attack. Much of this heated rhetoric appeared in the highly partisan press of the times.

The use of the campaign to reach, entertain, inform, and mobilize the general electorate began on a large scale in 1840. Festivals, parades, slogans, jingles, and testimonials were employed to energize voters. The campaign of 1840 is best remembered for the slogan "Tippecanoe and Tyler too"—promoting Whig candidates General William Henry Harrison, hero of the battle of Tippecanoe in the War of 1812, and John Tyler—and for its great jingles:

> **WHAT HAS CAUSED THIS GREAT COMMOTION?**
>
> (SUNG TO THE TUNE OF "LITTLE PIG'S TAIL")
>
> What has caused this great commotion, motion, motion,
> Our country through?
> It is the ball a rolling on, on.
> *Chorus*
> For Tippecanoe and Tyler too—Tippecanoe and Tyler too,
> And with them we'll beat little Van, Van, Van, [Martin Van Buren]
> Van is a used up man, And with them we'll beat little Van.[2]

The successful Whig campaign made it a prototype for subsequent presidential contests.

THE EVOLUTION OF PRESIDENTIAL CAMPAIGNS

The election of 1840 was also the first in which a party nominee actually campaigned for himself. General William Henry Harrison made twenty-three speeches in his home state of Ohio.[3] He did not set a precedent that was quickly followed, however. It was twenty years before another presidential candidate took to the stump and then under the extraordinary conditions of the onset of the Civil War and the breakup of the Democratic Party.

Senator Stephen A. Douglas, Democratic candidate for president, spoke out on the slavery issue to try to heal the split that it had engendered within his party. In doing so, however, he denied his own personal ambitions. "I did not come here to solicit your votes," he told a Raleigh, North Carolina, audience. "I have nothing to say for myself or my claims personally. I am one of those who think it would not be a favor to me to be made President at this time."[4]

Abraham Lincoln, Douglas's Republican opponent, refused to reply, even though he had debated Douglas two years earlier in their contest for the Senate seat from Illinois, a contest Douglas won. Lincoln, who almost dropped out of public view when the campaign was underway, felt that it was not even proper for him to vote for himself.[5] He cut his own name from the Republican ballot before he cast it for others in the election.[6] For their part, the Republicans mounted a massive campaign on Lincoln's behalf. They held what were called "Wide Awake" celebrations in which large numbers of people were mobilized. An account of one of these celebrations reported:

> The Wide-Awake torch-light procession is undoubtedly the largest and most imposing thing of the kind ever witnessed in Chicago. Unprejudiced spectators estimate the number at 10,000. Throughout the whole length of the procession were scattered portraits of Abraham Lincoln. Banners and transparencies bearing Republican mottoes, and pictures of rail splitters, were also plentifully distributed. Forty-three bands of music were also in the procession.[7]

FROM PORCH TO TRAIN

Presidential candidates remained on the sidelines until the 1880s. Republican James Garfield broke the tradition by receiving visitors at his Ohio home. Four years later in 1884, Republican James Blaine made hundreds of campaign speeches in an unsuccessful effort to offset public accusations that he profited from a fraudulent railroad deal. Benjamin Harrison, the Republican candidate in 1888, resumed the practice of seeing people at his home, a practice that has been referred to as front-porch campaigning. Historian Keith Melder writes that Harrison met with 110 delegations consisting of almost 200,000 people in the course of the campaign.[8] William McKinley received even more visitors at his front-porch campaign in 1896. He spoke to approximately 750,000 people who were recruited and in some cases transported to his Canton, Ohio, home by the Republican Party.[9]

McKinley's opponent in that election, William Jennings Bryan, actually traveled around the country making speeches at Democratic political rallies. By his own account, he logged more than 18,000 miles and made more than 600 speeches, and, according to press estimates, he spoke to almost 5 million people, nearly collapsing from exhaustion at the end of the campaign.[10]

In 1900, Republican vice presidential candidate Theodore Roosevelt took on Bryan, "making 673 speeches, visiting 567 towns in 24 states, and traveling 21,209 miles."[11] Twelve years later, ex-president Theodore Roosevelt once again took to the hustings, only this time he was trying to defeat a fellow Republican president, William Howard Taft, for his party's nomination. Roosevelt won nine primaries, including one in Ohio, Taft's home state, but was denied the nomination by party leaders. He then launched an independent candidacy in the general election, campaigning on the Progressive, or "Bull Moose," ticket. His Democratic opponent, Woodrow Wilson, was also an active campaigner. The Roosevelt and Wilson efforts ended the era of passive presidential campaigning. The last front-porch presidential campaign was waged by Warren G. Harding in 1920.

FROM RALLY TO RADIO AND TELEVISION

Harding's campaign was distinguished in another way: he was the first to use radio to speak directly to voters. This new electronic medium and television, which followed it, radically changed presidential campaigns. Initially, candidates were slow to adjust their campaign styles to these new techniques.[12] It was not until the candidacy of Franklin Delano Roosevelt in 1932 that radio was employed skillfully in political campaigns. Roosevelt also pioneered the "whistle-stop" campaign train, which stopped at railroad stations along the route to allow the candidate to address the crowds that came to see and hear him. In 1932, Roosevelt, who personally took a train to Chicago to accept his nomination, visited thirty-six states, traveling some 13,000 miles. His extensive travels, undertaken in part to dispel a whispering campaign about his health—he had polio as a young man, which left him unable to walk or even stand up unaided—forced President Herbert Hoover onto the campaign trail to defend his presidency and seek reelection.[13]

Instead of giving the small number of speeches he had originally planned, Hoover logged more than 10,000 miles, traveling across much of the country. He was the first incumbent president to campaign actively for reelection. Thereafter, with the exception of Franklin Roosevelt during World War II, personal campaigning became standard for incumbents and nonincumbents alike.

Harry Truman took campaigning by an incumbent a step further. Perceived as the underdog in the 1948 election, Truman whistle-stopped the length and breadth of the United States, traveling 32,000 miles and averaging ten speeches a day. In eight weeks, he spoke to an estimated 6 million people.[14] While Truman was rousing the faithful with his down-home comments and hard-hitting criticisms of the Republican-controlled Congress, his opponent, Thomas E. Dewey, was promising new leadership but providing few particulars. His sonorous speeches contrasted sharply and unfavorably with Truman's straightforward remarks.

The end of an era in presidential campaigning occurred in 1948. Within the next four years, television came into its own as a communications medium. The number of television viewers grew from less than half a million in 1948 to approximately 19 million in 1952, a figure that was deemed sufficient in the minds of campaign planners to launch a major television effort. The Eisenhower presidential organization budgeted almost $2 million for television, and the Democrats promised to use both radio and television "in an exciting, dramatic way" in that election.[15]

The potential of television was evident from the outset. Republican vice presidential candidate Richard Nixon took to the airwaves in 1952 to reply to accusations that he had appropriated campaign funds for his personal use and had received money and other gifts from wealthy supporters, including a black-and-white cocker spaniel named Checkers. Nixon denied the charges but said that under no circumstances would he and his family give up the dog, which his children dearly loved. A huge outpouring of public sympathy for Nixon followed his television address, effectively ending the issue, keeping him on the ticket, and demonstrating the impact television could have on a political career and a presidential campaign. Ironically, it was the televised Senate hearings into the practices of Nixon's 1972 reelection committee that informed the public of the dirty tricks in which his campaign had engaged and the taping system in the White House that revealed the president's culpability in the Watergate cover-up.

Television made mass appeals easier, but it also created new obstacles for the nominees. Physical appearance became more important as did oratorical skills. Instead of just rousing a crowd, presidential aspirants had to convey a personal message and a compelling image to television viewers. Television had other effects as well. It eventually replaced the party as the principal link between the nominees and the voters. It decreased the incentive for holding so many election events—rallies, parades, speeches—since many more people could be reached through this mass communications medium. It also required that campaign activities and events be carefully orchestrated and scripted, keeping in mind how they would appear on the screen and what images they would convey to voters. Off-handed comments and quips were discouraged because they invariably got candidates into trouble.

FROM ART TO SCIENCE

The people who organized and ran campaigns were also affected. Public relations experts were called on to apply mass-marketing techniques. Pollsters and media consultants supplemented and to some extent replaced old-style politicians in designing and executing campaign strategies. Even the candidates seemed a little different. With the possible exception of Lyndon Johnson and Gerald Ford, both of whom succeeded to the presidency through the death or resignation of their predecessors, incumbents and challengers alike reflected the grooming and schooling of the age of mass communications. And where they did not, as in the cases of Walter Mondale, Michael Dukakis, and Robert Dole, they fared poorly.

The age of television campaigning is obviously not over, but the revolution in computing, communications technology, and in the collection and integration of large data sets of personal information has provided political organizations in general and parties in particular with opportunities to target and communicate with individuals and groups to identify, persuade, and turn out voters. The use of the Internet as a vehicle to provide information, solicit contributions, gain volunteers, and mobilize voters has revolutionized contemporary campaigning. It has also rendered people skilled in this technology essential for modern presidential campaign organizations.

This chapter and the one that follows discuss these aspects of modern presidential campaigns. Organization, strategy, and tactics serve as the principal focal points of this chapter, whereas news coverage, image, and issue projection are addressed in the next one. The next section of this chapter describes the structures of modern presidential campaigns and the functions they perform. It examines attempts to create hierarchical campaign organizations but also notes some of the decentralizing pressures. The tensions between candidate organizations and the regular party structure are alluded to as well, as is the relationship between the campaign organization and the new administration.

The basic objectives that every strategy must possess—designing a basic appeal, creating a leadership image, sometimes coping with the incumbency factor, and building a winning geographic coalition—are addressed in the next section of the chapter. The last section deals with tactics: the techniques for communicating a candidate's message, the targeting and timing appeals, and, finally, the vote turnout operation.

CAMPAIGN ORGANIZATIONS AND OPERATIONS

Running a campaign is a complex, time-consuming, nerve-racking venture. Constant emergencies and unexpected events must be dealt with as well as the numerous personal issues, heightened by the pace of work, the hours spent at it, and the egos of the ambitious, mostly young people who get involved. Campaigns are hectic, fast-paced, and all-consuming experiences. Mistakes can be costly. Nonetheless, many of the people who work in political campaigns really enjoy the experience.

Campaign organizations engage in a variety of broad-based operations, including advance work, scheduling, press relations, issue research, speechwriting, polling and focus groups, media advertising, finances, legal issues, and more recently, computer-based technologies, Internet communications, and targeted outreach activities. All recent presidential campaigns have had large and increasingly specialized organizations. They are led by a chairperson who presides over the organization and usually acts as a liaison among the candidate, party, and public; a hands-on manager who oversees the operation; a senior strategist who coordinates the medium with the message; and a political director and several deputies who supervise day-to-day activities. There is also a press secretary, speechwriters, and a research team. In addition, there are division chiefs for special operations and a geographic hierarchy that reaches down to the state and local levels. Every campaign also has its professional pollsters, media consultants, social networking experts, strategists and grassroots organizers, plus an array of technical experts, including accountants, lawyers, computer geeks, and data analysts.

Within this basic structure, organizations have varied somewhat in style and operation. Most have been centralized, with a few individuals making the key strategic and tactical decisions; a few have been decentralized. Some have worked through or in conjunction with national and state party organizations; others have created their own field organizations. Some have operated from a comprehensive game plan; others have adopted a more incremental, design-it-as-you-go approach. In some, the nominees have assumed an active decision-making role; in others, the candidates defer to the principal campaign advisers, who collectively make major strategic and tactical decisions.

All recent presidential campaigns have maintained a war room that anticipates and reacts quickly to events in the news and to tactics used by their political opponents. Operating twenty-four hours a day, the war room is staffed by people who monitor Web sites, newspapers, magazines, talk shows, and even the late-night comics for comments and allegations about the candidates. The general rule is to leave no charge unanswered. Faxes and e-mails are sent by the war room to the news media on a regular, sometimes even hourly, basis, to alert them to mishaps, misstatements, and negative research that the staff dug up.

War Room

REPUBLICAN STRUCTURES AND STAFFS

The Goldwater (1964), Nixon (1972), Reagan (1984), George H. W. Bush (1988), and George W. Bush (2000 and 2004) campaigns all exemplify the tight, hierarchical model in which a few people control decision making and access to the candidate. In Goldwater's case, his chief advisers were suspicious of top party regulars, most of whom did not support the senator's candidacy. They opted for an organization of believers, one that would operate in an efficient fashion.[16]

The same desire for control and for circumventing the party was evident in Richard Nixon's reelection campaign in 1972. Completely separate from the national party, even in title, the Committee to Reelect the President (known as CREEP by its critics) raised its own money, conducted its own public relations (including polling and campaign advertising), scheduled its own events, and even had its own security division. It was this division, operating independently from the Republican Party, that harassed the Democratic campaign of George McGovern, heckling his speeches, spreading false rumors, and perpetrating other illegal acts, including the attempted bugging of the Democratic National Committee headquarters at the Watergate Office Building. The excesses perpetuated by individuals in this group illustrate both the difficulty of overseeing all the aspects of a large presidential campaign and the risk of placing nonprofessionals in key positions of responsibility. Had the more experienced Republican National Committee exercised greater influence over the president's reelection, there might have been less deviation from accepted standards of behavior.

The George W. Bush presidential campaigns of 2000 and 2004 were prototypes of well-run, well-coordinated political operations. Karl Rove, who had overseen Bush's gubernatorial campaigns, was the chief strategist and principal link to the candidate. He was assisted by an experienced team of campaign professionals and a large number of volunteers.

In 2004, the Bush reelection committee coordinated closely with the White House. Early on, a process was established to differentiate lines of authority and spheres of decision making between top campaign and White House officials. Karl Rove was the linchpin with joint responsibilities in both political and presidential spheres. Rove initiated a "Breakfast Club" of the president's top advisers that met on weekends at his home to evaluate the progress of the campaign and discuss strategy. White House communications chiefs Dan Bartlett and Karen Hughes, who traveled with the president, regularly interacted with top campaign officials. The fact that most of the principals had worked together on Bush's 2000 campaign and later on his White House staff facilitated their working relationships during the reelection campaign.

In 2007 and 2008, John McCain's campaign organization went through several iterations. The initial organization, established right after the 2006 midterm elections, was composed of people with whom the senator had worked closely in the past. Because McCain was viewed as the early front-runner, his staff planned the campaign accordingly with high fund-raising expectations and considerable spending on fund-raising events. But when contributions were disappointing and pledges weren't honored, McCain was forced to fire several of his top advisers and restructure his campaign.

Instead of maintaining a front-runner organization and strategy, McCain reverted to his insurgent-type candidacy of 2000. He got back on his "Straight Talk Express" bus and campaigned throughout New Hampshire, helped by only a few paid staff. He depended mainly on volunteers who had helped him in the past to turn out the vote. After winning in New Hampshire he set his sights on South Carolina. Unlike his campaign in that state in 2000, McCain got help from the Republican political organization in 2008 and won.[17] Even after his victories in these two early state contests, McCain still relied primarily on volunteers and his reputation and momentum to carry him to victory in the large state primaries that were held on Super Tuesday, although he had also raised some money to advertise in these states. Nonetheless, when he secured the Republican nomination on March 4, 2008, he had a staff of only 38 and

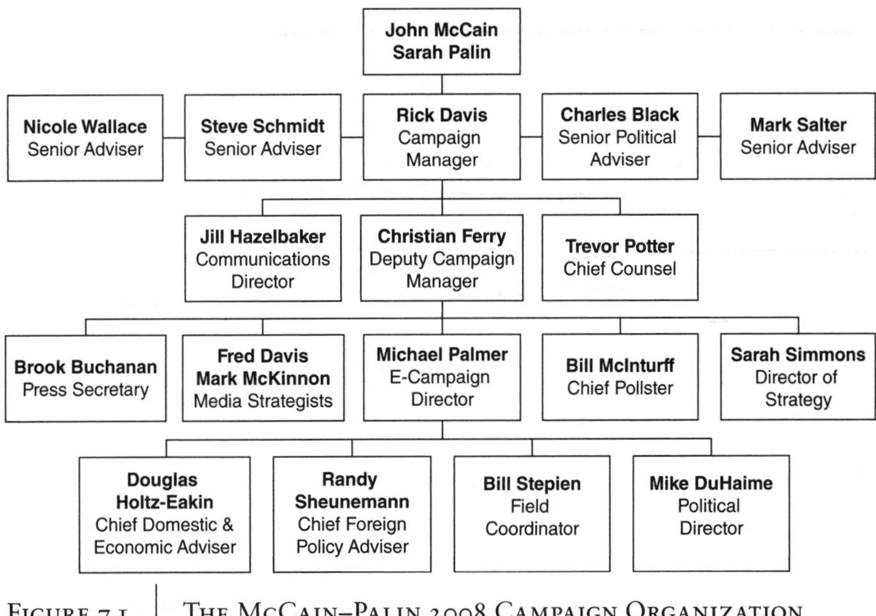

FIGURE 7.1 | THE MCCAIN–PALIN 2008 CAMPAIGN ORGANIZATION

virtually no money left in his campaign account. According to Steve Schmidt, who had been brought in to oversee day-today operations:

> You can't run a campaign with 38 people. So the campaign had difficulties through the spring. Lots of growing pains. Lots of execution failures from lighting to teleprompters, all evidence of a lack of money and staff. That issue was embedded in our operation all the way through.[18]

McCain used the spring and summer before the Republican convention to raise money for his travels, staff, and other expenses as well as funds for the Republican National Committee that planned to use those funds to supplement McCain's presidential campaign. He also expanded his campaign staff into a larger, more comprehensive organization. Figure 7.1 indicates the personnel, titles, and general structure of the McCain–Palin campaign organization.

The operation reflected the candidate. According to Rick Davis, the campaign manager, McCain "keeps his own counsel. He gets input from a lot of different sources and then he makes up his mind."[19] At several points in the campaign, the organization had to react quickly to unscripted statements that McCain made or actions he took, such as his announcement that he was suspending his campaign at the height of the financial crisis in mid-September.[20]

DEMOCRATIC STRUCTURES AND STAFFS

Democratic campaign organizations have tended to be looser in organization and more decentralized in operation than have the Republicans'. Until the 1970s, the Democrats had stronger state parties and a weaker national base. As a consequence, their presidential candidates tended to rely more on state party organizations to run their general election campaigns. Since then, Democratic presidential campaign structures have become stronger and more centralized. Most have designated regional and state coordinators to oversee campaign efforts in the individual states. These coordinators, usually placed on the payroll of the state parties to reduce administrative costs to the national campaign, also served as intermediaries between the state parties and the national campaign organization. Obama went a step further in 2008. His campaign recruited and ran its own statewide operations; it placed less reliance on outside groups, such as labor unions or party organizations, to mobilize voters.

The Obama campaign was a model of efficiency, with field operations its principal priority. David Plouffe, campaign manager, had closely studied the Bush turnout operation of 2004, and modeled his grass-roots operation on that Republican effort.[21] Using the Internet to identify volunteers, the Obama team conducted its own training sessions in door-to-door canvassing and persuasion. During the nominations, the goal was to expand the electorate; during the general election campaign, it was to secure the vote. In states that permitted early voting, Obama's volunteers were instructed to get their people to vote as soon as they decided on Obama. Plouffe and his chief of staff, Jim Messina, oversaw the general administration of the campaign. David Axelrod, senior political strategist, managed the message. Obama participated in an evening conference call with the senior staff but did not usually involve

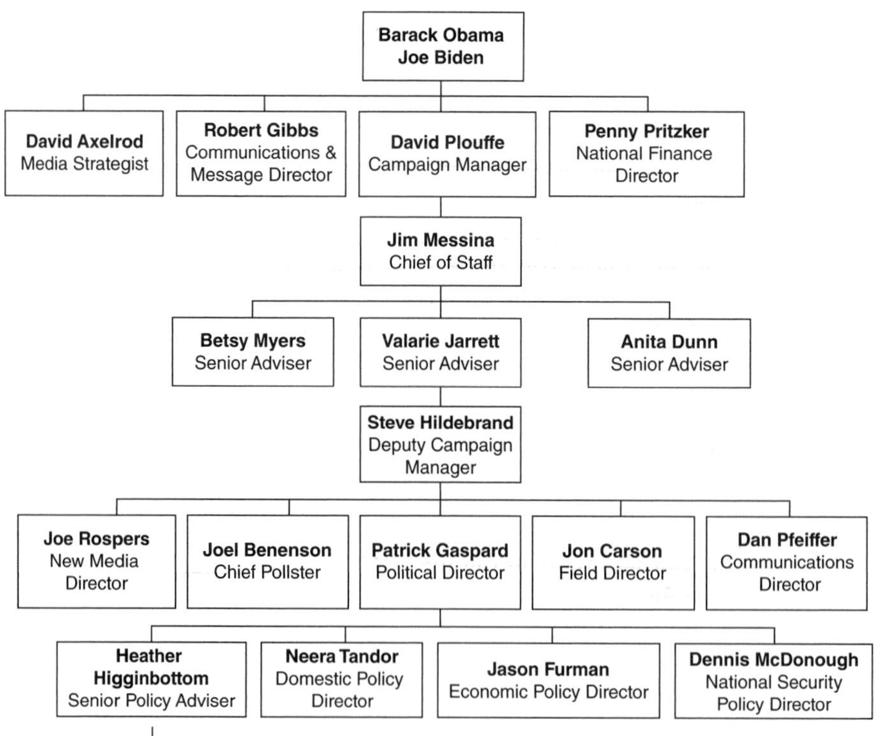

FIGURE 7.2 | THE OBAMA–BIDEN 2008 CAMPAIGN ORGANIZATION

himself in day-to-day details of running a campaign. Much like his campaign organization, he too was highly disciplined. Figure 7.2 indicates the organization and principal players in the 2008 Obama–Biden campaign.

As president, both Clinton and Obama helped plan their own reelections. Clinton ran weekly strategy sessions for the last two years of his first term.[22] Obama also worked closely with his political advisers. David Plouffe was the principal White House liaison with the Chicago-based reelection team.

Transitioning to Government

The organization of presidential campaigns, the key players in that organization, and their relationship to the candidate all have important implications for government. A campaign organization reflects the candidate's management style: his or her willingness to take advice, to delegate to others, and to make decisions and adhere to them or adjust them if the situation changes. Reagan's reliance on his campaign staff, his reluctance to second-guess his advisers, augured his White House staffing arrangement and his passive administrative style. Similarly, George W. Bush's hands-off style of management suggested the type of CEO approach he took in his presidency. In contrast, Clinton's penchant for getting into the details of operations and policy matters represented the other extreme. Moreover, his constant desire to assess the public mood before, during, and after he voiced his policy preferences was also reflected in the way in which he did business as president.

Obama falls in the middle of these extremes. When first advised by his newly chosen campaign manager, David Plouffe, "to let go and trust,"[23] Obama initially indicated the difficulty he would have doing so:

> I understand that intellectually, but this is my life and career. And I think I could probably do every job on the campaign better than the people I'll hire to do it. It's hard to give up control when that's all I've known in my political life. But I hear you and will try to do better.[24]

During his campaign, however, he did leave the operational details to Plouffe and his staff and stayed focused on the external aspects of the campaign: presentation and message. Although he did not design his campaign ads, he rewrote and edited those in which he appeared. According to Plouffe, "His [Obama's] primary role was to tone them down or ask us to hold off, a role he played when it came to speeches and remarks as well."[25] At the beginning of his presidency, he continued to emphasize his public role, particularly his explanations of public policy decisions. He set the policy priorities of his administration, but let others in the White House and Congress reach agreement on the specifics.

A second way in which campaigns affect governance is through the personnel. Presidents tend to hire their campaign workers not only to reward them for their efforts but also because they can depend on their loyalty and work ethic. Many of the principals in the campaign end up in the White House in administrative, policy, and public relations positions.

The relationship between the candidate's organization and the party's organization also impacts on governance. Candidates who circumvent their party and its elected officials in the planning and conduct of their presidential campaigns, as Richard Nixon did in 1972, Jimmy Carter in 1976, and, to a lesser extent, Bill Clinton in 1992, find it more difficult to mobilize the necessary political support in Congress. George W. Bush and Barack Obama, who both received strong partisan support in their election campaigns, were also able to rely on this support for achieving their policy goals.

STRATEGIC OBJECTIVES

Strategies are game plans, blueprints, and calculated efforts to convince the electorate to vote for a particular candidate. They include a basic appeal as well as a plan for implementing it.

Certain decisions cannot be avoided when developing an electoral strategy. These decisions stem from the rules of the system, the costs of the campaign, the character of the electorate, and the environment in which the election occurs. Each decision involves identifying objectives, allocating resources, and monitoring and adjusting that allocation over the course of the election. That is what a strategy is all about: It is a plan for directing campaign resources, targeting them to specific groups, and tracking their impact on the electorate.

Most strategies are designed well before the race begins; a few may be forged during the election itself. George H. W. Bush's campaign plan in 1988, Clinton's in 1992 and 1996, George W. Bush's in 2000 and 2004, and Barack Obama's in 2008 were formulated well before their respective conventions met. In fact, the people who were responsible for President George W. Bush's reelection campaign started almost immediately after the president took office in 2001 to plan for Bush's reelection.[26]

Obama's advisers began to design their campaign strategy in January 2007 even before Obama had committed himself to run. Plouffe, its primary architect, noted that the strategy, which had Obama fund-raising and campaigning in the four states that held early nomination contests, was tested many times, but designing it early was very important.[27] After winning the nomination, campaign planners had to recast the strategy for the general election, reflecting the larger and broader electorate, changes in the economic and national security environments, and the partisan opponents that they faced.

DESIGNING A BASIC APPEAL

The first step in constructing a campaign strategy is fashioning a basic appeal. This appeal has two principal components: partisan images and policy positions and priorities. The objective is to frame the electoral choice in as advantageous a manner as possible.

Partisan Images

All things being equal, the candidates of the dominant party have an advantage that they try to maximize by emphasizing their partisan affiliation, lauding their partisan heroes, and making a blatant partisan appeal. When the Democrats were the majority, their candidates traditionally clothed themselves in the garb of their party. During the same period, the Republicans did not. Eisenhower, Nixon, and Ford downplayed partisan references, pointing instead to their personal qualifications and policy preferences. As the partisan gap narrowed, Republican candidates became more willing to point to their partisan label. Today, GOP candidates wear that label proudly.

Since 2000, the major parties have been near parity with one another. In 2000, both major-party candidates moved toward the political center after they had won their party's nomination in order to appeal to independent voters and weak party identifiers. In 2004, Bush did not. Believing the electorate evenly and deeply divided, the Bush campaign tried to maximize its base by emphasizing conservative Republican social and national security policies. By 2008, the discontent directed toward the Bush administration led both Obama and McCain to emphasize their independence and, to some extent, their willingness to deviate from traditional partisan positions to achieve needed policy change. Obama advocated political change as well. He campaigned against "politics as usual" and said he would take a bipartisan approach if elected.

Regardless of how much emphasis is placed on partisanship, the popular images of the party still evoke strong feelings. For the Democrats, common economic interests are still the most compelling cue for most of their supporters. Perceived as the party of the average person, the party that got the country out of the Great Depression, the party of labor and minority groups, the Democrats do better after they have been out of power and when the economy has problems, as it did in 1992 and 2008. Democratic candidates tend to stress "bread-and-butter" issues, such as jobs, wages, education, and other benefits for the working and middle classes. The Democrats contrast their concern for the plight of average Americans with the Republicans' ties to the wealthy and especially to big business.

The Democrats' sympathy for the less fortunate, however, has been a mixed blessing. Beginning in the 1970s and continuing into the twenty-first century, this sympathy has been perceived by some as antithetical to the interests of the middle class, particularly if big government programs were involved. Exploiting this perception, Republicans have repeatedly criticized their liberal, "tax-and-spend" opponents.

Bill Clinton sought to reassert his party's middle-class appeal in his presidential campaigns. Calling himself a "New Democrat," Clinton took pains to distinguish his own moderate policy orientation from the more liberal views of his Democratic predecessors and the more conservative positions of his Republican opponents. He presented himself as a change-oriented candidate in 1992 and as a builder of progress in 1996. In contrast, Al Gore and John Kerry took more populist approaches, emphasizing their desire to help working families and average Americans. Obama also targeted those in the middle class with his campaign rhetoric and policy proposals, specifically his intent to raise the tax rates on individuals whose personal income exceeded $200,000 and families that earned more than $250,000 but not for those who earned less than that amount.

Whereas economic issues have tended to unite the Democrats, social issues have been more divisive. Since the 1970s, Republican presidential candidates have taken advantage of these divisions by focusing on those matters on which the Democrats' electoral constituency was divided, issues such as school vouchers, welfare programs, free trade, affirmative action, and same-sex marriage. In doing so, the Republicans appealed to the fears and frustrations of moderate and conservative Democrats and reaffirmed their support for the traditional American values of individual initiative, family responsibility, and local autonomy.

When foreign policy, national security, and, more recently, homeland security issues are salient, Republican candidates have traditionally done better. In 1952, Eisenhower campaigned on the theme "Communism, Corruption, and Korea," projecting himself as the candidate most qualified to end the war. Nixon took a similar tack in 1968, linking Humphrey to the Johnson administration and the war in Vietnam. Four years later, Nixon varied his message, painting George McGovern as the "peace at any price" candidate and himself as the experienced leader who could achieve peace with honor. Gerald Ford was not nearly as successful in conveying his abilities in foreign affairs but compensated for his shortcomings by relying on Dr. Henry Kissinger, his secretary of state and principal foreign policy spokesman. Ronald Reagan, despite his own lack of experience in foreign affairs, pointed to the Soviet invasion of Afghanistan and to the Iranian hostage situation to criticize Carter's foreign policy leadership. George H. W. Bush cited his experience in foreign affairs and his personal acquaintance with many world leaders in 1988, although his emphasis on foreign policy became a liability four years later with the Cold War over, the Persian Gulf War concluded, and the public preoccupied with a domestic economy in recession. Lacking his father's expertise in foreign affairs, George W. Bush did not stress foreign policy in his 2000 campaign, but did in 2004 in the light of the terrorist attacks and his declaration of a war on terrorism. He defended U.S. involvement in Iraq as a critical battlefield in that war. Foreign policy issues took a back seat to economic concerns in 2008, thereby reducing the advantage that McCain's experience in national security affairs might have given him had those issues been more salient.

The general perception that the Democrats are weaker in foreign and military affairs has prompted some of their recent standard-bearers to talk even tougher than their Republican opponents on national security issues. In his 1976 campaign, Carter vowed that an Arab oil embargo would be seen by his administration as an economic declaration of war. In 1984, Walter Mondale supported the buildup of U.S. defenses, including Reagan's strategic defense initiative. In 1988, Dukakis spoke about the need for the United States to be more competitive within the international economic arena, as did Clinton in 1992. Gore and Kerry emphasized the foreign policy expertise they gained in the Senate, their military service in Vietnam, and their support for a strong American presence around the world. With the nation involved in two wars in 2008, Obama took a less belligerent stand, promising to end the war in Iraq and bring U.S. forces home and give more resources to the war in Afghanistan, close the prison at the Guantánamo naval base in Cuba where accused enemy combatants were held, and revitalize America's image around the world.

Salient Issue Positions

The electoral environment affects the priorities and substance of a candidate's policy appeal. In 1992, the electorate was concerned about the economy, particularly the loss of American jobs at home and the growing federal budget deficit. In 1996, with the economy strengthened, unemployment low, inflation in check, and a strong stock market, the electorate in general expressed satisfaction with the country's economic condition, a situation that favored the incumbent. The salient issues in 2000 were how to improve education, provide tax relief, and put Social Security and Medicare on a firmer financial foundation; in 2004, the war in Iraq was a primary concern, along with continuing budget deficits, unequal economic growth, the shift of manufacturing jobs overseas, and social issues such as same-sex marriage. In 2008, it was the deep and broad economic recession that affected the entire country. Over the course of the election an average of six in ten Americans believed the economy to be the nation's most important policy problem.[28]

In general, economic issues tend to be the most recurrent themes in American elections. Ronald Reagan drove the economic problem home in 1980 with the question he posed at the end of his debate with President Jimmy Carter, a question he directed at the American people: "Are you better off now than you were four years ago?" Similarly, James Carville, Clinton's chief strategist in the 1992 campaign, kept a sign over his desk that read, "It's the economy, stupid." He did not want anyone in the Clinton organization to forget that the poor economy was the campaign's primary issue. In 2008 and again in 2010, the economy drove the election, hurting the party in power.

A strong economy helps the party in power but not to the extent that a weak one hurts it. Loss of jobs, increases in the cost of living and inflation, even skids in the stock market affect large numbers of people and become strong motivations for voting against the party and president on whose watch these problems occurred.

CREATING A LEADERSHIP IMAGE

Regardless of the partisan imagery and thematic emphases, candidates for the presidency must stress their own qualifications for the job and cast doubt on their opponents'. They must appear presidential, demonstrating those personal attributes and leadership qualities the voters consider essential and that the incumbent is perceived to lack.[29] In the words of David Axelrod:

> With very few exceptions, the history of presidential politics shows that public opinion and attitudes about who should next occupy the oval office are largely shaped by perceptions of the retiring incumbent. And rarely do the voters ask for a replica. Instead they generally choose a remedy, selecting a candidate who will address the deficiencies of the outgoing President.[30]

Accentuating the Positive

A favorable image, of course, cannot be taken for granted. It has to be created, or at least polished. Contemporary presidents are expected to be strong, assertive, and dominant, although if their policies are not successful, they may be criticized for the way in which they exercised power. During times of crisis or periods of social anxiety, these leadership attributes are considered absolutely essential. The strength that Franklin Roosevelt was able to convey by virtue of his successful bout with polio, Dwight Eisenhower by his military command in World War II, and Ronald Reagan by his tough talk, clear-cut solutions, and consistent policy goals contrasted sharply with the perceptions of Adlai Stevenson in 1956, George McGovern in 1972, Jimmy Carter in 1980, and Walter Mondale in 1984 as weak and indecisive. Kerry suffered as well from the perception, heightened by the Republican campaign, that he vacillated, pontificated, and made inconsistent policy judgments throughout his political career. McCain was also criticized for his erratic behavior in canceling and then resuming his campaign during the financial crisis in September 2008.

For challengers, the task of seeming to be powerful, confident, and independent (of being one's own person) can best be imparted by a no-nonsense approach, a show of optimism, a conviction that success is attainable, and a clear, coherent, and consistent vision that can be converted into specific policy positions. John Kennedy's rhetorical emphasis on activity in 1960 and Richard Nixon's tough talk in 1968 about the turmoil and divisiveness in the country helped to generate the impression of a take-charge personality. Kennedy and Nixon were seen as leaders who knew what had to be done and would do it. Ronald Reagan's simple but direct language, his strong, consistent anti-communist views, his optimism and belief in America's strength and ingenuity, and the confidence with which he presented his views contrasted sharply with Jimmy Carter's inaction during the Iranian hostage crisis, his penchant for self-criticism, his demands for sacrifice, and his bland, emotionless rhetoric.

In addition to seeming tough enough to be president, it is also important to exhibit sufficient knowledge and skills for the job. One of the reasons that the Obama campaign wanted the first presidential debate in 2008 to be on foreign policy was to demonstrate that their candidate was as knowledgeable and thoughtful as his older and more seasoned Republican opponent.[31] Experience can also become an issue for candidates who have not held national office. State governors, particularly those from small states, need to prove that they can handle a job as difficult, complex, and pressured as the presidency. Obama's limited experience as a U.S. senator was criticized by his nomination and general election opponents. However, the choice of Alaska Governor Sarah Palin as the Republican vice presidential nominee undermined McCain's argument on the importance of experience and also brought some attention to his age and health because Palin had even less governing experience and none at the national level.

What many candidates without national experience do is run against Washington, pointing out that they are not part of the problem so they are better able to fix it. Obviously, such a strategy works only if the public has a lot of grievances against those in power. This was the message Jimmy Carter presented after Watergate and Obama emphasized during the 2007–2008 economic recession when much of the discontent was directed toward President George W. Bush.

Empathy is also an important attribute for presidential candidates. People want a president who can respond to their emotional needs, one who understands what and how they feel. Roosevelt and Eisenhower radiated warmth. Carter, Clinton, and George W. Bush were particularly effective in generating the impression that they cared, whereas McGovern, Nixon, Dukakis, and Dole appeared cold, distant, and impersonal. Obama was also criticized for seeming distant and unemotional; Republicans accused him of being an elitist. In response to that criticism, Obama recounted his growing up as a child of a single mom, an absent father, and living abroad and later with his grandparents in very modest economic circumstances. He also used his story to convey his understanding of the problems ordinary people face and to provide hope that Americans of all walks of life could achieve their dreams and aspirations.

Candor, integrity, and trust emerge periodically as important attributes in presidential image building. Most of the time these traits are taken for granted. Occasionally, however, a crisis of confidence, such as Watergate or the Clinton impeachment, dictates that political skills be downplayed and these personal qualities stressed. Such crises preceded the elections of 1952, 1976, 2000, and 2008. In the first two of these elections, Dwight Eisenhower, a war hero, and Jimmy Carter, who promised never to tell a lie, both benefited from the perception that they were honest, decent men not connected with the "mess" in Washington. George W. Bush made much of the scandalous behavior in the Clinton administration during his nomination campaign but much less during the general election campaign. However, he often repeated the line that brought him the most accolades from Republican audiences: "When I put my hand on the Bible, I will swear to not only uphold the laws of our land, I will swear to uphold the honor and dignity of the office to which I have been elected, so help me God."[32]

In 2008, the issue was not integrity but judgment. The war in Iraq and the economic meltdown raised questions about President George W. Bush's decision making, whether he rushed to judgment in Iraq, was overly influenced by a "groupthink" mentality of his national security advisers, and understood the complexities of the economic problems at home. McCain ran as a maverick Republican and Obama as a cool, confident, change-oriented Democrat.

Character is important in elections when issues involving personal behavior preoccupy the administration in power. Character also tends to be more important when less is known about the candidates—at the beginning of their presidential quest. It is less important for incumbents running for reelection because the electorate has had time to evaluate their values and attributes in the presidency.

Highlighting the Negative

Naturally, candidates can be expected to raise questions about their opponents. These questions assume particular importance if the public's initial impression of the candidates is fuzzy, as it may be with outsiders who win their party's nomination. When Republican polls and focus groups commissioned by the Bush campaign in 1988 revealed Dukakis's imprecise image, Bush campaign advisers devised a strategy to take advantage of these perceptions and define

Dukakis in ways that would discredit him. The strategy was based on the premise that the higher the negatives of a candidate, the less likely that candidate would be to win. Lee Atwater, architect of this strategy, put it this way: "When I first got into politics, I just stumbled across the fact that candidates who went into an election with negatives higher than 30 or 40 points just inevitably lost."[33]

In 1992, when George H. W. Bush ran for reelection, he also challenged the qualifications of his opponents. But here his campaign ran into a public relations problem generated by adverse reactions to his negative Dukakis campaign four years earlier and to the allegations about Ross Perot that were leaked to the media by supporters of Bush. Fearing that his first negative commercials would be greeted by a "there he goes again" refrain by the press, the Bush campaign delayed airing these ads and when they did run them, they did so with a touch of humor to soften their effect. Still, voters were leery.[34] Unlike Dukakis, who chose initially not to dignify Bush's attacks by replying to them, Clinton helped defuse the attacks against him by reacting quickly and forcefully. His rapid reaction not only deflected criticism but it also enabled the Clinton campaign to keep the media focus on its main issue—the economy—not on the candidate's character.

The emphasis on negativity has continued in each subsequent election. In 1996, the Clinton campaign unleashed a barrage of press releases and advertisements that criticized Dole's voting record in the Senate. Dole countered with personal accusations against Clinton. In 2000, Gore's credibility, particularly his tendency to exaggerate his own importance and embellish stories he told, became the focus of Republican attacks after the first and second presidential debates in which the Democratic candidate misspoke several times. The Democratic criticism of George W. Bush was based on his competence, not his character.

Negativity played a major role in the 2004 election. George W. Bush repeatedly defined his opponent, John Kerry, in negative terms, calling him indecisive, inconsistent, and sometimes incoherent—a flip-flopper. Kerry, who wanted to wage an upbeat, positive, and optimistic campaign, was very critical of his opponent's economic and national security policies. His criticism was reinforced by news of the resistance in Iraq, spiking gasoline prices, and continuing problems of balancing the federal budget and international trade.

The Bush administration was also the target of criticism in 2008 even though the president was not eligible to seek reelection. Obama tried to tie his Republican opponent to the policies of the Bush administration while McCain pointed to his Democratic opponent's lack of experience and accomplishments in a not-so-subtle contrast to his own distinguished record of public service in the military and in the Congress.[35]

In summary, candidates try to project images of themselves that are consistent with public expectations of the office and its occupant and project images of their opponents that are inconsistent with those expectations. Traits such as inner strength, decisiveness, competence, and experience are considered essential for the presidency, as are empathy, sincerity, credibility, and integrity. Which traits are considered most important vary to some extent with the assessment of the strengths and weaknesses of the incumbent and the needs of the times. Challengers try to exploit an incumbent's vulnerabilities by emphasizing the very skills and qualities that the incumbent president is pereceived to lack.

DEALING WITH INCUMBENCY

Claiming a leadership image requires a different script for an incumbent than for a challenger. Until the mid-1970s, when the news media became more critical of presidential performance, incumbents were thought to have an advantage. Between 1900 and 1972, thirteen incumbents sought reelection and eleven won; the two who lost, Taft in 1912 and Hoover in 1932, faced highly unusual circumstances. In Taft's case, he was challenged by the independent candidacy of former Republican President Theodore Roosevelt. Together, Taft and Roosevelt split the Republican vote, enabling Democrat Woodrow Wilson to win with only 42 percent of the total vote. Hoover ran during the Great Depression, for which he received much of the blame. (Box 7.1 summarizes the advantages and disadvantages of incumbency in running for reelection.)

Following the 1972 election, however, incumbents have not fared as well. All have sought reelection, but only Reagan, Clinton, and George W. Bush have been successful. Adverse political and economic factors help explain the defeats. The worst political scandal in the nation's history and the worst economic recession in forty years hurt Ford's chances, as did his pardon of the person who had nominated him for the vice presidency, Richard Nixon. In 1980 and 1992, a weak economy, a loss of confidence in the president's leadership abilities, and an anti-Washington mood contributed to Carter's and George H. W. Bush's losses.

Today, incumbents are advantaged or disadvantaged based on their perceived performance in office. Having a good record contributes to a president's reelection potential just as a poor record detracts from it. Bad times almost always hurt an incumbent. A crisis, however, helps, at least in the short run. Rightly or wrongly, the public places more responsibility for economic conditions, social relations, and foreign affairs on the president than on any other person or government institution. That a president may actually exercise little control over some of these external factors seems less relevant to the electorate than do negative conditions themselves, the desire that they be improved, and the expectation that the president do something about them.

Attributes such as personal favorability appear to be less important. Both Carter and George H. W. Bush had favorable personal ratings, yet both were defeated in their reelection attempts. Clinton's favorability evaluation was much less positive, yet he was easily reelected in 1996. However, his highly negative ratings in 2000 may have hurt Gore, or so Gore feared when he designed a strategy to separate himself from Clinton.

BOX 7.1 | An Incumbency Balance Sheet

Incumbency can be a double-edged sword, strengthening or weakening a claim to leadership. Incumbents ritually point to their accomplishments, noting the work that remains and sounding a "stay-the-course" theme; challengers argue that it is time for a change and that they can do better.

Advantages of Incumbency

Being president is thought to help an incumbent in the quest for reelection more often than not. The advantages stem from the visibility of the office, the esteem it engenders, and the influence it provides. The president is almost always well known. A portion of the population may even have difficulty at the outset in identifying challengers, although the extended nomination process contributes to name recognition over time.

Moreover, incumbents are generally seen as experienced and knowledgeable, as leaders who have stood the tests of office in the office. Such a perception benefits them more often than not. Stability and predictability satisfy the public's psychological needs; the certainty of four more years with a known quantity is likely to be more appealing than the uncertainty of the next four years with an unknown one, provided the incumbent's performance in office during the past four years has been viewed as generally favorable. In the case of George W. Bush in 2004, partisans disagreed on his domestic record but were generally laudatory of his response to 9/11. Thus for him in that election, the challenge was to keep the primary focus on terrorism, relegating other concerns to secondary importance.

Translated into strategic terms, the public's familiarity and comfort with incumbents permit presidents running for reelection to highlight their opponent's lack of experience, leadership qualities, and clear policy options and contrast these deficiencies with their own experience, leadership, and record of policy achievements. Carter used a variation of this tactic in 1980. He emphasized the arduousness of the job in order to contrast his energy, knowledge, and intelligence with Reagan's. Clinton contrasted himself with his opponent in another way in 1996. He campaigned as the candidate for the future, casting his seventy-three-year-old opponent as a link to the past. George W. Bush and his father both ran for reelection on their national security records. For George H. W. Bush, that record was not sufficient because of the economic recession in 1992; for George W. Bush, it was, in large part because the economy was not in recession and other grievances were not of a magnitude to defeat the president. Democratic pollster Mark Mellman put it simply: "[T]he reality is the country was not feeling the level of pain to oust an incumbent president."[i]

The ability of presidents to make news, to affect events, and to dispense the "spoils" of government can also work to their advantage. Presidents are in the limelight and can maneuver to remain there. Having a "bully pulpit" gives them an advantage in setting the campaign agenda. All recent presidents who have campaigned for reelection have tried to utilize the symbolic and ceremonial presidency, signing legislation into law in the Rose Garden of the White House, meeting heads of state in Washington or their own capitals, making speeches and announcements, holding press conferences, honoring the military and civilians for their accomplishments while standing at a podium featuring the presidential seal.

Presidents have another trump card. Presumably, their actions can influence events. They try to gear economic recoveries to election years. They also use their discretionary authority to distribute resources such as grants, contracts, and emergency aid to their political advantage. They must be careful, however, not to seem

BOX 7.1 | AN INCUMBENCY BALANCE SHEET *continued*

overtly partisan when doing so. Actions they take that appear to be solely or primarily for political purposes, such as Ford's pardon of Nixon in 1974 or announcements of juicy federal government contracts during the electoral campaign, can backfire.

The incumbency advantages extend to vice presidents seeking their party's presidential nomination but not nearly as much to their general election campaign. Of the four most recent vice presidents who tried to succeed to the presidency directly from the vice presidency—Nixon (1960), Humphrey (1968), George H. W. Bush (1988), and Al Gore (2000)—only Bush was successful.

The difficulty that incumbent vice presidents face is that they cannot exert leadership from a position of followership. To establish their leadership credentials, vice presidents need to get out of their president's shadow; they have to separate themselves. If they do, it becomes that much more difficult for them to claim and share the successes of that administration. George H. W. Bush dealt with this problem by stating that he would pursue Reagan's agenda but do so in a kinder and gentler way. Al Gore, on the other hand, articulated a populist policy in contrast to the Clinton administration's more moderate, mainstream approach. Moreover, in his acceptance speech at the Democratic convention, Gore made a point of asking voters to support him on the basis of *his* policy goals, not Clinton's: "This election is not an award for past performance. I'm not asking you to vote for me on the basis of the economy we have. Tonight I ask for your support on the basis of the better, fairer, more prosperous America we can build together."[ii]

Disadvantages of Incumbency

The challenges that contemporary presidents face, the persistent media criticism they encounter, and the anti-Washington, antipolitician mood of the contemporary electorate can offset the usual incumbency advantage, particularly when the economy is weak.

In their campaigns for office, presidential candidates hype themselves, make promises, and create expectations. Once in office, however, they find these expectations difficult to meet. With the constitutional system dividing authority, the political system decentralizing power, and public opinion fluid, ambiguous, often inconsistent, and compartmentalized, it is difficult for presidents to build and maintain a governing consensus. Yet their leadership role demands that they do so—hence the gap between expectations and performance.

Persistent media criticism contributes to these difficulties. With radio and television talk-show hosts railing against them, their policies, and their behavior in office, with television and newspaper investigative reporters heightening public awareness of policy problems and inadequate governmental responses to them, and with network news coverage generally more critical of incumbents, particularly during presidential campaigns, presidents often find it hard to maintain a favorable leadership image, although Reagan was able to do so and Clinton gained high job approval ratings during his last five years in office. George W. Bush's image was mixed, as illustrated by his presidential approval scores that hovered around the 50 percent mark during his reelection campaign. On the issue of fighting terrorism, however, he received more praise than blame.

---

[i] Mark Mellman, quoted in Kennedy Institute, *Campaign for President: The Managers Look at 2004* (Landam, MD: Rowman and Littlefield, 2006), p. 138.

[ii] Al Gore, "Acceptance Speech to the Democratic National Convention" (Aug. 17, 2000). www.presidency.ucsb.edu/ws/index.php?pid=25963.

BUILDING A WINNING GEOGRAPHIC COALITION

In addition to designing a general appeal and addressing leadership and related incumbency issues, assembling a winning geographic coalition is also a critical strategic component of every presidential campaign. Since the election is decided in the Electoral College, the primary objective must always be to win a majority of the college, not necessarily a majority of the popular vote.

Electoral College strategies almost always require candidates to campaign in the most competitive states, giving priority to those with the most electoral votes. These states are the most important in an Electoral College system because of the winner-take-all method by which the votes are allocated in all but two states, Maine and Nebraska.

One criterion for assessing the level of competition, at least at the beginning of the election cycle, is the margin of victory in the previous presidential election. If that margin was within the range of ±6 percent, the state is considered competitive; if the margin of victory exceeded that amount, it would probably not be, unless a large influx or exodus of residents to or from that state occurred in the four years following the election. The influx of Hispanic immigrants into the Southwest, Colorado, and southern California is a case in point. States that had long-established Republican voting patterns, such as Arizona and Colorado, have become much more competitive as a consequence of immigration from south of the border, while California, which had been competitive, is now tilting Democratic at the presidential level because of the growth of its Hispanic population. In contrast, Louisiana, which had a long tradition of supporting Democratic presidential candidates, has become more Republican, particularly after the departure of thousands of African Americans in the aftermath of Hurricane Katrina.

Another strategic factor that can influence resource allocation strategies is the existence of a third-party or independent candidate such as H. Ross Perot in the 1990s and Ralph Nader in 2000 and 2004. As noted previously, Nader's vote in Florida substantially exceeded the margin of Bush's 2000 victory, yet the Gore campaign prematurely decreased its advertising in that state, unaware that the Nader vote could be the difference between victory and defeat. The Kerry campaign, determined not to make the same mistake four years later, worked hard at limiting Nader's ballot access and his popular vote in competitive states. Although Nader ran again in 2008, his campaign floundered. There was no major third-party effort in 2008.

In addition to the initial determination of how competitive the state may be, campaigns use public opinion polls to monitor continuously voter sentiment. Polls that indicate a closer-than-expected race can trigger the expenditure of more resources in the state; if the number of advertising buys or candidate appearances increases on one side, the opponent's campaign usually takes notice, conducts its own poll, and if the findings confirm that opinion is becoming closely divided, adjusts its Electoral College strategy accordingly. Resource calculations are made primarily on the basis of polling data, the relative strength or weakness of the party organization in the state, the number of electoral votes that are at stake, and the availability of funds.

In building their Electoral College coalitions, candidates start with their base—areas that have been traditionally favorable to their party's nominees. Following the Civil War, the Democrats could depend on the "Solid South," while Republicans were stronger in the Northeast. Beginning in the 1960s, these areas began to shift their partisan allegiances. By the mid-1990s, the South had become solidly Republican and the Southwest increasingly Republican, while the Northeast was becoming more Democratic. With the Rocky Mountain region strongly Republican and the Pacific Coast states leaning Democratic, the focus of recent campaigns has been the Midwest, America's so-called weather vane, a region that tends to reflect the country's mood.

Since 1968, Republicans who have won the presidency have concentrated their campaigns in the major battleground states in the Midwest. The Democratic victories by Carter in 1976 and Clinton in 1992 and 1996 were achieved by narrowing the Republican advantage in the South and winning a majority of the large industrial states. When the Republicans are not able to take the South for granted, they must devote more resources to this area. Doing so enables the Democrats to compete more effectively in other regions of the country.

In 2000 and 2004, both parties focused their efforts on a few key battleground states. Each side began its campaign with about twenty states in play. As the campaign progressed, the number of competitive states decreased. Initially in 2004, Florida, Pennsylvania, and West Virginia were considered highly competitive, as were Oregon and Washington. By the end, these states had shifted in the direction of one candidate or the other, and as a consequence, both campaigns directed most of their resources to a few Midwestern states—Ohio, Wisconsin, Missouri, Iowa, and Minnesota—plus three additional small states that polls indicated were too close to call: Nevada, New Hampshire, and New Mexico. Said Tad Devine, a senior Kerry adviser, "We were looking at the same geography. We knew ten months before that this thing was about winning two out of three of Ohio, Florida, and Pennsylvania. It wasn't that complicated."[36] In the end, only three states—New Hampshire, New Mexico, and Iowa—switched their votes from 2000 to 2004.

The enlargement of the Democratic electorate by the Obama campaign in the 2008 nomination process along with the discontent directed toward the Bush administration presented additional opportunities for the Democrats in the Electoral College. Not wanting to be dependent on a few states for victory, the strategists of the Obama campaign decided to expand the map.[37] To determine which additional states to target, Plouffe and his associates looked at past voting patterns, state turnout levels and registration figures, and statewide polling data on partisan and independent voters. They assumed that Obama could win the states Kerry carried in 2004 plus Iowa, a state in which Obama did well and McCain skipped during the nomination period, and New Mexico, a state that was moving into the Democratic column with its increasing Hispanic population. Winning these states would give Obama 264 of the 270 electoral votes he needed.[38]

To these traditionally Democratic states, the Obama campaign added Colorado and Nevada, two states with a growing number of Hispanic voters; Florida, Virginia, and North Carolina, states that have been trending less Republican; plus the states of Indiana, Montana, and Missouri, in which early preelection polls indicated that Obama had a chance to win. The plan was to use sufficient resources to be competitive in these states as well as to devote the resources necessary for the traditional battleground states of Ohio, Michigan, and Pennsylvania. Not only did the plan expand the map for the Democrats but it forced McCain to spend time and money in Republican (red) states, thus stretching his limited financial base even thinner. Plouffe also identified one electoral district in Omaha, Nebraska, in which he thought Obama could win. Nebraska is one of two states to allocate one electoral vote to the winner of each congressional district plus two votes for the statewide victor; the other is Maine.

The Democratic plan was largely successful. With the exception of Montana and Missouri, Obama won all the targeted states to which he allocated substantial funds and visited often. Table 7.1 indicates the advertising expenditures and presidential and vice presidential candidate visits to these battleground states as well as to the large industrial states of California, Texas, New York, and Illinois.

TACTICAL CONSIDERATIONS

Whereas the basic objectives set the contours of the campaign strategy, tactical considerations influence day-to-day operations, events, and future activities. Tactics are the specific ways in which strategic objectives are achieved. Unlike strategy, which can be planned well in advance, tactics change with the situation, the political environment, and the needs of the campaign.

COMMUNICATIONS

There are a variety of ways to convey a political message, including door-to-door canvassing, direct mail, e-mail and other communications on the Internet, and indirectly, through the news and entertainment media. At the local level, door-to-door personal contact is the best way to turn out voters and affect their voting decision. But it is also the most time-consuming and volunteer-intensive way to persuade would-be voters. Beginning in the 1960s and continuing through the 1980s, candidates and parties devoted more of their resources to mass-marketing techniques. Turnout dropped as a consequence.

Today, advances in communications technology, particularly the ability to direct appeals to specific groups of voters, have rejuvenated grassroots campaigns. Both parties have invested millions of dollars in new computer-based data sets and programs to identify potential supporters, persuade them of the merits of their candidates, and get them to vote. As mentioned previously, the Republican Party conducted a very effective turnout campaign in key states in 2004. It became the model for the Obama operation in 2008.

Table 7.1 | Campaign Advertising and Candidate Appearances in the Key States in 2008

	Obama–Biden		McCain–Palin	
	Ad Spending*	**State Visits†**	**Ad Spending**	**State Visits**
Battleground States				
Midwest				
Ohio	$25.7	22	$21	28
Michigan	12.1	10	12	9
Missouri	11.2	13	9.4	14
Indiana	16.78	3.1	5	
Wisconsin	12.4	7	9.1	7
Iowa	13.34	5.3	9	
Subtotal	$91.4	64	$59.9	72
South				
Florida	$36.8	12	$16.4	13
Virginia	25.4	19	12.5	10
North Carolina	15.1	12	6.5	8
Southwest				
Nevada	9.2	7	5.8	7
New Mexico	4.1	5	3.1	6
Others				
Pennsylvania	39.7	16	27.6	31
Colorado	10.2	8	9.2	13
Montana	11.3	3	9.4	0
Subtotal	$151.8	82	90.5	88
Total	**$243.2**	**146**	**$150.4**	**160**
Large Nonbattleground States				
California	$5.6	6	.005	8
Illinois	.002	13	.003	2
New York	1.4	4	–	11
Texas	8.9	2	–	2
Subtotal	$15.9	25	.008	23

*January 1, 2007–November 4, 2008

†June 8, 2008–November 3, 2008

Source: CNN.Politics.com http://edition.cnn.com/ELECTION/2008/map/adspending; http://edition.cnn.com/ELECTION/2008/map/visits. Kantar Media's Campaign Media Analysis Group. Used with permission.

Presidential Campaign Strategies in 2004 and 2008

The 2004 Election

George W. Bush: A New Strategy for Staying in Place

The components of Bush's 2004 election strategy were derived from the political environment in which the country found itself at the beginning of the twenty-first century, the character strengths George W. Bush demonstrated as president following the terrorist attacks on September 11, 2001, John Kerry's character weaknesses, and the advantages incumbents have in seeking reelection when national security issues are dominant.

The principal goal of the reelection strategy was to enlarge the Republican electorate since it was assumed that most voters had already made up their minds and were strongly inclined to cast ballots in accordance with their partisan loyalties. There simply were not that many undecided voters in 2004. This election strategy grew out of the failure of Bush's 2000 election campaign to win a popular vote victory. Republican strategists blamed themselves for not getting out more of the Christian fundamentalist vote in 2000. They were determined not to repeat this tactical error.[i]

Efforts to improve partisan turnout began immediately after the 2000 presidential campaign. Fifty million dollars were spent in 2002 alone, developing and testing "victory-type" programs.[ii] Convinced that the old-style programs—"the traditional buying ads on three channels, doing some robo-calls, and doing some paid mail as a voter contact"—were no longer sufficient,[iii] Republican political strategists decided on a multifaceted approach to identify and contact people with pro-Republican inclinations. They believed that it was important that the volunteers who did the contacting should be known, personally or by reputation, by the people they contacted and should live in the same communities.[iv]

The information necessary to identify the "right" people, those who would be most responsive, was available, but it had to be collected, integrated, and analyzed. Combining lists of people who attended church regularly, belonged to certain groups with Republican leanings, subscribed to certain publications, listened to or watched certain networks, stations, or programs, contributed to a Republican candidate in the past, and/or lived in certain areas, Republicans sought to identify these "lazy Republicans," make sure that they were registered to vote, and then get them out to vote.

The plan required well-trained and committed partisans who could be counted on to initiate and maintain contacts with members of the targeted group. In the past, both parties had turned to paid organizers, party professionals, labor unions, nonparty groups, and even profit-making firms to do so. The Republican plan deviated from past grassroots efforts by depending primarily on community-based volunteers.[v]

The strategy depended on strong positive feelings toward the president and his party. In 2004, those feelings were present; by 2006, they had weakened considerably. Democrats also felt strongly and, for the most part, negatively about Bush and/or his policies in 2004, but many of them did not feel as strongly about Kerry. In other words, Republicans displayed greater intensity toward Bush than Democrats did toward Kerry.

Another important component of the Republican ground campaign was its focus on the social issues. The eleven-state ballot initiatives against same-sex marriage, the

BOX 7.2 | **Presidential Campaign Strategies in 2004 and 2008** *continued*

president's repeated reference to a constitutional amendment that would define marriage as a union between man and woman, and his frequently stated beliefs about God and the sanctity of human life all contributed to the success of the Republican's get-out-the-vote strategy.[vi]

A second strategic thrust of Bush's reelection campaign was to emphasize leadership during crises. The president had established his leadership credentials following the terrorist attacks on the World Trade Center and the Pentagon. Even if people disagreed with his policies, they acknowledged his attributes of strength, conviction, determination, and purpose. Bush had passed the leadership test; Kerry had not taken it in the minds of the American people.[vii] The Bush campaign replayed its leadership qualities again and again, comparing the president's actions after 9/11 to his challenger's equivocation, lack of clarity, and penchant for reversing himself. The Republicans believed that on the national security issue, Kerry had not demonstrated qualities of leadership that would make him an acceptable alternative to Bush while international terrorism was still perceived to be a domestic threat.[viii] By keeping the focus on terrorism, Bush benefited even though the news from Iraq was generally negative. Moreover, since the end of World War II, the public has placed more confidence in the Republicans' ability in foreign affairs than the Democrats'.[ix]

Being the incumbent helped Bush as well. The Bush Reelection Committee tried to maximize its incumbency advantages by using the bully pulpit to frame the campaign debate, shielding Bush from the press, and using the backdrop of the White House and the presidential seal to distinguish George W. Bush from his Democratic challenger.

John Kerry's Strategy: "Anything You Can Do, I Can Do Better"

With the electorate divided evenly along partisan lines and Kerry's leadership qualities disputed, the Democratic challenger did not have an obvious or easy road to the White House. In fact, he began with several disadvantages. One was the five-week period following the Democratic convention and before the Republican one, a period during which the Democratic candidate did not want to spend his limited federal funds. Going silent after his acceptance speech undercut whatever momentum the convention gave to Kerry and made him a target for Republican opponents, especially the Swift Boat Veterans for Truth, who were critical of his war record and antiwar activities after he left the military.

A second problem for Kerry concerned the president's personal favorability ratings that precluded a campaign to demonize him. Kerry went after Bush's policies with some success among Democrats but not among Republicans. Nor was the proportion of undecided Independents large enough or angry enough at Bush for Kerry to gain a decisive edge.

Advocating leadership change in times of crisis is difficult for challengers unless they can demonstrate that the incumbent's policies or actions were responsible for the crisis and that the challenger has demonstrated superior leadership qualities to deal with such a crisis. The Kerry campaign did not try to tag Bush with the responsibility for 9/11, only with a failed policy in Iraq. In the end, Kerry was

continued

PRESIDENTIAL CAMPAIGN STRATEGIES IN 2004 AND 2008 *continued*

unable to convince a plurality of Americans that he could provide stronger, more dependable, more coherent leadership in the war on terrorism, an inability that proved fatal.

The 2008 Election

Obama: Empowering the People for Change

Every campaign tries to maximize its strengths. For Obama, the advantages were its financial resources, grassroots operation, and the high level of public dissatisfaction with the direction the country was heading.[x] Obama's Internet operation had raised record amounts of money during the nomination and his volunteers had enlarged the Democratic electorate by its registration and get-out-the-vote activities. The plan was to do the same in the general election. The campaign message was political and policy change. In appearance and in appeal, Obama distinguished himself from the unpopular incumbent, George W. Bush. He called for unity in a country deeply divided by partisanship and ideology and gave hope and conveyed optimism to a public increasingly nervous about the deteriorating economic conditions.

The emotion Obama generated provided his campaign with several strategic opportunities that his opponent lacked—a large war chest capable of expanding even further, virtual and actual on-the-ground campaign operations, and as we have noted, an ability to change the Electoral College map beyond the traditional battleground and Democratic states. "Our goal was to force them to defend Bush states," wrote David Plouffe in his book, *The Audacity to Win*. "We saw little to no evidence that they could add to the Bush Electoral College margin."[xi]

The rejection of federal funds was critical to the success of the campaign strategy. Not only would it give Obama a significant resource advantage but it would give the people who ran his campaign control over their own advertising and field operations. In the past, Democratic candidates relying on public funding were increasingly dependent on generic advertising by the Democratic National Committee and nonparty groups that by law could not coordinate most of their campaign activities with those of the presidential campaign. Democratic campaigns had also been dependent on state party organizations for mounting grassroots operations. Plouffe noted, "[W]e did not want to outsource our field organization because so many of those people were volunteering for Obama . . . [not] the Michigan State Democratic party . . . [or] the Democratic National Committee."[xii]

Initially, the message was about the need for change and who could best achieve it. Over time, the change message increasingly focused on the economy and the candidate and the party best able to fix it. After the mid-September financial crisis when McCain said, "the fundamentals of our economy are strong" and both major party candidates went to Washington to participate in the discussion of how to save the large investment and insurance firms threatened with bankruptcy, the Obama campaign began emphasizing McCain's ill-chosen words and his erratic behavior.

> Our response [to the statement] followed a standard formula. Insert a rebuttal to McCain's outrageous comment in Obama's next speech that day to create a back and forth, ensuring maximum coverage. Produce TV and radio ads for release by that afternoon and get them up in the states right away. Make sure all our volunteers and staff out in the states had talking points on this to drive home in their conversations with voters.[xiii]

BOX 7.2 Presidential Campaign Strategies in 2004 and 2008 *continued*

The Obama plan was successful, although it was obviously facilitated by the financial crisis and the deteriorating economic conditions that became evident in mid-September and continued through the election. A disciplined campaign, resource advantages, an appealing message, and a strong and energetic field organization contributed to Obama's victory. There was little that McCain could say or do that would improve the economy or shift the blame from the Republican administration of George W. Bush.

McCain's Campaign: An Experienced Maverick

Although John McCain wrapped up the Republican nomination in early March, he was not able to generate much enthusiasm for his candidacy from Republicans. His choice of Sarah Palin was intended to be a game changer. That she was a popular reform governor was thought to reinforce McCain's independent streak but, more importantly, energized partisans who agreed with her socially conservative policy views and liked her homey "hockey-mom" style. Christian Ferry, McCain's Deputy Campaign Manager, stated:

> She was a huge positive for our field operation. She generated incredible enthusiasm amongst our volunteers. Folks who probably were going to vote for McCain on election day were now saying, "I am going to work very hard for McCain," because of the type of affection they had not just for John McCain but for Sarah Palin.[xiv]

The initial enthusiasm for Palin's selection contributed to a first-time lead in the national public opinion polls for McCain following the Republican convention.

The choice of Palin also affected press coverage. The news media shifted its focus to Palin and the excitement she generated among Republicans. But with greater coverage came greater scrutiny. In one-to-one interviews with broadcast journalists Charlie Gibson and Katie Couric, Palin did not do as well as she had done reading prepared speeches and interacting with partisans. She did not seem to know the Bush Doctrine in foreign policy nor did she have a keen understanding of the complexities of other international or domestic policy issues. Her lack of knowledge raised questions about her suitability to be next in line for the presidency if McCain won. Late-night comedians had a field day.

Since McCain began the general election with a significant financial disadvantage, his campaign was forced to depend on the Republican National Committee to supplement the $84.1 million he received from the federal treasury's campaign fund. The plan involved launching a coordinated advertising campaign with the committee. To do so, however, required that the ads mention national party candidates as well as McCain. Sarah Simmons, director of strategy for McCain–Palin, noted the problem: "Every time we said John McCain's name, we had to say congressional Republicans or congressional liberals as a match. . . . In half our ads, it looked like we were running against Harry Reid."[xv] Moreover, the bulk of these "hybrid" ads had to be negative because of the low esteem in which Congress was held by the American people.[xvi] Negative ads appeal more to partisans than to Independents and partisans of the other party. The hybrid ads were not helping McCain to enlarge his base. By October, the campaign decided to drop them entirely and do its own advertising with the limited funds that were available.

continued

BOX 7.2

PRESIDENTIAL CAMPAIGN STRATEGIES IN 2004 AND 2008 *continued*

McCain's suspension of his campaign also adversely affected his on-the-ground operations. According to Ferry, "there was a great deal of confusion. . . . Our volunteers weren't certain what exactly that meant for them. We had a period of ten days when our voluntary activity went way down."[xvii] The campaign eventually was able to resume its field operations, but valuable time had been lost.

Nor did McCain's performance in the first two debates help close the lead that Obama built after the economic crisis imploded. The people who advised McCain concluded that they needed a new campaign narrative to change the perceptions of the electorate if their candidate was going to win. That narrative took the form of Joe the Plumber, a person who challenged Obama's economic policies at one of his campaign rallies. Joe became a symbol for middle-class workers who had lost their jobs and were angry that the government was bailing out the firms that caused the problem rather than helping average Americans. Joe was a guy with whom regular folks could relate and with whom McCain connected. Part of Obama's response to Joe, "I think when you spread the wealth around, it's good for everybody,"[xviii] raised the issue of wealth redistribution to which Republicans believed that most of the country was opposed.[xix]

Joe rallied Republicans but did not change the dynamics of the election. With the economy dominating the news, domestic terrorism less salient, and a Status of Forces Agreement reached with Iraq that would bring most U.S. forces home over the next few years, there was little McCain could do to reverse electoral trends and catch up. In the words of Steve Schmidt, a senior adviser and campaign operative for McCain: "The economic collapse blew up our strategy in the middle of September. We never went back to national security as an issue in the campaign, an issue [on which] we were strong."[xx]

---

[i]In the words of Ken Mehlman, who initially headed the political office in the Bush White House and later directed the president's reelection campaign:

> The 2000 campaign convinced us of a lot of different things, but one of the most important things was that we needed a plan to try to expand the electorate and particularly expand our part of the electorate. There was a four-year plan to accomplish that, which included lots of different things. Fundamentally, it included two big things: one, to use the 2001 and 2002 elections to test out all kinds of different political tactics and make sure that we were being most effective in 2004 . . . (turnout, television advertising—where we bought, how we bought it). But secondly, just as important, was a way of communicating to key audiences that would expand the electorate.

Quoted in *Campaign for President: The Managers look at 2004* (Lanham, MD: Rowman and Littlefield, 2006), p. 98.

[ii]Mehlman, Ibid., p. 102.

[iii]Mehlman quoted in Ibid., p. 103.

[iv]The turnout strategy was supported by experimental and field research that found personal contact is the key to turning out people who are less likely to vote. Donald P. Green and Alan S. Gerber, *Get Out the Vote: How to Increase Voter Turnout* (Washington, DC: Brookings Institution, 2004).

[v]Mehlman described it as a "bottom-up" effort:

> We did not have outsiders come in. This was bottom up, not top down. What we tried to do was to provide channels for those people all over the country that supported this president to get their energies and their enthusiasms involved, and to figure out metrics by which we could figure our resource allocation.

BOX 7.2 | Presidential Campaign Strategies in 2004 and 2008 *continued*

Mehlman quoted in *Campaign for President 2004*, p. 199.
[vi] Democrats pursued a similar strategy in the 2006 midterm elections, using ballot initiatives on minimum wage to get out their vote.
[vii] In the words of Matthew Dowd, a senior strategist for the Bush campaign:

> There were a lot of people who never knew if Kerry wanted to cut and run—they didn't know what he wanted to do. On Election Day, a lot of them questioned whether or not he had a different plan than the President. In the end, the majority of voters said, I trust the President more than John Kerry on Iraq.

Dowd quoted in *Campaign for President 2004*, p. 193.
[viii] Here's how Bush's campaign manager, Ken Mehlman, put it:

> If you look historically, when people reject an incumbent because they are worried about an issue that's out there, they reject the incumbent because they think the challenger has a certain quality that helps deal with the issue they are worried about. In 1980, the public viewed the Iranian Hostage Crisis as evidence that Jimmy Carter was a weak leader, which they always thought, and they wanted a strong leader, Ronald Reagan. In 1992, . . . when people heard economic news that they didn't think was good enough, they wanted a guy who was going to focus on the economy. That had always been Clinton's definition. . . . If people thought Iraq was really messed up and was a tougher battle than before, they wanted someone who would be a strong leader . . . [Kerry] did have national security experience, but he wasn't defined as a strong leader as the President was.

Mehlman quoted in *Campaign for President 2004*, pp. 114–115.
[ix] Lydia Saad, "Republican Party Favored on Security Issues, Foreign Policy," Gallup Poll (Jan. 15, 2004). www.gallup.com/content/?ci=10204&pg=1
[x] "Topics from A-Z: Satisfaction with United States," Gallup Poll (2008). www.gallup.com/poll/1669/General-Mood-Country.aspx
[xi] David Plouffe, *The Audacity to Win* (New York: Viking, 2009). p. 249.
[xii] David Plouffe quoted in *Campaign for President: The Managers Look at 2008* (Lanham, MD: Rowman and Littlefield, 2009). p. 181.
[xiii] Plouffe, *Audacity*, p. 332.
[xiv] Christian Ferry quoted in *Campaign for President: 2008*, p. 193.
[xv] Sarah Simmons quoted in *Campaign for President: 2008*, p. 184.
[xvi] Simmons in Ibid.
[xvii] Ferry quoted in *Campaign for President: 2008*, p. 193.
[xviii] Barack Obama quoted in Mark Impomeni, "Obama Explains 'Spread the Wealth" Comment, *Politics Daily*, October 22, 2008. www.politicsdaily.com/2008/10/22/obama-explains-spread-the-wealth-comment
[xix] These remarks were made at a campaign stop in Ohio. They were also taken out of context. His entire statement was as follows:

> My attitude is that if the economy's good for folks from the bottom up, it's going to be good for everyone. If you've got a plumbing business, you're going to be better off if you've got a whole bunch of customers who can afford to hire you. And right now, everybody's so pinched that business is bad for everybody. And I think when you spread the wealth around, it's good for everybody.

Barack Obama quoted by National Public Radio. www.npr.org/templates/story/story.php?storyId=95799684
[xx] Steve Schmidt quoted in Kathleen Hall Jamieson, ed. *Electing the President 2008: The Insider's View* (Philadelphia: University of Pennsylvania Press, 2009). p. 63.

Jon Carson, national field director for Obama, emphasized the importance of personal contact: "At the end of the day, the most effective thing someone was able to say at the door was why they were supporting Barack Obama. [What mattered] was the fact that their neighbor was there saying, 'this is okay, let's vote for this guy.'"[39]

The Obama campaign went to great lengths to get community-based volunteers into the field. They made them feel as if they were part of the campaign, even giving precinct leaders limited access to the campaign's data base. Large rallies were also used to generate enthusiasm and gain volunteers. Attendees who

BOX 7.3 | OBAMA'S INTERNET REVOLUTION

The Obama Web campaign began even before Obama declared his candidacy. Moved by his 2004 keynote address to the Democratic National Convention, several college students set up their own Obama blogs to drum up support for his presidential candidacy. Obama's Internet advisers took advantage of these blogs, integrating them into their campaign and encouraging others to pass the word about Obama.

The Internet component had a staff of ninety-five. They were charged with using the new technology to expand their electoral base, particularly with people under thirty years of age.[i] The official campaign site, mybarackobama.com, was intended to be multipurposed and user-friendly, a social networking site from which those who accessed it could participate in the campaign in any number of ways: they could start their own online discussion groups with their friends, register to vote, donate money, and volunteer their services. They got a steady flow of information from the campaign—speeches, advertisements, policy positions, and updated schedules of events. After Obama won the Democratic nomination, the campaign made available phone numbers to call and Web addresses to visit so that volunteers could work for the campaign from their own homes and neighborhoods, thereby constructing virtual and actual phone and e-mail banks.

"Obamaites" made millions of calls, 3 million during the last four days before the election. The campaign sent out more than 7,000 different messages.[ii] In total, over 1 billion e-mails landed in in-boxes.[iii] A million people participated in the campaign's text-messaging program. On the night Obama officially received the Democratic nomination, more than 30,000 cell phones among the crowd of 75,000 were used to text into the program. Text messaging continued through election day with

---

supported Obama were asked to call a number on their cell phones which then captured their numbers and enabled the Obama organization to continue to contact them over the course of the campaign. Similarly, visitors to the Obama Web site were also asked for their e-mail addresses. The campaign concluded with a data base of millions of e-mail addresses and cell numbers.

Developments in the communications media, specifically in satellite technology, also enable candidates to reach a wide audience. They can remain in a studio and talk with local anchors across the country. Electronic town meetings and press conferences have now become standard fare. The 2004 and 2008 elections saw the expansion of these activities on the Internet. (See Box 7.3.)

EVENT PLANNING AND SPEECHMAKING

Staging a campaign event is not easy. The appearance of the stage, the timing of the speech or rally, the dignitaries invited and their seating positions, the recruitment and composition of the audience, the facilities for press coverage, the videotaping of the event, and, of course, the candidate's dress, speech (and the sound bites written into it), and interaction with those present must be planned in detail and well ahead of the event. Nothing should be left to chance.

people who signed up, receiving five to twenty messages a month depending where they lived and the kind of messages they opted to receive.[iv]

Over the course of the campaign, Obama was profiled in more than fifteen online communities. The campaign also took advantage of YouTube for what amounted to free advertising and repeated showings of Obama's speeches. His address on race during the nomination period attracted 4 million television viewers and 6.7 million saw it on YouTube, for an estimated exposure of 14.5 million hours.[v]

By the end of the campaign, almost 40 percent of registered voters said that they had seen campaign videos online.[vi] There were 13 million e-mail addresses in the campaign's data base, compared to 3 million for Kerry in 2004 and 600,00 for Dean in 2000. The campaign created 35,000 voluntary groups and received more than $500 million in online contributions from approximately 6.5 million donors.[vii]

---

[i] Jose Antonio Vargas, "Obama's Wide Web," *The Washington Post* (Aug. 20, 2008), sec. C. www.washingtonpost.com/wp-dyn/content/article/2008/08/19/AR2008081903186.html

[ii] Jose Antonio Vargas, "Obama Raised Half a Billion Online" (Nov. 20, 2008). voices.washingtonpost.com/44/2008/11/20/obama_raised_half_a_billion_on.html

[iii] Ibid.

[iv] Ibid.

[v] Claire Cain Miller, "How Obama's Internet Campaign Changed Politics," *The New York Times* (Nov. 7, 2008). bits.blogs.nytimes.com/2008/11/07/how-obamas-internet-campaign-changed-politics

[vi] YouTube videos featuring the major presidential candidates were viewed 3.2 billion times, according to the measurement firm TubeMogul. David Carr and Brian Stelter, "Campaign in a Web 2.0 World," *The New York Times* (Nov. 2, 2008). www.nytimes.com/2008/11/03/business/media/03media.html

[vii] Steven Hill, "World Wide Webbed: The Obama Campaign's Masterful Use of the Internet." *Social Europe Journal* (April 8, 2009).

Source: Stephen J. Wayne, *Is This Any Way to Run a Democratic Election?* (Washington, DC: CQ Press, 2011), pp. 219–220.

Problems must be anticipated. The Bush campaign of 2004 took steps to ensure friendly crowds and no hecklers. Almost all Bush events required tickets, and the Republicans monitored their distribution. In most cases, tickets went to party workers, campaign volunteers, and political donors. Protestors, evident at some Bush events, were kept outside and at a distance; if one protestor or a small group of them managed to slip in and display critical posters, banners, or even T-shirts, they would be escorted out by campaign security personnel. Camera crews, hired by the Bush–Cheney campaign, recorded the events and distributed video film clips to local and regional television.

In addition to controlling their immediate environment, the campaign also needs to control its campaign narrative and, if possible, the news about their campaign. To do so, candidates must stay on message and avoid ad-lib remarks. When speaking to religious conservatives, George W. Bush would make frequent references to his basic Christian values. Barack Obama would give his regular stump speech, tweaking it to the particular group to which he was talking. Although he would refer to the ongoing debate and newsworthy events, he was careful not to step on the theme he wanted the press to highlight.

Despite all the planning, occasionally there are slipups. In 2000, George W. Bush did not realize a microphone in front of him was open and used a scatological metaphor to characterize a *New York Times* reporter to his running mate, Dick Cheney. Sixteen years earlier, Bush's father had used a similar epithet.[40] During the nomination process, Obama referred to people who live in small towns as "bitter" when manufacturers closed their factories and moved them abroad.

One-liners can also work to a candidate's advantage. When Republican vice presidential nominee Dan Quayle compared his Senate experience with John F. Kennedy's in his debate with Lloyd Bentsen, the Democratic candidate shot back, "I served with Jack Kennedy; I knew Jack Kennedy; Jack Kennedy was a friend of mine. Senator, you are no Jack Kennedy."[41] Quayle, shaken by Bentsen's blunt reply, remained on the defensive for the remainder of the debate.

Knowing that their opponents and the press will focus on inconsistencies and slipups, candidates are warned to stick to their prepared script that has been pretested before groups of voters. Frequently, speechwriters will insert code words to generate a reaction from a particular group. The message is often compartmentalized. Groups get information on those positions and priorities that the campaign has determined to be most in accord with their opinions and beliefs. Other candidate stands and beliefs are not conveyed. The problem with such specialized messages is that they can lead to unrealistic expectations that the newly elected or reelected president cannot achieve. Obama faced this problem in his early years in office. His transformational policy goals and "yes we can" optimism created unrealizable expectations and unrealistic time frames in which to achieve them. When he was unable to meet these expectations, his job approval declined.

In addition to what to say, how to say it, and to whom, timing is also an important consideration. Candidates naturally desire to build momentum as their campaigns progress. The 1996 Clinton campaign was one of the most successful in adhering to a timed plan for communicating various messages to the voters. In the year before the election, the president emphasized his centrist and moderate positions, co-opting many of the Republicans' policy stands in the process. As the nomination campaign got underway, he talked about family values and showcased himself in various presidential roles, in stark contrast to the Republican candidates, who were criticizing one another's qualifications for the presidency. During the general election campaign, Clinton remained on his presidential pedestal, emphasizing the accomplishments of his administration and his desire to build a "bridge to the future."

SUMMARY

Throughout much of the nineteenth century, presidential campaigns were run by the political parties on behalf of their nominees. The goal of the campaign was to energize and educate the electorate with a series of public activities and events. Beginning in the 1840s, but accelerating in the 1880s, presidential candidates themselves became increasingly involved in the campaign. By the 1920s, they had become active participants, using radio, later television, and more recently, the Internet to reach as many voters as possible.

Advances in transportation and communications have made campaigns more complex, more expensive, and more technologically sophisticated. These advances require considerable activity by the candidates and their staffs. Strategy and tactics are now more closely geared to the technology of contemporary politics and run by campaign professionals: pollsters, media consultants, direct mailers, grassroots organizers, lawyers, accountants, data collectors and analysts, and experts of the new media. Their inclusion in the candidate's organization has made the coordination of centralized decision making critical. It has also produced several complementary organizations and campaigns: those of the candidates, the parties, and outside groups. When an incumbent is running, the White House is also involved.

The job of campaign organizations is to produce a unified and coordinated effort. Most presidential campaigns follow a general strategy based on the prevailing political attitudes and perceptions of the electorate, the reputations and images of the nominees and their parties, and the geography of the Electoral College. The strategy includes designing a basic appeal, creating a leadership image, dealing with incumbency (if appropriate), and allocating campaign resources in the light of the Electoral College.

In projecting their basic appeals, Democratic candidates have emphasized their party label and those "bread-and-butter" issues that have held their electoral coalition together since the 1930s. Republican candidates, on the other hand, did not emphasize partisanship until the 1980s when the Republicans gained parity with the Democrats. They focused instead on domestic and foreign policy problems and character issues.

Part of the strategy of every presidential campaign is to project an image of leadership. Candidates do this by trumpeting their own strengths and exploiting their opponent's weaknesses. They try to project those attributes that the public desires in their president, traits that are endemic to the office and resonate with the public mood at that time. Being president, making critical decisions, and exercising the powers of the office are evidence of the leadership skills that incumbents have displayed and challengers have to demonstrate.

An established record, particularly by presidents seeking reelection, shapes much of that leadership imagery. That record may contribute to or detract from a candidate's reelection potential. In good times, incumbents have an advantage; in bad times, they do not. When national security issues are salient, incumbents usually benefit; when economic issues are paramount, they do not. Poor economies hurt an incumbent more than good economies help them or the candidate of their party.

When allocating resources, the geography of the Electoral College must always be considered. Each party begins with a base of safe states. In the 1980s, that base was thought to be larger for the Republicans than for the Democrats. Population movements to the South and the West resulted in a regional advantage for the Republicans, one that allowed them greater flexibility in designing their general election strategy. In the 1990s, however, the Democrats seemed to gain an advantage in the Northeast and the Pacific Coast region. In 2000 and 2004, the Electoral College was divided closely between red (Republican) and blue (Democratic) states, and there was stability in the states' voting preferences. In 2008, the Obama campaign made gains in the South and Southwest as well as in the traditional battleground states of the Midwest.

The level of competition within states is another factor that affects campaign strategy and resource allocation. Less than one-half of the states are truly competitive at the beginning of the race and usually less than half a dozen at the end. Time, effort, and money are concentrated within the most competitive states; the rest of the country witnesses the campaign primarily in the news and by word of mouth; they do not see the candidates in person except perhaps at a fund-raiser during the preelection period; they do not see many, if any, of the political commercials, except if they are controversial and become news, in and of themselves; and they receive less personal and computer-generated communication than do people in the key battleground states.

The candidates' strategies influence the conduct of their campaigns, the appeals they make, and the images they project. Their tactics have more direct effect on day-to-day events and get-out-the-vote activities. Key tactical decisions include what communication techniques are to be used, when, and to which groups of voters.

Campaign events are designed to project and reinforce the candidate's image and policy appeals and to critique those of the opponent. Everything is carefully planned, from the composition of the audience, to the positioning of the cameras, to the script for the candidate and others who may also address the crowd, to the seating arrangement on the platform. Spontaneity is discouraged.

In the end, the methods that mobilize the electorate by getting people excited about a candidate are likely to generate the most impact in turning out and influencing the vote. In 2004 and 2008, greater emphasis was placed on grassroots organizations and operations with the result that turnout increased. Much of the campaign, however, is still filtered through the news media. The next chapter explores this mediation and its impact on the election.

WHERE ON THE WEB?

Many of the *Where on the Web* sites listed in Chapter 5 will be useful to study the general election as well.

- **Campaigns and Elections**
  www.campaignline.com
  Posts articles that have appeared in the magazine *Campaigns and Elections.*
- **24-7 News Networks: CNN, Fox News, MSNBC**
  www.CNN.com
  www.foxnews.com
  www.msnbc.com
  Contain news, investigatory, and feature stories on the presidential campaign.
- **C-SPAN: The Road to the White House**
  www.cspan.org
  Provides C-SPAN programming on the campaign as well as candidate appearances, speeches, student surveys, and political debates.

- **Gallup Poll**
  www.gallup.com
  Contains the latest polling data on the campaign. Gallup is one of the premier polling organizations.
- **National Journal**
  www.nationaljournal.com
  Of the many news sources for following the presidential primaries and caucuses, the *National Journal's* site is one of the best.
- **New York Times**
  www.nytimes.com
  The New York Times prides itself on being a paper of record. You will find much information on the policy positions and speeches of the candidates in this newspaper as well as the latest delegate count and prenomination polls.
- **Politics1**
  www.politics1.com
  An online guide to current politics with links to other relevant sites for the presidential election.
- **Polling Report**
  www.pollingreport.com
  Summarizes ongoing public polls on the presidential election.

EXERCISES

1. Assess how the candidates targeted their appeals in the most recent presidential election. What appeals did they direct toward their own partisans, especially to the principal groups in their party's traditional electoral coalition, and how did they deal with Independents and others, including those who say they support third-party candidates?
2. Indicate the initial geographic strategies of the major-party candidates in 2008 and then how those strategies changed over the course of the campaign. Now compare these strategies to those you believe should or will be employed in 2012. Design a resource allocation memo for the candidate of your choice.
3. How has the Internet changed the tactics and operations of presidential campaigns in recent years? To what extent has this new technology affected the democratic character of presidential elections?
4. Write a memo for your party's presidential candidate on the most effective ways to use the Internet to reach, energize, and motivate partisans and those without partisan affiliations.
5. List the typical activities of a contemporary "war room" for a presidential candidate.

SELECTED READINGS

Campaign for President: The Managers Look at 2008. Lanham, MD: Rowman & Littlefield, 2009.

Heilemann, John, and Mark Halperin. *Game Change*. New York: HarperCollins, 2010.

Jamieson, Kathleen Hall, ed. *Electing the President 2008: The Insiders' View*. Philadelphia: University of Pennsylvania Press, 2009.

Melder, Keith. *Hail to the Candidate: Presidential Campaigns from Banners to Broadcasts*. Washington, DC: Smithsonian Institution Press, 1992.
Morris, Dick. *Behind the Oval Office*. New York: Random House, 1997.
Nader, Ralph. *Crashing the Party: Taking on the Corporate Government in an Age of Surrender*. New York: St. Martin's Press, 2002.
Ornstein, Norman, and Thomas Mann, eds. *The Permanent Campaign and Its Future*. Washington, DC: AEI/Brookings, 2000.
Plouffe, David. *The Audacity to Win*. New York: Viking, 2009.
Shaw, Daron R. *The Race to 270: The Electoral College and Campaign Strategies of 2000 and 2004*. Chicago: University of Chicago Press, 2006.
Tenpas, Kathryn Dunn. *Presidents as Candidates*. New York: Garland, 1997.
Troy, Gil. *See How They Ran: The Changing Role of the Presidential Candidate*. New York: Free Press, 1991.
White, Theodore H. *The Making of the President: 1960*. New York: Atheneum, 1988.
____________ *The Making of the President, 1964*. New York: Atheneum, 1965.
____________ *The Making of the President, 1968*. New York: Atheneum, 1969.
____________ *The Making of the President, 1972*. New York: Atheneum, 1973.
____________ *America in Search of Itself: The Making of the President, 1956–1980*. New York: Harper & Row, 1982.
Woodward, Bob. *The Choice*. New York: Simon & Schuster, 1997.

NOTES

1. Keith Melder, *Hail to the Candidate: Presidential Campaigns from Banners to Broadcasts* (Washington DC: Smithsonian Institution Press, 1992), pp. 70–74.
2. Ibid., p. 87.
3. Ibid., p. 88.
4. Marvin R. Weisbord, *Campaigning for President* (New York: Washington Square Press, 1966), p. 45.
5. Historian Gil Troy writes that Lincoln's avoidance of anything that smacked of political involvement was in fact a political tactic that he used throughout the campaign. Gil Troy, *See How They Ran: The Changing Role of the Presidential Candidate* (New York: Free Press, 1991), p. 66.
6. Weisbord, *Campaigning for President,* p. 5.
7. Melder, *Hail to the Candidate,* p. 104.
8. Ibid., p. 125.
9. Keith Melder, "The Whistlestop: Origins of the Personal Campaign," *Campaign and Elections,* 7 (May/June 1986), p. 49.
10. William Jennings Bryan, *The First Battle* (1896; reprint, Port Washington, NY: Kennikat Press, 1971), p. 618.
11. Melder, *Hail to the Candidate,* p. 129.
12. Weisbord, *Campaigning for President,* p. 116.
13. Franklin Roosevelt had been disabled by polio in 1921. He wore heavy leg braces and could stand only with difficulty. Nonetheless, he made a remarkable physical and political recovery. In his campaign, he went to great lengths to hide the fact that he could not walk and could barely stand. The press generally did not report on his disability. They refrained from photographing, filming, or describing him struggling to stand with braces.
14. Cabell Phillips, *The Truman Presidency* (New York: Macmillan, 1966), p. 237.
15. Stanley Kelley, *Professional Public Relations and Political Power* (Baltimore, MD: Johns Hopkins Press, 1956), pp. 161–162.

16. Karl A. Lamb and Paul A. Smith, *Campaign Decision Making: The Presidential Election of 1964* (Belmont, CA: Wadsworth, 1968), pp. 59–63.
17. Christian Ferry, Deputy Campaign Manager, in *Campaign for President: The Managers Look at 2008* (Lanham, MD: Rowman & Littlefield, 2009), p. 86.
18. Steve Schmidt in Kathleen Hall Jamieson, ed., *Electing the President 2008: The Insider's View* (Philadelphia: University of Pennsylvania, Press, 2009), pp. 55–56.
19. Rick Davis quoted in *Campaign for President: 2008,* pp. 170–171.
20. In mid-September 2008, at the peak of the economic crisis, McCain was quoted as saying, "As you know, there's been tremendous turmoil in our financial markets and Wall Street, and it is- its- people are frightened by these events. Our economy, I think, still the fundamentals are- of our economy are strong." Sam Stein, "McCain On 'Black Monday': Fundamentals Of Our Economy Are Still Strong," *Huffington Post* (September 15, 2008). www.huffingtonpost.com/2008/09/15/mccain-fundamentals-of-th_n_126445.html.
21. David Plouffe, in Jamieson, *Electing the President: 2008,* p. 40.
22. According to James Carville, Clinton's principal strategist in 1992:

    > By the time the convention had come, we had spent a lot of time, a lot of money, a lot of research on determining what it was that we wanted to do. By mid-June, . . . we had a pretty good idea of the things that we needed to accomplish, of the nature and depth of our problems, and how we wanted to solve them and accomplish our objectives. . . . Strategically, we knew 85 percent of what we wanted to do by late June.

    James Carville, in Charles T. Royer, ed., *Campaign for President: The Managers Look at '92* (Hollis, NH: Hollis Publishing, 1994), p. 194.
23. Plouffe continued, "Your staff will inevitably screw up. But the most precious resource in any campaign is time. The candidate's time. You have to be the candidate. Not the campaign manager, scheduler, or driver." David Plouffe, *The Audacity to Win* (New York: Viking, 2009), p. 8.
24. Barack Obama quoted in Plouffe, Ibid.
25. Plouffe, Ibid., p. 323.
26. George W. Bush believed that his father had made a major error by not considering his reelection as a component of the political power he was able to exercise as president. The younger Bush was determined not to repeat this error.
27. Plouffe, *Audacity,* p. 17.
28. "Topics from A-Z: Most Important Problem," Gallup Poll, 2008. www.gallup.com/poll/1675/Most-Important-Problem.aspx.
29. An excellent examination of presidential traits appears in Benjamin I. Page, *Choices and Echoes in Presidential Elections* (Chicago: University of Chicago Press, 1978), pp. 232–265.
30. David Axelrod quoted in Jamieson, *Electing the President: 2008,* p. 68.
31. If he did not do well, however, the early debate would have given him more time to recover and still demonstrate his competence.
32. George W. Bush, "Acceptance Speech at the Republican National Convention" (August 3, 2000). www.presidency.ucsb.edu/ws/index.php?pid=25954.
33. Lee Atwater, quoted in Thomas B. Edsall, "Why Bush Accentuates the Negative," *The Washington Post* (Oct. 2, 1988), p. C4.
34. A survey conducted by the Times Mirror Center for the People & the Press in early October 1992 found that 50 percent of those who saw the Bush advertisements felt that they were not truthful compared with 35 percent for the viewers of Clinton's ads. Times Mirror Center for the People & the Press, "Campaign '92: Air Wars" (Oct. 8, 1992), p. 2.

35. Obama was careful not to disparage McCain personally. He acknowledged his years of service and sacrifice to his country.
36. Tad Devine quoted in *Campaign for President 2004*, p. 196.
37. Plouffe, *Audacity*, p. 247.
38. Plouffe, Ibid., pp. 249–258.
39. Carson, in *Electing the President: 2008*, p. 44.
40. Another well-reported incident, this one involving Vice President Nelson Rockefeller, occurred in 1976. It, too, was precipitated by heckling. The Republican vice presidential candidate of that year, Senator Robert Dole, accompanied by Rockefeller, was trying to address a rally in Binghamton, New York. Constantly interrupted by the hecklers, Dole and then Rockefeller tried to restore order by addressing their critics directly. When this approach failed, Rockefeller grinned and made an obscene gesture. The vice president's response was captured in a picture that appeared in newspapers and magazines across the country, much to the embarrassment of the Republican ticket.

    Democrats have also had their share of off-color embarrassing remarks. In 1972, Senator George McGovern, the Democratic nominee, had been heckled continuously at events; it was later discovered that many of these hecklers had been campaign workers and volunteers for the Committee to Reelect the President and had been instructed to disrupt the McGovern campaign. In one incident, a sign-carrying heckler yelled an obscenity at the senator as he worked the crowd. McGovern replied with the off-color remark, "Kiss my ass," an assertion that suggested a forcefulness that many believed had been lacking in his campaign.

    Similarly, to evidence a macho character that critics believed he lacked, George H. W. Bush said he "intended to kick ass" in his debate with Democratic vice presidential nominee Geraldine Ferraro.
41. Lloyd Bentsen, "Transcript of the Vice Presidential Debate," *The Washington Post* (Oct. 6, 1988), p. A30.

MEDIA POLITICS

CHAPTER 8

INTRODUCTION

Media and politics go hand in hand. The press has served as an outlet for divergent political views from the founding of the Republic. When political parties developed at the end of the eighteenth century, newspapers became a primary means for disseminating their policy positions and promoting their candidates.

The early press was contentious and highly adversarial, but was not aimed at the masses. Written for the upper, educated class, newspapers contained essays, editorials, and letters that debated economic and political issues. It was not until the 1830s that the elitist orientation of the press began to change. Technological improvements, the growth in literacy, and the movement toward greater public involvement in the democratic process all contributed to the development of the so-called penny press, newspapers that sold for a penny and were directed at the general public.

THE MASS MEDIA AND ELECTORAL POLITICS: AN OVERVIEW

The penny press revolutionized American journalism. Newspapers began to rely on advertising rather than subscriptions as their primary source of income. To attract advertisers, they had to reach a large number of readers. To do so, newspapers had to alter what they reported and how they reported it. Prior to the development of the penny press, news was rarely "new"; stories were often weeks old before they appeared and were rewritten or reprinted from other sources. With more newspapers aimed at the general public, a higher premium was placed on gathering news quickly and reporting it in an exciting, easy-to-read manner.

PRINT MEDIA

Once newspapers became designed for the mass public, they began to help inform voting decisions for most of the electorate. The invention of the telegraph helped in this regard. The telegraph made it possible for an emerging Washington press corps to communicate information to the entire country. What was considered news also changed. Events replaced ideas; human-interest stories supplemented the official proceedings of government; and drama and conflict were featured. Stories of crime, sex, and violence captured the headlines and sold papers, not essays and letters on public policy. Joseph Pulitzer's *New York World* and William Randolph Hearst's *New York Journal* set the standard for this era of highly competitive "yellow journalism."[1]

Not all newspapers featured sensational news. In 1841, Horace Greeley founded the *New York Tribune,* and ten years later, Henry Raymond began the *New York Times*. Both papers appealed to a more-educated audience interested in the political issues of the day. After a change in ownership, the *New York Times* became a paper of record. Operating on the principle that news is not simply entertainment but valuable public information, the *Times* adopted the motto "All the news that's fit to print." It published entire texts of important speeches and documents and detailed national and foreign news. Toward the middle of the nineteenth century, newspapers began to shed their advocacy role in favor of more neutral reporting. The growth of news wire services, such as the Associated Press and United Press, and of newspapers that were not tied to political parties, contributed to these developments.

As candidates became more personally involved in the campaign, they too became the subject of press attention. By the beginning of the twentieth century, the focus had shifted to the nominees, so much so that at least one candidate, Alton Parker, Democratic presidential nominee for 1904, angrily criticized photographers for their unyielding efforts to take pictures of him while he was swimming in the nude in the Hudson River.[2] Despite the intrusion into their personal lives, candidates began taking advantage of the press's interest in them, using "photo opportunities" and news coverage to project their image and extend their partisan appeal.

BROADCAST MEDIA

With the advent of radio in the 1920s and television in the 1950s, news media coverage of campaigns changed once again. Radio supplemented the print media. Although it did not provide regular news coverage, radio excelled at covering special events as they were happening. The 1924 presidential election was the first to be reported on radio; the conventions, major speeches, and election returns were broadcast live that year. During the 1928 election, both presidential candidates, Herbert Hoover and Alfred E. Smith, spent campaign funds on radio advertising.

Radio lost its national audience to television in the 1950s but remained a favorite communications medium of candidates seeking to target their messages to specific groups in specific locations. A cheap and accessible electronic medium, radio continues to be used extensively. The amount of time that people spend commuting in their automobiles has increased the importance of radio as a communication vehicle.

The influence of television on presidential elections was first felt in 1952. The most important news event of that presidential campaign was a speech by General Dwight Eisenhower's running mate, Richard Nixon. Accused of obtaining secret campaign funds in exchange for political favors, Nixon defended himself in a television address. He denied accepting contributions for personal use, accused the Democratic administration of being soft on communism, criticized his campaign opponents, and vowed that he would never force his children to give up their dog, Checkers, who had been given to the Nixon family by political supporters. The emotion of the speech, and particularly the reference to Checkers, generated a favorable public reaction, ended discussion of the campaign funds, kept Nixon on the Republican ticket, and demonstrated the power of television for candidates in their campaigns.

Paid television advertising by the political parties also first appeared in the 1952 presidential campaign. The major broadcast networks extended their evening news reports to half an hour in 1963, and by the end of the 1960s, television had become the principal source of election news for most Americans. Presidential campaigns in turn became made-for-television productions. Their public events were staged with television in mind. On-air interviews, talk-show participation, even the entertainment format have become part and parcel of the modern electoral campaigns.

During the 1970s into the 1980s, the evening newscasts had the largest audience. Newspapers trailed, with radio and news magazines lower down on the list. One of the big changes during this period was the development and growth of cable news networks. Cable and satellite technologies began to acquire more subscribers and all-news formats, thereby fragmenting the number of news sources. That growth has continued. Today, almost 70 percent of television households are wired for cable, and 31.6 percent have alternative sources such as satellite dishes.[3]

THE INTERNET

The Internet has become an important primary and secondary source of news as well. In 2004, 21 percent cited the Web as their principal source; by 2008, that percentage had risen to 36, with 58 percent of voters under thirty indicating that the Internet was their major source of information about the election.[4] Besides being a relatively cheap and easy way to reach potential supporters, the Internet has become the most important way to target younger voters who might otherwise not see as much of the campaign, receive much of the direct mail, or be contacted personally by a campaign worker.

Contemporary campaigns use their own Web sites to provide up-to-date information, including the latest speeches, political news, forthcoming events, and all the political advertising aired on television and the documentaries made about their candidates, using the latest video streaming technology to do so. In 2008, Obama put an archive of all his speeches on the campaign's Web site; those who accessed it could also receive posters and flyers, a schedule of campaign events in their area, and talking points for canvassing by phone or visit. The Obama site received more than twice as many "hits" as did the McCain site, even after the latter was rejuvenated in the summer of 2008.[5] Both major-party candidates also ran Internet ads on the sites of major news organizations, designed to pop up in key battleground states as well as in searches in which targeted groups were mentioned.

This chapter examines these developments and their impact on presidential electoral politics. The first section discusses traditional "hard" news coverage of campaigns. It examines how network news organizations interpret political events and how candidates react to those interpretations. The "soft" news/entertainment format is explored in the second section. Here the chapter describes the techniques that candidates have used in recent campaigns to circumvent the national press corps. The third section turns to another news/entertainment feature—presidential debates. It describes the history of the debates and their structure, staging, and impact on the electorate. Political advertising is the subject of the fourth section, which describes some of the most successful commercials, examines the increasing emphasis on negativity, and assesses the effect of advertising on the voters' perceptions of the candidates. The final section looks at the media's cumulative impact on voting choice.

TRADITIONAL COVERAGE: HARD NEWS

The modus operandi of news reporting is to inform the public. But the press does so with its own professional orientation—one that affects what is covered and how it is covered.

HORSE RACE JOURNALISM

Political scientist Thomas E. Patterson argues that the dominant conceptual framework for election reporting is that of a game. The candidates are the players and their moves (words, activities, and images) are seen as strategic and tactical devices to achieve their principal goal, winning the election. Even their policy positions are frequently evaluated within this gaming framework; issue stands are described as calculated appeals to constituency groups. Although Patterson argues that the gaming aspect of electoral politics is most pronounced at the beginning of the presidential selection process, he also sees it as an organizing principle for the press throughout the entire election cycle.[6]

Why do the news media use the game metaphor ("horse race") as its primary one? The answer is entertainment. Races are exciting. Viewing elections as a game heightens viewers' interest. Heightened interest, in turn, increases the size of the audience and, of course, the profits, because advertising revenue is based on the estimated number of people watching or hearing a particular program or reading a paper. There is another reason for employing the game format. It lends an aura of objectivity to reporting. Rather than presenting subjective accounts of the candidates' positions and their consequences for the country, the news media can present quantitative data on the public's reaction to the campaign. Public opinion surveys reported as news are frequently the dominant story during the primaries and caucuses, sharing the spotlight with other campaign issues such as the candidates' character, strategies, and tactics.

Covering campaigns as if they were sporting events is not a new phenomenon. In 1976, Patterson found about 60 percent of television election coverage and 55 percent of newspaper coverage treated the campaign as if it were a sporting contest.[7] Michael J. Robinson's and Margaret Sheehan's analysis of the *CBS Evening News* during the 1980 election revealed that five out of six stories emphasized the competition.[8] The emphasis on the game of politics has continued (see Table 8.1). However, in the 2004 election, policy stories—the war on terror, the war in Iraq, spiraling oil prices, and a host of domestic issues combined—slightly exceeded the attention given to the "race" for president. In 2008, it was back to the game; the Project for Excellence found that 53 percent of the election stories were about strategy, tactics, and the horse race.[9] An analysis of television news by The Center for Media and Public Affairs had similar findings, as reflected in Table 8.1.

The problem with horse-race journalism is that it diverts public attention from substance to strategy. Instead of examining the merits and limitations of a candidate's proposal, journalists explore the underlying political motivations for making the proposal, moving from the *what* to the *why* in the process. Such a focus skews the information people receive; it also heightens the partisan political component of elections and reduces the substantive policy debate to which most people are exposed.

From 1988 until the election of 2004, there was a declining amount of campaign news that was available on the major broadcast networks. However, in 2004 and 2008, the amount of election news increased, reversing a decline that began in 1992. (See Table 8.1.) Once the campaign is underway, the principal candidates get approximately the same amount of coverage; third-party and independent candidates do not.[10] Contrary to popular belief, incumbents seeking reelection do not usually dominate the election news.

With the growth in the number of all-news networks on cable television and news sites on the Internet, the total amount of information available to the general public is much larger today than in the past. However, so are the options for avoiding election news programming entirely.

The growth of news sources has also created more pressure on the all-news networks to find a niche rather than aim for a general audience with a more

TABLE 8.1 | BROADCAST NETWORK EVENING NEWS COVERAGE OF PRESIDENTIAL ELECTIONS (LABOR DAY–ELECTION DAY), 1988–2008

Year	1988	1992	1996	2000	2004	2008
Amount						
Number of Stories	589	728	483	462	504	683
Stories per Day	10.5	11.5	7.7	7.3	9.0	9.4
Total Minutes	1,116	1,402	788	805	1,070	1,606
Focus (percent of stories)*						
Horse Race	58	58	48	71	48	55
Policy Issues	39	32	37	40	49	33
Candidate Sound Bite						
Length (seconds)	9.8	8.4	8.2	7.8	7.8	—
Percent of Air Time	n/a	12	13	12	12	—
Tone (percent of favorable comments)						
Democratic Nominee	31	52	50	40	59	68
Republican Nominee	38	29	33	37	37	33

*Stories can include one or both focuses. Numbers do not add up to 100.

Source: Stephen J. Farnsworth, and S. Robert Lichter, "The Nightly News Nightmare Revisited: Network Television's Coverage of the 2004 Presidential Election," paper presented at the annual meeting of the American Political Science Association, Washington, D.C., September 2005, Table 1, p. 31. Used with permission.; "Election Watch: Campaign 2008 Final: How TV News Covered the General Election Campaign," *Media Monitor* 23 (Winter 2009), pp. 2–4.

broad-brush, bipartisan approach. Fox News has successfully directed its news programming toward conservatives and Republicans; in contrast, MSNBC, CNN, and National Public Radio attract more liberal, Democratically-oriented viewers and listeners. According to Professor Diana C. Mutz, differentiated approaches and audiences have contributed to the partisan political divide in the United States today by facilitating selective exposure, which in turn reinforces rather than challenges the political attitudes that people have and has heightened the partisan basis of contemporary American politics.[11]

THE BAD NEWS SYNDROME

The tone of election coverage also tends to be negative. Incumbents usually receive more critical comments from nonpartisan sources—average Americans—than do challengers. In 1980, Jimmy Carter was treated more harshly than Ronald Reagan, and in 1984, Reagan was treated more harshly than Walter Mondale. Vice President George H. W. Bush, running for president in 1988, also fared poorly, but so did his Democratic rival, Michael Dukakis. Each received two negative comments for every positive one. In 1992 and 2004, the incumbents were also subject to more critical coverage than were their challengers. Only Bill Clinton in 1996 fared better than his Republican opponent Robert Dole.

More Republicans than Democrats perceive an ideological bias in political reporting. Most academic experts do not, although they admit that reporters and correspondents tend to be more liberal and Democratic. They also point out that the owners and editors are more Republican and conservative.[12] However, content analyses of the coverage of presidential elections on the major broadcast networks' evening news shows conducted by the Center for Media and Public Affairs indicate that in the elections of 1984, 1992, 1996, 2004, and 2008 the Democratic presidential candidate got a higher percentage of good press than did his Republican opponent. In 1980, 1988, and 2000, neither party's candidate was advantaged.[13] On the three broadcast networks Obama's coverage was twice as favorable as McCain's; on Fox it was nearly equal: 40 percent of McCain's coverage was favorable on that news network compared to 37 percent for Obama.

The Project for Excellence in Journalism reported findings similar to those of the Center for Media and Public Affairs. During the six-week period of its analysis, September 8–October 16, its researchers found that the amount of coverage was equal but the spin favored Obama. Part of the explanation for Obama's advantage stems from the horse race focus, in which the press reports which candidate is ahead; part of it also related to the economic downturn and the blame placed on the party that controlled the White House. Republican vice presidential nominee Sarah Palin also received more negative (39 percent) than positive (28 percent) and neutral (33 percent) coverage.[14]

Why the bad press? Most academic experts see it as a consequence of the news media's role as watchdog of government. They also believe it has something to do with the press's understanding of what is newsworthy and what is not. Put simply, bad news seems to be more newsworthy than good news. A fresh face winning and an experienced candidate losing are news; an experienced one winning and an unfamiliar one losing are not. Similarly, the first time a candidate states a position, it may be newsworthy; the second time, it is old news; the third time, it is not news at all. Since candidates cannot give new speeches every time they make an address, the news media that cover the candidates look for other things to report.

Verbal slips, embarrassing incidents, quotes taken out of context, inconsistent statements, and mistakes often become the focus of attention. Kiku Adatto found that "only once in 1968 did a network even take note of a minor incident unrelated to the content of the campaign."[15] In recent elections, however, there is much more frequent reporting of trivial slips.[16] The news media's penchant for reporting slips of the tongue and off-color communications encourages the candidates not to be spontaneous, not to be candid, and above all, not to make mistakes. It also encourages speechwriters to put in sound bites and applause lines that they want the press to highlight and that they will use for their ads.

Slipups are inevitable in a long campaign, however. But if poorly chosen words are used or salty private comments become public, candidates need to acknowledge mistakes and campaigns need to respond quickly to minimize the damage and return the focus to the desired narrative. In 2000, Al Gore admitted that he made factual errors during the first presidential debate; George W. Bush conceded that he had once been arrested for drunk driving many years earlier; in his first debate with Bush in 2004, John Kerry said, "When I talked about the $87 billion, I made a mistake in how I talked about the war." But he did not say whether his vote had been a mistake. Bush, however, refused to reply to accusations that appeared in internal National Guard memos, and highlighted by CBS News, that he had not fulfilled his Guard responsibilities in the 1970s; the memos turned out to be forgeries. In 2008, Obama admitted that he and his wife bought property adjoining their house in Chicago from Tony Resko, a person later convicted of mail fraud, wire fraud, corrupt solicitation, and a variety of other federal crimes. Republicans had to admit that Joe the Plumber's real name was not Joe. It was Samuel Joseph Wurzelbacher. And he was not a registered plumber nor did he own a plumbing firm.

A candidate's failure to provide the news media with information, pictures, or even the pose they desire can draw an admonishment from the press. Take the comment that ABC correspondent Sam Donaldson made to Michael Dukakis, who was playing a trumpet with a local marching band in the midst of his 1988 presidential campaign. Donaldson reported, "He played the trumpet with his back to the camera." As Dukakis played the Democratic victory tune, "Happy Days Are Here Again," Donaldson could be heard saying off-camera "We're over here, Governor."[17]

Television news has an additional bias. As an action-oriented, visual medium, its content must move quickly and be capable of projecting a strong visual image on a screen. Television emphasizes pictures and deemphasizes words; less attention is devoted to what candidates say and more to how people react to their words and images. That is why campaign speeches are laden with sound bites and catch phrases, such as "Where's the beef?" "It is morning in America," "Read my lips—No new taxes," "a bridge to the twenty-first century," "compassionate conservatism," the "war on terrorism," and "yes we can."

Emotion is more newsworthy than passivity; conflict is usually more newsworthy than consensus. Angry words and actions gain attention more easily than does reasoned debate. They also produce a more emotive response from the audience. Professor Diana C. Mutz argues that news coverage of strident rhetoric has contributed to partisan incivility and passionate politics that characterizes today's political environment in America.[18]

MEDIATED COVERAGE

From the candidates' perspectives, the bad news is magnified by the fact that they do not have the opportunity to tell their own stories in their own words on the news that is reported by the major news networks. The average length of a quotation from candidates on the evening news shows in 1968 was 42.3 seconds. Since 1988, it has been less than 10 seconds. What is worse from the candidates' perspective is that the reporters and correspondents are on camera much longer than are the candidates, approximately seven times longer for most campaign stories.[19] The bottom line is that the networks' anchors and correspondents present election news to the voters, not the candidates. How they do so has even become a subject of news media coverage.

The Story Line

In addition to the nature of network news and the format in which it is given, the news is also fitted into a framework. According to Patterson, a dominant story line emerges and much of the campaign is explained in terms of it. In 1992, it was Pat Buchanan's surprising showing against George H. W. Bush that was news, not Bush's easy wins over his Republican rival; it was the conservative-controlled Republican convention and platform that garnered the headlines during the summer of 1992, not the adulation that greeted Bush and his running mate, Dan Quayle, at the convention; it was the president's inability to turn the election around, to "hit a home run" during his debates with Clinton and Perot, that was news rather than Bush's plans for the future or even the character issues he raised about his opponents. In Patterson's words:

> Bush's bad press was mainly a function of journalistic values. The news form itself affected both the content and the slant of most of his coverage. Bush's story was that of a reelection campaign in deep trouble—much like the story of a baseball team that was favored to win the pennant but stumbled early and never regained its stride.[20]

Patterson describes this story line as the likely loser scenario. It was the story of the Dole campaign in 1996. Portrayed as a weak opponent, hopelessly trailing the incumbent president, Dole's position in the race was used as the basis for evaluating and assessing the status of his campaign. Unfortunately for Dole, that evaluation was harsh. The news media repeatedly referred to his struggling campaign and his attempts to "jump-start" it, as if it had stalled. Thus, the horse race metaphor contributed to the likely loser scenario into which the press fit the story of the Dole campaign.[21]

For Clinton, the story line was just the opposite. It was that of the front-runner who had a large lead and who had skillfully maneuvered to keep it. In this particular story, the press attributed Clinton's lead and inevitable success to a beneficial economic environment; superior resources, especially the perquisites of the presidency; and an extremely well-organized and well-run campaign. The news media's depiction of Ronald Reagan's 1984 presidential campaign was similar and provides yet another illustration of the press's use of the front-runner script. In 2008, public dissatisfaction with the Bush administration made the election Obama's to lose after the financial crisis in mid-September.

Two other narratives, according to Patterson, are the bandwagon, in which one candidate builds a larger and larger lead over the course of the campaign as people join the bandwagon, and the opposite scenario, the front-runner loses ground. In the first scenario, the image of strong and decisive leadership generates support; in the second, the image of weak and vacillating leadership contributes to the erosion. Jimmy Carter's primary spurt in 1976 provides an illustration of the bandwagon; his decline in the general election of 1980 exemplifies the losing-ground story.[22]

The story line in 2000 focused on the closeness of the race, attributed in part to the weaknesses of both candidates: Gore's personal shortcomings and Bush's lack of depth on the issues. A variant on the competition theme toward the end of the campaign was the spoiler scenario for Ralph Nader. In 2004, the focus was on leadership, Bush's leadership in the war against terrorism and the war in Iraq. In directing attention to the president, the news media made much of his polarizing candidacy to convey the hostile political climate in which the election was cast. Four years later, the story line was the failure of that leadership and the candidate best able to achieve policy and political change. Patterson's point is that the press fit the news of the campaign into the principal story rather than creating a new story from the changing events of the campaign. Naturally, the perceptions of the news media affect the electorate's understanding of what is happening.

THE DEMISE OF THE NEWS CYCLE

There used to be a news cycle, dictated in large part by when a particular medium had to ready itself for publication or airing. In the age of newspapers, the cycle ended when the morning and afternoon papers had to go to press. In the days when most Americans received their news from the evening broadcast networks, it ended midafternoon, depending on whether visuals, pictures, or film were to be included. Video cameras, mobile trucks, and helicopters extended the deadlines, as has satellite technology. Cable news networks that were on 24-7 reduced still further the deadlines for reporting speeches and campaign events. Anita Dunn, communications strategist for the Obama campaign, noted that 10 PM, when the first editions of the *New York Times* and *Washington Post* hit the streets, was decision time for designing next-day communications, ads, or speeches that responded to earlier events of the day.[23]

The Internet has made the contemporary news cycle continuous. Reporters are constantly updating their stories that appear within minutes on the news organization's Web site. Rumors on the Web seemingly move with the speed of light. The two-source rule that print reporters used to verify the accuracy of information has been abandoned to speed the news and stay competitive.

From the perspective of the campaign, the news flow is constant and often overwhelming. Nicole Wallace, McCain's communications strategist, put it this way:

> When you're in communications, you're drinking out of the fire hose. You've got all the news created by your own campaign to deal with, the ads, the ads that come from the other side. You've got the changing and evolving relationship with the political press. And then you're always on the front line of whatever is coming your way . . .[24]

Campaigns limit access and information to try to control their narrative. They discourage leaks unless they have made a decision to release certain information to a particular reporter. When they are successful, the press complains about lack of access and transparency; when they are not, the leaks are frequently driven by internal disputes within the campaign.

IMPACT OF THE NEWS MEDIA

What impact does the style and substance of election news coverage have on the voters? Studies of campaigning in the 1940s indicated that the principal effect of the print media was to activate predispositions and reinforce political attitudes rather than to convert voters. Newspapers and magazines provided information, but primarily to those who were most committed. The most committed, in turn, used the information to support their beliefs. Weeding out opposing views, they insulated themselves from unfavorable news and from opinions that conflicted with their own.[25]

Selective Perception

With the bulk of campaign information coming from the print media in the 1940s, voters, especially the most partisan voters, tended to minimize cross-pressures and strengthen their own preexisting judgments. In contrast, the less committed also had less incentive to become informed. They maintained their ignorance by avoiding information about the campaign. The format of newspapers and magazines facilitated this kind of selective perception and retention.

Television might have been expected to change this situation because it exposed the less committed to more information and the more committed to other points of view. Avoidance became more difficult, although the use of remote controls has rendered viewers less captive to the picture on a particular channel than they were when television first began to cover presidential campaigns. Similarly, the proliferation of cable channels provides viewers with many non-news options as well as a variety of 24-7 news networks that possess discernible and different ideological orientations.

Television news also compartmentalizes more than the print press. The evening news shows on the broadcast networks fit a large number of stories into their thirty-minute program (which includes only about twenty-three minutes of news). Of necessity, this limited time restricts the coverage that can be given to each item. Campaign stories average ninety seconds or less, the equivalent of only a few paragraphs of a printed account. Their brevity helps explain why viewers do not retain much information from this type of television coverage.

There has also been a fragmentation of news sources. The major broadcast networks have lost a substantial portion of the audience they had in the 1970s and 1980s to cable news networks and local news affiliates. The local affiliates in particular have become more important sources for news about campaigns in the region they cover. They devote more time to news coverage and have gained in audience size.[26] Viewers of cable news programs have also increased, with the Fox News Network enjoying the greatest growth. There has also been a polarization among regular viewers, with conservatives and Republicans preferring Fox and liberals and Democrats favoring MSNBC and CNN.

Television news is still important because more people follow presidential campaigns on television than through any other medium. It is the prime source of news for approximately two-thirds of the population. The Internet is second, followed by newspapers, radio, and magazines.[27] (See Table 8.2.)

TABLE 8.2 | PRINCIPAL SOURCES OF CAMPAIGN NEWS, 1992–2008

Question: How have you been getting most of your news about the presidential election campaign? From television, from newspapers, from radio, from magazines or from the Internet? [Up to two answers were accepted.]

Main Source	1992	1996	2000	2004	2008
Television	82%	72%	70%	76%	68%
Broadcast				29	18
NBC	–	–	–	13	8
ABC	–	–	–	11	7
CBS	–	–	–	9	6
Cable				40	44
FOX	–	–	–	21	22
CNN	–	–	–	15	21
MSNBC	–	–	–	6	9
Local News	–	–	–	12	10
Newspapers	57	60	39	46	33
Radio	12	19	15	22	16
Magazines	9	11	4	6	3
Internet	–	3	11	21	36

Source: "Voters Liked Campaign 2004, But Too Much 'Mudslinging': Moral Values: How Important?" Pew Research Center for the People & the Press, (Nov. 11, 2004), p. 8. www.peoplepress.org/reports/display.php3?ReportID=23; "High Marks for the Campaign, a High Bar for Obama: Republicans Want More Conservative Direction for GOP," Pew Research Center for the People and the Press, (Nov. 13, 2008). www.people-press.org/report/?pageid=1429. Used by permission.

Agenda Setting

Television news helps set the agenda for the campaign. It helps determine issue salience by emphasizing what is newsworthy and what is not. This emphasis frames the debate, the attention paid by candidates to specific policy and character issues, and to some extent, the kinds of responses they have to provide. Media expert Michael J. Robinson believes that this agenda-shaping function directly affects the political elites. He argues that the press influences how political elites "relate" to the mass public and how those elites communicate political options.[28] In this way, the news media affect the conduct of the campaign.

The news media may have a direct influence on voters as well. They provide information that colors public perceptions of the candidates and parties, particularly the candidates' qualifications for leadership. From the perspective of those running for office, this coverage is harsh and the reporters and commentators are adversarial. The candidates' motives are questioned, their speeches are summarized into a very few points or sound bites, their misstatements are highlighted, their character frailties stressed, and their policy positions criticized and often portrayed as inconsistent, or even hypocritical.

Media Bias

In a highly polarized political environment, the negativity of the press contributes to perceptions of media bias. In a survey taken after the 2004 presidential election, the Pew Research Center for the People and the Press found that 40 percent of Republicans felt that Bush's coverage was unfair;[29] and they were right according to the Center for Media and Public Affairs, which monitors the "spin" on the broadcast networks' evening newscasts. The Center found that only 37 percent of the comments on Bush were positive compared to 59 percent positive for Kerry.[30] In 2008, a majority of Democrats believed the news media were fair to Obama while only 22 percent of Republicans thought that they were fair to McCain.[31] Again, content analyses of the principal networks, with the exception of Fox News, provide support for these assessments (see Table 8.1).

Perceptions of media bias have led to a loss of confidence in the press. Thirty years ago, a majority of people thought that the news media got their facts right. Today, a majority believes that they do not, that the news media lack compassion, and that they are too negative. Confidence in the press has dropped more sharply than public confidence in other American institutions.[32]

Yet even with all the negative coverage, most candidates conclude that critical coverage is still better than no coverage at all, particularly in the early phases of the nomination process and especially for the candidates who do not begin with national reputations. At the outset of the process, media attention conveys credibility; it is an indication that the press take a candidate seriously. That is why candidates try their utmost to get coverage.

Although the news tends to be concentrated and focused on certain issues, events, and personal traits, the press does not speak in a single voice. The fragmentation of news sources and the orientations of news networks provide some balance to campaign coverage, although the self-selection process by which people choose the news outlets they regard as fair and most believable tends to reinforce the partisan and ideological perspectives that voters bring to the election campaign.

NONTRADITIONAL COVERAGE: SOFT NEWS AND LOCAL COVERAGE

The ways in which the news media cover elections and present criticism have encouraged candidates to find ways of circumventing the national press corps to reach their audiences directly. Since the 1990s, one of the methods for doing so has been appearances on talk-entertainment shows, the so-called soft news format. Another has been appearances on local news shows that carry a greater variety of human-interest stories in addition to the news within their regional focus.

Ross Perot pioneered the use of a soft news format on television, and Jerry Brown did so on radio. This new format provides a candidate-friendly environment in which to engage the electorate. Appearances on the morning and evening television news/talk shows and syndicated programs on these and other networks, including MTV, have now become commonplace, as have appearances on the late-night shows of Jay Leno and David Letterman and Comedy Central's *The Daily Show* with Jon Stewart.

Even incumbent presidents are expected to use this news/entertainment medium in their quest for reelection. President George H. W. Bush initially resisted in 1992, and when he finally consented to appear on talk shows, he seemed ill at ease, especially on MTV. Bill Clinton was just the opposite. His appearance on the *Arsenio Hall Show* before the Democratic convention in 1992, wearing sunglasses and playing his saxophone, portrayed him as a "real cool guy," someone with whom the audience could identify.

For Perot, talk-show appearances constituted much of his "live" campaign, beginning with his announcement that he might run for president on *Larry King Live* in 1992 and again in 1996. Chris Dodd announced his candidacy for the 2008 Democratic nomination on *Imus in the Morning*. Asked why he chose that radio venue for making his announcement, Dodd said: "CBS said they would give me three minutes. I got 20 minutes on Imus."[33] And the appearances on news/entertainment shows have continued, even accelerated, in subsequent presidential campaigns. When Oprah Winfrey endorsed Barack Obama and traveled with him to rallies, it was considered an important news item and political endorsement.

The talk-entertainment format offers a much less hostile environment than interviews by national reporters and network anchors. The candidates are treated better, more like celebrities than politicians. The hosts tend to be more cordial. They and the general public ask softball questions in comparison to the hardball, "gotcha" journalism of the national news media. Candidates also have more time to answer the questions on these shows than the brief comments that are allowed to air on the news networks.[34]

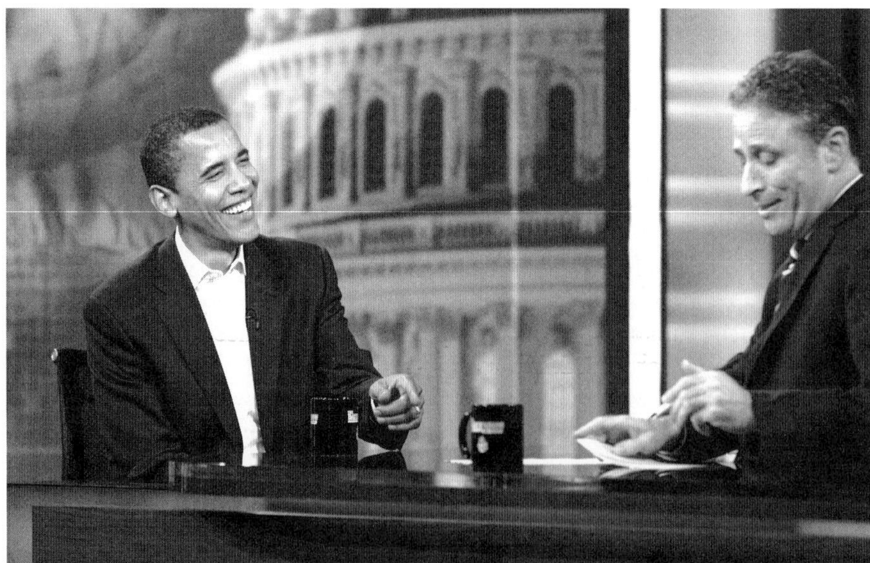

AP Photo/Jason DeCrow

Barack Obama on *The Daily Show* with Jon Stewart.

The audience differences are also important. People who watch these shows tend to be less oriented toward partisan politics; thus they may be more open to the information presented by the candidates who appear on these programs. Incidental learning occurs; candidate images improve as a consequence of the time and discretion they are given to talk about personal and family matters; they appear more lifelike and likeable, less like stereotypical politicians.[35]

Variations of the talk-entertainment format are town meetings and call-in programs in which candidates answer questions posed by citizens. By interacting with everyday folks, presidential candidates can demonstrate their responsiveness, sincerity, and empathy with the problems people face. Bill Clinton was particularly effective in such a setting during his two presidential campaigns.

Another advantage of doing the news-entertainment circuit is that the candidates' appearances themselves may become newsworthy, thereby generating an even larger impact for the candidates when clips of their comments are rebroadcast or summarized on the news. Nor are the expenses associated with these appearances comparable to the costs of staging a major media event or even designing, testing, and airing an advertisement.

The diverse audience, the higher comfort level, and the greater ability of candidates to project their desired images by presenting seemingly spontaneous but often carefully crafted answers suggest that the soft news format will continue to be used by presidential campaigns to circumvent the national press corps and reach a portion of the general public directly.

Local news outlets offer candidates many of the same advantages that news/entertainment shows provide: more time, greater visibility, less invasive questioning, a different audience, interaction with local luminaries, and an opportunity to illustrate their personal side.

PRESIDENTIAL DEBATES

Debates represent another "entertainment" component of presidential campaigns, one which candidates, particularly those who are behind, find useful. They see debates as an opportunity to improve their own images and damage their opponents'. Unlike most of their campaign rhetoric—speeches, statements, and responses to questions—debates are live and unedited, although the formats, agreed to beforehand, limit the time for responses. Moreover, the candidates' answers are usually prepared in advance; they are carefully crafted and well rehearsed. Nonetheless, debates give those running for office greater latitude to present their thoughts as they want them to be presented and in doing so demonstrate some of their personal qualifications for the job.

The news media like the debate format as well because it generates interest and facilitates comparison. A debate is a newsworthy event that fits within the game motif. Debates attract larger audiences than speeches or most news coverage, although they are not a source of revenue for the television networks because advertisements are not permitted during the debates.

The public likes debates because they are more exciting and "real" than staged campaign events and canned stump speeches. Debates provide voters with comparable information. They generate interest; they are a spectacle to be seen and heard.

The first series of televised debates occurred in 1960. John Kennedy used them to counter the impression that he was too young and inexperienced. Richard Nixon, on the other hand, sought to maintain his stature as Dwight Eisenhower's knowledgeable and experienced vice president and the obvious person to succeed his boss in office.

In the three elections that followed, Lyndon Johnson and then Nixon, both ahead in the polls, saw no advantage in debating their opponents and refused to do so. Gerald Ford, however, trailing Jimmy Carter in preelection polls, saw debates as his best opportunity to come from behind and win. The Carter camp, on the other hand, saw them as a means of shoring up Democratic support. In 1980, the rationale was similar. From Reagan's perspective, it was a way to reassure the electorate about himself and his qualifications for office. For Carter, it was another chance to emphasize the differences between himself and Reagan, between their parties, and between their issue positions and ideological perspectives.

By 1984, presidential debates had become so much a part of presidential campaigns that even incumbents could not avoid them without making their avoidance a major campaign issue. Thus, Ronald Reagan was forced by the pressures of public opinion to debate Walter Mondale, even though he stood to gain little and could have lost much from their face-to-face encounter. And in the 1992 election, George H. W. Bush's initial refusal to accept a plan for a series of campaign debates put forth by the Commission on Presidential Debates, a nonpartisan group that had organized the 1988 presidential and vice presidential debates, hurt him politically. Bill Clinton chided Bush repeatedly for his refusal to debate. Democrats dressed as chickens appeared at his campaign rallies. President Bush finally relented, telling his handlers, "I am tired of looking like a wimp."[36]

The issue in 1996 and again in 2000 was not whether to debate but whom to include. In 1992, Ross Perot and his running mate, Admiral James Stockdale, were invited to participate, and they did, to Perot's advantage but not to Stockdale's.[37] In 1996, Perot and his running mate, Pat Choate, were not asked. The Commission on Presidential Debates, composed of five Democrats and five Republicans, concluded that Perot's candidacy was not viable, that he had no chance of winning the election even though his name appeared on the ballot in all fifty states and the District of Columbia. The commission based its decision on Perot's standing in the polls, about 5 percent at that time, and on the judgment of a small number of political scientists and journalists, surveyed by the commission's staff and advisory council, who unanimously concluded that Perot not only could not win the election but would not carry a single state.[38]

The Commission on Presidential Debates has employed similar reasoning since then when excluding third-party candidates. In doing so, it has established three criteria for inclusion in the debates in addition to the Constitution's eligibility requirement (be a natural-born citizen, thirty-five years of age or older, and a resident of the United States for at least fourteen years).

To satisfy the commission's criteria, candidates had to be on the ballot in enough states to have a chance of winning a majority of the electoral votes, be organized in a majority of the congressional districts within the state, and demonstrate a sufficient level of electoral support by receiving an average of 15 percent or more in public opinion polls. That percentage was to be calculated by averaging preelection surveys of five different polling organizations. Not surprisingly, the only candidates to meet these criteria have been the Democratic and Republican presidential nominees.

By bringing the candidates together on the same stage at the same time, the debates become major news, routinely covered by the news media. They attract more viewers than any other single event of the campaign. In 2008, an average of 60.5 million people watched the debates. For the first time, the vice presidential debate between Senator Joe Biden and Governor Sarah Palin had the largest viewing audience of all the debates, almost 70 million viewers.[39] (See Table 8.3.)

Although presidential debates have now become part of the American electoral tradition, their number, scheduling, and format are still subject to arduous negotiation between the principal contenders and their staffs. In these negotiations, each side naturally wants to maximize its advantages. Candidates who are ahead in the polls when these negotiations occur, usually the incumbent, call the shots on the number of debates, their scheduling, and their rules. Ostensibly, the Commission on Presidential Debates hosts the events, but the candidates determine the procedures for conducting them. For example,

TABLE 8.3 | PRESIDENTIAL DEBATES, 1960–2008

Year		Number of Debates	Average Estimated Size of the Television Audience (in Millions)	Percent of Households Watching
1960	Kennedy v. Nixon	4	77	60
1976	Carter v. Ford	4*	65	51
1980	Carter v. Reagan	1	81	59
1984	Mondale v. Reagan	3*	66	46
1988	Dukakis v. Bush	3*	66	36
1992	Bush v. Clinton v. Perot	4*	66	42
1996	Clinton v. Dole	3*	40	29
2000	Gore v. G. W. Bush	4*	40.6†	26
2004	G. W. Bush v. Kerry	4*	53.5†	36.3
2008	Obama v. McCain	4*	60.5	37.6

*Includes one vice presidential debate.

†The average for just the three presidential debates.

Sources: Estimates of audience sizes for 1960–1992, "How Many Watched," *The New York Times* (Oct. 6, 1996), p. A25. Copyright © 1996 by the *New York Times*. Reprinted by permission. Estimates for 1996, "Debate Ratings Beat Baseball," Associated Press (Oct. 17, 1996). Copyright © 1996 by the Associated Press. Reprinted by permission. Estimates for 2000, 2004, and 2008 based on ratings by Nielsen Media Research. "Politics Unusual: Media and the Making of a President," Nielsen Company (November 7, 2008). blog.nielsen.com/nielsenwire/politics/politics-unusual-media-and-the-making-of-a-president

President Carter refused to include independent John Anderson in the 1980 debate; in 1984, 1988, 1996, and 2004, incumbents Reagan, Vice President Bush, Clinton, and George W. Bush set the parameters. There was little their opponents could do but concur.

It was a different story, however, in 1992. With President George H. W. Bush trailing in the polls, the campaign moving into the late September–early October period, and Clinton making an issue of Bush's refusal to debate, the president could not dictate the terms and had to accept a compromise that included formats that he and his advisers initially opposed.[40]

An agreement of understanding, drafted and approved by the major-party candidates, specifies the rules. In 2004, one rule was that only the person talking would be seen on television; no cutaways to the other candidate would be permitted. The television networks, however, were not parties to the agreement and did not abide by it. Sometimes they showed one of the candidates and sometimes both. Kerry took notes when Bush was talking; Bush did not, however, when Kerry spoke. To some, the president appeared bored, tired, or irritated. Moreover, during the first debate his suit jacket bulged in the middle of his back, suggesting to Democrats that he had a device feeding him the answers, an allegation that Bush's handlers vigorously denied. However, in the second and third debates, he wore a better-fitting suit.

In 2008, there were no major rules controversies.[41] There were also fewer distracting elements in the debates that caught press and public attention, although in the second one Senator McCain seemed to be wandering around the stage, leading some Democrats and late-night comics to suggest that he was lost.

PREPARATION

Despite the appearance of spontaneity, debates are highly scripted, carefully orchestrated events. The candidates are coached and rehearsed. They often sound like their stump speeches and political commercials. They articulate

AP Photo/Ron Edmonds

President Bush makes a point while Senator Kerry takes notes.

and rearticulate their campaign themes. There have been a few exceptions, however, to the extensive preparation. Richard Nixon in his first debate with Kennedy, and James Stockdale in the 1992 vice presidential debate, did not prepare extensively for them and suffered by comparison with their more polished opponents.[42]

To get ready for the debates, candidates go over briefing books that their aides prepare, view videotapes of their opponents, and engage in mock debates with stand-ins playing their opponent's part. This extensive preparation is designed to ensure that there are no surprises and that the candidates anticipate the questions and provide thoughtful answers that are consistent with their campaign themes, previous statements, and political advertising.

In addition to their concerns about substance and rhetoric, campaign media consultants also consider stylistic matters: how candidates look, how they dress, how they speak, and how they interact with the questioners and with their opponents. Kennedy and Carter talked faster than Nixon and Ford to create an action-oriented image in the minds of the viewers. Both tried to demonstrate their knowledge by citing many facts and statistics in their answers. Ford and Reagan spoke in more general terms, expressing particular concern about the size and structure of government. Reagan's wit and anecdotes in 1980, Bush's manner in 1988, and Perot's down-to-earth language and self-deprecating humor in 1992 conveyed a human dimension with which viewers could identify in contrast to their opponents' less "identifiable" responses. Dukakis was especially hurt by his reply to the question of whether he would favor an irrevocable death penalty for a person who raped and killed his wife. His matter-of-fact, rambling response sealed his technocratic, iceman image.

In 2004 and again in 2008, the goal of the Democratic nominees was to look presidential, sound authoritative, and evidence a command of the issues. In contrast, their more experienced Republican opponents wanted to emphasize leadership traits that had been successfully demonstrated—Bush's in his response to the terrorist attacks and McCain as a POW in Vietnam and later an influential senator. Presidential qualities were also an issue in the vice presidential debate, particularly for Governor Sarah Palin after questions were raised about her knowledge of world affairs. For Joe Biden, a more experienced national politician, the challenge was to give clear and concise answers. Biden has a tendency to be verbose and to occasionally put his foot in his mouth.

Strategy and Tactics

Much calculation goes into debate strategy and tactics. Candidates and their staffs need to decide which issues to stress and how to stress them, how to catch their opponents off guard or goad them into an error, and whether and how to respond to a personal attack and to criticism of their policy positions. In 1992, Clinton emphasized the need to change policy in his challenge to an incumbent. In 1996, he took credit for his policies and the good times that followed from them. In 1992, he was critical of Bush on the issues, especially the economy; in 1996, he took the high road as president and did not engage in personal allegations against his opponent, even when Dole criticized him personally.

A strategic goal of most candidates during debates is to overcome any negative perceptions about them that have developed and, at the same time, magnify their positive attributes. For George W. Bush in 2000, this meant demonstrating his presidential potential—his command of the issues, communication skills, and leadership abilities. As vice president, Gore had already established his mastery of the issues and become a policy and political spokesman for the administration. What the vice president needed to do was convey a more human side and approachable manner. Bush achieved his strategic goals; Gore did not.[43]

In 2004, the situation was reversed. It was Kerry who had to demonstrate presidential qualities; Bush had already proven his. Kerry did well in his first debate with the president. He looked and sounded sharper than Bush, jumping five points in the public opinion polls while Bush dropped three. But the surge was short-lived. In the second and third debates, the president held his ground and rebounded in the polls. He ended the debates with the same amount of support that he had going into them. What happened, according to Bush campaign manager Ken Mehlman, was that Kerry's base returned, but he did not gain among Independents and Republicans.[44]

The debates in 2008 also shored up support for the candidates, but the external environment was much more favorable to the Democrats. Although the campaigns had agreed that the first debate would focus on foreign policy and national security affairs, the deteriorating economy, congressional deliberations over the bailout by the Bush administration, and McCain's brief suspension of his campaign turned public attention to economic issues, which were discussed as much as foreign policy in the debate. The poor economy played to the Democratic candidate's strength. It allowed Obama to appeal to his core supporters, partisan Democrats, and to reinforce his theme of the need for policy change. He blamed the financial crisis on "eight years of failed economic policies promoted by George Bush [and] supported by John McCain."[45] Tying McCain to Bush blunted McCain's claim of being a maverick.

For his part, McCain presented himself as a reformer and Obama as a "tax and spend" Democrat with the most liberal voting record in the U.S. Senate. McCain pointed to his independent thinking as a senator, even opposing a president of his own party when he disagreed with that president's policy decision. When they debated foreign policy, Obama reiterated his belief that the war in Iraq was a mistake, that the United States should have finished the job in Afghanistan against al Qaeda and the Taliban. McCain contrasted his experience, knowledge, and judgment in national security affairs with Obama's, arguing that he was more qualified to make difficult foreign policy decisions.

The themes of both candidates were repeated in their second and third debates. After Obama again tied McCain to the policies of the past eight years, McCain responded, "Senator Obama, I am not President Bush. If you wanted to run against President Bush, you should have run four years ago. I'm going to give a new direction to this economy in this country."[46] The Obama campaign later used McCain's response in an ad called "90 Percent," which claimed that McCain backed Bush 90 percent of the time.

EVALUATION AND IMPACT

Debates usually help the challenger more than the incumbent, particularly in the first debate, because they provide a basis for comparison. Being on the same stage and answering similar questions enable a lesser-known candidate to clarify his image, emphasize leadership qualities, and articulate policy positions. Kennedy (1960), Carter (1976), Reagan (1980), and George W. Bush (2000) benefited from their initial debates with their incumbent presidential or vice presidential opponent because they were able to satisfy questions about their knowledge of the issues, their relevant political experience, and their qualifications for president. Similarly, John Kerry was able to demonstrate his presidential leadership qualities in his first debate with President Bush in 2004, and Barack Obama showed his knowledge, his confidence, and his communicative skills against the more experienced John McCain. The debates helped to solidify Obama's lead (see Table 8.4). In the words of David Axelrod, Obama's strategic adviser: "The debates, coupled with the financial crisis, gave people the sense of assurance they needed that this would be change, but it would be safe as well."[47]

In close races, debates can make a difference. They can convince the undecided for whom to vote and reinforce or counter preferences of weak partisans. They do so by increasing interest, clarifying issue positions, and shaping images. But debates rarely shift public opinion on a large scale because most voters have their minds made up or at least have their partisan predilections intact before viewing the debates. In fact, they are attracted to the debates precisely because of their partisan orientations. In general, people who are more interested in the election are more likely to watch the debates; people who are more knowledgeable are more likely to learn from them; and people who have strong partisan inclinations are more likely to be convinced by them. Partisans see the debate through a political lens and root for their own candidate. As a result, a single poor performance, such as Reagan's in his first debate with Walter Mondale and Bush's in his first debate with John Kerry, is unlikely to change the voting preferences of most partisans.

Normally, the vice presidential debate is not nearly as consequential as the presidential one. Fewer people watch it since that debate involves the number-two players on the teams. But the debate can still raise or allay doubts about the vice president's capacity to fill in if something were to happen to the president. In 1988, the vice presidential debate worked to Dan Quayle's disadvantage when his performance confirmed rather than challenged the impression that he was not up to the job. In 1992, Admiral James Stockdale, Perot's running mate, seemed unprepared, which left doubts in voters' minds whether he (and by implication, Perot) were qualified for the country's top two jobs. In 1996, Jack Kemp floundered on foreign affairs.[48] No such concerns were evident about either vice presidential nominee during their one debate in 2000, 2004, or 2008. Sarah Palin, for whom there were lower expectations going into the debate, performed adequately, although she was unable to change the stereotype held by Democrats and some in the news media that she was not qualified to be president.

TABLE 8.4 | THE IMPACT OF PRESIDENTIAL DEBATES ON ELECTORAL SUPPORT, 1992–2008

1992

Time Sequence	Bush	Clinton	Perot	Other/Undecided
Before the Debates	33%	51%	10%	6%
After the First	34	47	13	6
After the Second	31	43	18	8
After the Third	34	43	17	6

1996

Time Sequence	Clinton	Dole	Perot
Before the Debates	52%	37%	5%
After the First	54	38	5
After the Second	52	41	5

2000

Time Sequence	Gore	Bush	Nader	Buchanan
Before the First	49%	41%	2%	1%
After the First	41	48	4	1
After the Second	44	47	3	1
After the Third	41	50	3	1

2004

Time Sequence	Bush	Kerry
Before the First	52%	44%
After the First	49	49
After the Second	49	48
After the Third	52	44

2008

Time Sequence	Obama	McCain
Before the Debates	49%	44%
After the First	50	42
After the Second	52	41
After the Third	50	43

Sources: 1992 figures are based on the *Gallup Poll Monthly* (Sept. and Oct., 1992); 1996 figures are based on ABC News tracking poll of likely voters; 2000, 2004, and 2008 figures from Gallup Poll of likely voters, October 23, 2000, October 18, 2004, and October 17, 2008. www.gallup.com/poll/111241/Gallup-daily-little-impact-from-debate-far.aspx

CAMPAIGN ADVERTISING

Candidates are marketed much like any commercial product. Advertising is used to gain attention, make a pitch, and leave an impression. The goal, of course, is to get the electorate to do something—vote for a specific candidate on election day.

Advertising allows candidates to say and do what they want. The trick is to make the commercials look real. Candidate-sponsored clips are not unbiased, and the public knows it. To refine advertisements and improve the odds that they project the desired messages, which in turn produce the desired effects, ads are pretested before focus groups. When they are not, they can do more damage than good. Such was the case when Michael Dukakis's staff created a photo opportunity in which their candidate wore an army helmet and rode in a combat-ready tank. The objective of the advertisement was to demonstrate Dukakis's support for the military and for a strong national defense policy. The situation, however, looked so silly and contrived that the Republicans countered with a commercial of their own in which a scene from the Dukakis ad was featured along with information about the Democratic candidate's opposition to a long list of military programs and weapons systems.

Media consultants specializing in political advertising are hired to supplement regular campaign staff to design, produce, and target the advertisements as well as buy time on media markets in states on which the campaign is focusing. Each campaign normally retains an advertising firm to coordinate these activities.

Designing and airing political commercials constitutes the principal expense of contemporary presidential campaigns. In 2000, the total advertising by the candidates, parties, and nonparty groups on the race for the presidency amounted to $263 million; in 2004, the price tag was $620, an increase of 235 percent; in 2008, it was about the same. Obama, with the largest war chest, spent the most, approximately $226 million in the general election compared to McCain's and the Republican National Committee's $162 million.[49] Obama purchased over 436,000 airings; McCain and the RNC paid for 337,000.[50]

FORMAT AND TYPE OF ADS

Political commercials take many forms. Short spots are interspersed with other commercials in regular programming. Longer advertisements that preempt part of the standard broadcast fare and full-length productions, such as interviews, documentaries, and campaign rallies, have also been employed, although less in recent elections because of their expense. The benefits of the short spots are that they make a point, are cheaper to produce and air, and are usually viewed by a larger audience. Longer programs, which may go into greater detail about the candidate's career, qualifications, and beliefs, are generally seen by fewer people, although Ross Perot's novel media campaign in 1992 attracted and maintained an average audience of 11.6 million viewers even though most of his programs lasted thirty minutes or longer. Perot's simulcast, carried on ABC and CBS right before the election, had an audience size of 26 million. Obama also bought a half hour on the evening of October 29, a few days before the election. His program was seen by a total of 33.5 million people on broadcast and cable networks.[51]

From the perspective of content, there are basically three types of political commercials: those that praise candidates and their accomplishments (positive ads), those that contrast candidates to the obvious advantage of the ad's sponsor (contrast ads), and those that just criticize candidates on the grounds of their policy preferences or personal behavior (negative ads). In most campaigns, candidates use all three types, although of late, the emphasis has been on contrast and negativity.

Positivity

Positive campaign advertisements emphasize the strengths of a candidate. For presidents seeking reelection, or even vice presidents running for the top office, one of those strengths is clearly experience in high office, which incumbents always emphasize. One of Jimmy Carter's most effective commercials in 1980 showed him in a whirl of presidential activities ending as darkness fell over the White House. A voice intoned, "The responsibility never ends. Even at the end of a long working day, there is usually another cable addressed to the chief of state from the other side of the world where the sun is shining and something is happening." As a light came on in the president's living quarters, the voice concluded, "And he's not finished yet." Ronald Reagan in 1984 and George Bush in 1992 used a variation of the president-at-work ad.

Challengers need to stress their qualifications. They have to define themselves or risk having their opponents do it for them. Thus, the first task of most challengers is usually to present themselves to the American people by designing and airing biographical videos that feature their life story in a positive and compelling way.

A related task is to distinguish themselves from their opponents using comparison ads. In 1976, Carter emphasized his unusual leadership abilities. His slogan, "A leader, for a change," as well as his less formal appearance and even his decision to use green as the color of his literature in contrast to the traditional red, white, and blue, conveyed "freshness" and set him apart from old-style Washington politicians in general and the two Republican presidents who preceded him in particular.

In 1980, Reagan stressed different kinds of solutions to the nation's old and persistent policy problems, as did Perot in 1992. Perot's ads that year were among the most distinctive ever seen in a presidential campaign. Their amateurish quality was purposely designed to set them apart from the slick, smooth, professional commercials of his Republican and Democratic opponents. It was precisely this contrast that Perot wanted to convey to the American people.

In 2000, Bush's ads emphasized his likeability and trustworthiness; Gore's stressed his knowledge, experience, and caring and crusading spirit as a fighter for the working class. Both candidates ran more positive than negative commercials until the final two weeks of the campaign. Their national party organizations, however, went negative much earlier.

The 2004 campaign was more negative than the 2000 campaign. Bush began attacking Kerry in March of the election year and continued to do so until election day. Only twenty-three of his eighty ads were positive.[52] The Democratic National Committee and the 527 groups that supported Kerry went after Bush, but the Kerry campaign stayed positive in an effort to build up his resume.

The Bush campaign began and ended with the president's response to the terrorist attacks of September 11, 2001. The first ads aired in March 2004, and the final ones near the end of the campaign recalled the president's strong leadership after the attacks. But it was a commercial by a 527 group supporting Bush that received the most attention and seemed to have the greatest emotional impact. The ad showed the president giving a big hug to Ashley, a little girl whose mother died in the collapse of the World Trade Center. "I know that's hard. Are you all right?" Ashley replied, "He's the most powerful man in the world and all he wants to do is make sure I'm safe." Ashley's father added: "What I saw was what I want to see in the heart and in the soul of the man who sits in the highest elected office in our country."[53]

Twenty million dollars was spent on the air buys for "Ashley." There were 7,000 showings in Ohio alone. Seventy percent of the people polled in that state remember seeing the ad.[54] Said Kerry's media adviser, Bob Strum, '"Ashley' was real, was human, people could relate to it. 'Ashley' probably cost us Ohio and cost us the presidency!"[55]

The goal of Obama's advertising was to draw a sharp distinction between the change he offered and the continuation of Bush's policies that a vote for McCain would represent. Throughout the nomination and general election, the campaign emphasized togetherness, honesty, optimism. Jim Margolis, one of the architects of this media strategy, said:

> There were three essential pillars that we communicated throughout the course of this campaign. The first was the unity pillar. We need a president who's going to unite us, not divide us. . . . Second, we need a president who will change the ways of Washington and will focus on middle-class concerns. . . . Third, we need a president who will be honest with you, who will talk straight to you. And overall, . . . we tried to express optimism.[56]

One ad that captured these points and that spirit, "Our Moment Is Now," had Obama saying:

> We are in a defining moment in our history. Our nation is at war. The planet is in peril. The dream that so many generations fought for feels as if it's slowly slipping away. And that is why the same old Washington textbook campaigns won't do. That's why telling the American people what we think they want to hear, instead of telling the American people what they need to hear just won't do. America, our moment is now. I don't want to spend the next year or the next four years refighting the same fights we had in the 1990s. I don't want to pit red America against blue America. I want to be the President of *the United States of America*. [Italics added.][57]

McCain's positive ads reinforced his independence, experience, and service. The goal was to present him as more qualified for the job of president. One ad, that featured these themes, had an announcer telling McCain's story.

> Shot down, bayoneted, tortured. Offered early release, he said, "No." He'd sworn an oath. Home, he turned to public service. His philosophy: before party, polls and self—America. A maverick, John McCain tackled campaign reform, military reform, spending reform. . . . a man who has always put his country and her people before self, before politics. . . . Don't hope for a better life. Vote for one. McCain.[58]

Unlike Obama, McCain was usually pictured but did not talk in the ads. It was a grave-sounding announcer who added drama and ostensibly the objectivity of an informed observer to them.

Negativity

Negative ads exploit a candidate's weaknesses by focusing on character deficiencies, issue inconsistencies, and/or false leadership claims. They are not new. There has always been much negativity in American political campaigns. George Washington was called a philanderer and a thief; Andrew Jackson was accused of marrying a prostitute; at the outset of the Civil War, Abraham Lincoln was charged with being illegitimate and black; Theodore Roosevelt was said to be a drunkard; Herbert Hoover, a German sympathizer during World War I; and Franklin D. Roosevelt, a lecher, lunatic, and a closet Jew whose real name was Rosenfeldt.

What seems to be different today is the increasing emphasis placed on negative advertising and the use of fear to heighten its effect. Most negative ads provide contrasts that benefit the ad's sponsor. Clinton's 1996 ads against Robert Dole are a good illustration. Instead of criticizing Dole personally, the ads criticized the policy positions he took and the votes he cast in the Senate. One ad, "Wrong in the Past," went through a litany of popular education and health care programs that Dole ostensibly opposed. The announcer ended the ad by repeating the theme "Bob Dole, wrong in the past, wrong for our future." This ad was shown 6,780 times in seventy-five media markets.[59]

In the negative ads of 2000, Democrats challenged George W. Bush's record in Texas, accused him of being a captive of special interests, and chided him for proposing policies that would help the rich, bankrupt Social Security, and take away badly needed funds from public schools for private school vouchers. Republicans, in turn, characterized Al Gore as a proponent of big government, big spending, and big giveaway programs.

The 2004 Bush campaign was designed to contrast Bush's proven leadership skills with Kerry's policy inconsistencies, using Kerry's words and votes against him to achieve that contrast. One ad pictured Kerry windsurfing, going back and forth on the waves. It was a perfect metaphor—Kerry the patrician, the elitist candidate who claimed he represented the common person, and Kerry the flip-flopper, the candidate who couldn't make up his mind.

Most of McCain's ads were negative (as were Reagan's in 1984, Clinton's in 1996, and Bush's in 2004). One reason for the negativity of McCain's ads was their hybrid nature. Another was to change the focus from public dissatisfaction with the Republican administration of George W. Bush to questions about Obama, particularly his lack of experience in national security affairs and his expansive domestic policy agenda. To get at the inexperience issue, a McCain ad began with Joe Biden saying, "Mark my words. It will not be six months before the world tests Barack Obama. The world's looking. We're going to have an international crisis to test the mettle of this guy. I guarantee you it's gonna happen." The announcer then said: "It doesn't have to happen. Vote McCain," as McCain appears with the required acknowledgement, "I'm John McCain, and I approve this message."[60] To get at Obama's domestic policy agenda, McCain ads reinforced the Republican stereotype of Democrats as big taxers and spenders.

The Obama ads against McCain sought to paint him as McSame, using statements that McCain made during the presidential debates and during his quest for the Republican nomination. Here is the dialogue from one of the ads:

Barack Obama: "I'm Barack Obama, and I approve this message."
John McCain: "Senator Obama, I am not President Bush."
Announcer: True, but you voted with Bush 90 percent of the time. Tax breaks for big corporations and the wealthy. But almost nothing for the middle class. Same as Bush. Keep spending $10 billion a month in Iraq while our own economy struggles? Same as Bush. You may not be George Bush but
John McCain: "I voted with the President over 90 percent of the time, more than—a lot of—even my Republican colleagues."[61]

Practically every contrasting ad the Obama campaign aired emphasized that McCain was more of the same, picturing him with George W. Bush in the ads.

Emotive Content

The 2004 Bush ads also played on the fear generated by the terrorist attacks. One ad, entitled "Risk," included pictures of terrorist attacks, frightened children, and a warning:

> After September 11, our world changed. Either we fight terrorists abroad or face them here. John Kerry and liberals in Congress have a different view. They opposed Reagan as he won the Cold War, voted against the first Gulf War, voted to slash intelligence after the first Trade Center attack, repeatedly opposed weapons vital to winning the war on terror. John Kerry and his liberal allies: Are they a risk we can afford to take today?[62]

The negative ads against Bush were less effective, and for the most part, less scary, although one of them showed a soldier shooting into the air and a car bursting into flames with the announcer saying, "Now Americans are being kidnapped, held hostage—even beheaded."[63] McCain's negative ads in 2008 were not as emotive as Bush's. Ironically, the successful surge of U.S. forces in Iraq, which McCain supported and Obama opposed, helped reduce the saliency of the Iraq war as a political issue.

At the end, the issue for Obama was to reassure Americans about himself. He did so with an ad in which he spoke directly to the accusations and fears expressed by Republicans.

> John McCain wants to scare you. I want you to know what I believe. I believe in the dignity of work. I believe in tax cuts for the middle class. I believe people who break the law should be punished. And the terrorists who plot against us should be hunted down before they strike. I believe we need to fund our schools. But that no money can take the place of a parent taking responsibility for their child. And I believe in you and our ability to make America even better.[64]

In his infomercial aired three days before the election, Obama rephrased Ronald Reagan's famous question at the end of his debate with Jimmy Carter, "Are you better off now than you were four years ago?" Rephrasing the question as "Will our country be better off four years from now?" he answered by reiterating his middle-class appeal, his opposition to new taxes (except for the wealthy), to the war in Iraq, and to the special interest politics that has dominated Washington for so many years.

CONTENT ACCURACY

Since the 1988 election, the public has become more leery of negative ads. Part of its skepticism stems from the legacy of negative advertising, particularly in that year. Part of it results from the exaggeration and hyperbole that are contained in shrill accusations.

The 2004 and 2008 campaigns were no exception. In 2004, Bush charged that Kerry had proposed "government-run health care," wanted "higher taxes," and had voted in favor of "slashing intelligence" and "reckless defense cuts." Kerry in turn accused Bush of having "the worst economic record since Hoover"; he also claimed that Bush "intended to reinstitute the draft" and "cut Social Security benefits by 30 to 45 percent."

In 2008, it was more of the same. Table 8.5 quotes some of the charges and their accuracy according to FactCheck.org, an organization sponsored by the Annenberg Public Policy Center.

Although these accusations did not go unchallenged by the campaigns at which they were directed and by reporters covering them, the repetition of the claims in speeches and in the ads themselves drowned out the media's attempt to set the record straight. People believed the ads. According to Kathleen Hall Jamieson and Brooks Jackson:

> More than half of U.S. adults (52 percent) said the claim that Sen. Barack Obama's tax plan would raise taxes on most small businesses is truthful, when in fact only a small percentage would see any increase.
>
> More than two in five (42.3 percent) found truth in the claim that Sen. John McCain planned to "cut more than 800 billion dollars in Medicare payments and cut benefits," even though McCain made clear he had no intent to cut benefits.[65]

Table 8.5 | Charges and Accuracy of 2008 Advertisements

McCain's Charges Against Obama

- "Obama supports tax increases for working families making over $42,000 a year and for seniors;"
- "Obama's proposed tax credits for health insurance really provide welfare benefits;"
- Obama has a close personal relationship with former 1970s radical Bill Ayers.

FactCheck's Contention About the Truth of these Charges

- "Obama's plan would raise taxes only on individuals making more than $200,000 a year, or couples or families making more than $250,000."
- "[R]efundable tax credits are a key feature of McCain's own health care plan, except that he calls them 'reform.' In an early version of Obama's plan, only a tiny portion of his tax credits would have gone to anyone who didn't work, and advisers quickly announced that they had added a work requirement even for that one (a tax credit to benefit homeowners who don't itemize deductions)."
- "They [Obama and Ayers] met in 1995, when Obama was asked to head the board of a school reform group, the Chicago Annenberg Challenge, that Ayers had helped start. The organization, formed to dispense grants in an effort to improve the city's schools, was hardly radical; its board included a number of well-regarded Chicago establishment types. Also, Obama and Ayers overlapped for two years on the board of another foundation, and Ayers hosted a coffee in his home when Obama was running for the Illinois state legislature."

Obama's Charges Against McCain

- "Millions of seniors would see their Medicare payments cut and investments in Social Security diminished if Social Security was privatized, a policy McCain supported;"
- "McCain's health care plan would be the largest middle-class tax increase in history;"
- McCain opposes stem cell research.

FactCheck's Contention About the Truth of these Charges

- "The Bush plan, which McCain embraced, would not have allowed anybody born before 1950 to have private accounts, so nobody retired on Social Security today could possibly be relying on private accounts for even a small portion of his or her benefit check."
- "It's true that McCain would, for the first time, require workers to pay federal income tax on the value of their employer-provided health insurance. But that's offset by the tax credits he'd provide of up to $2,500 per individual and $5,000 per couple or family—and most people would come out ahead."
- "Technically, the carefully-worded phrase is correct: McCain *has* opposed embryonic stem cell research. But not since 2001, when he became convinced, he says, that the potential good it could do outweighed other considerations."

Source: "The Whoppers of 2008—The Sequel," FactCheck.org www.factcheck.org/elections-2008/the_whoppers_of_2008

Why do people believe false charges? One reason is that reports on the accuracy of speeches and ads are usually single stories but the speeches and the ads are voiced and shown many times over, which gives them greater impact. Professors Jamieson and Jackson report that the FactCheck Web site was accessed by 462,678 visitors on its "best day" while the Obama campaign ran for a total of 17,614 times two commercials that said McCain would cut Medicare benefits.[66]

Secondly, partisan orientations and political beliefs also condition what people believe. The sad truth is that people shield themselves from information that challenges their beliefs and believe information that supports their views. The Annenberg postelection polls found "nearly one in five (19 percent) falsely think Obama is a Muslim, and even more (22 percent) find truth in the claim that he's nearly half Arab. Republicans were 2.8 times more likely than Democrats to buy the Muslim claim, and just over twice as likely to swallow the half-Arab notion."[67]

TACTICAL CONSIDERATIONS

Targeting

Another characteristic of contemporary political advertising is the degree to which it is targeted to the most competitive states. In their study of advertising in the 2004 national election, Michael M. Franz, Joel Rivlin, and Kenneth Goldstein describe the geographic focus:

> . . . only 21 states received *any* advertising at all during the 2004 presidential campaign. More than half of all Americans—57 percent of the electorate—did not see a single ad broadcast in their home media market. And during the final month of the campaign, 87 percent of all presidential ads were concentrated in just 44 media markets in a shrinking number of battleground states, home to only 27 percent of the electorate.[68]

Within the competitive states, campaigns are targeted to specific groups by advertising on niche cable channels and local television stations. If, for example, men were the targeted audience, then commercials might be aired during sporting events; if women were to be targeted, then channels such as E!, WE, and Lifetime might be used. Daytime programs would attract homemakers; prime-time evening, which is more expensive, would reach a larger audience. Similarly, ads would be placed on the Black Entertainment Television (BET) to reach African Americans, on Univision or other Spanish language channels to reach Hispanics, and on Comedy Central or Discovery to reach younger people. Ads placed on cable news networks reach a more attentive public, but also one that may be more ideologically oriented, with Fox attracting conservatives; MSNBC, liberals; and CNN, moderates and liberals.[69]

Naturally, the content of the ads is designed with the audience in mind. Take the Republican turnout effort in 2004. Using data that broke down the electorate into different demographic groupings in different states, the Republican campaign targeted specific messages to African Americans and Hispanics interested in education and health care. Each group received information about Bush's policies in those issue areas but not in others. The vote of these groups for Bush increased from its 2000 level.[70] Obama also engaged in "microtargeting," and likely increased his share of the vote as a result.[71] In their book *The Obama Victory: How Media, Money, and Message Shaped the 2008 Elections,* Kate Kenski, Bruce W. Hardy, and Kathleen Hall Jamieson conclude that Obama's microtargeting combined with his spending advantage over McCain in advertising "shifted vote preference in his direction," perhaps giving him victories in close states such as Indiana, North Carolina, Florida, and Virginia that he might otherwise have lost.[72]

Newsworthiness

The most effective ads are those that reinforce or become news. Since the beginning of television advertising, three political commercials have made news, which extended their reach and potential impact. The first one to do so was the Democrats' 1964 ad suggesting that Barry Goldwater might get the country involved in a nuclear war. Designed to reinforce the impression that Goldwater was a trigger-happy zealot who would not hesitate to unleash nuclear weapons against a communist foe, the ad pictured a little girl in a meadow plucking petals from a daisy. She counted to herself softly. When she reached nine, the picture froze on her face, her voice faded, and a stern-sounding male voice counted down from ten. When he got to zero there was an explosion, the little girl disappeared, and a mushroom-shaped cloud covered the screen. Lyndon Johnson's voice was heard: "These are the stakes—to make a

Courtesy of the Democratic National Convention

A still from the "Daisy Girl" anti-Goldwater ad.

world in which all of God's children can live, or go into the dark. We must either love each other, or we must die." The ad ended with an announcer saying, "Vote for President Johnson on November 3. The stakes are too high for you to stay home." The commercial was run only once. Goldwater supporters were outraged and protested vigorously, but their protestations actually kept the issue alive. Parts of the ad were shown on television newscasts. The Democrats had made the point, and the news made it stick.[73]

The second infamous ad, "Willie Horton," featured a mug shot of an African American prisoner who had raped a white woman while on a weekend furlough from a Massachusetts jail. Aimed at those who were fearful of crime, and especially of African American males, the ad, sponsored by a PAC supporting George H. W. Bush in 1988, was supplemented by other prisoner ads designed by the Bush campaign. The cumulative impact of these ads left the impression that Dukakis was a liberal do-gooder. By the end of the 1988 presidential campaign, 25 percent of the electorate knew who Willie Horton was, what he did, and who furloughed him; 49 percent thought Dukakis was soft on crime.[74]

The third ad that became news was run in August 2004, right after the Democratic Convention in which Kerry had emphasized his Vietnam military record in his acceptance speech. He had been awarded two Purple Hearts and a Bronze Star for his valor in commanding a Navy gunboat under attack. A group consisting of some Vietnam veterans, calling themselves Swift Boat Veterans for Truth, disputed Kerry's claims and brought attention to his antiwar efforts after his release from active duty. Shown in August during the lull between major party conventions, the ad captured national attention. The decision of the Kerry campaign not to respond to the charge gave the ad credibility and undermined the image that the Democrats were trying to project about Kerry.

The reach and potential impact of the first Swift Boat ad, which was shown in just seven small media markets (Charleston, Dayton, Green Bay, La Crosse, Toledo, Wausau, and Youngstown) was enormous. The Swift Boat Veterans gave over 1,000 interviews on talk radio, appeared on network newscasts, and raised $19 million, which they used to run other anti-Kerry ads. Although news reporters raised questions about the validity of the allegations, the attention that the press gave to the charges actually extended and may have enhanced the ad's impact.

Kerry's campaign tried to create news of its own by running ads on its Web site that were designed for television but not shown to the public. The ads directly responded to charges leveled against Kerry by the Bush campaign, the Republican National Committee, and Republican-oriented 527 groups. After discovering that the ads were not aired, the press complained bitterly about these fake video releases.

Timing and Sequencing

The timing of the Swift Boat ads right after the Democratic convention was perfect. Since both Democratic and Republican nominees planned to accept federal funds, the Kerry team, which had to stretch their dollars over five more

BOX 8.1 SWIFT BOAT VETERANS FOR TRUTH—ANTI-KERRY AD

Script: "Even before Jane Fonda went to Hanoi to meet with the enemy and mock America, John Kerry secretly met with enemy leaders in Paris though we were still at war and Americans were being held in North Vietnamese prison camps. Then he returned and accused American troops of committing war crimes on a daily basis. Eventually, Jane Fonda apologized for her activities. But John Kerry refuses to. In a time of war, can America trust a man who betrayed his country?"

Picture: Jane Fonda in Hanoi in 1972 with clapping North Vietnamese soldiers in the background; the scene then shifts to John Kerry with scenes of war in the background and then turns to Kerry testifying before the Senate committee investigating the Vietnam War. Jane Fonda is then pictured at a news conference, followed by Kerry before the Senate committee with the words "betrayed his country," superimposed on him.

weeks than the Republicans, decided to stay off the air in August to save money and also not compete with the summer Olympics.[75] Kerry's advisers hoped that nonparty groups would fill the void, but the BCRA prohibited them from coordinating campaign efforts with the Kerry campaign or the Democratic National Committee. The 527s did run ads during this period, but only one of them responded to the accusations made by the Swift Boat Veterans for Truth (see Box 8.1). The Kerry experience is one of the reasons that Obama chose private funding. Plouffe and his associates wanted to exercise control over the content and timing of all their ads.

Most advertising content is sequenced. At the outset, it is necessary to provide biographical information about family, experience, and qualifications for the office. The Clinton biographical ads were particularly effective in 1992. His biography, entitled *The Man from Hope*, presented the personal Clinton from his childhood in Hope, Arkansas, the town in which he was born and initially raised, to his governorship of that state. The film used the town's name to convey Clinton's optimism and his life story to demonstrate his ability to achieve his dreams and the country's. Both Obama and McCain ran biographical ads at the start of their general election campaigns that detailed their life history in such a way as to make it seem like each candidate was on a natural progression to the presidency.

Once the personal dimension has been established, the policy orientations of the candidates and their priorities for the coming years are articulated. In this phase of advertising, themes are presented and policy positions noted. The second stage of ads usually presents the candidate's policy agenda, the principal issues, and what should be done about them. These ads are also designed to position candidates for the debates with their opponent. They provide a programmatic foundation upon which to stand. In the third stage, the candidate frequently goes on the offensive, running a series of ads in which the reasons not to vote for the opponent are stressed. Candidates who are behind frequently "go negative" earlier.

By going negative at the end, the advertising campaigns had come full circle. From initially trumpeting their candidate's strengths, the campaigns end by blasting their opponent's weaknesses. The choice had come down to which candidate is the lesser of two evils.

THE IMPACT OF ADVERTISING ON TURNOUT AND VOTING BEHAVIOR

There has been a major debate within the discipline of political science about the impact of negative advertising and negative news. Has the increased amount of negativity made the electorate more cynical? Stephen Ansolabehere and Shanto Iyengar believe that it has. Their experimental studies of negative political commercials found that these ads adversely affect turnout, increase cynicism, and decrease feelings of efficacy, especially for those with no partisan allegiances. In other words, the ads are a turnoff; people who see them lose interest in voting.[76]

Other political scientists, however, are not so sure. In fact, much of the theoretical and empirical evidence suggests quite the opposite effect, that negative ads stimulate turnout. For knowledgeable partisans, their primary effect is to reinforce rather than challenge their inclinations to support their party's nominees. Negative advertisements in particular seem to generate a strong response from partisans, which solidifies their vote. In this sense, the ads "work." They prime the electorate; they provide clues for seeing and images for evaluating; and they turn out party voters.[77]

Do ads change opinions? The evidence here is less clear. Ads would seem to have a greater affect on people who had not made up their minds and lacked the information provided in the advertisement. However, the ad is only one message, although it can be a continuing one. In an increasingly complex communications' environment in which personal contact, new stories in a variety of media, and live debates are seen and heard by people, it is very hard to pinpoint the impact of each of these factors on voters. Besides, most voters come into the election with preexisting political attitudes, opinions on the issues, and even judgments on the candidates, all of which may affect their judgments when they vote.

THE CUMULATIVE EFFECT OF THE MASS MEDIA ON ELECTIONS

The time, money, and energy spent on media by the candidates suggest that the mass media do condition campaigns and affect voting behavior. Why else would so many resources be devoted to them? Yet it is difficult to document the media's precise effect.

Much of the candidates' concern focuses on news coverage. The negativism of the press, the tendency to highlight inconsistencies and misstatements, even the propensity to interpret rather than report events, have led many people, especially candidates and their handlers, to conclude that coverage is biased, has adversely affected their campaigns, and unduly influences the electorate.

Are the media, particularly the news media, really that powerful? Do they affect voter choice? The answer is probably yes, although their impact may depend on the level of public knowledge, strength of partisan attitudes of the electorate, and the initial judgments voters make even before the campaign begins.

There is evidence that voters do learn from campaigns and use that knowledge to make an informed judgment on election day. What they learn tends to reinforce their political attitudes because people are more attracted to news sources that reflect their beliefs than those that challenge them. Not only has the proliferation of news networks facilitated the selective exposure of political partisans but it has also widened the levels of knowledge between activists and those people who are less interested, involved, and informed about campaign politics.

Despite the discernible orientations of news sources and the distortion and bias of political commercials, voters still assert that they have enough information to make an enlightened voting decision in presidential elections. When asked if they learned enough in the 2000, 2004, and 2008 campaigns to make an informed choice, over 80 percent said they had.[78] Of course, how much information people *really* need to make such a judgment continues to be subject to much debate.[79]

SUMMARY

The mass media have a profound effect on presidential elections: on the organization, strategy, and tactics of the campaign, the distribution of resources, and directly or indirectly on the electorate's voting decisions. That is why so much of a presidential campaign is devoted to media-related activities.

First newspapers, then radio and television, and more recently, the Internet have provided the primary communication channels through which information about the campaign is transmitted to voters. The multiplication of news networks on cable and news sites on the Internet, the increasing importance (and length) of local news shows, and the entertainment/news format have provided additional, and for the most part, more favorable opportunities for candidates to reach the electorate than they had when the broadcast news networks monopolized campaign reporting. The news cycle has evolved into one of continuous coverage.

The news media see and report the campaign as a game, fitting statements, events, and activities into various story lines. Their schema highlights drama and gives controversial statements and events the most attention but also downplays in-depth discussions of policy issues. Campaign coverage also plays up personalities and gives disproportionate attention to blunders, factual errors, personal exaggerations, and slips of the tongue; reporters focus on conflict and emphasize the contest.

Candidates naturally try to improve the coverage they receive by planting stories, leaking opposition research, scripting their speeches with sound bites, orchestrating events with the mass media in mind, minimizing spontaneity to prevent embarrassing words or situations, and creating good visuals. But even with all this preparation and staging, the news of their campaign may not be accurate or complete, and from the candidates' perspective, it is never good enough.

For this reason, candidates also try to circumvent the national news media to reach the voters directly. People like to be entertained, so candidates have resorted to various popular interview and even comedy shows to convey a message, project a personal image, energize their supporters and make them feel part of the campaign, and extend their appeals to those who do not regularly tune in to national news programming.

In the past, parades, rallies, and other campaign events were the principal vehicles by which these objectives were achieved. The party conventions and presidential debates also provide large-audience opportunities and format-friendly environments for candidates to make appeals, look presidential, and expand and excite their partisan base. Debates, especially, facilitate candidate comparisons that usually work to the advantage of challengers who need to present themselves as the equal of their incumbent opponents. The news media play a role here as well, covering the debates and often participating in them by asking questions and reporting the candidates' responses, the public's reaction, and their own evaluations in terms of winners and losers. They then integrate the debate into the ongoing story of the campaign.

In a very close race, debates can make a difference. Usually, however, they do not. Partisans disproportionately comprise the debate audience; they tend to root for *their* candidates while handlers from the campaigns and significant others "spin" the results to their political advantage. As a consequence, bounces from the debates tend to be short-lived and fade into the political environment that helps shape the election and condition its outcome.

Since campaign news is often bad from the candidate's perspective, campaigns try to make their own news and direct their messages through advertising. More money is spent on this campaign activity than on any other. Although political commercials tap both positive and negative leadership dimensions, the amount of negativity has increased in recent elections.

Voters have become increasingly leery about the claims of these ads, but the political commercials still seem to have an impact. Campaigns target their ads to specific groups of voters in specific localities with messages tailored to the group. The challenge is to win over Independents and weak partisans and reinforce the partisan base.

In 2008, public discontent led to a message of change, with all candidates claiming that they were the leader who could achieve it. In the end, Obama's money and message, and the skill with which he articulated it, combined with a political environment that benefited the Democrats, enabled him to carry the day.

WHERE ON THE WEB?

In addition to the media outlets mentioned in previous chapters, here are some others to explore.

- **Associated Press**
  www.ap.org
  The largest news service in the United States provides fast-breaking information on its wire service and Web site.
- **Center for Media and Public Affairs**
  www.cmpa.com
  Conducts studies on television coverage of the campaign and the "spin" that the candidates and their stands on the issues get.
- **Commission on Presidential Debates**
  www.debates.org
  Plans the debates, selects the cities, decides which candidates can participate, and moderates the discussion format between the principal candidates. The commission also provides transcripts of past and present presidential debates.
- **The Freedom Forum**
  www.freedomforum.org
  Provides information on freedom of the press issues, with links to the Newseum, the Media Studies Center, and the First Amendment Center, all sponsored by the Gannett news organization.
- **FactCheck.org**
  www.factcheck.org
  A nonpartisan, nonprofit group organized by the Annenberg Public Policy Center at the University of Pennsylvania that evaluates the accuracy of political advertising.
- **Living Room Candidate**
  www.livingroomcandidate.org
  An online site for televised presidential candidate commercials since 1952.
- **National Annenberg Election Survey**
  www.annenbergpublicpolicycenter.org
  Conducts ongoing national surveys over the course of the campaign that measures information acquisition, voters' attitudes, and the news media's and advertising's impact.
- **New York Times**
  www.nytimes.com
  A paper of record, the *New York Times* is the newspaper most likely to carry the transcripts of the candidate's major speeches.
- **The Pew Research Center for the People & the Press**
  www.people-press.org
  A nonpartisan research organization sponsored by the Pew Charitable Trusts that surveys public opinion on politics and the media.
- **Politics Online**
  www.politicsonline.com
  Tracks presidential campaigning on the Internet.

- **Washington Post**
  www.washingtonpost.com
  A good source of information about the campaign and the mindset of the Washington political establishment.

EXERCISES

1. Compare the amount of television coverage given to the horse race and to issues of candidate personality, policy, and strategy and tactics by examining the analysis performed by the Center for the Media and Public Affairs (www.cmpa.com). Do you feel the coverage was balanced or unbalanced? Did it provide voters with sufficient information to make an intelligent judgment on election day? Did the press display an ideological bias?
2. Take any major event in the presidential campaign and compare coverage of it by a national newspaper, television broadcast network, a national cable news network, and a major source of information on the Internet. Which coverage was better? Which was more interesting? Why?
3. View one of the presidential debates and note the principal points the candidates made. If elected, did the candidate follow through on the positions he or she advocated? (These tapes should be available in the C-SPAN archives and at the Commission on Presidential Debates web site at www.debates.org.)
4. Contrast the advertisements of the presidential candidates on the basis of their messages, presentations, and targeted groups. Note also the media on which the advertisements ran. These ads should also be available on the candidates' Web sites.
5. Check the accuracy of the ads you have discussed in the first question by using FactCheck.org. Which ads appear to be more accurate? Do you think that these ads are also more effective? Explain.
6. Compare the blogs of the principal candidates running for president. Which one do you find the most interesting? Which do you think is the most informative? Which one generates the most enthusiasm among bloggers? Which of the current campaign organizations do you think has best been able to convert this Web-based enthusiasm into a grassroots movement?

SELECTED READINGS

Ansolabehere, Stephen, and Shanto Iyengar. *Going Negative*. New York: Free Press, 1995.

Buchanan, Bruce. *Renewing Presidential Politics: Campaigns, Media, and the Public Interest*. Lanham, MD: Rowman & Littlefield, 1996.

Davis, Richard, and Diana Owen. *New Media and American Politics*. New York: Oxford University Press, 1998.

Denton, Robert E., Jr. *The 2008 Presidential Campaign: A Communication Perspective*. Lanham, MD: Rowman & Littlefield, 2009.

Devlin, L. Patrick."Contrasts in Presidential Campaign Commercials of 2004," *American Behavioral Scientist,* 49 (Oct. 2005): 279–313.

Farnsworth, Stephen J., and S. Robert Lichter. *The Nightly News Nightmare: Network Television Coverage of Presidential Elections, 1988–2004*. Lanham, MD: Rowman & Littlefield, 2006.

Geer, John G. *In Defense of Negativity: Attack Ads in Presidential Campaigns*. Chicago: University of Chicago Press, 2006.

Goldstein, Ken, and Paul Freedman. "Campaign Advertising and Voter Turnout: New Evidence for a Stimulation Effect." *The Journal of Politics,* 64 (Aug. 2002): 721–740.

Graber, Doris A., Denis McQuail, and Pippa Norris, eds. *The Politics of News: The News of Politics*. Washington, DC: CQ Press, 2007.

Hart, Roderick. *Campaign Talk: Why Elections Are Good for Us*. Princeton, NJ: Princeton University Press, 2000.

Huber, Gregory, and Kevin Arceneaux. "Identifying the Persuasive Effects of Presidential Advertising." *American Journal of Political Science* 51 (2007): 957–977.

Iyengar, Shanto, and Donald Kinder. *News That Matters: Television and American Opinion*. Chicago: University of Chicago Press, 1987.

Jamieson, Kathleen Hall. *Everything You Think You Know about Politics and Why You're Wrong*. New York: Basic Books, 2000.

——— *Packaging the Presidency: A History and Criticism of Presidential Campaign Advertising*. Oxford, UK: Oxford University Press, 1996.

——— *Dirty Politics: Deception, Distraction, Democracy*. Oxford, UK: Oxford University Press, 1996.

——— and David S. Birdsell. *Presidential Debates*. New York: Oxford University Press, 1988.

Kaid, Lynda Lee, and Anne Johnston. "Negative versus Positive Television Advertising in U.S. Presidential Campaigns, 1960–1988." *Journal of Communications,* 41 (Summer 1991): 53–64.

Kenski, Kate, Bruce W. Hardy, and Kathleen Hall Jamieson. *The Obama Victory: How Media, Money, and Message Shaped the 2008 Election*. Oxford, UK: Oxford University Press, 2010.

Lau, Richard R., Lee Sigelman, and Ivy Brown Rouver. "The Effects of Negative Political Commercials: A Meta-Analytic Reassessment." *Journal of Politics,* 69 (Nov. 2007): 1176–1209.

Mark, David. *Going Dirty: The Art of Negative Campaigning*. Lanham, MD: Rowman & Littlefield, 2006.

Mutz, Diana C. "How the Mass Media Divide Us," in Pietro S. Niola and David W. Brady, eds. *Red and Blue Nation? Characteristics and Causes of America's Polarized Politics*. Washington, DC: Brookings/Hoover, 2006, pp. 223–262.

Patterson, Thomas E. *Doing Well and Doing Good: How Soft News and Critical Journalism Are Shrinking the News Audience and Weakening Democracy—And What News Outlets Can Do about It.* Cambridge, MA: Joan Shorenstein Center on the Press, Politics, and Public Policy, 2000.

——— *Out of Order.* New York: Knopf, 1993.

Schroeder, Alan. *Presidential Debates: Forty Years of High-Risk TV*. New York: Columbia University Press, 2000.

Shaw, Daron R. "The Effect of TV Ads and Candidate Appearances on Statewide Presidential Votes, 1988–1996." *American Political Science Review,* 93 (Dec. 1999): 957–977.

West, Darrell M. *Air Wars: Television Advertising in Election Campaigns, 1952–2004,* 4th ed. Washington, DC: CQ Press, 2005.

Notes

1. The term *yellow journalism* comes from the comic strip "The Yellow Kid," which first appeared in Joseph Pulitzer's *New York World* in 1896. The kid, whose nightshirt was colored yellow in the paper, was an instant hit in the black-and-white newspapers of the day and sparked a bidding war for the comic strip between Pulitzer and William Randolph Hearst. Although the strip's popularity lasted only a few years, the competition between these two media titans continued for decades.

2. David Stebenne, "Media Coverage of American Presidential Elections: A Historical Perspective," in *The Finish Line: Covering the Campaign's Final Days*, ed. Martha FitzSimon (New York: Freedom Forum Media Studies Center, 1993), p. 83.
3. "Utilization of Selected Media, 1980–2007," *Statistical Abstract of the United States* (2010), Table 1095. www.census.gov/compendia/statab/2010/tables/10s1095.pdf.
4. "High Marks for the Campaign, a High Bar for Obama," Pew Research Center for the People and the Press (Nov. 13, 2005). www.people-press.org/report/?pageid=1429.
5. "McCain vs Obama on the Web," Project for Excellence in Journalism (Sept. 15, 2008). www.journalism.org/node/12772
6. Thomas E. Patterson, *Out of Order* (New York: Knopf, 1993), pp. 53–133.
7. Thomas E. Patterson, "Television and Election Strategy," in *The Communications Revolution in Politics*, ed. Gerald Benjamin (New York: Academy of Political Science, 1982), p. 30.
8. Michael J. Robinson and Margaret A. Sheehan, *Over the Wire and on TV: CBS and UPI in Campaign '80* (New York: Russell Sage Foundation, 1983), p. 148.
9. "Winning the Media Campaign," Project for Excellence in Journalism (Oct. 22, 2008). www.journalism./node/13307.
10. When running for their party's nomination, candidates receive coverage roughly in proportion to their popular standing, with the front-runners getting the most attention. After the conventions are over, it becomes primarily a two-person contest. The amount of speaking time candidates receive on the national news is roughly proportional to their media coverage. Stephen J. Farnsworth and S. Robert Lichter, "*The Nightly News Nightmare* Revisited: Television's Coverage of the 2004 Presidential Election." Paper presented at the annual meeting of the American Political Science Association, Washington DC, Sept. 2005.
11. See Diana C. Mutz, "How the Mass Media Divide Us," in Pietro S. Nivola and David W. Brady, eds., *Red and Blue Nation? Characteristics and Causes of America's Polarized Politics*. (Washington, DC: Brookings/Hoover, 2006), pp. 224–240.
12. S. Robert Lichter, Stanley Rothman, and Linda S. Lichter, *The Media Elite* (Bethesda, MD: Adler & Adler, 1986).
13. Farnsworth and Lichter, "*The Nightly News Nightmare*," p. 15.
14. "Winning the Media Campaign." www.journalism./node/13307.
15. Kiku Adatto, "The Incredible Shrinking Sound Bite," *New Republic* (May 28, 1990), p. 22.
16. Roger Ailes, media director for George Bush's 1988 campaign, explained this phenomenon in the following manner:

    > Let's face it, there are three things that the media are interested in: pictures, mistakes, and attacks. That's the one sure way of getting coverage. You try to avoid as many mistakes as you can. You try to give them as many pictures as you can. And if you need coverage, you attack, and you will get coverage.
    >
    > It's my orchestra pit theory of politics. If you have two guys on stage and one says, "I have a solution to the Middle East problem," and the other guy falls in the orchestra pit, who do you think is going to be on the evening news?
    >
    > David R. Runkel, ed., *Campaign for President: The Managers Look at '88* (Dover, MA: Auburn House, 1989), p. 136.

17. Adatto, "Sound Bite," p. 22.

18. Mutz, "How the Mass Media Divide Us," p. 246.
19. "Journalists Monopolize TV News," Center for Media and Public Affairs, p. 21; Patterson, *Out of Order,* p. 106.
20. Patterson, *Out of Order,* p. 106.
21. Ibid., pp. 119–120.
22. Ibid., pp. 118–119.
23. Anita Dunn in Kathleen Hall Jamieson, *Electing the President 2008: The Insiders' View* (Philadelphia, University of Pennsylvania Press, 2009), p. 140.
24. Nicole Wallace quoted in Jamieson, *Electing the President 2008*, p. 138.
25. Paul Lazarsfeld, Bernard Berelson, and Hazel Goudet, *The People's Choice* (New York: Columbia University Press, 1948); Bernard Berelson, Paul Lazarsfeld, and William McPhee, *Voting: A Study of Opinion Formation in a Presidential Campaign* (Chicago: University of Chicago Press, 1954).
26. Martin Kaplan, Ken Goldstein, and Matthew Hale, "Local News Coverage of the 2004 Campaign: An Analysis of Nightly Broadcasts in Eleven Markets" (Lear Center, Local News Archives, Feb. 15, 2005). www.localnewsarchive.org
27. The Nielsen Company reported that 163.6 million watched the results of the 2008 election on television or the Internet (134.8 million on television alone and 5.2 million on the Internet alone).
28. Michael J. Robinson, "Mass Media and the Margins of Democratic Politics: Non-Transformations in the USA," (unpublished paper, March 1993), pp. 81–83.
29. "Voters Liked Campaign 2004, But Too Much 'Mudsling,'" Pew Research Center for the People and the Press (Nov. 11, 2004), p. 8.
30. Stephen J. Farnsworth, and S. Robert Lichter, *The Nightly News Nightmare,* p. 31.
31. "Election Watch: Campaign 2008 Final: How TV News Covered the General Election Campaign," *Media Monitor* 23 (Winter 2009), pp. 2–4.
32. "Topics A–Z: Confidence in Institutions," Gallup Poll, 2010. www.gallup.com/poll/1587/confidence-institutions.
33. Chris Dodd quoted in Dan Balz, "Democratic Senator Dodd Enters Presidential Race," *The Washington Post* (Jan. 12, 2007), p. A6.
34. In his initial quest for the presidency in 2000, George W. Bush spoke for thirteen minutes on a single appearance on the *Late Show with David Letterman*—longer than the total time he appeared on the evening news of three television broadcast networks during the *entire* month of October. Similarly, Gore appeared on Letterman's show in September for more time than he appeared on the three evening news shows during that whole month combined. "Journalists Monopolize TV News," Center for Media and Public Affairs, p. 27.
35. Matthew A. Baum, "Talking the Vote: Why Presidential Candidates Hit the Talk Show Circuit," *American Journal of Political Science,* 49 (April 2005), pp. 213–234.
36. Peter Goldman, Thomas M. DeFrank, Mary Miller, et al., *Quest for the Presidency: 1992* (College Station: Texas A&M Press, 1994), p. 535.
37. Admiral Stockdale had not been briefed by Perot's handlers prior to the debate. He was unable to answer questions about Perot's policy positions. At one point when the moderator asked him a question, he said that he could not hear it because his hearing aid was not on. Viewers did not come away with confidence that he could be an effective vice president, much less president.
38. Perot complained bitterly, first appealing to the Federal Communications Commission and then instituting legal action to prevent the debates from being held if he could not participate. Although he failed to stop the debates, he used his

exclusion to emphasize one of his campaign themes—the self-serving nature of the two-party system and the need to reform it. The reason that Perot was so agitated was that participating in the debates was part of his 1996 campaign strategy. He had boosted his popularity significantly in 1992 by his performance in the presidential debates and hoped to do so again in 1996.

39. "Politics Unusual: Media and the Making of a President," Nielsen Company (Nov. 7, 2008). blog.nielsen.com/nielsenwire/politics/politics-unusual-media-and-the-making-of-a-president.
40. In 2000, the Commission on Presidential Debates proposed four 90-minute debates, three involving the presidential candidates and one, the vice presidential nominees. Al Gore accepted immediately, but George W. Bush did not. Instead, Bush proposed debates on two network talk shows, *Meet the Press* and *Larry King Live,* and wanted only to participate in one of the commission's debates. With Gore enjoying a better reputation than Bush as a skilled and knowledgeable debater, the press interpreted the Republican candidate's counterproposal as an attempt to make the debates less formal, limit the size of the viewing audience, and reduce their impact on the electorate. Although the vice president had stated that he would debate his opponent in any venue, including news shows, he refused to accept Bush's invitation unless and until the governor agreed to accept the commission's entire debate proposal, which Bush eventually did.
41. The McCain campaign initially proposed that the major-party candidates appear at ten town meetings, McCain's favorite venue. The Obama campaign rejected the proposal in favor of the traditional debate format, which included one town meeting–styled debate. McCain had little choice but to agree.
42. Nixon had closeted himself alone in a hotel before his first debate with Kennedy. He received only a ten-minute briefing. Moreover, he had bumped his knee on a car door going into the television studio and was in considerable pain. Theodore H. White, *The Making of the President, 1960* (New York: Atheneum, 1988), p. 285.
43. Helped by the low expectations that accompanied his appearance and his opponents' aggressive style and factual embellishments, Bush seemed the equal of his opponent on the issues and the nicer person in the give-and-take, especially during their first debate when Gore's sighs and expressions of dismay, heard while Bush was talking, produced a negative public reaction among viewers, particularly women. In the words of Bush adviser, Matthew Dowd, "His 'sighs' and bearing made him look like he wasn't a nice person, and at points, when he answered questions, he lectured. He actually did more damage to himself than we did to him." Kathleen Hall Jamieson and Paul Waldman, *Electing the President 2000: The Insiders' View* (Philadelphia: University of Pennsylvania Press, 2001), p. 22.
44. Ken Mehlman in *Campaign for President: The Managers Look at 2004* (Lanham, MD: Rowman and Littlefield, 2006), p. 144.
45. "Debate Transcript," Commission on Presidential Debates (Sept. 26, 2008). www.debates.org/index.php?page=2008-debate-transcript.
46. "Debate Transcript," Commission on Presidential Debates (Oct. 15, 2008). www.debates.org/index.php?page=october-15-2008-debate-transcript
47. David Axelrod quoted in Jamieson, *Electing the President 2008*, p. 76.
48. Kemp's performance so dismayed Republican strategists who were watching it on television that Haley Barbour, the chair of the Republican National Committee was heard to remark, "I told you we should have kept the ball game [the National League playoffs] on one channel!" Haley Barbour, quoted in Evan Thomas, *Back from the Dead* (New York: Atlantic Monthly Press, 1997), p. 184.

49. "Political Advertising in 2008," University of Wisconsin Advertising Project, March 17, 2010. wiscadproject.wisc.edu.
50. Ibid.
51. "Obama's Oct. 29 Simulcast Follows in Perot's Footsteps," Nielsen Wire (Oct. 30, 2008). blog.nielsen.com/nielsenwire/media_entertainment/obama%e2%80%99s-oct-29-simulcast-follows-in-perot%e2%80%99s-footsteps/.
52. L. Patrick Devlin, "Contrasts in Presidential Campaign Commercials of 2004," *American Behavioral Scientist,* 49 (Oct. 2005), p. 283.
53. Living Room Candidate.org. www.livingroomcandidate.org/commercials/2004/ashleys-story.
54. The poll was conducted by Public Opinion Strategies. Devlin, "Contrasts in Presidential Campaign Commercials of 2004," p. 296.
55. Bob Strum quoted in Devlin, "Contrasts in Presidential Campaign Commercials of 2004," p. 296.
56. Jim Margolis in Jamieson, *Electing the President 2008,* p. 123.
57. "Defining Moment," Living Room Candidate.org. www.livingroomcandidate.org/commercials/2008.
58. "Love 60," Living Room Candidate.org. www.livingroomcandidate.org/commercials/2008/love-60.
59. L. Patrick Devlin, "Contrasts in Presidential Campaign Commercials of 1996," *American Behavioral Scientist,* 40 (Aug. 1997): p. 1064.
60. "Listen to Biden," in Jamieson, *Electing the President 2008,* p. 117.
61. "90 Percent," Living Room Candidate.org. www.livingroomcandidate.org/commercials/2008/90-percent.
62. Lynda Lee Kaid, "Videostyle in the 2004 Presidential Advertising," in Robert E. Denton, Jr., ed. *The 2004 Presidential Campaign: A Communication Perspective.* Lanham, MD: Rowman & Littlefield, 2005, p. 292.
63. Jim Rutenberg, "Scary Ads Take Campaign to a Grim New Level," *The New York Times* (Oct. 17, 2004), p. A1.
64. "What I Believe," in Jamieson, *Electing the President 2008,* p. 130.
65. Kathleen Hall Jamieson and Brooks Jackson, "Our Disinformed Electorate," December 12, 2008. FactCheck.org. www.factcheck.org/specialreports/our_disinformed_electorate.html.
66. Ibid.
67. Ibid.
68. Michael M. Franz, Joel Rivlin, and Kenneth Goldstein, "Much More of the Same: Television Advertising Pre- and Post-BCRA" in Michael J. Malbin, ed., *The Election after Reform* (Lanham, MD: Rowman & Littlefield, 2006), p. 147.
69. Kate Kenski, Bruce W. Hardy, and Kathleen Hall Jamieson, *The Obama Victory: How Media, Money, and Message Shaped the 2008 Election* (Oxford, UK: Oxford University Press, 2010), p. 279.
70. Chris Cillizza, "Romney's Data Cruncher," *The Washington Post* (July 5, 2007), pp. A1 and A6. www.washingtonpost.com/wp-dyn/content/article/2007/07/04/AR2007070401423.html.
71. For an excellent discussion of microtargeting in the 2008 presidential campaign, see Kenski, Hardy, and Jamieson, *The Obama Victory*, pp. 265–285.
72. Ibid., p. 284.
73. A daisy girl look-alike advertisement was aired in several battleground states in 2000 by a nonprofit, Republican-oriented group from Texas. Like its famous predecessor, the ad featured a young girl plucking the petals of a daisy, a countdown, and a nuclear explosion. The message was that the Clinton–Gore administration had jeopardized the nation's security by providing nuclear secrets to China

in exchange for campaign contributions, thereby giving China the capacity to unleash a nuclear attack against the United States. The ad ended with the words "Don't take a chance, please vote Republican." Leslie Wayne, "Infamous Political Commercial Is Turned on Gore," *The New York Times* (Oct. 27, 2000), p. A26.

74. Edwin Diamond and Adrian Marin, "Spots," *American Behavioral Scientist,* 32 (March/April 1989), p. 386.
75. Gore had run into trouble in 2000 when early spending by the Democrats in that election left them unable to match the funds the Bush campaign put into Florida and the other key battleground states at the end. The Kerry advertising team was determined not to repeat this mistake.
76. Stephen Ansolabehere and Shanto Iyengar, *Going Negative: How Political Advertisements Shrink and Polarize the Electorate* (New York: Free Press, 1995), pp. 147–150.
77. Ken Goldstein and Paul Freedman, "Campaign Advertising and Voter Turnout: New Evidence for a Stimulation Effect," *Journal of Politics* 64 (Aug. 2002), pp. 122–123. See also Steven Finkel and John Geer, "A Spot Check: Casting Doubt on the Demobilizing Effect of Attack Advertising," *American Journal of Political Science,* 42 (June 1988), pp. 573–595; Paul Freedman and Ken Goldstein, "Measuring Media Exposure and the Effects of Negative Campaign Ads," *American Journal of Political Science,* 43 (Sept. 1999), pp. 1189–1208; Kim Fridkin Kahn and Patrick Kenney, "Do Negative Campaigns Mobilize or Suppress Turnout? Clarifying the Relationship between Negativity and Participation," *American Political Science Review,* 93 (Dec. 1999), pp. 877–890; Martin Wattenberg and Craig Brians, "Negative Campaign Advertising: Demobilizer or Mobilizer?" *American Political Science Review,* 93 (Dec. 1999), pp. 891–900; John G. Geer, *In Defense of Negativity: Attack Ads in Presidential Campaigns* (Chicago: University of Chicago Press, 2006).
78. "High Marks for the Campaign, a High Bar for Obama," Pew Research Center for the People & the Press (Nov. 13, 2008). www.people-press.org/reports/questionnaires/471.pdf.
79. For a very interesting article on this subject, see Larry M. Bartels, "Uninformed Votes: Information Effects in Presidential Elections," *American Journal of Political Science,* 40 (Feb. 1996), pp. 194–230.

The Election

PART IV

9 CHAPTER

Understanding Presidential Elections

INTRODUCTION

Predicting the results of an election is a favorite American practice. Politicians do it; the news media do it; even the public tries to anticipate the outcome far in advance of the event. It is a form of entertainment—somewhat akin to forecasting the winner of a sporting contest.

Presidential elections are particularly prone to such predictions. National surveys now report continuously on the opinions of the American public during the campaign.[1] On election night, television news commentators project a winner before most of the votes are counted. Election day surveys of voters exiting the polls assess the mood of the electorate and present the first systematic analysis of the results. Subsequently, more in-depth studies that include the same respondents in the pre- and postelection surveys reveal shifts in opinions and attitudes.

Predictions and analyses of the electorate based on survey data are not conducted solely for their entertainment or news value, although many are. They provide important information to candidates running for office and to those who have been elected. For the nominees, surveys of public opinion indicate the issues that can be effectively raised and those that should be avoided.

They also suggest which audience might be most receptive to specific policy positions, even the words and expressions they should use. For the successful candidates, analyses of voter preferences, opinions, and attitudes provide an interpretation of the vote, indicate the range and depth of public concern on the key issues, and signal the amount of support newly elected presidents are likely to receive on these issues as they begin their term in office.

This chapter examines the presidential vote from three perspectives. The first anticipates the vote by examining the environment and public opinion as the election approaches. There are many ways to assess the electoral environment. The first part of this section looks at how political scientists have tried to do so, the models they have used, and the success that they have had in predicting the outcome of the popular vote. The focus then shifts to the public, its attitudes, beliefs, and opinions. Here we look at snapshots of the public over the course of the election campaign. This part of the chapter discusses national opinion polls, describes their methodologies, and evaluates their predictive success. We then turn to the news media's election forecasts and analyses based on the large poll that is taken primarily on election day as voters exit the voting booths.

The second section turns to an examination of the vote itself. After discussing election day surveys, it reports on the American National Election Studies (ANES), which have been conducted since 1952 by researchers at the University of Michigan and, since 2005, along with researchers at Stanford University. These studies, which survey voters before and after the election, provide basic data that scholars have used to analyze elections and understand voting behavior and how the campaign affected the outcome. The principal findings of these analyses are summarized for each presidential election since 1952.

The final section of the chapter turns to the relationship between campaigning and governing, between issue debates and public policy making, between candidate evaluations and presidential style. Do the campaign issues determine the new agenda of the administration? Does the projected or perceived image of the candidates affect the tone of the presidency or the actions of the winner in office? Can an electoral coalition be converted into a governing coalition? Do the selection process expectations help or hinder the president in meeting them? These questions are explored in an effort to determine the impact of the election on the operation of the presidency, the behavior of the president, and the functioning of the political system.

PREDICTING PRESIDENTIAL ELECTIONS

Political scientists have had a long-running debate about how much campaigns do really matter. Do they dictate, influence, or have relatively little impact on the outcome of the election?

There are several principal schools of thought. One argues that campaigns usually do not matter all that much and that the environment in which elections occur shapes the electorate's judgment and augurs the outcome of the vote; another suggests that it is the preexisting political views that matter;

a third alternative is that campaigns can be decisive, particularly when the electorate is closely divided. These contending points of view are not necessarily inconsistent with one another, but they do reflect differences in the perceptions of what the most important influences on voting are—economic, social, and political conditions; political attitudes, salient issues, and personalities of the candidates or the conduct of the campaign itself.

FORMAL MODELS

Those in the environment-conditions-results school have constructed formal models by which they forecast election outcomes. They identify critical variables that measure or reflect the economic, social, and political environment in which an election occurs; place these variables in their model; and use them to predict the percentage of the popular vote that the winning candidate should receive. To ensure that they have the right combination of factors in their model, the researchers usually test its accuracy on the basis of how their model would have predicted past elections.

Since economic performance is a major criterion by which the electorate evaluates the party in power and its candidates for office, especially if the incumbent is running for reelection, almost all the election models contain measures of the economy; some modelers also try to anticipate how the economy will perform in the year of the election and how the public thinks it will perform.[2] Economic indicators include the Gross National Product (GNP), Gross Domestic Product (GDP), rate of economic growth, level of unemployment, number of new jobs created since the previous election, rate of inflation, consumer confidence index, and forecasts about the country's economic future.

If the indicators are favorable, the models assume that the electorate will make a retrospective judgment and reward the party in control of the White House and the incumbent; if they are unfavorable, the expectation is that the electorate would vote for the other party's candidates in the hope that they will improve conditions. When an incumbent president is not on the ticket, the electorate looks more to the future and may make a prospective judgment based on the promises and qualifications of the candidates seeking the presidency. In making a prospective voting decision, people need to have knowledge about the candidates, their parties, and their policies in order to judge them.

But how much knowledge is really necessary? In the 2008 election, a survey by the Annenberg Public Policy Center found that more than half the people could identify Obama's and McCain's positions on seven major policy issues. Of those who could not do so, however, the survey found little learning taking place during the general election campaign.[3]

A second set of variables concerns the political environment: the public's evaluation of the current president, the electability of the candidates running for the nomination, and the party that has been in control of the White House, sometimes for an extended period of time. The principal measure for judging the president's job approval is the answer to the question, "Do you approve or disapprove of the job the president is doing?" High approval ratings (over 50 percent) are normally considered a positive sign for an incumbent seeking reelection. Similarly, the relative ease or difficulty of winning the party's nomination may also indicate how well that candidate will do in the general election.[4] People like to support a winner or at least a candidate who has a reasonable chance of winning.

Another variable is the number of terms a party controls the White House. Assuming that the public tires of one-party control for an extended period, the "get-tired effect" should kick in after two or more presidential terms, thereby reducing the vote of the candidate of the party in power. However, the candidate of a party that has recently gained control of the White House should not be affected in a quest for reelection. Of the presidents who were elected in the twentieth and twenty-first centuries, only Jimmy Carter was defeated after his and his party's first term in the White House; the other incumbents who lost—William Howard Taft (1912), Herbert Hoover (1932), and George H. W. Bush (1992)—did so after an extended period of their party's control of the presidency.

Models forecast popular vote results. Their success in doing so depends on the relevance of the measures they use as criteria by which the voters will decide, the period during which data have been collected for these measures, and the assumption that the campaigns of the two major candidates will effectively cancel each other out. If the measures do not incorporate the principal issues of the campaign, if the data on which they are based are collected too early, then the forecast may not be accurate, particularly if other events, including the campaign itself, affect the judgment of the voters.

Prior to the 2000 presidential election, all the models predicted a Gore victory over Bush by 52.8 percent to 60.3 percent of the popular vote. They did so because the measures they used reflected the booming economy, the absence of a national security threat and the position of the United States as the only remaining superpower, and President Bill Clinton's high job approval ratings, although his personal favorability ratings were much lower. Nonetheless, Al Gore seemed to be in a strong position to take advantage of these favorable factors, or so the models forecast. What went wrong? Why were the modelers' predictions inaccurate? Gore actually received 48.4 percent of the total vote, 50.2 percent of the two-party vote.

Some critics attributed the incorrect estimates of the final popular vote to ideological bias. They see political scientists as liberal-leaning and Democratic—hence more favorable to Gore than Bush. Others, however, contended that the 2000 election was unique, or at least different from previous elections. Bill Clinton's personal digressions may also have been a factor that none of the models included. Perhaps the economy didn't help the Democrats because the prosperity had lasted too long and people had gotten used to it.

The electorate apparently believed that either of the candidates could and would continue the good economic times, thereby decreasing the incumbent vice president's initial advantage. In addition, the vice president's inability or unwillingness to take credit for the successful economic policies of the Clinton years may also have affected the results.

In their postmortems following that election, the modelers pointed to a variety of factors that impaired their collective judgment: they used the wrong combination of variables; they calculated presidential approval but not Clinton's personal unfavorability; they overemphasized economic factors and underestimated moral and social ones; and finally, they failed to consider the uniqueness of the 2000 election. Dr. Christopher Wlezien concluded an analysis of why his and other models did not capture the final result more accurately with the following admonition:

> All that forecasting models can offer well in advance of an election is some sense of the advantage or disadvantage candidates have as the campaign begins. They offer a starting point of sorts, not the final resting place. Campaigns matter. They always have and always will. If this wasn't already clear before the 2000 election, it is now.[5]

In 2004, the modelers did better. They all forecast that Bush would win the popular vote, receiving anywhere from 49.9 percent to 57.6 percent of the two-party vote. The average forecast was 53.8 percent; Bush actually received 50.7 percent of the total vote, 51.2 percent of the two-party vote.[6]

The outcome of the 2008 presidential election was not hard to predict, particularly after the financial crisis of mid-September of that year. But even before that crisis, a Democratic victory seemed probable with economic growth declining, an unpopular, two-term president in the White House, and a war in progress that a majority of Americans had come to believe was a mistake. Most of the political science forecasters predicted an Obama victory by an average of 52 percent of the two-party vote.[7]

The imponderables that the 2008 models could not predict were further economic developments and candidate-related matters. Of these, Obama's race was the most indeterminable factor. Since he was the first African American to receive a major-party nomination, there were no historical data that could be used to anticipate how voters would react to such a candidate at the presidential level.[8] In the end, the economy got worse, race was not a factor, and Obama's vote exceeded predictions, but not by much. He received 52.9 of the total vote and 53.7 of the two-party vote.

PUBLIC OPINION POLLS

In addition to using formal models to forecast the vote, political scientists and journalists also depend heavily on public opinion surveys to anticipate election outcomes and gain information about the political views of the electorate. The public is naturally interested in who is going to win. The news media and candidates are obsessed with the answer to the question of who will win, hence their reliance on and reporting of poll results.

Polls also provide the major-party candidates with information about the perceptions and concerns of the public over the course of the election cycle, how specific appeals resonate with specific groups, and the electoral opportunities that information provides the campaign. For example, the Obama campaign conducted a national survey in May 2008 to discern whether the groups that supported and opposed Obama during the Democratic nomination process would continue to do so in the general election. Joel Benenson, the campaign's pollster, was surprised to find considerable support from the groups that backed Hillary Clinton: senior women, noncollege women, Hispanics, and union households. Catholics were the only Clinton group with which the poll indicated Obama might have difficulty winning.[9]

There are hundreds of public opinion surveys. In 2008, there were 221 separate national polls and 975 state polls between Labor Day and election day.[10]

A Brief History of Election Polling

Although the number of polls has mushroomed in recent years, polling itself is not a new phenomenon. There have been nationwide assessments of public opinion since 1916. The largest and most comprehensive of the early surveys were the straw polls conducted by the *Literary Digest,* a popular monthly magazine. The *Digest* mailed millions of ballots and questionnaires to people who appeared on lists of automobile owners and in telephone directories. In 1924, 1928, and 1932, the poll correctly predicted the winner of the presidential election. In 1936, it did not: a huge Alfred Landon victory was forecast, and a huge Franklin Roosevelt victory followed.

What went wrong? The *Digest* mailed 10 million questionnaires over the course of the campaign and received 2 million back. As the ballots were returned, they were tabulated. This procedure, which provided a running count, blurred shifts in public opinion that may have been occurring during the campaign. But that was not its only problem. The principal difficulty with the *Digest*'s survey was that the sample of people who responded was not representative of the voting public. Automobile owners and telephone subscribers were simply not typical voters in 1936, since most people did not own cars or have telephones. This distinction mattered more in 1936 than it had in previous years because of the Great Depression. There was a socioeconomic cleavage within the electorate. The *Literary Digest* sample did not reflect this cleavage; thus its results were inaccurate.

While the *Digest* was tabulating its 2 million responses and predicting that Landon would be the next president, a number of other pollsters were conducting more scientific surveys and correctly forecasting Roosevelt's reelection. The polls of George Gallup, Elmo Roper, and Archibald Crossley differed from the *Digest*'s in two principal respects: they were considerably smaller, and their samples were more representative of the population as a whole, allowing more accurate generalizations to be made.

The *Digest* went out of business, but Gallup, Roper, and Crossley continued to poll and to improve their sampling techniques. In 1940, Gallup predicted Roosevelt would receive 52 percent of the vote; he actually received 55 percent. In 1944, Gallup forecast a 51.5 percent Roosevelt vote, very close to his actual 53.2 percent. Other pollsters also made predictions that closely approximated the results. As a consequence, public confidence in election polling began to grow.

The confidence was short-lived, however. In 1948, all major pollsters forecast a victory by Republican Thomas E. Dewey. Their errors resulted from poor sampling techniques, from the premature termination of polling two weeks before the end of the campaign, and from incorrect assumptions about how the undecided would vote.

In attempting to estimate the population in their samples, the pollsters had resorted to filling quotas. They interviewed a certain number of people with different demographic characteristics until the percentage of these groups in the sample resembled that percentage in the population as a whole. Simply because the percentages were approximately equal, however, did not mean that the sample was representative of the population. For example, interviewers avoided certain areas in cities, and their results were consequently biased.

Moreover, the interviewing stopped several weeks before the election. In mid-October, the polls showed that Dewey was ahead by a substantial margin. Burns Roper, son of Elmo Roper, polling for *Fortune* magazine, saw the lead as sufficiently large to predict a Dewey victory without the need for further surveys. A relatively large number of people, however, were undecided. Three weeks before the election, Gallup concluded that 8 percent of the voters had still not made up their minds. In estimating the final vote, Gallup and other pollsters assumed that the undecided would divide their votes in much the same manner as the electorate as a whole. This assumption turned out to be incorrect. Most of those who were wavering in the closing days of the campaign were Democrats. In the end, most of them voted for Truman or did not vote at all.

The results of the 1948 election once again cast doubt on the accuracy of public opinion polls. Truman's victory also reemphasized the fact that surveys reflect opinion at the time they are taken, not necessarily days or weeks later. Opinion and voter preferences may change.

Contemporary Polling

To improve their monitoring of shifts within the electorate, pollsters changed the method of selecting people to be interviewed. They developed a more effective means of anticipating who would actually vote and polled continuously to and through election day to identify more precisely and quickly shifts in public sentiment and reactions to campaign events. Obviously, polls conducted closer to the day on which people vote are more likely to forecast the actual results more accurately than polls taken months before.

These changes, plus the continued refinement of the questions, have produced better and more accurate polls as the election approaches. Between 1936 and 1950, the average error of the final Gallup preelection poll was 3.6 percent; since then it has usually been 2 percent or less. (Table 9.1 indicates the final Gallup Polls and the election results since 1936. Table 9.2 lists the final preelection polls and results in 2008.)

Very close elections in 1960, 1968, and 1976, however, resulted in several pollsters' making wrong predictions. In 1980, the size of Reagan's victory was substantially underestimated in some nationwide polls; in 1992 and 1996, Clinton's margin was overestimated, whereas in 2000, Gore's was underestimated by some pollsters.

Why do pollsters underestimate or overestimate the results? Although opinions can change between a poll and the actual vote, that change should be small since most pollsters now conclude their surveys on or near election day. They also try to identify the voting patterns of people who tell interviewers

TABLE 9.1 | GALLUP POLL ACCURACY RECORD, 1936–2008 (IN PERCENTAGES)

Year	Final Survey	Election Results	Deviation
2008	Obama 55	Obama 53	+2
	McCain 44	McCain 46	−2
2004	Bush 49	Bush 50.7	−2
	Kerry 49	Kerry 48.3	+1
2000	Bush 48	Bush 47.9	+0
	Gore 46	Gore 48.4	−2
	Nader 4	Nader 2.7	+1
1996	Clinton 52	Clinton 50.1	+1
	Dole 41.0	Dole 41.4	−0
	Perot 7	Perot 8.5	−1
1992	Clinton 49	Clinton 43.3	+5
	Bush 37	Bush 37.7	−0
	Perot 14	Perot 19.0	−5
1988	Bush 56	Bush 53.0	+2
	Dukakis 44	Dukakis 46	−2
1984	Reagan 59	Reagan 59.2	0
	Mondale 41	Mondale 40.8	0
1980	Reagan 47	Reagan 50.8	−3
	Carter 44	Carter 41	+3
	Anderson 8	Anderson 6.6	+1
	Other 1	Other 1.6	−0
1976	Carter 48	Carter 50.1	−2
	Ford 49	Ford 48.1	+0
	McCarthy 2	McCarthy .9	+1
	Other 1	Other .9	+0
1972	Nixon 62	Nixon 61.8	+0
	McGovern 38	McGovern 38.2	−0
1968	Nixon 43	Nixon 43.5	−0
	Humphrey 42	Humphrey 42.9	−0
	Wallace 15	Wallace 13.6	+1
1964	Johnson 64	Johnson 61.3	+2
	Goldwater 36	Goldwater 38.7	−2
1960	Kennedy 51	Kennedy 50.1	+0
	Nixon 49	Nixon 49.9	−0

continued

TABLE 9.1 | GALLUP POLL ACCURACY RECORD, 1936–2008 (IN PERCENTAGES) *continued*

Year	Final Survey	Election Results	Deviation
1956	Eisenhower 59.5	Eisenhower 57.8	+1
	Stevenson 40.5	Stevenson 42.4	−1
1952	Eisenhower 51	Eisenhower 55.4	−4
	Stevenson 49	Stevenson 44.6	+4
1948	Truman 44.5	Truman 49.5	−5
	Dewey 49.5	Dewey 45.1	+4
	Wallace 4	Wallace 2.4	+1
	Other 2	Other 3	−1
1944	Roosevelt 51.5	Roosevelt 53.8	−2
	Dewey 48.5	Dewey 46.2	+2
1940	Roosevelt 52	Roosevelt 55	−3
	Willkie 48	Willkie 45	+3
1936	Roosevelt 55.7	Roosevelt 62.5	−6
	Landon 44.3	Landon 37.5	+6

Source: "Election Poll Accuracy," The Gallup Poll. www.gallup.com/poll/9442/Election-Polls-Accuracy-Record-Presidential-Elections.aspx

TABLE 9.2 | ACCURACY OF THE FINAL 2008 PREELECTION POLLS

Poll	Date*	Obama	McCain	Unsure/ Undecided/ Other
Actual Results		52.9	45.7	1.4
Polls				
Marist	11/3	52	43	5
American Research Group	11/3	53	45	2
Fox/Opinion Dynamics	11/2	50	43	7
NBC/Wall Street Journal	11/2	51	43	6
CBS	11/2	51	42	7
Democracy Corps (D)	11/2	51	44	5
Ipsos/McClatchy	11/2	50	42	8
CNN/Opinion Research	11/1	53	46	1
Pew Research Center	11/1	49	42	9

*Election day was November 4, 2008.

Source: "White House 2008: General Election Trial Heats," Polling Report.com www.pollingreport.com/wh08gen.htm

that they plan to vote early or by absentee ballot. They also must consider turnout, who will vote, and how the undecided voters will break.

Anticipating likely voters is a tricky business. Simply asking people whether they plan to vote is not sufficient because as we noted in Chapter 2, more people will say that they intend to vote than actually do so. Pollsters usually ask a battery of questions to determine the likelihood of the respondent actually voting. If their allocation formula proves to be incorrect, then their sample is likely to deviate from the actual vote. This happened in 2000 when some pollsters split the undecided vote between Gore and Bush. By doing so, they failed to capture the extent of the late surge for Gore. Similarly in 1992, pollsters made an incorrect judgment about the Perot vote. Based on the experience of other third-party and independent candidates whose support had declined as election day approached, pollsters underestimated the popular vote that Perot received. Not only did Perot's support not decline but his campaign also succeeded in attracting a large number of first-time voters whose turnout was difficult to anticipate.

A potential problem in 2008 was anticipating the so-called Bradley effect. In 1982, California polls predicted that Los Angeles mayor Tom Bradley, an African American, would be elected governor of California. But they were wrong. Bradley lost a close election. Similarly, other state polls overestimated the vote African American candidates would receive for mayor of Chicago in 1983, governor of Virginia in 1989, and mayor of New York City, also in 1989. The underestimation of the vote for African American candidates seemed to suggest that people, not wanting to be perceived as racially biased, did not tell pollsters the truth about how they intended to vote. In the 1990s, racial attitudes began to change. Daniel Hopkins's study of 133 elections between 1989 and 2006 found little evidence of a "Bradley effect" after the early 1990s.[11]

New communication technologies have posed other problems for pollsters (see Box 9.1).

TELEVISION FORECASTS

Forecasts continue right to the end, until all the votes are tabulated. The final projections are presented by the major television broadcast and cable networks during the night of the election. In airing the results, the news media have four objectives: to report the vote, to forecast the winners, to analyze the returns, and to do so ahead of the other networks.

Beginning in the 1960s, the major networks and news services established a consortium, the News Election Service (NES), to pool their resources in reporting the vote count. Thousands of reporters were assigned to precincts and county election boards around the country to relay the presidential, congressional, and gubernatorial votes as soon as they were tallied.

If all the news media wanted to do was report the results, this type of reporting would suffice. But they want to do more. They want to analyze the vote and explain its meaning. To do so, they need more information than the vote itself. They need to know the reasons people voted for or against particular candidates. The best way to obtain this information accurately is to get it from the people themselves right after they exit the voting area.

BOX 9.1

Communications Technology and Survey Research

Changing communications technology has presented new challenges to survey researchers, particularly in the conduct of the interview and the selection of the sample. In the early polls, personal interviews were held in people's homes, a method that put respondents at ease. Establishing a personal relationship with the people being interviewed was thought to contribute to the truthfulness of their responses.

But home interviewing was slow and costly. During the 1980s, telephone interviews replaced personal visits; computers were used to analyze and tabulate the data more quickly and accurately. Random-digit dialing reached both listed and unlisted numbers.

Automated dialing, recorded messages, and eventually computerized calling greatly increased the number of phone calls people received, especially in the evening when they returned home from work. Complaints about being constantly disturbed by callers, particularly telemarketers, led Congress to enact legislation that allowed people to place their phone numbers on the Federal Communication Commission's "Do Not Call List." Survey researchers, nonprofit organizations, bill collection agencies, and companies with whom a person had done business were exempted from the call prohibition. These exceptions encouraged some telemarketers to pretend they were conducting a survey in order to gain information about respondents and also to sell a product to them.

As the calls persisted, the "hang up" rate and number of noncompleted surveys rose to around 70 percent. In addition to increasing the number of calls pollsters had to make to reach the required sample size, they also had to discern whether the people who completed the call were different demographically and attitudinally from those who refused to do so.

At the beginning of the twenty-first century, a similar issue arose with cell phone users. The number of homes *without* a land-line phone has increased sharply. Initially, pollsters were discouraged from calling cell phones because federal law prohibits the use of automated dialing devices to reach cell numbers; manual dialing is much more expensive, increasing the costs of the poll. Survey researchers also felt they had to provide a small financial incentive to the cell user because their charges are based on time used. It costs survey researchers four to five times as much to call a cell number as a land-line phone.

The Pew Research Center has found demographic differences between cell and land-line users. People who rely on cell phones primarily or exclusively tend to be younger; a smaller proportion of them are married; and a larger percentage of cell phone users are minorities, particularly African Americans and Hispanics. According to Scott Keeter, director of survey research for Pew, the number of exclusive cell phone users has been small and attitudinal differences not sufficiently large to offset the statistical weighting of the sample.[i] However, increasing cell phone usage presents a continuing financial problem for survey researchers, a problem that could also challenge the accuracy of their polling results.

---

[i]Scott Keeter, "How Serious Is Polling's Cell-Only Problem?" Pew Research Centerfor the People and the Press (June 20, 2007). pewresearch.org/pubs/515/polling-cell-only-problem; "The Cell Phone Challenge to Survey Research," Pew Research Center for the People and the Press (May 15, 2008). people-press.org/report/276/the-cell-challenge-to-survey-research

The first exit poll was conducted by Walter Mitofsky for CBS News in 1968. Other news networks followed. But this type of polling is expensive and requires large numbers of people who have to be trained for one day's work. It also requires sophisticated computer equipment and programming as well as considerable historical data on state precincts and their voting trends. To save money, the major news organizations formed a consortium, Voter Research and Survey (VRS), to collect the data, project the winners, and explain the outcomes. In the early 1990s, the NES became part of the new consortium.

Initially, the participating organizations maintained their own decision desks to call the elections. The competition among them resulted in several incorrect projections. Responding to external and internal criticism, the VRS exit polling operation was overhauled after the 2000 election at a cost of approximately $10 million. The new system failed completely in the 2002 midterm elections. Poll takers could not get through on the phone lines, the computers crashed, and the analysis could not be completed.

The consortium then decided to contract with Edison Research to do its exit polling. That firm has conducted exit polls for the major broadcast and cable networks as well as Associated Press and several large newspapers since 2004.[12]

How Exit Polls Work

A large number of precincts across the country are randomly selected. The random selection is made within states in such a way that principal geographic units (cities, suburbs, and rural areas), size of precincts, and their past voting records are taken into account. Several thousand representatives of the polling organization administer the poll to voters who are chosen in a systematic way (for example, every third, fourth, or fifth person) as they leave the voting booths. Voters are asked to complete a short questionnaire (thirty to forty items) that is designed to elicit information on their voting choices, political attitudes, and candidate evaluations and feelings, as well as their own demographic characteristics. Several times over the course of the day, the questionnaires are collected, tabulated, and their results telephoned to a central computer bank where they are analyzed using various statistical measures.

A variety of models are used to compare the returns from the precincts to those of past elections and to returns from other parts of the state. The sequence of the votes, the order in which they are received, is also considered in the analysis. Then, after most or all of the election polls in a state have been completed, the findings of the exit poll are made public by the news media. Over the course of the evening, the networks adjust the exit poll data to reflect the actual results as those results are tabulated.

The exit poll is usually very accurate. Because it is conducted over the course of the day, there may be a little bias that would underrepresent or overrepresent certain types of voters who cast their ballots at different times of the day. By the end of the day, however, this bias should be eliminated.

Only voters are sampled and in large numbers, thereby reducing the error to much less than that of the national surveys conducted before the election. In addition, the exit poll provides a sample of sufficient size to enable analysts to discern the attitudes, opinions, and choices of smaller groups and subgroups (such as white southern Protestants; African American males; and unmarried, college-educated women) within the electorate. In 2008, the sample size of exit poll interviews and telephone survey of people who said they voted early was more than 17,000.[13] (See Table 9.3 later in this chapter.)

Controversies About Early Vote Projections

Early projections of the winner on election night based on exit polling have generated considerable criticism, primarily on the grounds that they discourage turnout and affect voting in states in which the polls are still open. This controversy was heightened in 1980. When the early returns and polls conducted for the networks and major newspapers all indicated a Reagan landslide, the networks projected his victory early in the evening while voting was still occurring on the West Coast and in Hawaii. At 9:30 PM Eastern Standard Time (EST), President Jimmy Carter appeared before his supporters and conceded defeat. Almost immediately, Carter's early announcement incurred angry protests, particularly from defeated West Coast Democrats, who alleged that the president's remarks discouraged many Democrats from voting. It is difficult to substantiate their claim, however.[14] Researchers who have studied the impact of the 1980 television projections on voting have found a small reduction in turnout in the West, but little evidence of vote switching or turnout bias toward or against the projected winner as a result of the early projections.[15]

The minimal effect of the election reporting on the outcome of the election seems to be related to the fact that relatively few people watch the broadcasts and then vote. Most people vote first and watch the returns later in the evening. Perhaps this pattern of voting and then watching or listening to the returns explains why George H. W. Bush's projected victory on the networks in 1988 before the polls closed on the West Coast did little to change the results in three out of four Pacific states (Washington, Oregon, and Hawaii) that voted for Michael Dukakis. Nonetheless, sensitivity to the criticism that early returns affect turnout and voting behavior led the networks to agree prior to the 1992 election not to project winners in any election within a state until its polls had closed. In states with different time zones, a majority of its polls have to close before winners would be projected.

The networks amended their pledge to make a national prediction in 1996 even as people were voting on the West Coast. Promptly at 9 PM EST, they forecast a Clinton victory. In anticipation of this early forecast, Republicans bitterly criticized the practice of "calling" the election before the polls had closed and warned of possible legislation to prevent it from happening again. No such legislation has been enacted, however, although congressional hearings were held.

Another early prediction controversy in which speed and accuracy collided occurred in 2000. Early in the evening of the election (7:50 PM EST), the television broadcast networks forecast a victory for Al Gore in Florida on the basis of exit polls even though residents in the central time zone living in the Florida Panhandle were still voting. The announcement elated

Democrats. However, as the evening wore on, a discrepancy became evident between the actual returns and the exit polls. On the basis of this discrepancy, CNN retracted its prediction of a Gore victory. The other networks quickly followed suit. At 2:16 AM EST, the Fox News channel declared Bush the winner on the basis of tabulated returns. Again, the other networks quickly followed.

Hearing the news, Vice President Gore called Governor George W. Bush to concede the election and was on his way to make a public announcement to his supporters. Before he did so, however, he learned that the election was still too close to call. Gore then telephoned Bush again and retracted his concession while the networks retracted their prediction of a Bush victory.[16] In the end, the closeness of the Florida vote, combined with the voiding of thousands of improperly punched ballots, precluded a valid exit poll prediction.

Despite the fact that the exit polling operation was overhauled after the 2000 election and Edison Research was conducting the poll, the results in 2004 were also controversial. The first release of the exit data at 12:59 PM showed Kerry with a small but statistically insignificant lead.[17] By midafternoon, however, his lead had jumped to 3 percent, a percentage that was statistically significant. Democrats were gleeful; Republicans were puzzled because their poll watchers were reporting very high turnouts in Republican districts. Reporters began drafting their Kerry victory stories. Although Kerry's lead in the exit polls diminished over the rest of the day and into the evening, and the final exit poll released at 1:33 AM confirmed Bush's popular and Electoral College wins, reporters and politicians were miffed at being misled.

Why would such a large sample of randomly selected voters be incorrect? Some poll takers complained that they were kept at a distance from the polling centers (as prescribed by state law to prevent electioneering at the polls) and thus had difficulty interviewing the requisite number of voters as well as adhering to the instructions determining which people to interview. Moreover, in the morning, Democrats, especially women voters, seemed more willing to complete the interview and then the requisite questionnaire than men, thereby skewing the results in Kerry's favor because women tend to vote more Democratic than men. The morning numbers may also have overrepresented certain areas, such as cities and close-in suburbs, which also tend to be more Democratic.

There are other problems with exit polls. An increasing number of people vote before election day. In 2004, approximately 22 percent of the electorate voted early; in 2008, that proportion had increased to over 30 percent. Early voting has required the exit poll to add a telephone survey to discern the demographic characteristics, attitudes, and voting behavior of these early voters. The time span between actual voting and the telephone interview affects the memory of respondents and the accuracy of the information they provide.

Paul Gronke's research indicates that "early voters are more partisan and live in areas with a higher average commute."[18] Other studies have found that these early voters tend to be older than election day voters.[19] (Table 9.3 reports the results of the exit polls in the past three presidential elections.)

INTERPRETING THE ELECTION RESULTS

In addition to predicting the results, the television networks and major newspapers also provide an instant analysis of results on election night and the morning after. This analysis, based primarily on exit poll data, relates voting decisions to the issue positions, ideological perspectives, and partisan preferences of the electorate. Patterns among demographic groups, issue stands, and electoral perceptions and choices are noted and used to explain why people voted for particular candidates.

Although exit polls present a detailed picture of the electorate on election day (see Table 9.3), they do not provide an explanation of how the campaign has affected the outcome of the election. To understand changes in public attitudes and opinions during the campaign, it is necessary to survey people over the course of the election cycle, asking the same questions. The nationwide polls conducted by major commercial polling organizations—such as Gallup, Zogby, the Pew Research Center, plus those designed for major news organizations—often repeat questions, but they do not do so with the same respondents. Two national surveys, the American National Election Studies (ANES), conducted by researchers at the Universities of Michigan and Stanford, and the National Annenberg Election Survey (NAES) do. They interview and reinterview many of the same people before and after the election. As a consequence, they can analyze opinion change during the campaign. The wealth of data that these surveys produce has allowed political scientists to construct theories of why people vote as they do.

MODELS OF VOTING BEHAVIOR

There are two basic models of voting behavior: the *prospective,* which emphasizes the issues and looks to the future, and the *retrospective,* which emphasizes the candidates and their parties and looks to the past results of their policies and actions.[20]

In the prospective voting model, voters compare their beliefs and policy preferences with those enunciated by the parties and their nominees. They make a determination of which party and which candidates espouse positions that are closer to their own and thus would more likely pursue those positions if elected. In other words, voters make a judgment on the prospects of obtaining future policies they desire based on the current positions of the candidates and their parties and the policies they promise to pursue.

To make a prospective judgment, voters must have discernible beliefs and opinions of their own; they must be able to differentiate the beliefs and opinions of the candidates from one another; and finally, voters must be able to make a judgment about which party and candidate is closer to their own views on the issues they deem most important.

If people were only concerned with a single issue, the choice might be easy. But alas there are usually multiple issues upon which the voters are interested and candidates and parties take positions. To simplify the task for voters, the issues are frequently bundled together by the parties and their nominees and given an ideological label. Since the 1980s, voters have no difficulty discerning the Democratic Party as more liberal and the Republican Party as more conservative. The issues have changed but the ideological orientation of the parties has not. In fact, it has become clearer. Thus people who think of themselves as conservative and would like the next government to pursue conservative policies tend to vote Republican and people who identify themselves as liberal tend to vote Democratic. Exit poll data in Table 9.3 indicate a high correlation between ideology and voting behavior.

Not everyone has an ideological orientation, however. There are many people who think of themselves as moderate, a plurality of people according to the 2008 exit poll. People who do not have strong ideological inclinations or whose views fall between the positions of the major-party candidates need to consider other factors in deciding how to vote.

Another way to make a voting decision is to evaluate current economic, social, and political conditions and determine which party is primarily responsible for them. People who determine how they are going to vote in this manner are making a retrospective judgment. History serves as a prologue for the future. Unlike the prospective voters who compare their policy preferences with those of the candidates running for office, retrospective voters make a decision on the basis of who was in power, what they achieved, and whether the outcome was good or bad.

If the economy is strong, society harmonious, and the nation secure and at peace, people assume that their leaders, particularly the president, must be doing a good job. If conditions are not good, then the president gets much of the blame.[21] Thus, the key question that voters ask themselves when making a retrospective evaluation is "Am I and my country better off now than before the party now in power and its presidential and vice presidential candidates won control of the White House?"

If an incumbent president or even vice president is running, then this retrospective judgment should be closely related to the voting decision, especially if the electorate sees the most important problems the country is facing as similar to those that occurred during the incumbent's term. If, however, there is no incumbent seeking reelection (such as in 1952 and 2008), then the retrospective judgment may be a little less relevant for voters, although partisanship continues to link the incumbent to the candidate of his party, whether that candidate likes it or not. John McCain stressed his independence when he said in one of the presidential debates, "Senator [Obama], I am not President Bush," but the Democrats and the news media continued to emphasize his Republican connection, and the electorate perceived it as well.

In both the prospective and retrospective models, partisanship is apt to be an important influence on the evaluations people make to arrive at their voting decision. As noted in Chapter 3, political attitudes are relatively stable, although they tend to be activated and can be modified over the course of an election cycle.[22] They also can be changed, but how quickly and under what circumstances has been subject to some debate.[23] A partisan orientation provides voters with a lens through which campaigns can be filtered, candidates and issues evaluated, and electoral judgments made.

In the retrospective model, partisanship itself is the consequence of evaluations of the past performance of parties. It therefore functions as a summary judgment of how the parties and the candidates have done and as a basis for anticipating how they will do in the future.[24] Partisans who make a retrospective evaluation are more apt to rate presidents of their party more favorably before, during, and after the election and those of the other party less favorably. They also tend to see themselves as closer to the positions of their candidate and party than to the opposition. And they believe and value those positions.

Since the identification people have with political parties is the most stable and resilient factor affecting the voting decision, it is considered to be the single most important long-term influence on voting. Orientations voters have toward the candidates and issues are short-term factors that fluctuate from election to election.

One of the most significant developments within the American political environment has been the growing polarization of the parties and their elected officials. This polarization has produced greater policy differences between the parties and more issue consistency within them. In reinforcing partisanship, ideology has also linked a collection of issue positions more tightly to political attitudes, making the issues less of an independent factor in determining election outcomes. In other words, the partisan prism through which most voters view the election is more compelling than it was two or three decades ago. That prism exerts more influence on their evaluation of the candidates, the issues, and subsequently, the voter's electoral choice.

EXPLAINING CONTEMPORARY PRESIDENTIAL ELECTIONS: 1952–2008

Since a majority of the electorate continues to identify with a political party or leans in a partisan direction, the candidate of the dominant party should have an advantage—all things being equal. But as we have noted throughout this book, the major parties are at rough parity with one another, although there are usually small, ongoing shifts in partisan identities and party images that occur between election cycles. As a consequence, all things are rarely equal. Candidates change, issues come and go, and the public mood changes in intensity and direction. Thus, it is important to understand how the electorate evaluates these changes, how people feel about the candidates, how they perceive and judge candidates and their issue stands, and how the electorate's perceptions and evaluations affect their voting decisions and the election outcomes.[25] The next section discusses the interplay of these components in presidential elections since 1952.

1952–1956: The Impact of Personality

In 1952, the Democrats were the dominant party, but the Republicans won the presidential election and gained a majority in both houses of Congress. The issues of that election—the fear of communism at home and abroad, the presence of corruption in high levels of government, and the United States involvement in the Korean War—benefited the GOP, as did the popularity of its presidential candidate, former General Dwight D. Eisenhower. These short-term factors offset the Democrats' longer-term, partisan advantage and enabled the Republicans to win.[26] The electorate saw the Republicans as better able to deal with the problems of fighting communism, promoting efficiency in government, and ending the war.[27]

President Eisenhower's reelection four years later was also a consequence of his personal popularity, not his party's. He was evaluated favorably by the voters, while his opponent, Adlai Stevenson, was not. The Republicans did not win control of Congress, however, as they had in 1952. Their failure to do so in 1956 testified to the continuing partisan advantage that the Democrats enjoyed among the American electorate at that time.

1960–1972: The Increasing Importance of Issues

Beginning in 1960, the issues of the campaign seemed to play a more important role in the election's outcome than they had since the New Deal realignment. Noneconomic policy issues undercut the impact of partisanship forged on economic ties. In general, these issues contributed to the defection of Democrats from their party's presidential candidates in 1960, 1968, and 1972 and to defections by Republicans (and southern Democrats) in 1964.

John Kennedy's Catholicism was a primary concern to many voters in 1960 and helps explain the closeness of that election as a whole. Despite the Democrats' dominance within the electorate, Kennedy received only 115,000 more votes than Richard Nixon, 0.3 percent more of the total vote. Kennedy's Catholicism cost him votes in the heavily Protestant South. Outside the South, Kennedy actually picked up Democratic votes because of the massive support he received from Catholics and the concentration of this religious group in the cities in the large industrial states.[28]

Although Kennedy barely won in 1960, Lyndon Johnson won by a landslide four years later. Short-term factors contributed to the magnitude of the Johnson victory.[29] Barry Goldwater was perceived as a minority candidate within a minority party, ideologically to the right of most Republicans. Moreover, he did not enjoy a favorable public image as Johnson did. Policy attitudes also favored the Democrats, even in foreign affairs. Goldwater's militant anticommunism scared many voters. They saw Johnson as the peace candidate.

Two groups of voters began to change their voting preferences and eventually their partisan orientation in the mid 1960s. White southern Democrats, opposed to their party's civil rights initiatives, cast a majority of their votes for Goldwater, and moderate, northern Republicans, who disagreed with Goldwater's conservative policy positions, voted for Johnson. For the first time since the New Deal, five states in the solidly Democratic South (plus Goldwater's home state of Arizona) went Republican, auguring the major regional realignment that was to occur in the elections that followed.

In addition to civil rights, a new set of foreign policy issues also split the Democrats in 1968. The Vietnam War and the unrest and protests on college campuses that followed from it increased Democratic defections as that party's share of the vote declined 19 percent. The Republican vote, however, increased by only 4 percent. The third-party candidacy of George Wallace accounted for much of the difference between Democratic defections and the Republican vote. Wallace's support was issue based. Although he did not have much personal appeal, his policy positions did, particularly among white southerners, young new voters, and some blue-collar workers.[30] Had Wallace not run, the Republican presidential vote undoubtedly would have been larger because Nixon was the second choice of most Wallace voters.

The results of the 1968 presidential election thus deviated from the partisan alignment of the electorate. A significant number of voters had grievances against the Democratic Party and against Lyndon Johnson's conduct of the Vietnam War. Some of these voters supported Wallace and, to a lesser extent, Nixon. The Democratic candidate, Hubert H. Humphrey, suffered accordingly. A decline in the intensity of partisanship and a growth in the number of Independents contributed to issue voting. Had it not been for the Democrats' large partisan advantage and the overwhelming African American vote that Humphrey received, the presidential election would not have been nearly so close.

The trend away from partisan presidential voting for the majority party's candidate continued in 1972. With a nominee who was ideologically and personally unpopular, the Democrats suffered their worst presidential defeat since 1920. Richard Nixon enjoyed a better public image than George McGovern. Nixon was seen as the stronger of the two presidential candidates. These perceptions, positive for Nixon and negative for McGovern, contributed to Nixon's large victory in the 1972 election. More of the electorate saw the Republican standard-bearer as closer to their own positions than the Democratic candidate. McGovern was perceived as liberal on all issues and ideologically to the left of his own party. Democrats defected in considerable numbers; Republicans voted for their nominee.[31]

1976–1996: The Evaluation of Performance

Issue differences narrowed in 1976. Neither Gerald Ford nor Jimmy Carter emphasized the social and cultural concerns that played a large role in the previous presidential contest. Both focused their attention on trust in government and on domestic economic matters. In the wake of Watergate and a recession that occurred during the Ford presidency, it is not surprising that these issues worked to the Democrats' advantage. Carter was also helped by a slightly more favorable personal assessment than that given to Ford.[32] The latter's association with the Nixon administration, highlighted in the public mind by his pardon of the former president, his difficult struggle to win his own party's nomination, and his seeming inability to find a solution to the country's economic woes adversely affected his presidential image.[33]

With sociocultural issues muted and the Vietnam War over, economic concerns divided the electorate along partisan lines. This division put the candidate of the majority party back in the driver's seat. Carter won primarily because he was a Democrat and secondarily because his personal evaluation was more favorable than Ford's. Carter was also helped by being a southerner. He received the electoral votes of every southern state except Virginia. In an otherwise divided Electoral College, this southern support proved to be decisive.

When Carter sought reelection four years later, being a Democrat, an incumbent, and a southerner was not sufficient to win. Poor performance ratings overcame the advantage that partisanship and incumbency normally bring to a president of the majority party. In 1976, Carter was judged on the basis of his potential *for* office, and he beat Ford. In 1980, Carter was judged on the basis of his performance *in* office, and he lost badly to challenger Ronald Reagan. Carter's vote fell behind his 1976 percentages in every single state, and in approximately half the states, it dropped at least 10 percent. Why did he lose so badly?

Personal evaluations of Carter and assessments of his policies were not nearly as favorable as they had been four years earlier. Personal assessments of Ronald Reagan were also low, but in contrast to Carter's, they improved over the course of the campaign. Economic conditions—high inflation, large-scale unemployment, and the decreasing competitiveness and productivity of American industry—worked to the advantage of the party out of power. For the first time in many years, the Republicans were seen as the party better able to invigorate the economy, return prosperity, and lower inflation.

In addition, dissatisfaction with the conduct of foreign affairs culminating in frustration over the Soviet Union's invasion of Afghanistan, and especially in the failure of the United States to obtain the release of American hostages held in Iran, contributed to Carter's negative evaluation and to changing public attitudes toward defense spending and foreign affairs. In 1980, most Americans supported increased military expenditures, a position with which Reagan was closely identified, combined with a less conciliatory approach and a tougher, more militant posture in dealing with problems abroad. These issues, together with the negative assessment of Carter as president, explain why the Democratic candidate lost in 1980.

John Anderson, a former Republican member of Congress, also ran in that election as an Independent. A protest candidate who drew equally from Democrats and Republicans, Anderson was unable to attract a solid core of supporters. Nor was he able to differentiate his policy positions sufficiently from Carter's and Reagan's to generate an issue-oriented vote. In the end, his failure to win any electoral votes and only 6.5 percent of the popular vote demonstrated the resiliency of the major parties and the legitimacy that their labels provided candidates for national office.

In summary, in 1980, Carter was repudiated by the voters because of their negative retrospective evaluation of his presidency. Reagan appeared to offer greater potential for leadership.[34]

Four years later, voters rewarded President Reagan for a job well done with a huge victory. It is interesting to note that ideology did not work to Reagan's advantage in either 1980 or 1984. It was conditions more than Reagan's positions on the issues that apparently influenced the electorate's judgment. A resurgent economy, strengthened military, and renewed feelings of national pride brought the president broad support. Although voters agreed with Mondale more than with Reagan on many of the specific problems confronting the nation, they viewed Reagan as the person better able to deal with those issues. Leadership was a dominant concern. Voters evaluated Reagan's leadership skills much more highly than Mondale's. It was a retrospective vote. The electorate supported Reagan primarily for his performance in office. In other words, they voted *for* him in 1984 just as they had voted *against* Carter four years earlier.

The trend of retrospective voting continued in 1988 with the election of Reagan's vice president, George H. W. Bush. Bush won because the electorate evaluated the Reagan administration positively, associated Bush with that administration, and concluded that he, not Michael Dukakis, would be better able and more likely to maintain the Reagan revolution and the good times people associated with Reagan's presidency.[35] That Bush was not as favorably evaluated as Reagan had been four years earlier partially accounts for his narrower victory.[36]

Partisanship affected voting behavior more in 1988 than it had in any election since 1960.[37] In the past, a high correlation between partisan identities and voting behavior worked to the Democrats' advantage. In 1988, it did not. An increase in Republican allegiances and a decline in Democratic support produced an almost evenly divided electorate. There were slightly more Democrats but greater turnout and less defection among Republicans. In the end, neither candidate enjoyed a partisan advantage, but among Independents, Bush held a solid lead.

Ideological orientations worked to reinforce partisan voting patterns in 1988, with Republican candidate George H. W. Bush winning overwhelmingly among Republicans and conservatives, and Democratic candidate Dukakis doing almost as well among Democrats and liberals. The problem for Dukakis, however, and any liberal for that matter, was that the proportion of people who considered themselves liberal had declined substantially. In 1988, almost twice as many voters considered themselves conservative than liberal.

Four years later, with the economy in recession, budget and trade deficits rising, and layoffs of white-collar managers and blue-collar workers dominating the news, Bush was judged on his own performance in office, and that judgment was negative. He received only 37.4 percent of the popular vote in a three-person contest and 168 electoral votes (only 31 percent of the total). His 1992 vote declined among every population group.

Clinton was clearly helped by his partisan affiliation and his southern heritage in 1992. With slightly more Democrats in the electorate than Republicans, Clinton received the votes of three out of four Democrats. For the first time since 1964, Republican defections actually exceeded those of Democrats. Turnout, traditionally seen to advantage the Republicans, was neutralized in 1992 with Democratic turnout up and Republican turnout down.

Still, Clinton's partisan advantage could have been offset by a lopsided vote of Independents against him, but they divided their support among the three candidates (the third being Ross Perot), giving Clinton a plurality of their vote (38 percent) with Perot and Bush splitting the rest. Nor did ideology work to the incumbent president's advantage as it had in previous elections. Although liberals and conservatives continued to support, respectively, Democratic and Republican candidates, Perot cut into both groups, dropping Bush's support among conservatives about 15 percent from his 1988 level. Moreover, Clinton did comparably better among moderates than previous Democratic candidates, substantially leading Bush and Perot among self-identified moderates.

Although Bush was credited with a successful foreign policy, the lower salience of foreign policy issues in 1992 undercut Bush's achievements in this policy realm and even served to highlight his inattention to domestic matters. The economy was the principal issue and Clinton its principal beneficiary.[38] Although he received only 43 percent of the vote, his popular vote margin over the president was 5.6 percent. In the Electoral College, he won thirty-two states and the District of Columbia, for a total of 370 votes.

By 1996, domestic concerns were still dominant, but the economy was stronger, crime had decreased, and the nation remained at peace—all conditions that favored the incumbent. Voters responded accordingly, reelecting the Democratic president but also a Republican congressional majority. Clinton's popular and electoral vote exceeded his 1992 totals, although the regional composition of his vote was essentially the same as it had been four years earlier.

Despite misgivings about some aspects of the president's character, notably his personal integrity, honesty, and willingness to stand up for his beliefs, voters saw Clinton as more caring, more in touch with the times, and more visionary than his Republican opponent. But it was the nation's economy, not the president's character, that proved to be the critical factor in determining the outcome of the election. Those who perceived themselves to be better off (about one-third of the electorate) supported the president; those who saw themselves as worse off (about 20 percent) supported his opponent.

In short, the 1996 election was a referendum on the Clinton presidency, and Clinton won. Not only did the electorate evaluate his first term favorably but they saw the president as more capable of understanding and handling the challenges of the 1990s and building a bridge to the twenty-first century than either of his opponents.

2000–2008: Party Polarization and Personal Performance

Although the 2000 election could have been another referendum on the Clinton presidency, it was not for many voters. Vice President Al Gore's decision to emphasize the differences between himself and Governor George W. Bush rather than contrast the economic, social, and international conditions at the end of 2000 with those of 1992, the last time the Republicans controlled the White House and a Bush was in the presidency, focused the attention of the electorate on the future, not the past. Encouraging voters to make more of a prospective choice than a retrospective judgment turned out to be a poor strategic decision for the vice president. Gore's proportion of the Democratic vote dropped below Clinton's. By severing his ties with the Clinton administration, Gore hurt his own candidacy.[39]

Nonetheless, many of the same voting patterns emerged in 2000 that were evident in previous presidential elections, particularly during the 1990s (refer to Table 9.3). The electorate was clearly and evenly divided. Parity between the major parties contributed to this division. Partisans overwhelmingly supported their party's nominee, while Independents were almost evenly split between Bush and Gore.

A large, persistent gender gap increased in size to 11 percent in 2000, with a majority of women supporting Gore and Lieberman and a majority of men backing Bush and Cheney. Other groups within each party's electoral coalitions also voted in record proportions and along party lines, with racial and ethnic minorities and organized labor voting Democratic and Christian fundamentalists and evangelicals voting Republican. There was also a sectarian-secular divide; people who attended religious services more regularly voted more Republican than those who attended less regularly or not at all. The Democrats did better in the Northeast and Pacific Coast and the Republicans in the South and Rocky Mountain areas and in the Midwest.

Third-party candidates Ralph Nader and Pat Buchanan attracted much less attention and support than in the years when Perot ran on the Reform Party ticket. Neither one of them had funds that were comparable to Perot's in 1992 or even 1996. However, the closeness of the 2000 election enhanced the influence of these third-party candidacies, especially Nader's.[40] Had Nader not been on the Florida ballot, Gore would have probably won that state and thereby the Electoral College. In the exit polls conducted on election day, 70 percent of those who said that they voted for Nader indicated that they would still have voted had he not run. Of this group, Gore was preferred over Bush by a margin of two to one.

The nation's bitter political divisions that emerged during the Clinton presidency continued through the 2000 election and fueled the political controversy over the Florida vote. Were it not for the strong economy, the general contentment of the society, and people's optimism about the future, these divisions might have generated the same level of intensity within the population as they had among the political elites in Washington during the 1990s. Fortunately, however, they did not, and the electorate was able to get over its angst from the Florida vote controversy as the new president took office and began to exercise power. Politics returned to normal until the terrorist attacks of September 11, 2001.

The election of 2004 extended and reinforced most of the cleavages within the body politic. The major parties remained at parity with one another, divided by ideology. The president was viewed as a highly polarizing figure; Republicans overwhelmingly supported him, and Democrats overwhelmingly disapproved of his presidency. With the proportion of Independents shrinking and the intensity of party allegiances increasing, the election outcome turned on efforts to maximize partisan bases and persuade the relatively few undecided whom to vote for. The Republicans bested the Democrats in the turnout contest in the key battleground states, and Republican partisans were slightly more loyal to their party's nominees than were Democratic partisans to theirs.

Familiar cleavages within the electorate on religion, marital status, and gender persisted although the gender gap was reduced. The president received a larger proportion of the vote of married women than he did four years earlier, thereby increasing his proportion of the female vote.[41] The religious divide remained, however, with the level of religious activity being the key differential. The more regularly people went to their house of worship or engaged in congregation-related activities, the more likely they were to vote Republican.[42] Minority racial and ethnic groups continued to support the Democratic candidate. African Americans voted overwhelmingly for Kerry. Hispanics also favored the Democrat but by a lesser amount.[43]

The reasons for Bush's victory are more speculative than the findings about who voted for him. The president and his supporters benefited from a strong campaign that activated and extended the Republican base, undercut his opponent's leadership image, and took advantage of the incumbency factor. The ability of the president to focus public attention on the terrorism issue combined with perceptions of his strong leadership following the attacks on September 11, 2001, also worked to Bush's advantage. Nonetheless, the popular vote was close and the red state (Republican)–blue state (Democratic) division persisted. Only three states—Iowa, New Hampshire, and New Mexico—switched their presidential vote between 2000 and 2004.

President Bush ran into more political difficulty in his second term than in his first. His domestic policy initiative to privatize Social Security failed; his administration's response to Hurricane Katrina was late and ineffectual; public opinion turned against the war in Iraq; and the economy was faltering, the budget deficit was getting larger, and during the 2008 election, there was a financial crisis. As the 2008 election campaign got underway, the president's approval ratings dropped to the low 30s. On election day, 72 percent of the population disapproved of the job he was doing.

Beginning in 2006 and continuing through 2008, a majority of Americans believed that the Democrats would do a better job than the Republicans of keeping the country prosperous.[44] Democratic partisans increased by 3 percent during this period. A larger proportion of people also identified as Independents while the Republican base shrank.[45] All of these factors worked to the Democratic presidential candidate's advantage in the 2008 election. Add to the unsatisfactory economic conditions and the partisan shifts that accompanied those conditions, the grassroots support Obama was able to generate, the large war chest he had raised, and the more disciplined, thematic campaign he mounted, his electoral victory was not surprising. He won 52.9 percent of the popular vote (69,456,897) and 67.8 percent of the electoral vote (365).

Although Obama's election was described as historic—the first African American to be elected president—trends evident in past elections persisted. New voters, particularly those under thirty, favored the Democratic candidate by more than two to one. So did Hispanic voters. The gender gap, which had been 11 percent in 2000 and 5 percent in 2004, expanded to 13 percent in 2008, with 56 percent of women voting for Obama. The male vote was evenly divided, although white males favored McCain by about 5 percent.

The Republican lock on certain states was also broken with Democratic victories in Virginia, North Carolina, Colorado, and Indiana. Obama won all the competitive battleground states in the Midwest with the exception of Missouri. He won Florida, all the states in the Northeast and middle Atlantic region with the exception of West Virginia, and the three states on the Pacific Coast. Partisan and ideological voting patterns, evident since the 1980s, continued although conservatives voted slightly more Democratic in 2008 than in the two previous presidential elections. It was the vote Obama received from moderates and Independents that made the difference, however, and contributed to his substantial victory. (See Table 9.3.)

TABLE 9.3 | PORTRAIT OF THE AMERICAN ELECTORATE, 2000–2008 (IN PERCENTAGES)

		2000			2004			2008		
Percentage of 2008		**Bush**	**Gore**	**Nader**	**Bush**	**Kerry**	**Other**	**Obama**	**McCain**	**Other**
	Total Vote	48%	48%	3%	51%	48%	1%	53	46	1
Gender										
47	Men	53	42	3	55	44	1	49	48	3
53	Women	43	54	2	48	51	1	56	43	1
Race and Ethnicity										
74	Whites	54	42	3	58	41	1	43	55	2
13	Blacks	9	90	1	11	88	1	95	4	1
9	Hispanics	35	62	2	44	53	3	67	31	2
2	Asians	41	55	3	44	56	–	62	35	3
3	Others							66	31	3
Marital Status										
66	Married	53	44	2	57	42	1	47	52	1
34	Unmarried	38	57	4	40	58	1	65	33	2
Age										
18	18–29 Years	46	48	5	45	54	1	66	32	2
29	30–44 Years	49	48	2	53	46	1	52	46	2
37	45–64 Years	49	48	2	52	47	1	50	49	1
16	65+ Years	47	50	2	52	47	0	45	53	2

Education										
4	Not H.S. Grad	38	59	1	49	50	0	63	35	2
20	H.S. Grad	49	48	1	52	47	1	52	46	2
31	Some College	51	45	3	54	46	0	51	47	2
28	College Grad	51	45	3	52	46	1	50	48	2
17	Postgraduate	44	52	3	44	55	1	58	40	2
Religion										
54	Protestant*	56	42	2	59	40	0	45	54	1
27	Catholic	47	50	2	52	47	1	54	45	1
2	Jewish	19	79	1	25	74	–	78	21	1
6	Something Else	28	62	1	23	74	1	73	22	5
12	None	30	61	7	31	67	2	75	23	2
Labor Unions										
21	Union Household	37	59	3	40	59	1	59	39	2
Income										
6	Under $15,000	37	57	4	36	63	1	73	25	2
12	$15,000–$29,999	41	54	3	42	57	1	60	37	3
19	$30,000–$49,999	48	49	2	49	50	1	55	43	2
21	$50,000–$74,999	51	46	2	56	43	1	48	49	3
15	$75,000–$99,999	52	45	2	55	45	0	51	48	1
14	$100,000–$149,999	54†	43†	2†	57	42	1	48	51	1
6	$150,000–$199,999				58	42	0	48	50	2
6	$200,000+				63	35	1	52	46	2

continued

TABLE 9.3 | PORTRAIT OF THE AMERICAN ELECTORATE, 2000–2008 (IN PERCENTAGES) *continued*

		2000			2004			2008		
Percentage of 2008		**Bush**	**Gore**	**Nader**	**Bush**	**Kerry**	**Other**	**Obama**	**McCain**	**Other**
Family's Financial Situation is										
24	Better Today	36	61	2	80	19	1	37	60	2
34	Same Today	60	35	3	49	50	1	45	53	2
42	Worse Today	63	33	4	20	79	1	71	28	1
Region										
21	Northeast	39	56	3	43	56	1	59	40	1
24	Midwest	49	48	2	51	48	1	54	44	2
32	South	55	43	1	58	42	0	45	54	1
23	West	46	48	4	49	50	2	57	40	3
Party										
32	Republicans	91	8	1	93	6	1	9	90	1
29	Independents	47	45	6	48	49	3	52	44	4
39	Democrats	11	86	2	11	89	0	89	10	1
Ideology										
22	Liberals	13	80	6	13	85	2	89	10	1
44	Moderates	44	52	2	45	54	1	60	39	1
34	Conservatives	81	17	1	84	15	1	20	78	2

Employment Status										
65	Work Full-Time for Pay	48	49	2	53	45	1	55	44	1
35	Do Not Work Full-Time	48	47	3	51	49	0	50	48	2
New Voters										
11	First-Time Voters	43	52	4	46	53	1	69	30	1
Incumbency Evaluation										
27	Approve of Incumbent's Performance	20	77	2	90	9	1	10	89	1
71	Disapprove of Incumbent's Performance	88	9	2	6	93	1	67	31	2
Most Important Issue for Voting										
7	Energy Policy (2008)/ Education (2004)				26	73	1	50	46	4
10	War in Iraq				26	73	1	59	39	2
63	The Economy				18	80	1	53	44	3
9	Terrorism				86	14	0	13	86	1
9	Health Care				23	77	0	73	26	1

*Includes all Protestants.

†For the 2000 election, these numbers represent the response for "Income $100,000 or more," as the last three income categories were not split out at that time.

Source: General Exit Poll in 2000 conducted by VNS, a consortium of the major news organizations-ABC, CBS, CNN, FOX, NBC, the Associated Press; General Exit Poll in 2004 and 2008 conducted by Edison Media Research and Mitofsky International for the National Election Pool and found on the Web sites of major news organizations following the election.

The religious division remained; a majority of Protestants voted for the Republican candidate while Catholics, closely divided in 2000 and 2004, voted more heavily Democratic due in large part to the increase of Hispanics in the electorate. Jews and most other religious groups remained strongly Democratic. For the first time, the exit poll included a category of "none" when voters were asked to identify their religion. Of the 12 percent who checked this box, 75 percent voted for Obama, continuing evidence of a sectarian-secular divide.

The electorate made a retrospective judgment in 2008. More than three out of four voters thought that the country was "seriously off on the wrong track" and most blamed the Bush administration for the unsatisfactory conditions. People wanted change, and they saw Obama as the candidate most likely to initiate and achieve it. There was some prospective voting. The electorate was closer to McCain than Obama on the issues; however, the high level of dissatisfaction directed toward the Bush administration and the deteriorating economy proved to be more influential on the election outcome than policy preferences.[46] Those preferences, however, were to become a problem for Obama when he pursued his government-oriented domestic policy agenda.

CONVERTING ELECTORAL CHOICE INTO PUBLIC POLICY

It is not unusual for the meaning of the election to be ambiguous. The reasons that people vote for presidents vary. Some do so because of their party affiliation, some because of issue stands, and some because of their assessment of the candidates' potential and their past performance. For most people, a combination of factors contributes to their voting decision. That combination makes it difficult to discern exactly what the electorate means, desires, or envisions by its electoral choice.

The President's Imprecise Mandate

The president is rarely given a clear mandate for governing. For a mandate to exist, the presidential candidates must take discernible and compatible policy positions and the electorate must vote for them because of those positions. Moreover, the results of the election must be consistent. If there is a discrepancy between the popular and the electoral vote, or if one party wins the White House and another wins the Congress, it is difficult for a president to claim a mandate.

Few elections meet the criteria for a mandate. Presidential candidates usually take a range of policy positions, often waffle on a few highly divisive and emotionally charged issues, may differ from their party and its other candidates for national office in their priorities and their issue stands, and rarely have coattails long enough to sweep congressional candidates into office. In fact, the presidential candidates tend to run behind the congressional candidates of their own party in those candidates' legislative districts.

Mandates may not exist, but that has not prevented presidents from claiming them. They do so largely for political reasons. Winning a large popular and electoral vote and gaining control of Congress creates opportunities and expectations that a newly elected president might want to seize to change national policy. Such an incentive would be enhanced if the victor defeated an incumbent.

Professor Patricia H. Conley argues that the elections of 1952, 1964, and 1980 encouraged the winners to claim a policy mandate. Eisenhower's campaign promise to go to Korea, Goldwater's strong opposition to Johnson's domestic legislative program, and Reagan's rejection of the ideology, policies, and programs of the Carter administration provided the electorate with a clear choice of which policy direction it preferred. The winners' sizable victories were interpreted as mandates for these presidents to pursue their policy orientation and achieve their stated goals.[47]

The election results in 1948 and 1992 were not quite as clear, according to Conley, but they still offered Truman and Clinton opportunities to claim a mandate and use it as evidence of popular support.[48] Democratic majorities in both houses of Congress furthered the claim that the voters had made a policy choice in their electoral decisions. Clinton's failure to achieve many of his promises, such as to cut middle-class taxes, stimulate the economy, "change welfare as we know it," reform the nation's health care system, and eliminate discrimination on the basis of sexual orientation, shows the flip side of a mandate claim—the magnification of failure if expectations are not met.

George W. Bush was careful not to claim a mandate in 2000 as he pursued his campaign promises. However, prior to September 11, 2001, he had achieved only one legislative campaign promise—a large tax cut. After his reelection in 2004, however, the president expressed more confidence. At a press conference held two days after his reelection, Bush said:

> . . . when you win there is a feeling that the people have spoken and embraced your point of view. And that's what I intend to tell the Congress. That I made it clear what I intend to do as the president. . . . I've earned capital in this election. And I'm going to spend it for what I told the people I'd spend it on, which is, you've heard, the agenda: Social Security and tax reform, moving this economy forward, education, fighting and winning the war on terror.[49]

But did the people embrace the president's point of view on Social Security, tax reform, and the economy? Did he really have more political capital? Data collected from the exit polls and postelection surveys reveal a mixed electoral message at best. On the issues such as fighting the war on terror and supporting family values, the electorate expressed more confidence in Bush than Kerry; on the economy and a range of other domestic issues, voters said that they had more confidence in Kerry. Neither Social Security nor tax reform was cited as a principal reason for voting for Bush.

Confusing hope with fact, claiming a mandate when none exists, contending that the electorate supports most or all of the winner's policy agenda, and assuming that members of Congress will dutifully follow a president's lead are fraught with danger, as Bush found out in his second term and Obama in his first. Even when there is electoral support for specific policies, that support can wane quickly in the face of unexpected events, changing conditions, and shifts in public sentiment.

Take health care reform, for example. Two-thirds of the electorate in 2008 indicated they were worried about being able to afford the health care services they needed;[50] 54 percent saw it as a responsibility of the federal government to make sure that all Americans have health care coverage.[51] With a high percentage of Democrats and the president personally favoring health care reform, Obama pursued and achieved his initiative. But public support declined, even before the legislation was enacted, with a plurality opposing the legislation.[52] Did the president really have a mandate to reform health care?

Presidents must adapt to situational and opinion changes or their job approval ratings and their political influence will suffer. Bill Clinton and Barack Obama found this out in their first two years in office. Their stimulus and health care programs clashed with growing public concerns about big government and budget deficits. Until their policies produced results, and they modified their government-oriented agendas, they were in trouble.

In short, elections provide a window of opportunity for presidents but not much more than that. And the time frame for that opportunity may be short. The longer the period after the election, the less the election will serve as a guide to priorities and policy decisions for the government.

CAMPAIGN PROMISES AND PRESIDENTIAL PERFORMANCE

What presidential candidates promise and parties pledge in their platforms matters because elected officials try to redeem their promises. If they did not, their credibility would be challenged. Political scientist Jeff Fishel found that from 1960 to 1984, presidents "submitted legislation or signed executive orders that are broadly consistent with about two-thirds of their campaign pledges."[53] Of the more than 500 promises candidate Barack Obama made in his 2008 election campaign, he had kept 132 of them, broken 28, compromised on 41, had 220 in the works, and was stalled on 82 by the end of his second year in office, according to Politifact.com, a Web site maintained by the *St. Petersburg Times* that tracks the president's promises and performance.[54]

Although these figures do not reveal the importance of promises, their scope, or their impact, they do suggest that, in general, campaign platforms and candidate pledges are taken seriously by those in power. They provide a foundation from which an administration's early policy initiatives emanate.

EXPECTATIONS AND LEADERSHIP

When campaigning, candidates also try to create an aura of leadership, conveying such attributes as assertiveness, decisiveness, compassion, and integrity. Kennedy promised to get the country moving, Johnson to continue the New Frontier–Great Society programs, Nixon to "bring us together," and George H. W. Bush to maintain the Reagan policies that produced peace and prosperity for the eight previous years but do so in "a kinder and gentler" way. In 1992, Clinton pledged policy change in a moderate direction and an end to gridlock between Congress and the presidency; in 1996, he promised to build a bridge to the twenty-first century. In 2000, George W. Bush promised to defuse the strident partisan political climate in Washington, and in 2004, to "do whatever it takes" to win the war on terror. Barack Obama promised to change policy and politics in his 2008 campaign and conveyed a "yes we can" optimism that with public support he would be able to achieve these changes.

These promises created performance expectations. In the 1976 election, Jimmy Carter heightened these expectations by his constant reference to the strong, decisive leadership he intended to exercise as president. His decline in popularity stemmed in large part from his failure to meet these leadership expectations. When George W. Bush, reelected in large part because voters saw him as a stronger leader than his Democratic opponent, did not exercise such leadership in the aftermath of Hurricane Katrina, his job approval suffered significantly. Barack Obama was thinking of the expectations he created and the short time frame the public would give him to meet them when he said in his election victory speech at Grant Park in Chicago, "The road ahead will be long. Our climb will be steep. We may not get there in one year or even one term, but America—I have never been more hopeful than I am tonight that we will get there."[55]

All new administrations, and to some extent, most reelected ones, face diverse and often contradictory desires. By their ambiguity, candidates encourage voters to see what they want to see and believe what they want to believe. Disillusionment naturally sets in once a president begins to make decisions. Political scientist John E. Mueller has referred to the disappointment that people may experience with a president as "the coalitions of minorities variable." In explaining declines in popularity, Mueller notes that presidents' decisions inevitably alienate parts of the coalition that elected them. This alienation can produce a drop in popularity over time, although as the Reagan and Clinton presidencies demonstrate, such a drop is not inevitable, if good times prevail.[56]

The campaign's emphasis on personal and institutional leadership also inflates performance expectations. By creating the aura of assertiveness, decisiveness, and potency, candidates help shape what the public anticipates they will do in office. Most presidents contribute to the decline in their own popularity by promising more than they can deliver. The question is, can the promise of leadership be conveyed during the campaign without creating unrealistic and unattainable expectations for the new president? For most candidates, especially challengers, the answer clearly seems to be "no."

THE ELECTORAL COALITION AND GOVERNING

Not only does the selection process inflate performance expectations and create a set of diverse policy goals but also it may decrease the president's power to achieve them. Moreover, the anti-Washington, antigovernment mood of the electorate, evident since the 1980s, has given outsiders, who are less experienced in national politics and may as a result be less able to meet the demands of the office when they first assume it, an electoral advantage. Carter in 1976, Clinton in 1992, and Obama in 2008 made much of the fact that they did not owe their nomination to the power brokers within their own party.

But even an experienced Washington hand would face difficulties. The political muscle of the White House has been weakened by the growth of autonomous state and congressional electoral systems; the proliferation of well-organized, well-funded, and well-led interest groups that pursue their own policy goals; and the decentralization and compartmentalization of power within the government.

Presidential candidates begin their quest for office largely on their own. They essentially designate themselves to run. They create their own organizations, choose professionals to run them, mount their own campaigns, and make their own promises. So do most members of Congress. Moreover, the coattails that tied party partisans to the winning presidential candidate have all but dissipated. Members of Congress can choose to follow the president's lead or choose not to do so; either way, it is their partisan constituency that will decide their fate, not the president.

To win elections, presidential candidates have to mobilize a broad constituency. Nonparty groups play a large role in that mobilization process; they run campaigns within campaigns—contributing and spending money, communicating with their members and sympathizers, and turning out the vote. But they do so with strings attached. They encourage candidates to take policy positions they favor and, if elected, to pursue policies they advocate. Presidents who deviate from their campaign agenda do so at the risk of alienating these support groups. The interest groups' struggle enlarges the arena of policy making, raises the political stakes, and contributes to the multiplicity of forces that converge on most presidential decisions. They limit a president's policy options.

Presidential campaigns encourage candidates to promise new programs and project an image of leadership. Normally, candidates indicate what they will do if elected, but rarely do they add the caveat "if Congress is willing to do so, if the bureaucracy follows my lead, or if the courts deem it constitutional." There is a disconnect between the campaign promises and leadership images of those who run for the presidency and the reality of the American constitutional system, which divides powers to prevent any one institution from dictating public policy on its own.

SUMMARY

Americans are fascinated by presidential elections. They want to know who will win, why the successful candidate has won, and what the election portends for the next four years. Their fascination stems from four interrelated factors about elections: they are dramatic, decisive, participatory, and affect future political leadership, public policy, and coalition building.

Using past elections as a guide, political scientists have tried to construct models to anticipate how the electorate will react to economic, political, and, to a lesser extent, social conditions. The models provide formulas for calculating the percentage of the vote the winning candidate is likely to receive on the basis of a combination of quantifiable indicators such as per capita income, level of employment, rate of inflation, popularity of the president, and the number of terms the president's party has controlled the White House. These models have been reasonably accurate, although they overestimated the size of Gore's popular vote in 2000 and Bush's in 2004. But the United States does not elect a president by direct popular vote. And campaign strategies are based on the politics of the Electoral College. Campaigns matter, more so when environmental factors do not overwhelmingly favor one candidate over another.

To discern how campaigns affect the electorate, researchers monitor public opinion over the course of an election. They do so by analyzing data from national and state opinion polls of likely voters. Polls are also important to candidates for discerning what to emphasize and how to prioritize, articulate, and target their policy and personal appeals. National opinion polls have become fairly accurate measures of the public mood and candidate preferences at the time the polls are taken. They provide data that can be employed to help explain the meaning of an election: the issues that are most salient, the positions that are most popular, and the hopes and expectations that are initially directed toward the elected leaders of government.

The personality of the candidates, the issues of the campaign, and the evaluation of the administration in power have dominated recent elections and the voting decisions of the electorate. Singularly and together, these factors, as seen through the prism of partisanship, explain the outcome of the vote. In 1960, it was Kennedy's Catholic religion that seemed to account for the closeness of the popular vote despite the large Democratic majority in the electorate. In 1964, it was Goldwater's uncompromising ideological and issue positions that helped provide Johnson with an overwhelming victory in all areas but the deep South. In 1968, it was the accumulation of grievances against the Democrats that spurred the Wallace candidacy and resulted in Nixon's triumph. In 1972, ideology, issues, and the public's perception of McGovern's incompetence split the Democratic Party and culminated in Nixon's reelection landslide. In 1976, however, partisanship was reinforced by issue, ideological, and personal evaluations to the benefit of the majority party's nominee, Jimmy Carter. Dissatisfaction with Carter's performance in 1980 and satisfaction with Reagan's in 1984 overcame the Democrats' decreasing numerical advantage within the electorate, leading voters to cast their ballots for Reagan as the person they thought would be best qualified to lead. By 1988, the Democrats appeared to lose their partisan advantage entirely. The retrospective evaluation of the Reagan years gave the incumbent vice president an advantage that his campaign maximized.

In a certain sense, the 1992 election was a rerun of 1980. The incumbent was rejected on the grounds that his performance in dealing with the nation's most pressing issue, the economy, was unsatisfactory. In choosing between his two opponents, the public voted for Clinton primarily because of his partisan affiliation. Perot ran a strong race, but third-party candidates are disadvantaged because the electorate does not think that they can win, a perception that has its roots in the operation of the Electoral College system and the dominance of the two major parties. If the 1992 election was a rejection of George H. W. Bush, the 1996 election marked the approval of Bill Clinton. Helped by a strong economy, a skilled campaign, and effective use of the presidential office, Clinton augmented his partisan support from Democrats with a successful appeal to moderates and to independent voters.

Partisan divisions, issue differences, and mixed performance evaluations of the Clinton presidency carried over into the 2000 election, although the focus tended to be more on future policies and leadership than on past performance. The electorate was evenly divided between the major parties. Disputes over the vote count and the discrepancy between the popular and electoral vote heightened these partisan divisions, clouded the election results, and delayed the designation of a president-elect.

The 2004 election revealed the cleavages evident since the 1980s. The parties remained evenly divided with each retaining the bulk of its core supporters. Contributing to the president's victory was a larger Republican turnout and a slightly more loyal Republican electorate. The ideological divide also worked to the Republicans' advantage as conservatives continued to outnumber liberals.

In 2008, public discontent with the war in Iraq and a deteriorating economy, exacerbated by the financial crisis six weeks before election day, created an environment that strongly favored the Democrats. An effective campaign by Barack Obama, who promised policy and political change, conveyed hope and unity, and tied his opponent, John McCain, to the "failed" policies of the Bush administration, resulted in a substantial victory. An increase in Democrats, decrease in Republicans, and a growth in the number of Independents and proportion voting Democratic gave Obama a 7 percent popular vote victory and two-thirds of the electoral vote.

Although the map of the Electoral College changed significantly in the 2008 election, many of the voting trends since the 1980s continued: partisan and ideological divisions, the sectarian-secular divide, and the gender gap. Racial, ethnic, and religious minorities continued to vote heavily Democratic while the Protestant, white majority stayed Republican. It was a retrospective vote, as it had been in 2004, but the judgment was different—a vote against the policies and leadership of George W. Bush.

The dire economic situation, large Democratic congressional majorities, and campaign promises to change policy prompted President Obama to pursue a liberal policy agenda that included major government initiatives to stimulate the economy, help the states, extend unemployment payments, bail out two of the big three U.S. automobile companies, aid homeowners, reform defense acquisitions, extend wilderness areas, and regulate credit card companies and the financial community, at substantial cost to the taxpayers. He also achieved major health care reform, but his initiatives inflamed the partisan and ideological divisions within the country.

Had the president misread the results of the 2008 election? When the electorate voted for Obama, did they also vote for his policy agenda? The president acted as if they did. The reality was that voters were dissatisfied with conditions at the time of the election, blamed those conditions on the previous administration, and wanted change but did not agree on the substance of those changes.

Most elections do not provide a mandate, much less a clear message. Moreover, the public usually has a diverse and inflated set of expectations about the president and the policies that president will pursue. Yet presidents are still expected to take the lead and fulfill their promises. Their success depends on the public's evaluation of conditions they were elected to fix and the way in which they went about fixing them. That evaluation is reflected in a president's job approval ratings and the results of subsequent elections.

WHERE ON THE WEB?

Public Opinion

Access the latest polls about the election from the following sites:

- **Gallup Organization**
  www.gallup.com
- **CBS News Poll**
  www.CBSNews.com
- **The Pew Research Center for the People & the Press**
  www.people-press.org
- **Pollingreport.com**
  www.pollingreport.com
- **Roper Center for Public Opinion Research at the University of Connecticut**
  www.ropercenter.uconn.edu
- **Zogby International**
  www.zogby.com

Election Results

The Web sites of most major news organizations will have the unofficial results as collected by the Associated Press just as soon as the election is over and the results have been tabulated. These results usually do not include absentee ballots, which are counted later, or the results of any vote challenges. The official results are available from the Federal Election Commission (www.fec.gov) later in the year.

Election Analysis

Most major news organizations usually carry the final election exit poll in whole or in part on their Web sites. In addition, data from the American National Election Studies (www.electionstudies.org) are made available to faculty and students at universities and colleges that are members of the Inter-University Consortium for Political and Social Research about six months after the election is completed. Data from the National Annenberg Election Surveys are also available from the Annenberg Web site (www.annenbergpublicpolicycenter.org/NewsDetails.aspx?myId=263).

EXERCISES

1. Look at polls over the course of the election, and try to explain opinion shifts on the basis of events in the campaign or in the country as a whole. You can obtain a graph of Gallup polling over the course of the election at that organization's Web site (www.gallup.com).
2. Look at the results of several national polls at different points in the election cycle to determine how they contrast and compare to one another. If the polls show different results for the same period, try to ascertain who the respondents were (the general public, the electorate, registered voters, or most likely voters), whether the same questions were asked in the polls, how many people were surveyed, and the extent to which the results were within the margin of the sampling error.
3. After the election has concluded, access the large exit poll that will appear on the Web sites of most major news networks. Analyze the election results on the basis of this poll. In your analysis, note how major demographic groups voted, what the primary issues were, how important partisanship and ideology seemed to be, and the feelings voters had toward the candidates and their parties. Are the divisions, evident in past elections, continuing, or do you see changes in the voting patterns of the American electorate?
4. On the basis of the results of the presidential election, write a memo for the winning candidate explaining the meaning (mandate) of the election for governance. In your memo, indicate what the people expect the new president to do and the order in which they expect the president to do it.

SELECTED READINGS

Abramson, Paul R., John H. Aldrich, and David W. Rohde. *Change and Continuity in the 2008 Elections*. Washington, DC: CQ Press, 2010.

Campbell, James E. "An Exceptional Election: Performance, Values, and Crisis in the 2008 Presidential Election." *The Forum,* 6 (2008, No.4), Article 7. www.bepress.com/forum/vo6/iss4/art7.

Ceaser, James W., and Daniel DiSalvo. "The Magnitude of the 2008 Democratic Victory: By the Numbers." *The Forum,* 6 (2008, No.4), Article 8. www.bepress.com/forum/vo6/iss4/art8.

Conley, Patricia Heidotting. *Presidential Mandates: How Elections Shape the National Agenda*. Chicago: University of Chicago Press, 2001.

Dahl, Robert A. "Myth of the Presidential Mandate." *Political Science Quarterly,* 105 (Fall 1990): 355–372.

Erikson, Robert S. "The 2000 Presidential Election in Historical Perspective." *Political Science Quarterly,* 116 (Spring 2001): 29–52.

Fiorina, Morris. *Retrospective Voting in American National Elections*. New Haven, CT: Yale University Press, 1981.

Jacobson, Gary C. "The Effects of the George W. Bush Presidency on Partisan Attitudes." *Presidential Studies Quarterly*, 39 (June 2009): 172–206.

Leal, David L., Matt A. Barreto, Jongho Lee, and Rodolfo O. de la Garza. "The Latino Vote in the 2004 Election." *PS: Political Science and Politics* (Jan. 2005): 41–49.

Miller, Arthur H., and Martin P. Wattenberg. "Throwing the Rascals Out: Policy and Performance Evaluations of Presidential Candidates, 1952–1980." *American Political Science Review,* 79 (1985): 359–372.

Popkin, Samuel L. *The Reasoning Voter*. Chicago: University of Chicago Press, 1991.

Wattenberg, Martin P., ed. "2004 Presidential Election." *Presidential Studies Quarterly*, 36 (June 2006): 137–296.

Weiner, Marc D., and Gerald M. Pomper. "The 2.4% Solution: What Makes a Mandate?" *The Forum*, 4 (2006). www.bepress.com/forum/vo4/iss2/art4.

Winneg, Kenneth, and Kathleen Hall Jamieson. "Party Identification in the 2008 Presidential Election." *Presidential Studies Quarterly*, 40 (June 2010): 247–263.

NOTES

1. Most surveys that report daily results use a rolling poll in which one-third of the initial sample (usually around 500 respondents) is replaced each day. By the fourth day, no respondents from the initial sample are left.
2. Public expectations about the economy may be revealed by survey data, such as responses to the following question: "Now looking ahead, do you think that a year from now you (and your family living here) will be better off financially, or worse off, or about the same as now?"
3. Kate Kenski and Kathleen Hall Jamieson, "American Public Still Has Much to Learn about Presidential Candidates' Issue Positions as Campaign End Draws Near, Annenberg Survey Shows," Annenberg Public Policy Center (Oct. 29, 2008). www.annenbergpublicpolicycenter.org/Downloads/Political%20Knowledge%20Round%20II.pdf.
4. According to political scientist Helmut Norpoth, "How well presidential candidates do in primary elections foretell their prospects in the November election with great accuracy." Using a measure of the primary vote as his independent variable, Norpoth claims that his model predicted the winner of every presidential election since 1912 with the exception of the election of 1960. Helmut Norpoth, "From Primary to General Election: A Forecast of the Presidential Vote," *PS: Political Science and Politics,* 37 (Oct. 2004), pp. 737–740.
5. Christopher Wlezien, "On Forecasting the Presidential Vote," *PS: Political Science and Politics,* 34 (March 2001), p. 30. For an extended discussion by the modelers of what went wrong, see the March 2001 edition of *PS: Political Science and Politics,* pp. 9–75, and Christopher Wlezien, "Presidential Election Polls in 2000: A Study in Dynamics," *Presidential Studies Quarterly,* 33 (March 2003), pp. 172–187.
6. For a discussion and synopsis of the 2004 model forecasts, see Alan I. Abramowitz, James E. Campbell, Robert S. Erikson, Thomas M. Holbrook, Michael S. Lewis-Beck, Helmut Norpoth, Charles Tien, and Christopher Wiezien, "Forecasting the 2004 Presidential Election," *PS: Political Science and Politics,* 37 (Oct. 2004), pp. 733–767.
7. "Forecasting the 2008 National Elections," *PS: Political Science and Politics,* 41 (Oct. 2008), pp. 679–707.
8. Kate Zernike, "Do Polls Lie About Race?" *The New York Times* (Oct. 12, 2008), pp. wk1 and wk4.
9. The poll also showed that Obama was more clearly defined in the public's mind than McCain. He was perceived to have more of the leadership skills needed to affect policy change in all areas but national security. Joel Benenson in Kathleen Hall Jamieson, ed., *Electing the President 2008: The Insider's View* (Philadelphia: University of Pennsylvania Press, 2009), p. 94.
10. Costas Panagopoulos, "Preelection Poll Accuracy in the 2008 General Election," *Presidential Studies Quarterly,* 39 (Dec. 2009), p. 879.

11. Daniel J. Hopkins, "No Wilder Effect, Never a Whitman Effect: When and Why Polls Mislead about Black and Female Candidates," *Journal of Politics*, 71 (2009, No. 3), pp. 769–781.
12. For an excellent study of the evolution of exit polling and the difficulties it has encountered, see Robin Sproul, "Exit Polls: Better or Worse Since the 2000 Election?" Joan Shorenstein Center on the Press, Politics and Public Policy, Harvard University (2008). www.hks.harvard.edu/presspol/publications/papers/.../r33_traugott.pdf.
13. Edison Research described its exit polling operation in 2008 as follows: The National Exit Poll for 2008 was one of the most logistically complex and challenging studies ever undertaken, with over 3,000 people conducting exit polls, reporting votes and analyzing the results of over 100,000 election day interviews. In addition, Edison conducted over 15,000 telephone interviews across the United States to measure early and mail-in voting which accounted for approximately one-third of all votes cast in the 2008 presidential election."2008 National Election Data," Edison Research (accessed Jan.10, 2010). www.edisonresearch.com/2008_elections.php.
14. In general, turnout declined more in the East and Midwest than it did in the West in 1980. Even if there was a decline after Carter's concession, there is little evidence to suggest that Democrats behaved any differently from Republicans and Independents. Hawaii, the last state to close its polls, voted for Carter.
15. Raymond Wolfinger and Peter Linquiti, "Tuning In and Turning Out," *Public Opinion,* 4 (Feb./March 1981), pp. 57–59; Harold Mendelsohn and Irving Crespi, *Polls, Television, and the New Politics* (Scranton, PA: Chandler, 1970), pp. 234–236.
16. Sandra Sobieraj, "The Story Behind the Near-Concession." Associated Press, (Nov. 8, 2000). www.ap.org.
17. Although voters are questioned throughout the day of the election, the poll data are not supposed to be released until voting in a state has been completed. Early results, however, were made available to the news organizations that subscribed to the poll to give reporters a head start in writing their stories. In 2004, these early voting trends spread quickly on the Internet.
18. Paul Gronke, "Early Voting Reforms and American Elections," *William and Mary Bill of Rights Journal* 17 (2008), p. 450.
19. D. M. Merkle and Murray Edelman, "A Review of the 1996 Voter News Service Exit Polls from a Total Survey Error Perspective," in Paul J. Lavakas and Michael Traugott, eds., *Election Polls, the News Media, and Democracy* (New York: Chatham House, 2000), p. 81.
20. Morris P. Fiorina, *Retrospective Voting in American National Elections* (New Haven, CT: Yale University Press, 1981).
21. Presidents will not be blamed for natural disasters or even acts of terrorism over which they have no control, but they will be evaluated on how quickly and effectively they react to cataclysmic events, empathize with the victims, and provide the help to them.
22. Kenneth Winneg and Kathleen Hall Jamieson, "Elections: Party Identification in the 2004 Elections," *Presidential Studies Quarterly,* 35 (Sept. 2005), pp. 576–589.
23. Among political scientists, there are two schools of thought. One believes that partisan change results from revolutionary events and government actions to deal with them. These events and policies divide and realign the electorate. The Depression of the 1930s and the Roosevelt administration's New Deal policies resulted in such a realignment along economic lines, with the Democrats

becoming the majority party. The civil rights movement of the 1950s and 1960s, the Democrats' embrace of that movement, and the civil rights and voting rights laws that followed produced a new division within the electorate, particularly in the South, that led to the Republicans gaining ascendancy in that region of the country and reduced Democratic support among blue-collar workers.

There have been no major realigning events since then, yet partisan attitudes have continued to shift, prompting some to postulate that partisan loyalties are also subject to evolutionary change. As the product of a collective body of political experience, these attitudes can strengthen or weaken as a consequence of how well the parties deal with contemporary conditions and events and how well they reflect the public moods and beliefs. However partisanship takes hold, both schools of thought agree that party allegiances do affect voting behavior; the stronger the allegiances, the greater the effect.

24. It can also be seen as a social identity and value. Partisans vote on the basis of their identities and beliefs.
25. For a very interesting article on the impact of emotions on learning, perceptions, and voting, see George E. Marcus and Michael B. Mackuen, "Anxiety, Enthusiasm, and the Vote: The Emotional Underpinnings of Learning and Involvement During Presidential Campaigns," *American Political Science Review,* 87 (Sept. 1993), pp. 672–685.
26. For an analysis of the components of the 1952 presidential election, see Angus Campbell, Philip E. Converse, Warren E. Miller, and Donald Stokes, *The American Voter* (New York: Wiley, 1960), pp. 524–527.
27. Eisenhower was also perceived in a more favorable light than his opponent, Adlai Stevenson. Although the public still regarded Democrats as more capable of handling domestic problems, the appeal of Eisenhower, combined with the more favorable attitude toward the Republican Party in the areas of foreign affairs and government management, resulted in the victory of the minority party's presidential candidate.
28. Kennedy's Catholicism may have enlarged his Electoral College total by 22 votes. See Ithiel de Sola Pool, Robert P. Abelson, and Samuel Popkin, *Candidates, Issues, and Strategies* (Cambridge, MA: MIT Press, 1965), pp. 115–118.
29. For a discussion of the 1964 presidential election, see Philip E. Converse, Aage R. Clausen, and Warren E. Miller, "Election Myth and Reality: The 1964 Election," *American Political Science Review,* 59 (June 1965), pp. 321–336.
30. Philip E. Converse, Warren E. Miller, Jerrold G. Rusk, and Arthur C. Wolfe, "Continuity and Change in American Politics: Parties and Issues in the 1968 Election," *American Political Science Review,* 63 (Dec. 1969), p. 1097.

    Wallace claimed that there was not "a dime's worth of difference" between the Republican and Democratic candidates and their parties. He took great care in making his own positions distinctive. The clarity with which he presented his views undoubtedly contributed to the issue orientation of his vote. People knew where Wallace stood and liked him or didn't like him because of his policy positions.
31. Arthur H. Miller, Warren E. Miller, Alden S. Raine, and Thad A. Brown, "A Majority Party in Disarray: Policy Polarization in the 1972 Election," *American Political Science Review,* 70 (Sept. 1976), pp. 753–778.
32. Arthur H. Miller and Warren E. Miller, "Partisanship and Performance: Rational Choice in the 1976 Presidential Elections," paper presented at the annual meeting of the American Political Science Association, Washington, DC, September 1–4, 1977.
33. Nonetheless, Ford was probably helped more than hurt by being the incumbent. He gained in recognition, reputation, and stature. He benefited from having a podium with a presidential seal on it. His style and manner in the office contrasted

sharply with his predecessor's—much to Ford's advantage. As the campaign progressed, his presidential image improved. It just did not improve quickly enough to allow him to hold on to the office.

34. Warren E. Miller, "Policy Directions and Presidential Leadership: Alternative Interpretations of the 1980 Presidential Election," paper presented at the annual meeting of the American Political Science Association, New York, September 3–6, 1981.
35. J. Merrill Shanks and Warren E. Miller, "Alternative Interpretations of the 1988 Election," paper presented at the annual meeting of the American Political Science Association, Atlanta, Georgia, August 31–September 3, 1989, p. 58.
36. Paul R. Abramson, John H. Aldrich, and David W. Rohde, *Change and Continuity in the 1988 Elections* (Washington, DC: CQ Press, 1990), p. 195.
37. Ibid., p. 212.
38. Had Perot not run, it is unlikely that the results of the election would have been any different. Exit polls of Perot voters indicate that they would have divided their votes fairly evenly between Clinton and Bush, although the number of people casting ballots would undoubtedly have declined.
39. Gore's advisers contended that they had no choice. Their surveys indicated that Clinton was a liability, that he turned off swing voters, and that the electorate was tired of his scandal-plagued administration and wanted a change. What they did not calculate was the extent to which Clinton energized the Democratic base.
40. For an excellent discussion on the influence of third-party candidates, see Samantha Luks, Joanne M. Miller, and Lawrence R. Jacobs, "Who Wins? Campaigns and the Third Party Vote," *Presidential Studies Quarterly*, 33 (March 2003), pp. 9–30.
41. See Susan J. Carroll, "Security Moms and Presidential Politics: Women Voters in the 2004 Election," paper prepared for delivery at the 2005 annual meeting of the American Political Science Association, Washington, DC, September 1–4, 2005.
42. Within the religious community, there was an additional distinction between traditionalists and modernists. Protestant fundamentalists and evangelicals, Latter-day Saints, traditional Catholics, and orthodox Jews gave more support to the president than those with more nuanced and moderate sectarian beliefs. James L. Guth, Lyman A. Kellstedt, Corwin E. Smidt, and John C. Green, "Religious Influences in the 2004 Presidential Election," *Presidential Studies Quarterly*, 36 (June 2006), pp. 223–242.
43. According to the exit poll, the president gained a larger proportion of the Hispanic vote (44 percent) than he received in 2000 (35 percent). However, experts disagree over the size of the increase because of the small subset of self-identified Hispanic voters who were polled.
44. "Topics from A-Z: Party Images," Gallup Poll (2010). www.gallup.com/poll/24655/Party-Images.aspx#2.
45. Kenneth Winneg and Kathleen Hall Jamieson, "Party Identification in the 2008 Presidential Election," *Presidential Studies Quarterly*, 40 (June 2010), pp. 205–251.
46. Paul R. Abramson, John H. Aldrich, and David W. Rohde, *Change and Continuity in the 2008 Elections* (Washington: DC: CQ Press, 2010), p. 168.
47. Patricia Heidotting Conley, *Presidential Mandates: How Elections Shape the National Agenda* (Chicago: University of Chicago Press, 2001), pp. 77–115.
48. Ibid., pp. 116–145.
49. George W. Bush, "Press Conference," November 4, 2004 as quoted in *The New York Times* (Nov. 5, 2004), p. A16.

50. The question on the 2008 exit poll was, "How worried are you about being able to afford the health care services you need?" The responses were as follows: Worried 66 percent, not worried 33 percent. Sixty percent of voters who were worried voted for Obama and 42 percent of those who were not worried voted for him.
51. "Topics A-Z: Healthcare System," Gallup Poll (2010). www.gallup.com/poll/4708/Healthcare-System.aspx.
52. Jeffrey M. Jones, "In U.S., 46% Favor, 40% Oppose Repealing Healthcare Law," Gallup Poll (Jan. 7, 2011). www.gallup.com/poll/145496/Favor-Oppose-Repealing-Healthcare-Law.aspx.
53. Jeff Fishel, *Presidents and Promises* (Washington, DC: Congressional Quarterly, 1994), pp. 38, 42–43.
54. Politifact.com (Jan. 7, 2008). www.politifact.com/truth-o-meter/promises/obameter.
55. Barack Obama, "Victory Speech," *Huntington Post* (Nov. 4, 2008). www.huffingtonpost.com/2008/11/04/obama-victory-speech_n_141194.html.
56. John E. Mueller, *War, Presidents, and Public Opinion* (New York: Wiley, 1973), pp. 205–208, 247–249.

10 CHAPTER REFORMING THE ELECTORAL SYSTEM

INTRODUCTION

The American political system has evolved significantly since the second half of the twentieth century. Party rules, finance laws, and media coverage are now very different from what they were before the 1960s. The composition of the electorate has changed as well, with the expansion of suffrage to all citizens eighteen years of age or older and the continuing reduction of legal obstacles to voting. Campaigning for president has changed, and new communications technologies have enabled the parties and their nominees to measure public opinion, focus resources in the most competitive states, and target appeals to specific groups of voters within the electorate.

Have these changes been beneficial or harmful? Have they improved the democratic character of the political system? Have they made the electoral process operate more efficiently and represent more effectively the interests of the population? These questions have elicited a continuing, and sometimes spirited, debate.

Critics have alleged that the electoral process is too long, too costly, too burdensome, too error prone, and too easily subject to discretionary decisions by state election officials and to manipulation by the parties, candidates, and their supporters. They claim that it wears down candidates and numbs voters and that it results in too many personal accusations and too little substantive discussion, too much name-calling and "sound bite" rhetoric, and too little real debate on the issues. They have said that many qualified people are discouraged from running for office and much of the electorate is uninformed, uninterested, and uninvolved, as evidenced by the fact that a sizable number of people do not vote on a regular basis.

Other criticisms are that the system benefits the wealthy and the special interests, encourages factionalism, weakens the party's control over the campaign of its presidential and vice presidential nominees, overemphasizes personality and underemphasizes policy, encourages deceptive claims and allegations and that it is unduly influenced by a news media motivated more by economic gain than public service.

In contrast, proponents argue that the political system is seen as more legitimate and operates more democratically than ever before. There are relatively few disputed elections; people abide by the results; more, not fewer, people have voted in recent elections; and more, not fewer, partisans participate in the nomination phase. Candidates, even lesser-known ones, now have an opportunity to run for office and in the process, demonstrate their competence, endurance, motivation, and leadership skills. Parties remain important as vehicles through which the system operates and by which governing is accomplished. Those who defend the electoral system believe voters do receive as much information as they desire and enough to make informed and reasoned judgments. Most voters believe that as well according to postelection surveys conducted by the Pew Research Center for the People and the Press.[1]

The old adage "where you stand influences what you see" is applicable to the debate about electoral reform. No political process is completely neutral. There are always winners and losers. To a large extent, the advantages that some enjoy are made possible by the disadvantages that others encounter. Rationalizations aside, much of the debate about the system—about equity, representation, and responsiveness—revolves around a very practical, political question: who gains, and who loses?

Proposals to change the system need to be assessed in the light of this question. They should also be judged on the basis of how such changes would affect the operation of the electoral system, the agenda and composition of government, and the public policy made by elected officials. This chapter discusses some of these proposals and the effect they could have on the road to the White House. The chapter is organized into two sections: the first deals with the more recent developments and proposals in party rules, campaign finance, and media coverage; and the second examines the long-term, democratic issues of citizen participation, representation, and equity in the electoral process. Throughout this discussion, basic questions central to a democratic electoral process are addressed.

MODIFYING RECENT CHANGES IN PARTY RULES

Of all the changes that have recently occurred, the reforms in the nomination process, particularly the selection of delegates, have engendered the most controversy and resulted in the most persistent fine-tuning. Designed to encourage grassroots participation and broaden the base of representation, these reforms have also extended the nominating period, made the campaign more expensive, and made the need for early money more critical. They have also generated candidate-based organizations, weakened the influence of some state and local party leaders, converted conventions into coronations, and loosened the ties between the parties and their nominees. All of these consequences have made governing more difficult.

Since 1968, when the Democrats began to rewrite their rules for delegate selection, the parties have suffered from unintended repercussions of the rules changes. Each succeeding presidential election has seen reforms to the reforms, modifications that have attempted to reconcile expanded participation and representation with the traditional need for party unity and campaign oversight, with the goal of successfully pursuing a partisan agenda in government. Although less reform-conscious than the Democrats, the Republicans have also tried to steer a middle course between greater rank-and-file involvement and more equitable representation on the one hand and the maintenance of successful electoral and governing coalitions on the other.

How to balance these often competing goals has been a critical concern. Those who desire greater public participation have lauded the trend toward having more primaries and a larger percentage of delegates selected in them. Believing that the reforms have opened up the process and made it more democratic, participatory democracy advocates favor the continued selection of delegates based on the proportion of the popular vote that they or the candidate to whom they are pledged receive. In contrast, those who believe that greater control by state and national party leaders is desirable argue that the reforms have gone too far. They would prefer fewer primaries, a smaller percentage of delegates selected in them, more unpledged delegates and party leaders participating in the nominating conventions, and a larger role for state and national party organizations during the entire presidential campaign.

WHO SHOULD PARTICIPATE IN THE CAUCUSES AND PRIMARIES?

Party rules have consistently sought to limit participation in its primary elections to registered or self-declared partisans, although such restrictions are difficult to enforce in practice. The participation of Independents and crossover voting by the partisans of the other party has remained a contentious issue and a strategic choice that candidates for the nomination must consider. Do they direct their appeals to independent and independent-minded partisan voters as John McCain and Barack Obama did in 2008 or appeal primarily to their own party partisans as Hillary Clinton and most Republican candidates did in their party's 2008 nomination process?

From the party's perspective, the issue of allowing nonpartisans to participate dilutes the influence of party regulars and creates the possibility of selecting a nominee who does not best reflect the interests, needs, or ideological views of most of the party's rank and file. A special fear is that adherents of the other party will cross over to vote for the weaker opposition candidate in order to enhance their own nominee's chances in the general election.

On the other hand, from the perspective of the citizenry, a primary closed to all but registered partisans precludes much of the population from participating and reduces the incentive for nonparticipants to become informed and get involved during the election. Moreover, it allows party elites who have financial and organizational backing to extend their clout over the process and the outcome; it also permits partisan activists, who tend to have the strongest ideological convictions, to exercise disproportionate influence on the candidates, encouraging them to adhere to the beliefs and issue positions of a narrower group of partisans rather than a broader cross section of the party and the electorate. Political parties can benefit from an open primary system if it leads to the recruitment of more active supporters or makes their nominees more electable.

How Should the Votes Be Allocated?

Another rules issue concerns the allocation of votes in primaries. Since 1992, the Democrats have used a straight proportional voting system that allocates pledged delegates according to the percentage of the popular vote they or the candidate to whom they are committed receives. The Republicans have permitted the states to decide on the method of allocation, which could be proportional or winner-take-all within districts or on an at-large basis; in 2012, however, new GOP rules will require states that hold their contests in March to select convention delegates on the basis of a proportional vote.

Proportional voting more closely reflects the view of a state's primary electorate, but it also could have the effect of extending the nomination, delaying a consensus on the eventual nominee, and costing more money, as it did in 2008 for the Democrats. The more divided the party going into its nominating convention, the weaker its candidates are likely to be in the general election, or so the thinking has been within the national leadership of both major parties. The election of Barack Obama, after an extended and highly competitive nomination process, may lead party leaders to reconsider their judgment that a divisive nomination is harmful to the party's chances in the general election. The elimination of unpledged delegates by the Democrats would seem to be a step in the direction of a more democratic selection process.

Should the Nomination Process Be Shortened?

Some people have urged that the period during which presidential nominations occur be condensed. Professor Thomas E. Patterson has argued that an extended nomination "disrupts the policy process, discourages the candidacies of responsible officeholders, and wears out the voters."[2] It also diverts public attention from issues of government to campaign-related controversies and does so many months before the general election campaign begins. Moreover, Patterson notes that a long election cycle generates more negative news about the candidates as the campaign progresses, thereby souring voters on the choices they have on primary day and creating image problems for the candidates in the general election.[3]

Several proposals have been made for addressing the issue of excessively long campaigns. Some have even been introduced in the form of legislation in Congress. A simple change would be to limit the period in which caucuses and primaries can be scheduled to two or three months and perhaps also shorten the period during which candidates can raise money for their nomination campaigns. As we noted, the invisible primary starts for most candidates at the beginning of the year preceding the election. A second proposal would cluster primaries and caucuses, forcing states in designated regions or groups to hold their elections on the same day. A third plan, which is already in effect, provides incentives for states to schedule their contests later in the spring, but there have been few takers. A fourth idea is to create a national primary.

On the other hand, spreading out the caucuses and primaries reduces the impact of front-loading. It gives more candidates a better chance to demonstrate their qualifications. It provides more time for voters to evaluate the candidates. It also weakens the news media's influence on public opinion, which is greatest at the beginning of the nomination process.

Both major parties have attempted to frame their nomination process by specifying the time frame in which primaries and caucuses can be held. But getting states to adhere to these scheduling rules is difficult. The threat of reducing or eliminating their convention delegation has not prevented states, such as Michigan and Florida, in 2008, from holding elections before the window officially opens. If conventions were decision-making bodies, if the winning candidate did not care about unifying the party, if the states that violated party rules were not seen as critical in the general election, then a party's sanctions might be sufficient to bring recalcitrant states in line. But alas, they have not been.

As consequence, both Democratic and Republican party rules now permit four states (Iowa, New Hampshire, Nevada, and South Carolina) to hold their nomination selection process before the other states may do so. They have also tried to push the starting date back a month later than in 2008, but whether states will comply with the new calendar is another matter. Moving the caucuses and primaries later in the year may increase public awareness, but it may also provide more time for raising and spending money. What seems probable, however, is that the first day that all states are allowed to hold their caucus or primary, the first Tuesday in March 2012, will have a disproportionate number of contests; it will be Super Tuesday.

CAN FRONT-LOADING BE PREVENTED?

Front-loading, which has continued to increase over the years,[4] creates inequities. It gives greater influence to those states that hold their contests earlier and less to those that hold them later. To the extent that partisans in the early states are not representative of the party's rank and file, much less the electorate, they can generate momentum for a candidate who may not be the first or most acceptable choice for the party as a whole.

Front-loading helps well-known and well-financed candidates. Conversely, it hurts long shots who must raise more money more quickly and must also enter more contests before they have had ample opportunity to demonstrate their electability. The stepping-stones to the nomination have become more compressed, and as a result, the prospects that a non-front-runner can win the nomination have become more remote.

Front-loading moves the campaign forward, well into the year before the general election, in order to raise the money, get the endorsements, and build the organizations necessary to run in a large number of states simultaneously. Not only does it extend the nomination but it also shortens the competitive phase of the process. In 2004, the competitive period lasted only six weeks; in 2008, it lasted longer—two months for the Republicans and five months for the Democrats. With candidates beginning their campaigns in the year before the nomination, the process now extends from one year to about eighteen months. Thus candidates for their party's nomination have to begin their quest for the nomination earlier, and if successful, continue it longer.

Front-loading also forces candidates to campaign in many states simultaneously, if they can afford to do so. If not, then they must make strategic choices of where to spend their time and resources. Without a strong on-the-ground effort, they must rely on mass media to reach voters. Retail politics, in which candidates interact with voters in small groups and informal settings, suffers as a consequence.

From the perspective of a democratic political system, perhaps the most negative aspect of front-loaded campaigns is that the decisive stage of the nomination process occurs before most people are paying attention to electoral politics. By the time the party's electorate tunes in during and after the Iowa caucuses and the New Hampshire primary, the field has been thinned out. Moreover, there is little incentive for the public to stay attentive or even turn out to vote in later primaries once the winner has been effectively determined. Add to this problem the fact that front-loading presidential contests so early also separates the presidential nomination process from other state nominations, thereby reducing the link between the party's presidential candidate and other party nominees seeking elective office.

Should Regional Primaries Be Instituted?

Nomination contests could be formally regionalized, with states in different regions required to hold their nomination contests on the same day. Since the 1980s, there have been agreements among states in some regions to do so. The case for regional primaries is based on the assumption that such a system would be more equitable for the states and provide more focus for the candidates.

As long as the regions adopted some plan to rotate their nomination dates, which they do not do at present, each region over time would be able to exercise approximately equal influence over the selection of a party's nominees. Moreover, candidates would be forced to address regional concerns and appeal to regional interests. A nomination that extended to the four regional primaries would probably ensure that the winning candidate had broad-based geographic support, the kind of support that is necessary to win in the Electoral College.

But regionalization is not without its critics, who fear that it would exacerbate sectional rivalries, encourage local or area candidates, and produce more candidate organizations to rival those of the state and national parties. Moreover, like straight proportional voting, a regional primary system could impede the emergence of a consensus candidate, thereby extending the process to the convention and increasing, not decreasing, costs, time, and media attention. In addition, regional primaries help the best-organized and best-financed candidates because they require more resources to be devoted to the mass media.

SHOULD A NATIONAL PRIMARY BE HELD?

Another option, and the one that represents the most sweeping change, would be to hold a national primary. The heavily front-loaded schedule in 2008 created a *de facto* jumbo primary on February 5, much to the dismay of the leaders of both major parties, who objected to the early date and the concentration of so many contests on the same day.

Congress has been cool to idea of a national primary, but the general public seems to favor it. Gallup Polls taken over the past two decades indicate that almost two-thirds of the electorate prefers such an election to the present patchwork system.[5] Most proposals for a national primary call for it to be held in the late spring or early summer, followed by party conventions. Candidates who wanted to enter their party's primary would be required to obtain a certain number of signatures. Any aspirant who won a majority of that party's vote would automatically receive the nomination. In some plans, a plurality would be sufficient, provided it was at least 40 percent. In the event that no one received 40 percent, a runoff election could be held several weeks later between the top two finishers, or the national nominating convention could choose from among the top two or three candidates. In any event, nominating conventions would continue to be held to select the vice presidential candidates, to decide on the platforms, and determine rules.

A national primary would be consistent with the "one-person, one-vote" principle that guides most aspects of the U.S. electoral system. All participants would have an equal voice in the selection. No longer would voters in the states that held the early caucuses and primaries exercise more influence.

It is also likely that a national primary would stimulate turnout. It would give more people more incentive to get involved. Greater involvement might motivate more people to work for their party and its candidates. A national primary would probably result in a nomination by a more representative electorate than is currently the case.

A single primary election for each party would accelerate a nationalizing trend. Issues that affect the entire country would be the primary focus of attention. Thus, candidates for the nation's highest office would be forced to discuss the problems they would most likely address during the general election campaign and would most likely confront as president.

Moreover, the results of the election would be clear-cut. The person with the most votes would be the winner. The media could no longer interpret primaries and caucus returns as they see fit. An incumbent's ability to garner support through the timely release of grants, contracts, and other spoils of government might be more limited in a national contest, but it would not be eliminated entirely.

On the other hand, such an election would undoubtedly discourage challengers who lacked national reputations. No longer could an early victory catapult a relatively unknown aspirant into the position of serious contender or jeopardize a president's chances for renomination. In fact, lesser-known candidates, such as George McGovern, Jimmy Carter, Michael Dukakis, and even Bill Clinton in 1992, might find it extremely difficult to raise money, build an organization, and mount a national campaign. Barack Obama would certainly have had more difficulty challenging Hillary Rodham Clinton without his victory in Iowa.

From the standpoint of the major parties, a national primary might further weaken the ability of party leaders to influence the selection of the nominees. Moreover, a postprimary convention could not be expected to tie the nominee to the party, although it might tie the party to the nominee, at least through the general election.

Whether a national primary winner would be the party's strongest candidate is also open to question. With a large field of contenders, those with the most devoted or ideological supporters might do best. On the other hand, candidates who do not arouse the passions of the diehards, but who are more acceptable to the party's mainstream, might not do as well. Everybody's second choice might not even finish second, unless systems of approval voting or cumulative voting were used.[6] Approval or cumulative voting systems, however, complicate the election, confuse the electorate, question the result, undercut its legitimacy, and perhaps add to its costs.

A national primary would lessen the ability of states to determine when and how their citizens would participate in the presidential nomination process, although they would still be responsible for holding caucuses and primaries for other candidates for federal and state office.

Finally, a national primary would in effect produce two presidential elections every four years. Could public attention be maintained throughout such an elongated election cycle? Could sufficient money be raised? If so, by which candidates—those who are personally wealthy or who have the reputation and position to attract money? Could the candidates' grassroots organizations handle such a task, not once but twice? These questions have tempered widespread support within the parties for such a plan despite the general appeal of the idea to the public.

Recently, several political scientists have proposed a combination of rotating small-state primaries followed by a national primary.[7] Their plan calls for randomly selecting about one dozen small states and allowing them to hold their contests—caucuses or primaries—in which candidates would compete. Later in the spring or early summer, a national primary would be held in which voters in all states would be able to participate.[8] The parties could limit the number of candidates based on their success in the small-state contests or allow anyone to enter. If no one received a majority, a runoff election could be held or the national nominating convention could decide among the top candidates.

The architects of this plan believe that partisans of both the small and large states would benefit. The small states would essentially narrow down the field, and people in all the states could then decide on the nominee. This idea reverses the logic of delegates at the Constitutional Convention in 1787 who thought that the large states, with the most electoral votes, would choose the top candidates, but in all likelihood, no one, other than George Washington, would have the required majority. Thus the House of Representatives, voting by states, would select the president and vice president.

The merits of combining a state and national vote are that it might contribute to a more representative selection process in which partisans in both small and large states would exercise more equal influence over the selection of the nominee than occurs in the current nomination process. Not only would a national primary encourage more people to participate but it might also put them in a position to select the most qualified candidate based on candidate performance in the small-state elections.[9]

There are several problems with this hybrid selection process, however. Would the small states, such as Iowa and New Hampshire, agree to a selection lottery? Would the large states be willing to allow the small states to participate twice? Would a combined process save money or be more expensive? Would it extend or shorten the nomination process? Would it favor front-runners or provide greater opportunities for non-front-runners than currently exist? Would it make for a more enlightened public choice? Would people who consider themselves to be Independent be able to vote in a national primary or would that vary, as it currently does, from state to state?

THE PERILS OF CAMPAIGN FINANCE

Closely related to the delegate selection process are the laws governing campaign finance. These laws were first enacted in the 1970s in reaction to the secret and sometimes large illegal bequests to candidates, the disparity in contributions and spending among the candidates, and the spiraling costs of modern campaigns, particularly television advertising. The finance laws were designed to improve accountability and transparency, reduce spending, subsidize nominations, and fund the general election. Some of these objectives have been achieved, but unintended consequences have also resulted, and campaign finance remains a persistent problem.

The laws have taken campaign finance out of the back rooms and put much of it into the public spotlight. They have also, however, created a nightmare of compliance procedures and reporting requirements. Detailed records of practically all contributions and expenditures of the presidential campaign organizations must now be kept and periodically reported to the Federal Election Commission.[10] Good accountants and attorneys, specializing in election law, are now as necessary as pollsters, image makers, mass marketers, grassroots organizers, and experts in the new communications technologies.

Can Campaign Contributions and Expenditures Be Effectively Limited?

The hard-money, soft-money, independent-spending conundrum remains. In addition, the Supreme Court has said that corporations, and by inference, labor unions, may engage in free speech without limits imposed on their campaign spending. Although these groups remain subject to the disclosure provision of the Bipartisan Campaign Reform Act (BCRA), they can circumvent these provisions by giving money to intermediaries—nonparty groups—which spend some or all of it on political activities during election campaigns and even after them.

Can these loopholes be closed? Yes, say some members of Congress who introduced legislation to limit spending by corporations that receive $50,000 or more in government contracts or corporations that are owned or controlled by foreigners. The legislation, known by its acronym DISCLOSE (Democracy Is Strengthened by Casting Light on Spending in Elections), would also increase disclosure requirements. It was enacted by the House of Representatives in 2010 when the Democrats were in control, but not by the Senate.

Soft money, given to 527s and 501c groups, continues to be an issue although it was not as much of a problem during the 2007–2008 election cycle as it was four years earlier. Nonetheless, the prohibition on nonparty groups coordinating their spending with parties and candidates has led to confusion by voters and complaints by candidates that they are unable to control the information, imagery, and political discourse in their election campaigns. In addition, the soft money seems to be spent disproportionally on negative advertising, ads that can mislead and turn off voters.

One fear, that has not come to pass, however, is that the ban on the national parties soliciting soft money would hurt their fund-raising. Since 2004, the major parties have raised more in hard money than they had in hard money and soft money combined previously. And in 2008, candidates for their party's nomination, and Barack Obama in the general election, raised record amounts. Even in the 2007–2008 recession, the total amount of campaign revenues and expenses was higher than ever, dwarfing public funding and threatening to render it obsolete.

Can Public Funding Be Saved?

The BCRA did not intend to cripple the public-funding provision, but it may have done so inadvertently by doubling the amount that individuals could contribute and adjusting that amount to the rate of inflation. The increase in the size of contributions combined with the use of Internet technology has made it easier for candidates to raise large amounts of private funds. Their success in 2004 and 2008 has increased the incentive for rejecting federal funds and thus being subject to the spending limits that accepting those funds imposed. Even John McCain, a sponsor of the law, did not take public funds in his nomination campaign. He did so in the general election primarily because he believed he could not match his opponent's private fund-raising. In all likelihood, McCain will be the last major-party candidate to accept federal funds in the general election unless the law is changed to increase greatly the federal funds given to major-party candidates and to permit private money to supplement the government contribution.

Despite the benefits of public funding—it has made presidential elections more equitable, broadened the field of potential contenders by giving non-front-runners a chance, increased competition at the beginning of the process, lessened, to some extent, candidates' dependence on large contributions from wealthy donors and people with access to them, and at least initially, reduced the amount of time candidates had to spend raising funds—there has been little public outcry about the demise of public funding. Suspicion of politicians, opposition to federal "give-away programs," and fear of tax increases and larger budget deficits that would be required to replenish the campaign fund have lessened public support for federal funding.[11] Today, only about 7 percent of taxpayers check off the box on their tax form that allows $3 of their taxes to go to the national campaign fund.

Can public funding be saved? Ironically, the Obama campaign's success in seeking multiple small donations, often from the same donors, may offer a way out of this dilemma for those who believe in public support of political campaigns. In a joint project sponsored by the Campaign Finance Institute, American Enterprise Institute, and the Brookings Institution, four political scientists (Anthony J. Corrado, Michael J. Malbin, Thomas E. Mann, and Norman J. Ornstein) have proposed a series of changes in campaign finance law that would broaden the base of participation. They recommend that the law be changed to encourage candidates to seek a larger number of small donors, using the advances in telecommunications and Internet technology to do so. Here's part of what they recommend:

- Provide multimatching funds, but only for small contributors. For example, instead of matching the first $250 of every contribution a candidate receives from an individual donor (the current law), double, triple, or quadruple individual donations of $50 or less.
- Provide the funds for candidates who qualify for them earlier in the nomination process rather than waiting until the calendar year of the election. Since campaigns have been starting one or two years prior to the election, the FEC should start dispersing the funds earlier in the election cycle when candidates need them the most to gain visibility and set up a broad-based, small-donor operation.
- Instead of limiting campaign spending, limit the number of large donations a candidate may accept. Such a limit would force candidates who need additional funds to seek them from small donors and thus reduce their dependence on individuals who contribute the maximum amount of money, and especially individuals and organizations that bundle these maximum-sized contributions from their friends and associates to give them to the candidates.
- Place a ceiling on the amount of public funds a candidate may receive but allow them to continue to raise small private donations.[12]

Alternatively, Congress could follow the lead of several European countries by prohibiting private contributions entirely and providing the parties or their candidates with a specified amount of money to campaign—if there were public support for increasing the amount of money candidates receive from the government. But alas, there does not appear to be.

The campaign finance quandary at its most basic level is one of competing values: the freedom to spend on behalf of one's interests, beliefs, and opinions versus the equality of citizens in affecting campaign issues, debate, and election outcomes. In a democratic political system in which the vote and presumably the voice of all citizens should be equal, the wealthy should not have an advantage, but in a free and open society, everyone should be able to voice their opinions and spend their own resources to the extent that they desire to do so. Here is the problem: how to ensure that candidates have sufficient funds, that freedom of speech is protected, that political equality is promoted, and that the public has sufficient information to make an informed judgment. No wonder campaign finance reform has proven to be so difficult, so controversial, and seemingly insoluble.

PUBLIC AWARENESS AND KNOWLEDGE

For the electorate to make an enlightened judgment, people must have sufficient and accurate information about the candidates and parties, their policy positions, and campaign promises. They also must have some knowledge about the candidates' past experience and the parties' record while governing. Past performance is a criterion for anticipating future behavior.

Is the amount and type of information available in contemporary campaigns sufficient for people to make an informed judgment when voting? As noted in Chapter 5, most voters continue to answer "yes" to this question, but political scientists and other students of election behavior are not so sure. Almost everyone agrees that the more information people have about the candidates, issues, and parties, the better able they will be to cast an enlightened vote. But how much information is necessary and desirable? And what type of information does the electorate currently receive?

Changes in communication technology have made more information available and accessible, but that information has not necessarily produced a more educated electorate. A study of the communications during the 2008 campaign by three scholars at the Annenberg Public Policy Center at the University of Pennsylvania (Kate Kenski, Bruce W. Hardy, and Kathleen Hall Jamieson) concludes that microtargeting messages to groups of voters combined with the differential in campaign spending gave Obama a huge and, from a democratic perspective, unfair advantage in persuading voters of the merits of his candidacy and policies.[13] They wrote:

> . . . a better-financed candidate will microtarget in ways that draws voters to his candidacy based on unrebutted deception. Alternatively, "soft" voters will be more readily persuaded not by the merits of one case over another but by better microtargeted messaging and larger-volume ad buys.[14]

To prevent financial inequities from being used to skew the public debate, to preclude voters from getting unbalanced, incomplete, or even erroneous information, the authors of this study urge the communications media to provide free time or that public funds be used to buy it to enable candidates to get their messages across and respond to allegations and claims by their political opponents.[15]

But would a profit-oriented news media comply? Would the corporations that own the major news networks give free and equal access to all candidates or just major-party presidential candidates? A law that forced the news media to provide free time might even be counterproductive, reducing rather than increasing the amount of public communications during the campaign. Television and radio stations would undoubtedly be discouraged from selling time to nonparty groups and individuals if they were under obligation to provide it free to the person or party who was the object of the commercial. A decrease in media advertising would reduce the information available to the public and increase the electorate's dependence on the news media.

Besides, the appearance of candidates on talk/entertainment shows beginning in the early 1990s and the proliferation of all-news cable channels have already given major candidates more "free" time to respond to questions about their policy positions and personal character. But it has also given the producers, hosts, and commentators on these shows subtle ways of influencing the amount and content of the information by the wording and sequencing of questions to the candidates, by the choice of whom to interview and when to do so, and by the comments they make after the candidates respond to their questions.

Is Campaign News Coverage Satisfactory?

Critics say "no." They point to media bias and spin and to the emphasis on the horse race, campaign strategy, and personal behavior at the expense of more substantive discussion of policy issues.

To augment public knowledge, scholars have suggested that the major news networks and wire services assign special correspondents to cover the policy issues of the campaign, much as they assign people to report on its color, drama, and personal aspects. Others have suggested that the press place greater emphasis on campaign coverage, that they assess the accuracy of the statements and advertising claims of the candidates, and that they indicate the potential costs and benefits of the policy proposals the candidates offer.

To their credit, some newspapers, such as the *Washington Post* and the *New York Times,* major television networks, and public interest groups have begun to do ad checks on a regular basis. If other news organizations lack the resources to check the advertising, they could rely on FactCheck, a nonpartisan organization run by the Annenberg Public Policy Center at the University of Pennsylvania. The news media also provide analyses of the campaign issues.

In addition to criticizing press coverage of the campaign, academicians and others have called into question the amount and accuracy of election reporting. Other than requiring fairness, preventing obscenity, and ensuring that public service commitments are met, there is little the government can do to regulate the news media without impinging on the First Amendment that protects freedom of the press. The news media can choose which elections and candidates to cover, what kind and how much coverage to provide them, how to interpret the results of primaries and caucuses, and even predict who will win before the election is concluded. These choices, however, tend to be exercised by the news networks with public preferences in mind. Not only do corporations that own media affiliates engage in constant private polling to discern the interests of their viewers, listeners, and readers but people "vote" every day when they turn on a particular program on radio or television or buy a particular newspaper or magazine.

There is much that candidates can do, however, to affect the coverage they receive. If their words are unreported or not reported correctly, or if their ideas are misinterpreted or their motives suspected, they can seek other mass media formats to reach the general public, as they have done by using the entertainment and talk shows and maintaining their own Web sites. They can also employ satellite technology to reach local and regional audiences directly and thereby circumvent the national networks and news services. Unfortunately, candidates can also restrict press access to them, make unsubstantiated claims and accusations about an opponent, and provide or leak negative and inaccurate information to the news media. The reduction of news staffs by the major print media has also reduced their investigative capacities and made them more dependent on information they receive from others involved in the campaigns.

Does Early Exit Poll Reporting Affect Voting Decisions and Election Outcomes?

Another media-related issue is the election-night forecasts based on exit polling data that the networks air before all voting has been completed. Beginning in 1984, the networks promised not to forecast the results in any state until a majority of its polls had closed, although they violated that promise in reporting the exit poll results and projecting the winner in Florida in 2000. Opponents of the early reporting and predictions claim that it discourages turnout in states in which the polls are still open. The networks respond that the election-night forecasts are news, they have a right to report them, and people want to know the winners and losers as soon as possible.

Is there really a problem with the early forecasts? After all, public opinion polls on the election's probable outcome are being reported right up to election day. Political scientists have found that the early forecasts may depress turnout in states in which the polls are still open, but they have not found evidence that the predictions affect the overall results of the election.[16] Nonetheless, the perception that a problem exists is itself a problem, one that has forced Congress several times to hold hearings on the matter.

One proposed solution is to prevent the networks from making any forecasts about the outcome in a state until *all* its polls have closed; similarly, national predictions could not be made until all the voting in the United States has been completed. However, the number of time zones would effectively prevent any national prediction until the next morning Eastern Standard Time. Some have even suggested a uniform closing hour for the entire country, but even if there were one, could Congress compel the news networks to abide by it before reporting their exit poll results, given the competitive character of news reporting? Besides, people enjoy the election-night broadcasts and are eager to learn the results and celebrate or commiserate, accordingly.

Moreover, exit polls have considerable value for the information they provide about the beliefs, attitudes, and motivations of the voters. Much of the initial analyses of presidential elections and their meaning are based on that poll data. In a democracy, it is essential to get as clear a reading of the pulse of the electorate as possible.

Should Election-Night Reporting Be Changed?

Americans are glued to their television sets on election night. They want to know who has won. The national news networks with their anchors and well-known reporters provide a running account replete with victory and concession statements by the candidates, remarks by campaign aides, and commentary by political experts. Exit poll data are often reported, usually more to predict outcomes than to understand who voted for whom and why. Viewers and listeners have to trust that the data are accurate and that the sample is sufficiently large and properly weighted to permit generalizations—assumptions that are not always true. Local stations are given a few minutes to report local results, but the major networks focus on the presidential election and, to a lesser extent, that of the Congress. The print media, especially the major national newspapers, can do a more comprehensive job.

What is not provided in election-night coverage is in-depth analyses of the policy implications of the election outcome for the country. In addition to a demographic analysis, who voted for whom and why, the public would benefit from a more sophisticated understanding of what public perceptions were at the time of the election, the policy preferences of the newly elected public officials, the new administration's legislative and executive priorities, the compatibility of the people who were elected with one another and those who remain in the government, and the likelihood of the newly elected or reelected president and Congress being able to form governing coalitions along partisan, issue, or ideological lines. But whether reporters, weary of the campaign and eager to end the election story, are in a position to provide such information and the electorate is willing to absorb it is another matter.

ENHANCING THE DEMOCRATIC CHARACTER OF PRESIDENTIAL ELECTIONS

How can the structure and conduct of presidential elections be more consistent with a democratic electoral process? Increasing voter turnout, improving the quantity and quality of information that is available to the electorate, and having the results reflect public opinion more closely would help promote democratic values and produce a more democratic electoral process.

IS NONVOTING A PROBLEM IN U.S. ELECTIONS?

Many political scientists would say "yes."[17] They would point to the gap between those eligible to vote and those who actually do so. This gap, which will always exist in a system that does not compel voting, widened during the last forty years of the twentieth century. In 1996, for the first time since 1920, more than half of those eligible chose not to vote; in 2008, 43 percent of the voting-age population and 38 percent of the voter-eligible population did not do so; in the 2010 midterm elections, about six in ten people who were eligible did not vote.[18]

Low turnout in a free and open electoral system has been a source of embarrassment to the United States and of concern to its political leaders for several reasons. It weakens their credibility when promoting democracy abroad if it is practiced so lackadaisically at home. Moreover, the demographic differences between voters and nonvoters—those in the electorate are more educated with higher incomes than the general population—increase the influence gap within the political arena, advantaging the advantaged. Those with more education and higher incomes regularly exercise more influence over the outcome of elections, the agenda of government, and its public policy decisions. Disparities in political participation reinforce and even widen the division between the "haves" and "have-nots," resulting in alienation, apathy, and cynicism among people at the lower end of the socioeconomic continuum.

If nonvoting is a problem, then what can and should be done about it? Should people be encouraged to vote? Should they be forced to do so?

HOW CAN MORE CITIZENS BE ENCOURAGED TO VOTE?

The national government and many of the states have been trying to make it easier for people to vote. We have discussed some of the ways in which Congress has tried to facilitate voting.

Ease Government-Imposed Regulations

The enactment of the "motor-voter" bill in 1993 has made registration easier. The Help America Vote Act (HAVA) in 2002 provided money to computerize and consolidate state voter registration lists, make voting more accessible to the disabled and to non-English-speakers, protect the integrity of the voting process, and permit provisional voting by people whose registration is challenged at the time they vote. The law also created the U.S. Election Assistance Commission (EAC) to oversee its implementation. Thus far, the law has helped improve the accuracy of registration lists, provided money for new voting machines, and has reduced the number of incidences of voter intimidation and fraudulent voting practices.

More needs to be done, however, according to the Commission on Federal Election Reform, which studied voting problems and electoral issues following the 2004 election. The commission recommended a series of measures: a universal system of voter registration for the entire country, uniform procedures for counting provisional ballots and determining voter eligibility, a countrywide system of voter identification, and civic education programs for the general public. It also urged states to restore voting rights to ex-felons who have served their sentences.[19] Other suggestions include electronic voting machines with a paper ballot backup system.[20]

Although the commission's proposals would improve the integrity of voting in the United States, might make it easier for people (especially minorities) to vote, and could reduce the economic discrepancies between voters and nonvoters, it is unlikely that the proposals would eliminate these problems entirely or vastly increase turnout. Making it easier to vote is not the same thing as encouraging people to vote. Besides, Congress has not acted on the commission's report, and with turnout increasing, there is little likelihood the Congress would do so in the foreseeable future.

Other proposals to make registration automatic, as it is in many European countries, or extending it to election day itself, as is already permitted in a few states, have also been advanced. Counties or states that have facilitated registration in these ways have considerably higher levels of turnout than those that do not. But whether these states are better governed and/or their elections are perceived as more legitimate by the people is another question, one about which there may not be sufficient data to answer.

Make Election Day a Holiday or Nonworkday

Another idea to enhance turnout would be to make election day a national holiday or move it to Veterans Day, which comes later in the month. Presumably, either change would prevent work-related activities from interfering with voting as much as they do now for the bulk of the population.

Many countries follow the practice of holding their elections on a holiday or Sunday. The problem here is that an additional national holiday would cost employers millions of dollars in lost revenue and productivity, with no guarantee that turnout would increase. Moreover, veterans would probably oppose having politics obscure the meaning for which the holiday was intended—to honor those who served and sacrificed for their country. For workers in certain service sectors, the holiday might be a workday anyway.

Some states have extended the period for voting up to twenty-one days prior to the election to increase the number of voters. Others have enacted a "no-fault" absentee ballot system for those who find it difficult or inconvenient to get to the polls on election day. Under a liberalized absentee voting procedure, any eligible voter can obtain an absentee ballot with no questions asked. Twenty-two states currently provide one or both of these options, and voting turnout in those states has increased.[21] Oregon has gone so far as to institute a mail ballot, and turnout in that state now exceeds the national average.

But extending the voting period and balloting by mail are not without their costs. Fear of fraud if the ballots get into the wrong hands is one concern. Voting without all pertinent information is another. People who vote early do so without knowing what may be revealed or happen at the end of the campaign. They may be, in effect, captured by a candidate's targeted advertising and grassroots activity, make a spur-of-the-moment decision, and then, if state law permits, asked or taken to vote. Candidates who lack the money and field organization to match their opponents, such as Kerry in Ohio in 2004 and McCain in several of the close competitive states in 2008, are disadvantaged. Besides, for the candidates themselves, there is the added cost of distributing thousands of sample ballots or other information to voters and appealing to the electorate to use them when voting. Nonetheless, the benefit of increasing turnout has motivated more states to modify their single-day voting tradition. And as we have noted, about 30 percent of the votes in 2008 were cast before election day.

However, political scientist Adam J. Berinsky claims that electoral reforms that have already occurred have actually reinforced rather than reduced the education and income gap between the electorate and the population as a whole. He writes:

> No matter how low the direct costs to casting a ballot are set, the only way to accomplish both goals of increasing turnout and eliminating socioeconomic biases in the voting population is to increase the engagement of the broader mass public with the political world. Political information and interest, not the high tangible costs of the act of voting, are the real barriers to a truly democratic voting public.[22]

Conduct Citizen Education Campaigns

Educating the people on the merits of participating and the responsibilities of citizenry might also generate greater involvement and a higher turnout. If the public better understood what difference it makes who wins, if people had greater confidence that elected officials would keep their promises and that government would address salient issues, then more people might vote.

Professor Heather Gerken, an elections expert at Yale Law School, has put forth a novel idea. She suggests that states and localities calculate how democratic their elections systems actually are by using an index that would be determined on the basis of how many eligible people were registered, how many of those registered had actually voted, and how accurately the votes were tabulated. Implementing a democracy index would not require national legislation, although it might require additional funding to collect the data necessary for the index. Gerken is counting on the competitive instincts of state and local officials and the people they represent. She sees bragging power and community pride in being more democratic than others.[23]

But invigorating the electoral environment and encouraging more people to participate is not an easy task. If it were, it would have already been accomplished. It is difficult to convince nonvoters to spend the time and effort necessary to educate themselves on the candidates and the issues, to donate money or get involved in the campaign, and to vote unless they can see what difference it would make if they voted.

If, however, more people voted on a regular basis, the parties and candidates would have to broaden, not narrow, their appeals. They would have to address the needs and desires of all the people and not concentrate on those who are most likely to vote for their candidates. Those who have not participated as frequently in the current voluntary system of voting—the poorer, less educated, less fortunate, and younger—would receive more attention not only from candidates but from elected officials. More equitable public policies might result.

Encourage Grassroots Campaigns

Another way to increase turnout is for party and nonparty groups to continue to devote more resources to get-out-the-vote activities as was done in recent elections. Turnout increased in both 2004 and 2008, particularly in the competitive battleground states. In the nonbattleground states, however, the increase was more modest. Nonetheless, by maximizing a vote base and appealing to new voters as well as Independents, Bush in 2004 and Obama in 2008 enlarged their electorate.

But too much emphasis placed on maximizing a partisan base, as the Republicans did successfully in 2004, combined with effective microtargeting, which Obama did in 2008, might also divide the electorate into warring camps and give party activists and interest group leaders more influence. Such a result could further polarize the electorate, create a more contentious political environment, and perhaps produce a government in which public officials are less open to compromise and to incremental policy decisions. In a contentious political environment, such as the United States has experienced since the 1990s, shifts in party control are also apt to be more disruptive and result in greater shifts in public policy.

Change the Electoral System Entirely

The Electoral College does not encourage turnout in the noncompetitive states. Neither does having noncompetitive, single-member, legislative districts. Replacing the Electoral College with a direct popular vote and either making single-member districts more competitive or converting them into multimember districts in which congressional candidates would be chosen on the basis of the proportion of the vote that they or their party receive would increase turnout.

But systemic changes are difficult to accomplish. They upset the established political order and are likely to generate opposition from those who fear change and those who prefer and believe they profit from the current arrangement. Moreover, reforming the electoral system in this manner would probably require a constitutional amendment, which is always more difficult than enacting legislation. As a consequence, these proposals are not likely to be implemented in the short run or in the absence of other changes.

Require Voting as an Obligation of Citizenship

Another proposal would be to compel people to vote as an obligation of citizenship. Penalties could be imposed on those who refused to do so. Australia, Belgium, and Chile require voting, and their turnout is very high.

One obvious problem with forcing people to vote is the compulsion itself. Some people may be physically or mentally incapable of voting. Others may not care, have little interest, and have very limited information. They might not even know the names of the candidates. Would the selection of the best-qualified person be enhanced by the participation of uninformed, uninterested, and uncaring voters? Might demagogy be encouraged or even slicker and more sophisticated advertising be designed and targeted to different groups in different areas? Would government be more responsive and more popular, or would it be more prone to what British philosopher John Stuart Mill referred to as "the tyranny of the majority"?

Finally, is it democratic to force people to vote? If the right to vote is an essential component of a democratic society, then what about the right not to vote; isn't that an important right that should be protected as well? In short, the turnout issue is a difficult one to resolve. There are costs and benefits in enlarging the electorate as well as in the ways that this enlargement is achieved. Greater participation would probably produce a more representative election outcome but not necessarily a more informed or enlightened electorate. It would reduce the bias that now exists between the voters and nonvoters, but it might also result in a more contentious political environment that spills over into the operation of government. It would probably result in a more representative government but not necessarily a more efficient one or one capable of making better public policy decisions.

Should the Electoral College Be Modified or Abolished?

In addition to the problem of who votes, another source of contention is how the votes should be aggregated. Theoretically, the Constitution allows electors chosen by the states to vote as they please. In practice, most votes are cast for the popular-vote winner of the state. Electors are chosen for their partisan allegiances and are expected to vote for their party's nominees.

This *de facto* system has been criticized as undemocratic, unrepresentative of minority views within states, and potentially unreflective of the nation's popular choice. Candidate strategies to win the Electoral College vote focus on the key battleground states in which less than one-third of the population lives.[24]

The campaign's concentration on the competitive states not only excludes most Americans from seeing the presidential candidates up close or in television advertising but it also skews the campaign toward the issues in the battleground states, discourages people in the nonbattleground states from voting, and creates the false impression that the results of the election represent a national voting decision and, correspondingly, give the winner a national mandate.

Over the years, there have been numerous proposals to alter the presidential voting system. The first was introduced in Congress in 1797. Since then, there have been more than 500 others. In urging changes, critics have pointed to the Electoral College's archaic design, its electoral biases, and the undemocratic results it can produce and did in 2000 (see Chapter 1).

Abolish the Electors

The electors in the Electoral College have been an anachronism since the development of the party system. Their role as partisan agents is not and has not been consistent with their exercising an independent judgment. In fact, twenty-four states plus the District of Columbia prohibit such a judgment by requiring electors to cast their ballots for the winner of the state's popular vote. The Supreme Court has upheld such laws in its decision in the case of *Ray v. Blair* 343 U.S. 214 (1952) but has not ruled on the penalties that these laws prescribe for faithless electors.

One proposal is to simply do away with the electors entirely and the danger that they may exercise their personal preferences rather than the preferences of the people who elected them. First proposed in 1826, this suggestion has received substantial support, including the backing of Presidents John Kennedy and Lyndon Johnson. The Automatic Plan, as it is called, keeps the Electoral College intact but eliminates the electors. Electoral votes are automatically given to the candidate who has received the most popular votes in the state.

Other than removing the potential problem of faithless or unpledged electors, which has not been a major problem to date, the plan would do little to change the system as it currently operates. There have in fact been only a few faithless electors who failed to vote for their party's nominees—eight since 1948.[25] In 2000, one District of Columbia elector submitted a blank ballot to protest the District's lack of voting representation in Congress. Four years later, one Democratic elector from Minnesota made a mistake and voted for John Edwards for president and John Kerry for vice president.[26] In short, the problem of the faithless electors has not been much of a problem nor one of sufficient magnitude to justify a constitutional amendment.

Apportion the Electoral Vote to the Popular Vote

Electing the entire slate of presidential electors has also been the focus of considerable attention. If the winner of a state's popular vote takes all the electoral votes, the impact of the dominant party is increased within that state, and the larger, more competitive states, where voters tend to be more evenly divided, benefit.

From the perspective of the other major party and minor parties within the state, this winner-take-all system is neither desirable nor fair. In effect, it does not provide representation for people who do not vote for the winning candidate. And it does more than that: it discourages a strong campaign effort by a party that has little chance of winning the presidential election in that state, such as Democrats in Utah or Alaska or Republicans in Hawaii or Rhode Island. Naturally, the success of other candidates of that party is affected as well. The winner-take-all system reduces voter turnout.

One way to rectify this problem would be to have proportional voting. Such a plan has been introduced on a number of occasions in Congress; in 2004, it appeared as an initiative on the Colorado ballot. But the voters of that state wisely rejected it because it would have reduced Colorado's influence in the Electoral College. A proportional voting system only makes sense for individual states if *all* states adopt such a system. Under a proportional system, the electors would be abolished, the winner-take-all principle would be eliminated, and a state's electoral vote would be divided in proportion to the popular vote the candidates received within the state. A majority of votes in the Electoral College would still be required for election. If no candidate obtained a majority, most proportional voting plans call for a joint session of Congress to choose the president from among the top two or three candidates.

The proportional proposal would have a number of major consequences if adopted on a nationwide basis. It would decrease the influence of the most competitive states and increase the relative importance of the least competitive ones, where the voters are likely to be more homogeneous. Having the electoral vote proportional to the popular vote provides an incentive to all the parties, not simply the dominant one, to mount a more vigorous campaign and establish a more effective organization. This incentive could strengthen the other major party within the state, but it might also help third parties as well, thereby weakening the two-party system. Ross Perot, who received no electoral votes under the present winner-take-all system, would have received approximately 102 under the proportional plan in 1992 and 49 in 1996. More important, Bill Clinton would not have received a majority in 1992 or 1996 if electoral votes were distributed according to the proportion of the vote candidates received in individual states. (See Table 10.1.) Under these circumstances, third-party candidates, such as Perot and Nader, might have the power to influence the election between the major-party candidates by instructing their electors to support one of the other candidates or by forcing the House of Representatives to determine the winner.

Selection by the House weakens a president's national mandate and might encourage the major-party candidates to make promises or grant favors to legislators in exchange for their support. Such actions could decrease presidential influence during the initial period of an administration and reward regional or state interests at the expense of the national interest. And what happens if the leading candidate is of one party and a majority of state delegations in the House is controlled by the other party? Would legitimacy of the result be enhanced under that arrangement?

Operating under a proportional plan would in all likelihood make the Electoral College vote much closer, thereby reducing the claim most presidents want to make that they have received broad public backing for themselves, their new administration, and the policy proposals they have advocated during their campaign. George H. W. Bush would have defeated Michael Dukakis by only 43.1 electoral votes in 1988, Jimmy Carter would have defeated Gerald Ford by only 11.7 in 1976, and Richard Nixon would have won by only 6.1 in 1968. The election of 2000 would have been even closer, with Bush winning by less than 1 electoral vote; in 2004, he would have won by 16.9. And in at least one recent instance, a proportional electoral vote in the states might have changed the election results. Had this plan been in effect in 1960, Richard Nixon would probably have defeated John Kennedy by 266.1 to 265.6. (See Table 10.1.)

TABLE 10.1 | VOTING FOR PRESIDENT, 1956–2008: FOUR METHODS FOR AGGREGATING THE VOTES

Year	Electoral College	Proportional Plan	District Plan	Direct Election Percentage of Total Votes
1956				
Eisenhower	457	296.7	411	57.4
Stevenson	73	227.2	120	42.0
Others	1	7.1	0	0.6
1960				
Nixon	219	266.1	278	49.5
Kennedy	303	265.6	245	49.8
Others (Byrd)	15	5.3	14	0.7
1964				
Goldwater	52	213.6	72	38.5
Johnson	486	320.0	466	61.0
Others	0	3.9	0	0.5
1968				
Nixon	301	231.5	289	43.2
Humphrey	191	225.4	192	42.7
Wallace	46	78.8	57	13.5
Others	0	2.3	0	0.6
1972				
Nixon	520	330.3	474	60.7
McGovern	17	197.5	64	37.5
Others	1	10.0	0	1.8
1976				
Ford	240	258.0	269	48.0
Carter	297	269.7	269	50.1
Others	1	10.2	0	1.9
1980				
Reagan	489	272.9	396	50.7
Carter	49	220.9	142	41.0
Anderson	0	35.3	0	6.6
Others	0	8.9	0	1.7
1984				
Reagan	525	317.6	468	58.8
Mondale	13	216.6	70	40.6
Others	0	3.8	0	0.4

continued

Table 10.1 | Voting for President, 1956–2008: Four Methods for Aggregating the Votes *continued*

Year	Electoral College	Proportional Plan	District Plan	Direct Election Percentage of Total Votes
1988				
Bush	426	287.8	379	53.4
Dukakis	111	244.7	159	45.6
Others	1	5.5	0	1.0
1992				
Bush	168	203.3	214	37.5
Clinton	370	231.6	324	43.0
Perot	0	101.8	0	18.9
Others	0	1.3	0	0.6
1996				
Clinton	379	262.0	345	49.2
Dole	159	219.9	193	40.7
Perot	0	48.8	0	8.4
Others	0	7.3	0	1.7
2000				
Gore	266*	259.9†	250	48.4
Bush	271	260.3	288	47.9
Nader/Others	0	17	0	2.7
2004				
Kerry	251‡	258.3	221	48.3
Bush	286	275.2	317	50.7
Nader	0	4.5	0	1.0
2008				
Obama	365	283.4	301	52.9
McCain	173	246.9	237	45.7
Others	0	8.5	0	1.4

*One Democratic elector in the District of Columbia cast a blank electoral vote to protest the District's absence of voting representation in Congress.

†If the vote were divided just between the two major candidates in 2000, the respective vote received would be Gore 268.77 and Bush 269.23.

‡A Minnesota elector mistakenly voted for Edwards for president and Kerry for vice president.

Sources: Figures on proportional and district vote for 1952–1980 were supplied to the author by Joseph B. Gorman of the Congressional Research Service, Library of Congress. Calculations for 1984–1992 were made on the basis of data reported in the *Almanac of American Politics* (Washington, DC: National Journal, annual) and by the Federal Election Commission. Calculations since 1996 have been made on the basis of the "Official General Election Results for United States President," Federal Election Commission. www.fec.gov/pubrec/fe2004/2004pres.pdf; www.fec.gov/pubrec/fe2008/2008pres.pdf

Choose Electors in the Same Way as Members of Congress

Another proposal aimed at reducing the effect of winner-take-all voting is to choose electors in the same way a state chooses its members of Congress. Instead of selecting the entire slate on the basis of the statewide vote for president, only two electoral votes would be decided in this manner. The remaining votes would be allocated on the basis of the popular vote for president within individual districts (probably congressional districts). Maine and Nebraska currently employ such a district voting system.

In 2008, one of Nebraska's congressional districts, the one that included the city of Omaha and surrounding areas, voted for Obama while the other two congressional districts and the state overall voted for McCain, giving the Republican candidate four of the state's five electoral votes. Under this plan, a majority of the electoral votes would still be necessary for election. If the vote in the Electoral College were not decisive, then most district plans call for a joint session of Congress to make the final selection.

For the very smallest states, those with three electoral votes, all three electors would have to be chosen on a statewide basis. For others, however, the combination of district and at-large selection would probably result in a split electoral vote, especially in the larger states. On a national level, this change should make the Electoral College more reflective of the partisan division of the newly elected Congress rather than of the popular division of the national electorate.

The losers under such an arrangement would be the large, competitive states and, most particularly, the cohesive, geographically concentrated groups within those states. The winners would include small states. Third parties, especially those that are regionally based, might also be aided to the extent that they were capable of winning specific legislative districts.

It is difficult to project whether Republicans or Democrats would benefit more from such an arrangement, since much would depend on how the legislative districts within the states were apportioned and how those districts tended to vote. If the 1960 presidential vote were aggregated on the basis of one electoral vote to the popular-vote winner of each congressional district and two to the popular-vote winner of each state, Nixon would have defeated Kennedy 278 to 245, with fourteen unpledged electors. In 1976, the district system would have produced a tie, with Carter and Ford receiving 269 votes each (see Table 10.1).

Elect the President by Direct Popular Vote

Of all the plans to alter or replace the Electoral College, the direct popular vote has received the most attention and support. Designed to eliminate the College entirely and count the votes on a nationwide basis, it would elect the popular-vote winner provided the winning candidate received a certain percentage of the total vote. In most plans, 40 percent of the total vote would be necessary.[27] In some, 50 percent would be required. In the event that no one got the required percentage, a runoff between the top two candidates would be held to determine the winner.[28]

A direct popular vote would, of course, remedy a major problem of the present system—the possibility of electing a nonplurality president. It would better equalize voting power both among and within the states. The large competitive states would lose some of their electoral clout by the elimination of the winner-take-all system. Party competition within the states and perhaps even nationwide would be increased. A direct election would force the candidates to campaign in population centers, appeal to urban-suburban voters, and provide more justification for claiming a national mandate.

Critics, however, see a direct popular vote, particularly a close one, as more likely to nationalize and thereby aggravate such problems as determining voter eligibility, possible vote fraud, and vote tabulation errors like the ones that Florida experienced in 2000. A national election would probably cost more and might take longer. Less populated, rural areas, particularly in the mountain states, Hawaii, and Alaska, might be neglected. An election decided primarily by voters concentrated on the Atlantic and Pacific coasts would not provide the geographic balance and federal character that the current system provides. Finally, a plurality winner might not receive a majority of the votes as the Electoral College requires today. In seven out of the twenty-five elections in the twentieth century and one out of three in the twenty-first century, the winner did not receive 50 percent of the popular vote.

A direct election, however, might also encourage minor parties to enter and compete more vigorously, which could weaken the two-party system. The possibility of denying a major-party candidate 50 percent of the popular vote might be sufficient to entice a proliferation of candidates and produce a series of bargains and deals in which support was traded for favors with a new administration. The new administration might even look more like a coalition government in a multiparty system than one in a two-party system.

The organized groups that are geographically concentrated in the large industrial states would have their votes diluted by a direct election. Jewish voters, for example, highly supportive of the Democratic Party since World War II, constitute less than 2.5 percent of the total population but 14 percent in New York, one of the larger states. Thus, the impact of the New York Jewish vote is magnified under the present Electoral College arrangement, as is that of Hispanic voters in Florida, Texas, and California, and Christian fundamentalists and evangelicals in the South.[29]

There are partisan issues as well. Republicans perceive that they benefit from the current arrangement, which provides more safe Republican states than Democratic ones. They also fear that demographic trends, especially the increase in the Hispanic population, might work against them. The last two nonplurality presidents, Benjamin Harrison and George W. Bush, were both Republicans.

A very close popular vote could also cause problems in a direct election. The winner might not be evident for days, even months. Voter fraud could have national consequences. Under such circumstances, large-scale challenges by the losing candidate would be more likely and would necessitate national recounts rather than confining such recounts to individual states, as the current Electoral College system does.

The provision for the situation in which no one received the required percentage of the popular vote has its drawbacks as well. A runoff election would extend the length of the campaign and add to its cost. Considering that some aspirants begin their quest for the presidency a year or two before the election, a further protraction of the process might unduly tax the patience of the voters and produce an even greater numbing effect than currently exists. Moreover, it would also reduce an already short transition period for a newly elected president and would further drain the time and energy of an incumbent seeking reelection.

There is still another difficulty with a contingency election. It could reverse the order in which the candidates originally finished. This result might undermine the ability of the eventual winner to govern successfully. It might also encourage spoiler candidacies. Third parties and Independents seeking the presidency could exercise considerable power in the event of a close contest between the major parties. Imagine what Perot's influence would have been in a runoff between Clinton and Bush in 1992.

Nonetheless, the direct election plan is supported by public opinion and has been ritualistically praised by contemporary presidents. Gallup Polls conducted over the past three decades have consistently found the public favoring a direct election over the present electoral system by substantial margins, as indicated in Table 10.2. Former presidents Carter and Ford have

TABLE 10.2 | PUBLIC OPINION AND THE ELECTORAL COLLEGE

Year	Favor Direct Election	Oppose Direct Election	No Opinion
1944	65%	23%	13%
1967	58	22	20
1968			
May	66	–	–
November	80	–	–
1977	73	–	–
1980	67	–	–
Year*	**Amend the Constitution**	**Keep the Current Electoral System**	**Neither/Both/ No Opinion**
2000			
November 11–12	61	35	4
December 15–17	59	37	4
2004 October 11–14	61	35	4

*Gallup changed the question in 2000: "Thinking for a moment about the way in which the president is elected in this country, which would you prefer: to amend the Constitution so the candidate who receives the most total votes nationwide wins the election, or to keep the current system, in which the candidate who wins the most votes in the Electoral College wins the election?"

Source: Frank Newport, "Americans Support Proposal to Eliminate Electoral College System," Gallup Poll, January 5, 2001, www.gallup.com/poll/releases/pr010105.asp; Darren K. Carlson, "Public Flunks Electoral College System," Gallup Poll, November 2, 2004. www.galluppoll.com/content/Default.aspx?ci=13918 (accessed December 27, 2006). Used with permission.

both urged the abolition of the Electoral College and its replacement by a popular vote.

In 1969, the House of Representatives actually voted for a constitutional amendment to establish direct election for president and vice president, but the Senate refused to go along. Despite public opinion, it seems unlikely that sufficient impetus for a change that requires a constitutional amendment will occur until the issue becomes salient to more people and states that believe they currently have an advantage with the Electoral College system decide to forgo their perceived advantage in the interest of a larger democratic objective. Don't hold your breath!

With the likelihood of a constitutional amendment remote, proponents of a direct popular vote have come up with another plan to achieve the same goal—an interstate compact in which states would agree to join together to pass identical laws that award all of their electoral votes to the presidential candidate who won the most popular votes in the country as a whole. The compact would not take effect, however, until it was agreed to by states that constituted a majority of the Electoral College. Otherwise, there would be no assurance that the candidate with the most popular votes would win in the Electoral College.[30]

The practical merit of such a plan is that it would not require a constitutional amendment; it would also allow states to retain their authority for choosing their electors and for deciding how they should vote. The problem thus far is that only six states plus the District of Columbia have formally agreed to join such a compact, although legislatures in others are considering the plan. At the end of 2010, the compact had only about one-fourth of the support it needed to go into effect.

SUMMARY

There have been changes and continuities in the way we select a president. In general, the changes have made the system more democratic. The continuities link the system to its constitutional roots and its republican past.

The nomination process has been affected more than the general election. Significant modifications have occurred in the rules for choosing delegates, in the laws and judicial decisions regulating contributions and expenditures, and in ways in which campaign appeals are made, targeted, and evaluated; voters are informed; and elections reported to the public.

Supporters of the parties' rules changes contend that they have taken the nomination out of the back rooms and into the public arena, provided more opportunities for more candidates to compete, and given partisans more of a voice in choosing their party's nominees. In contrast, critics allege that the party rules still favor nationally recognized candidates, allow activists to exercise more influence over the selection of delegates and the eventual standard-bearer, and do not encourage participation in the states that hold their contests later in the process after the nominee has been effectively determined.

The campaign finance system has also been problematic. Many of the undemocratic features of the private funding system remain even though the size of individual and group contributions to candidates and parties have been limited, spending restrictions have been imposed on federally funded candidates, public funding has provided greater opportunities for more candidates to run for their party's nomination and has also helped to equalize campaign expenditures, and most campaign financial activity is now subject to full public disclosure. However, inequities continue to exist; loopholes in the law have permitted groups to skirt the federal funding contributions limits; Supreme Court decisions allow unlimited independent spending by individuals, nonparty groups, and corporations; federal funding is now jeopardized by candidates' abilities to raise large amounts of private money; and each presidential campaign is more expensive than the last one, often by significant amounts.

The public's ability to make an informed, enlightened judgment has also been called into question by the amount and quality of the communications received from the candidates and parties and coverage of the election by the news media. The channels of communication have increased, but the bulk of the communication is skewed toward specific groups that receive appeals designed to gain their attention and support. This information is often incomplete and one-sided. Candidates with the most money have the loudest voice, which they can use to drown out their opponents' claims and accusations.

In addition to being highly targeted, political commercials have become increasingly negative and emotionally charged and receive very little evaluation of their claims and allegations by nonpartisan, neutral sources. The news media seem more concerned with reporting entertaining campaign news than educating the public on the principal issues of the day, the way candidates would deal with these issues, and the impact that their policies would have on the country in the short term or long term. Moreover, the constitutional protections of freedom of the press severely limit what government can do to improve the coverage and ensure that the people get the information they need to cast an informed vote.

Have these changes been beneficial or harmful? Have they functioned to make the system more efficient, more responsive, and more likely to result in the choice of a well-qualified candidate? Politicians, journalists, and political scientists disagree in their answers.

Who votes and how votes should be aggregated continues to prompt debate and elicit concern. The expansion of suffrage has made the election process more democratic in theory, but the actual rates of participation have reduced this theoretical gain. Although the failure to vote of a substantial portion of the adult population has been a source of embarrassment and dismay to proponents of a democratic electoral process, there is also little agreement on how to deal with the problem in a federal system that values individual initiative, civic responsibility, and states' rights simultaneously.

Finally, the equity of the Electoral College has also been challenged once again by the results of the 2000 election, but none of the proposals to alter or abolish it, except the direct election of the president, has received much public backing. With no outcry for reform, Congress has been reluctant to alter the system by initiating an amendment to the Constitution and seems unlikely to do so until another electoral crisis and/or unpopular result creates sufficient public pressure to force Congress's hand. Proponents of direct election have thus recommended that states form an interstate compact among themselves and agree to have their electors support the popular-vote winner, but thus far, only a few states have done so.

Does the electoral process work? Yes. Can it be improved? Of course, it can. Will it be changed? Probably, but if the past is any indication, there is no guarantee that legally imposed changes will produce only, or even, their desired effect. If politics is the art of the possible, then success is achieved by those who can adjust most quickly to the legal and political environment and turn it to their electoral advantage.

WHERE ON THE WEB?

Public Interest Groups

- **Center for Responsive Politics**
  www.opensecrets.org
- **The Center for Voting and Democracy**
  www.fairvote.org
- **Common Cause**
  www.commoncause.org
- **National Popular Vote**
  www.nationalpopularvote.com
- **Public Citizen**
  www.citizen.org

Think Tanks

- **The American Enterprise Institute for Public Policy**
  www.aei.org
  A moderate, Republican-leaning institute interested in public policy.
- **The Brookings Institution**
  www.brookings.org
  Washington's oldest think tank; it has a moderate, centrist orientation.
- **Cato Institute**
  www.cato.org
  A libertarian-oriented institute that examines contemporary public policy issues.
- **Center for American Progress**
  www.americanprogress.org
  A liberal-oriented, Democratic-leaning think tank that examines contemporary issues and provides reports and op-ed articles.
- **Heritage Foundation**
  www.heritage.org
  A conservative group concerned with salient public policy issues.
- **Joint Center for Political and Economic Studies**
  www.jointctr.org
  A liberal-oriented think tank specializing in issues of particular concern to minority groups.

- **Urban Institute**
  www.urban.org
  A nonpartisan institute for the study of domestic public policy.

Government Sources

- **Congress**
  www.thomas.gov or www.house.gov and www.senate.gov
- **Presidency**
  www.whitehouse.gov

EXERCISES

1. From the perspective of American democracy, explain what you consider to be the major problem facing the presidential electoral system today and why you think it is such a problem. Then describe whether (and if so, how) liberal, moderate, and conservative groups as well as the Democratic, Republican, and minor parties see the issue you have identified and indicate any solutions they have proposed to fix it. Which of their proposals do you think is best and why? If you do not think any of their proposals will be effective, then propose one of your own.
2. Examine the legislation Congress has enacted in the twenty-first century to reform the electoral system. Indicate the major provisions of the legislation and how they have been implemented to date. What else do you think that Congress should do?
3. From the perspective of the presidential candidates, what is the most odious feature of the current presidential electoral system? Under the existing law, advise the candidates how to deal with this problem and/or propose reforms to reduce or eliminate it.

SELECTED READINGS

Bennett, Robert W. *Taming the Electoral College*. Stanford, CA: Stanford University Press, 2006.

Bugh, Gary, ed. *Electoral College Reform*. Farnham, Surrey, UK: Ashgate, 2010.

Center for Voting and Democracy. *The Shrinking Battleground: The 2008 Presidential Election and Beyond*. 2005. www.fairvote.org/shrinking

Corrado, Anthony J., Michael J. Malbin, Thomas E. Mann, and Norman J. Ornstein. *Reform in an Age of Networked Campaigns: How to Foster Citizen Participation Through Small Donors and Volunteers*. Washington DC: A Joint Project of the Campaign Finance Institute, the American Enterprise Institute, and the Brookings Institution, 2010.

Edwards, George C., III. *Why the Electoral College Is Bad for America*. 2nd. ed. New Haven, CT: Yale University Press, 2011.

Gerken, Heather K. *The Democracy Index: Why Our Election System Is Failing and How to Fix It*. Princeton, NJ: Princeton University Press, 2009.

Issacharoff, Samuel, Pamela S. Karlan, and Richard H. Pildes. *When Elections Go Bad: The Law of Democracy and the Presidential Election of 2000*. New York: Foundation Press, 2001.

Kenski, Kate, Bruce W. Hardy, and Kathleen Hall Jamieson. *The Obama Victory: How Media, Money, and Message Shaped the 2008 Election*. Oxford, UK: Oxford University Press, 2010.

Koza, John R., et al. *Every Vote Equal: A State-Based Plan for Electing the President by National Popular Vote*. Los Altos, CA: National Popular Vote Press, 2006.

Panagopoulos, Costas. "Are Caucuses Bad for Democracy?" *Political Science Quarterly*, 125 (Fall 2010): 425–442.

Polsby, Nelson W. *Consequences of Party Reform*. New York: Oxford University Press, 1983.

Schumaker, Paul D., and Burdett A. Loomis, eds. *Choosing a President: The Electoral College and Beyond*. New York: Chatham House, 2002.

Tolbert, Caroline J., Amanda Keller, and Todd Donovan. "A Modified National Primary: State Losers and Support for Changing the Presidential Nominating Process." *Political Science Quarterly*, 125 (Fall 2010): 393–424.

Tolbert, Caroline J., and Peverill Squire, eds. "Reforming the Presidential Nomination Process." *PS: Political Science and Politics*, 42 (Jan. 2009): 27–79.

Wayne, Stephen J. *Is This Any Way to Run a Democratic Election?* 4th ed. Washington, DC: CQ Press, 2010.

Notes

1. "High Marks for the Campaign, a High Bar for Obama," Pew Research Center for the People and the Press (Nov. 13, 2008). people-press.org/report/471/high-bar-for-obama.
2. Thomas E. Patterson, *Out of Order* (New York: Knopf, 1993), p. 210.
3. Ibid.
4. In 1976, 10 percent of the delegates were selected by the first Tuesday in March; in 2008, more than 70 percent were chosen by that date.
5. Darren K. Carlson, "Public Flunks Electoral College System," Gallup Poll, November 2, 2004. www.galluppoll.com/content/Default.aspx?ci=13918.
6. Approval voting allows the electorate to vote to approve or disapprove each candidate who is running. The candidate with the most approval votes is elected. In a system of cumulative voting, candidates are rank-ordered, and the ranks may be averaged to determine the winner.
7. Caroline J. Tolbert, Amanda Keller, and Todd Donovan, "A Modified National Primary: State Losers and Support for Changing the Presidential Nominating Process," *Political Science Quarterly*, 125 (Fall 2010), pp. 393–424.
8. Ibid, 421. The small states that held preprimary contests could allocate half their delegates to their early election and half to the national primary or they could allocate all of them to either election if they were to choose to do so. It would be up to the state.
9. Ibid.
10. It normally takes the Federal Election Commission up to two years to complete an audit of the expenses and determine which of them may not have been in compliance with the law.
11. For another perspective, see "Three Decades of Opinion Polls Indicate Substantial Popular Support for Threatened Presidential Election Public Financing Program," Campaign Finance Institute (Oct. 20, 2005.) www.cfinst.org/Press/PReleases/05-10-20/Three_Decades_of_Opinion_Polls_Indicate_Substantial_Popular_Support_for_Threatened_Presidential_Election_Public_Financing_Program.aspx.
12. Anthony J. Corrado, Michael J. Malbin, Thomas E. Mann, and Norman J. Ornstein, *Reform in an Age of Networked Campaigns: How to Foster Citizen Participation Through Small Donors and Volunteers* (Washington DC: A Joint Project of the Campaign Finance Institute, the American Enterprise Institute, and

the Brookings Institution, 2010). www.cfinst.org/books_reports/Reform-in-an-Age-of-Networked-Campaigns.pdf.

13. Kate Kenski, Bruce W. Hardy, and Kathleen Hall Jamieson, *The Obama Victory: How Media, Money, and Message Shaped the 2008 Election* (Oxford, UK: Oxford University Press, 2010).
14. Ibid., p. 313.
15. Ibid., p. 314.
16. "Eleven Recommendations for Improving Election Night Television," Cambridge, MA: The Joan Shorenstein Center on the Press, Politics, and Public Policy, Kennedy Institute, Harvard University (2004).
17. APSA Task Force on Inequality and American Democracy, "American Democracy in an Age of Rising Inequality," *Perspectives on Politics*, 2 (Dec. 2004), pp. 647–690.
18. Turnout expert Michael P. McDonald calculated turnout for the 2010 general election as 41.6 percent of eligible voters and 37.8 percent of the voting-aged population. Michael P. McDonald, "2010 General Election Turnout Rates," (updated Dec. 13, 2010). www.gmu/.edu/Turnout_2010G.html.
19. Excluded would be those convicted of a capital crime and sex offenders. "Building Confidence in U.S. Elections," Report of the Commission on Federal Election Reform (Sept. 2005). In forty-eight states, incarcerated felons cannot vote. In eleven states, ex-felons are permanently barred from voting. The prohibitions against felons apply to about 5.3 million people living in the United States.
20. There have been accuracy and security problems with electronic voting. Computer scientists contend that the current system is vulnerable to hidden programming by the designers of such systems as well as to outside hacking. A small error in the programming could switch hundreds, if not thousands, of votes. They also claim that the voting machines have not been adequately tested, a claim that the Election Assistance Commission supported when it decertified the main company testing the machines on the grounds that it did not adequately document the tests it was doing on the equipment. Christopher Drew, "Citing Problems, U.S. Bars Lab From Testing Electronic Voting," *The New York Times* (Jan. 4, 2007), pp. A1, A14.

    Another issue has been the absence of a paper trail to use when determining the accuracy of electronic machines in tabulating the vote. Without such a trail, it is difficult to check whether all the votes have been properly recorded and tabulated.

    Voting on the Internet is even more suspect. Problems with security prompted the Department of Defense to cancel the implementation of a Web-based system to allow members of the armed forces stationed abroad to vote via the Internet.
21. Thirty-one states currently allow early voting without excuses, and an additional three states provide it with excuses. Twenty-eight states permit absentee voting; twenty-two of them, however, require excuses; six do not. "Early Voting," *Wikipedia* (accessed Jan. 19, 2008). en.wikipedia.org/Early_voting.
22. Adam J. Berinsky, "The Perverse Consequences of Electoral Reform in the United States," *American Politics Research*, 33 (July 2005), pp. 471–491.
23. Heather K. Gerken, *The Democracy Index: Why Our Election System Is Failing and How to Fix It* (Princeton, NJ: Princeton University Press, 2009).
24. The Center for Voting and Democracy reports that more than 30 percent of the nation's white population lives in the battleground states compared to just

21 percent of African Americans and Native Americans, 18 percent of Latinos, and 14 percent of Asian Americans. "Presidential Election Inequality: The Electoral College in the 21st Century," *A Report by the Center for Voting and Democracy* (Takoma Park, MD: Center for Voting and Democracy, 2006), p. 13.

25. According to Fairvote.org, a group that wants to replace the Electoral College with a direct popular vote or, in the absence of a constitutional amendment, an agreement among the states to have their electors vote for the national popular-vote winner regardless of how their state votes, there have been 157 faithless electors. Seventy-one changed their votes because the candidate for whom they were going to vote died before they were to cast their votes. In the other cases, the electors simply decided on their own not to vote for their party's designated candidate. archive.fairvote.org/index.php?page=973.
26. The same problem occurred in 1988, although in that case, the reversal of presidential and vice presidential votes was done purposefully by a Democratic West Virginia elector.
27. Abraham Lincoln was the only plurality president who failed to attain the 40 percent figure. He received 39.82 percent in 1860, although he probably would have received more had his name been on the ballot in nine southern states.
28. Other direct election proposals have recommended that a joint session of Congress decide the winner. The runoff provision was contained in the resolution that passed the House of Representatives in 1969. In 1979, a direct election plan with a runoff provision failed to win the two-thirds Senate vote required to initiate a constitutional amendment.
29. John Kennedy carried New York by approximately 384,000 votes. He received a plurality of more than 800,000 from precincts that were primarily Jewish. Similarly, in Illinois, a state he carried by less than 9,000, Kennedy had a plurality of 55,000 from the so-called Jewish precincts. Mark R. Levy and Michael S. Kramer, *The Ethnic Factor* (New York: Simon & Schuster, 1972), p. 104.
30. *Every Vote Equal: A State-based Plan for Electing the President* (Los Angeles: National Popular Vote Press, 2006), pp. 243–274.

Appendix

RESULTS OF PRESIDENTIAL ELECTIONS, 1900–2008

	Candidates		Electoral Vote		Popular Vote	
Year	Democrat	Republican	Democrat	Republican	Democrat	Republican
1900	William J. Bryan	William McKinley	155	292	6,358,345	7,218,039
	Adlai E. Stevenson	Theodore Roosevelt	35%	65%	45.5%	51.7%
1904	Alton B. Parker	Theodore Roosevelt	140	336	5,028,898	7,626,593
	Henry G. Davis	Charles W. Fairbanks	29%	71%	37.6%	56.4%
1908	William J. Bryan	William H. Taft	162	321	6,406,801	7,676,258
	John W. Kern	James S. Sherman	34%	66%	43.0%	51.6%
1912	Woodrow Wilson	William H. Taft	435	8	6,293,152	3,486,333
	Thomas R. Marshall	James S. Sherman	82%	2%	41.8%	23.2%
1916	Woodrow Wilson	Charles E. Hughes	227	254	9,126,300	8,546,789
	Thomas R. Marshall	Charles W. Fairbanks	52%	48%	49.2%	46.1%
1920	James M. Cox	Warren G. Harding	127	404	9,140,884	16,133,314
	Franklin D. Roosevelt	Calvin Coolidge	24%	76%	34.2%	60.3%
1924	John W. Davis	Calvin Coolidge	136	382	8,386,169	15,717,553
	Charles W. Bryant	Charles G. Dawes	26%	72%	28.8%	54.1%
1928	Alfred E. Smith	Herbert C. Hoover	87	444	15,000,185	21,411,991
	Joseph T. Robinson	Charles Curtis	16%	84%	40.8%	58.2%
1932	Franklin D. Roosevelt	Herbert C. Hoover	472	59	22,825,016	15,758,397
	John N. Garner	Charles Curtis	89%	11%	57.4%	39.6%
1936	Franklin D. Roosevelt	Alfred M. Landon	523	8	27,747,636	16,679,543
	John N. Garner	Frank Knox	98%	2%	60.8%	36.5%

1940	Franklin D. Roosevelt	Wendell L. Willkie	449	82	27,263,448	22,336,260
	Henry A. Wallace	Charles L. McNary	85%	15%	54.7%	44.8%
1944	Franklin D. Roosevelt	Thomas E. Dewey	432	99	25,611,936	22,013,372
	Harry S Truman	John W. Bricker	81%	19%	53.4%	45.9%
1948	Harry S Truman	Thomas E. Dewey	303	189	24,105,587	21,970,017
	Alben W. Barkley	Earl Warren	57%	36%	49.5%	45.1%
1952	Adlai E. Stevenson	Dwight D. Eisenhower	89	442	27,314,649	33,936,137
	John J. Sparkman	Richard M. Nixon	17%	83%	44.4%	55.1%
1956	Adlai E. Stevenson	Dwight D. Eisenhower	73	457	26,030,172	35,585,245
	Estes Kefauver	Richard M. Nixon	14%	86%	42.0%	57.4%
1960	John F. Kennedy	Richard M. Nixon	303	219	34,221,344	34,106,671
	Lyndon B. Johnson	Henry Cabot Lodge	56%	41%	49.8%	49.5%
1964	Lyndon B. Johnson	Barry Goldwater	486	52	43,126,584	27,177,838
	Hubert H. Humphrey	William E. Miller	90%	10%	61%	38.5%
1968	Hubert H. Humphrey	Richard M. Nixon	191	301	31,274,503	31,785,148
	Edmund S. Muskie	Spiro T. Agnew	36%	56%	42.7%	43.2%
1972	George McGovern	Richard M. Nixon	17	520	29,171,791	47,170,179
	Sargent Shriver	Spiro T. Agnew	3%	97%	37.5%	60.7%
1976	Jimmy Carter	Gerald R. Ford	297	240	40,828,657	39,145,520
	Walter F. Mondale	Robert Dole	55%	45%	50.1%	48.0%
1980	Jimmy Carter	Ronald Reagan	49	489	35,483,820	43,901,812
	Walter F. Mondale	George Bush	10%	90%	41.0%	50.7%

continued

RESULTS OF PRESIDENTIAL ELECTIONS, 1900–2008 *continued*

	Candidates		Electoral Vote		Popular Vote	
Year	Democrat	Republican	Democrat	Republican	Democrat	Republican
1984	Walter F. Mondale	Ronald Reagan	13	525	37,577,137	54,455,074
	Geraldine Ferraro	George Bush	2%	98%	40.6%	58.8%
1988	Michael S. Dukakis	George Bush	111	426	41,809,074	48,886,097
	Lloyd Bentsen	Dan Quayle	21%	79%	45.6%	53.4%
1992	Bill Clinton	George Bush	370	168	44,909,889	39,104,545
	Al Gore	Dan Quayle	69%	31%	43.0%	37.5%
1996	Bill Clinton	Robert Dole	379	159	45,628,667	37,869,435
	Al Gore	Jack Kemp	70%	30%	49.2%	40.7%
2000	Al Gore	George W. Bush	266	271	50,996,039	50,456,141
	Joseph Lieberman	Dick Cheney	49.4%	50.4%	48.4%	47.9%
2004	John Kerry	George W. Bush	251	286	59,028,444	62,040,610
	John Edwards	Dick Cheney	46.7%	53.2%	48.3%	50.7%
2008	Barack Obama	John McCain	365	173	69,456,897	59,934,814
	Joe Biden	Sarah Palin	67.8%	32.2%	52.9%	45.7%

Index